WITH THE IRA IN THE FIGHT FOR FREEDOM

WITH THE IRA IN THE FIGHT FOR FREEDOM

1919 TO THE TRUCE

INTRODUCTION BY GABRIEL DOHERTY

MERCIER PRESS
Cork
www.mercierpress.ie

Trade enquiries to CMD BookSource,
55a Spruce Avenue, Stillorgan Industrial Park,
Blackrock, County Dublin

Originally published by *The Kerryman*

This edition published by Mercier Press, 2010

ISBN: 978 1 85635 687 9

10 9 8 7 6 5 4 3 2 1

A CIP record for this title is available from the British Library

Printed and bound in the EU.

CONTENTS

INTRODUCTION

Gabriel Doherty

In its review of the first edition of *With the IRA in the Fight for Freedom* the *Irish Press* noted that the title of the work alone was 'irresistible'. Certainly any work with the subtitle *The Red Path of Glory* was designed to catch the eye, all the more so when it was conjoined with a cover featuring the shadowy outlines of IRA volunteers, homesteads ablaze, and stark, lurid red streaks suggestive of many things, not least, of course, the copious amounts of blood shed during that fight.

It is an oblique commentary on the evolution of elite attitudes within the independent Irish state since the 1970s that some would now be tempted to dismiss the work out of hand for precisely the same reasons that drew in that original reviewer – that it is an unreconstructed, one-dimensional expression of a narrow republican interpretation of 'the Irish question' as it stood in the early to mid-twentieth century, an interpretation, moreover, which was and is positively irresponsible in its unqualified endorsement of the physical force tradition within Irish politics.

It would be naïve to dismiss or endorse such a view out of hand as being utterly devoid of merit. The work *is* of its time, certainly – but from a historiographical view that adds to, rather than diminishes, its interest and significance. It is an excellent – one might say classic – example of the dominant school of writing on the War of Independence during the middle decades of the twentieth century (or at least of those studies whose origins lay in a southern nationalist perspective), and, as such, it provides useful insights into that still grossly researched topic in Irish history: *mentalité*. This approach was characterised by an episodic approach to the war, the utilisation of first-hand accounts by eye-witnesses or veterans, a clear preference for engagements from which the IRA emerged victorious (and preferably unscathed), a southern focus, and rendered in the form of succinct 'racy' narrative, unencumbered by extensive footnotes or other indications of source material. It was a form of history antithetical to the austere precepts of the *Irish Historical Studies* school, one which, furthermore, was ideally suited to, and undoubtedly shaped by, the journalistic milieu through which many of the accounts first saw the light of day and whose influence in shaping popular understanding of the independence struggle has yet to be adequately assessed. (It is no coincidence in this respect that *With the IRA in the Fight for Freedom* first appeared under the imprint of *The Kerryman* newspaper.)

The book does not claim the status of a fully fledged history of the War of Independence, but presents itself, rather, as 'a portion' of that history in its reflection of the values and mores, as well as the actions, of that element of the revolutionary generation in Ireland who took an active part in the republican military campaign. It thereby excludes a great deal that is interesting about this period – the constructive political agenda of Dáil Éireann, British political and military strategy, the evolution of public opinion in Ireland and Britain, and – to reiterate the point made above – the situation in Ulster. Its other elisions are also significant, most especially the studied refusal to accord the Civil War even the briefest of mentions – but in bringing together committed partisans on both sides of that Civil War the reconciliatory and harmonious potential of a book whose focus is violence and death should not be entirely overlooked.

The work contains details of some familiar engagements of national significance (Kilmichael, Crossbarry, Bloody Sunday, the burning of Cork) and others of more parochial renown. The list of contributors could hardly be more impressive, and includes such luminaries as Piaras Béaslaí, Tom Barry, Simon Donnelly, Dan Breen, Oscar Traynor and Seán MacEoin amongst others. Their recollections are reproduced here as part of Mercier Press' enlightened policy of making available to the reading public, after a gap of some decades, once-standard works on the Irish revolution (and for those who wish to delve deeper into the subject one need look no further than the excellent reissues of the *Fighting Stories* series).

Of course, such testimonies are not contemporaneous with the episodes themselves (few combatants in any war have the luxury, when the bullets start flying, of having notepaper, pen *and* rifle, close to hand), and they inevitably suffer from the same potential flaws as all accounts of events that are recounted after the fact – and in this case many years after. The influence of intervening events, failing memory, an understandable inclination in some cases to exaggerate one's personal role, a desire, perhaps, to 'put the record straight' – all such factors can, in different ways for different accounts, conspire to place question marks over the specifics of recollection of any historical event. When that event, moreover, was a life-and-death military engagement (during which the belligerent's need to keep his head down far exceeded the chronicler's hankering after a panoramic view of proceedings) the risk of inadvertent (and usually inconsequential) misrepresentation is obviously enhanced. For these reasons the accounts presented here need to be checked and cross-referenced against other source material pertaining to each action before they can be considered definitive.

But such concern with the minutiae of historical methodology runs the risk of losing sight of what it is that attracted previous generations of the reading public in Ireland to chronicles such as the one presented here, and which seems to be drawing in new devotees with each passing year. The answer is surely that the work fits comfortably in a historiographical tradition – the *heroic* – whose impeccable pedigree (dating back as it does to the origins of the historical discipline in classical times) and emotional power has guaranteed its survival when more modern, 'professional' and restrained approaches to the discipline have stalled or withered completely. This heroic tone, to be sure, has many flaws (it can, for example, simply degenerate into the 'Great Man' school of historical causation, and most assuredly omits due consideration of dissenting voices) but perhaps it is time for professional historians in Ireland to recognise, or rather rediscover, its many virtues in the eyes of the general public – and what better place to start than here, by retracing steps on that 'red path of glory'?

ORIGINAL PREFACE

For many years *The Kerryman* Ltd, through its newspapers and in book form, has been telling the story of the struggle, made by men and women of our time, which brought into being our modern Irish state. If these men and women did not achieve all that they aimed at, they achieved more than any other generation had done in the centuries-old fight to throw off an alien yoke.

The book we now present to the public continues this policy of our House. We had, however, an additional object in view when publishing it at this time.

Since the end of the Second World War there has been a spate of books upon various aspects of the fighting and about the exploits of those who – individually or in combative units – distinguished themselves in the course of it. In particular, much has been written about the actions of those partisan or resistance groups who waged a ceaseless fight against enemy occupying forces. It seemed to us that in the face of this publicity for the actions of patriot forces attempting to re-establish the independence of their country it was timely to give a record of the fight put up by men and women of our own race against greater odds than any of those groups had to face.

Those resistance groups were lavishly supplied by powerful allies with adequate quantities of the most modern arms and equipment; their attacks on the enemy were supported and helped forward by strategic bombing and diversionary actions; their morale was sustained by a propaganda campaign which was almost worldwide in extent; and, finally, they were fighting an enemy who was new and strange to their country and who had to operate very much in the dark.

How very different was the task set before our own fighters for freedom! They had to fight an enemy who had been entrenched in the country for centuries, whose administration covered the land, who had friends in high places and in low places. They had to face him without the help of powerful allies, in the teeth of a campaign of misrepresentation, with arms which, for the most part, had to be taken from him in hard fighting. And the enemy they fought was the first imperial power in the world at the time. Only idealism and courage on the part of the fighters and the steadfast support of the people could have carried such an unequal struggle through to the end.

Let us not forget that struggle. That is the message of this book. In its pages we have tried to present a representative picture of the fight put up by the army of the Republic and of the campaign of terror so unflinchingly endured by the civilian population. Within the compass we had to prescribe for ourselves we could not, of course, give anything like an exhaustive account of the fight for independence. Some actions have been omitted because they have already been well publicised, and we felt that others, less well known, should take their place; some other actions, which we would like to have included, we have had to leave out because, for one reason or another, we found ourselves unable to gather the necessary information. In all instances the scene of a fight was visited and inspected, and every effort was made to check and verify information – wherever possible we endeavoured to get the officer in charge or a participant to tell the story of an engagement – and we are confident that the matter appearing in the book is as accurate as research and hard work could make it.

This book does not purport to be a history of the War of Independence, but it is a portion of that history. We offer it to the public in that light in the hope that, in its own small way, it may help to keep alive in the breasts of our people a remembrance of one of the most glorious periods in our history.

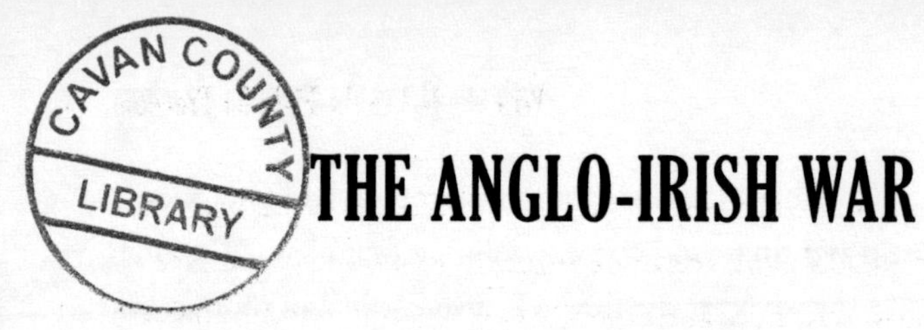

THE ANGLO-IRISH WAR

by Piaras Béaslaí

(member of GHQ, 1918 to the Truce; formerly editor An t-Óglach*; Director of IRA Publicity and member of Dáil Éireann)*

THE HEROIC GESTURE of Easter Week 1916 and England's barbaric revenge on the noble men who had led a heroic and chivalrous fight against overwhelming odds, had a tremendous effect upon the thoughts and feelings of the people of Ireland. The many who had been seduced from their allegiance to the cause of complete Irish independence by the propaganda of the Irish Parliamentary Party, now saw things in a different light. This change of mood was first reflected in the election of Count Plunkett, father of the executed Joseph Plunkett, and later of Joseph McGuinness, a convicted rebel 'felon' then serving time in Lewes prison, as proper representatives of the Irish people in preference to candidates of the Irish Parliamentary Party.

Later in 1917 came the East Clare by-election in which Éamon de Valera, just released from Lewes prison, was returned by an overwhelming majority; and a month later another 1916 rebel, William T. Cosgrave, was elected for Kilkenny. The Sinn Féin organisation, with Mr de Valera as president and Arthur Griffith as vice-president, now clearly represented the views and aims of the majority of the Irish people.

The change of feeling was further strengthened when the British government, early in 1918, endeavoured to make Irishmen liable to compulsory service in the British army in the war with Germany; and later when they arrested and deported to prisons in England over eighty men prominent in the national movement, including the heads of the Sinn Féin organisation, under the pretence that they were engaged in a plot to bring about a German invasion.

The Irish Volunteers, whose organisation had been secretly started again, and who had held a convention in Dublin, now, in the face of the menace of conscription, grew rapidly in strength, though still sadly deficient in arms and equipment.

Finally the end of the war, and the general election which followed in England and Ireland in December 1918, gave the Irish people their opportunity. In practically every constituency outside Ulster deputies were elected and pledged to refuse to attend the British parliament or recognise England's right to govern Ireland. In January 1919, those deputies who were at liberty (only about half of those elected) met in Dublin, constituted Dáil Éireann and declared Ireland *de jure* an independent Republic. Meeting secretly, the same deputies elected Cathal Brugha (then Chief of Staff of the Irish Volunteers) as president, and he appointed his cabinet. A significant fact was that he appointed a Minister for Defence (General Mulcahy) and the Irish Volunteers came under the authority of Dáil Éireann and became the army of the Irish Republic. In April 1919, after the release of the prisoners, a full meeting of deputies was held. Éamon de Valera was elected president and he appointed Cathal Brugha Minister for Defence. The Volunteers had become the army of the Irish Republic and later they pledged their allegiance to the elected government of Ireland.

Although the Volunteers were now the army of the Irish Republic, the title 'IRA' was never officially adopted by them. It was simply a popular name for them, which gradually came into use among the people in the year 1919 and is now used even by historians. Popular usage established the name without any formal vote by any representative body.

Ireland had now an elected parliament, a government accepted by the great majority of the people and an army responsible to that government, but the British were still in military occupation of the country. Large bodies of soldiers held strongholds and vital centres, and a network of smaller posts throughout the country was held by the Royal Irish Constabulary, with full control of every branch of civil administration and an elaborate system of espionage. To break down that regime and, as far as possible, obtain control in various ways was now a task in which the army of the Irish Republic had to play the leading part. The national policy adopted was a combination of defensive and offensive tactics, the old Sinn Féin policy of passive resistance, with a readiness to use force when feasible and strike the enemy at vital and vulnerable points.

It was realised that the most essential element of the British system of governing and oppressing Ireland was the force known as the Royal Irish Constabulary. It was the British propagandist device to refer to these men as 'policemen', a very misleading term; and when people abroad were told of 'policemen' being shot, it suggested the lawless violence of bandits. The 'RIC' were never policemen in the proper sense of the term, and bore no analogy to the Garda Síochána of these days. It is not too much to say that they were the arms, the eyes and the ears of the British administration in Ireland. They were a military force, armed with rifles and living in barracks, whose task it was to hold the country in subjection to England. They were kept at strength out of all proportion to that of a normal police force – over 12,000. There was hardly a village without an RIC barracks, manned by stalwart young men armed with rifles, in districts where ordinary crime was almost unknown. These men were all of native stock, but their training was calculated to eliminate all national or local sympathies. It was a regulation of the force that no constable could be stationed in his native county. It was his business to enforce British rule on the people; and it was also his duty to spy on the people. In every district the activities of all persons were watched and reports sent regularly to Dublin Castle. All who were connected with national organisations and even those who attended Irish language classes or debating societies were reported on. If this statement sounds exaggerated, let me quote the words of one of the last British chief secretaries of Ireland, Mr Birrell, who told a Royal Commission: 'We have the reports of the RIC, who send us in, almost daily, reports from almost every district in Ireland, which enable us to form a correct general estimate of the feeling of the countryside in the different localities.' An official record of the RIC in

1919 said: 'Against political agitations the RIC have invariably proved themselves most effective. It is largely due to the efficiency of their excellent organisation that the rebellion in Easter Week 1916, was kept within bounds and speedily suppressed throughout the country.'

It was obvious that the RIC was the most essential component of the machinery of British administration in Ireland and that action must first be taken against that force. Dáil Éireann passed a decree of social ostracism against members of the RIC, and the enforcement of this decree had a considerable effect, causing many men to resign from the force and making it increasingly difficult to obtain recruits. In some cases armed attacks resulted in the killing or wounding of constables and already in the summer of 1919, RIC barracks in Cork and Clare had been taken by surprise and destroyed, the constables being disarmed and released. These activities increased the unpopularity of the force and accelerated the resignations. In August 1919, what we regarded as the first step in evacuation was taken, when a large number of smaller barracks in outlying districts were closed down by the British authorities.

In Dublin, a genuine police force, the Dublin Metropolitan Police, functioned in place of the RIC, and the political espionage work was done by detectives. Already Michael Collins, Adjutant General, Director of Organisation and later Director of Intelligence, was in touch with some of these men, who had actually become agents of ours, whose services were invaluable; and through these men he was able to nullify the efforts of those who were working against us and to learn the secrets of the enemy. Later, after repeated warnings, some of the most dangerous enemy agents met their deaths. The city was afterwards filled with intelligence officers and Secret Service men from England, but these, for the most part proved very ineffective, and those who proved dangerous were finally baffled and unmasked, and paid the penalty.

To finance the various activities of the Irish government, including the army, a National Loan was floated, the target for Ireland being £250,000. The British declared the loan illegal and used every means in their power to suppress the work and capture those engaged in it; but, despite these efforts, the Minister for Finance, Michael Collins, raised in Ireland a sum of £379,000.

In the United States, to which Mr de Valera had secretly made his way in the summer of 1919, it was at first proposed to raise a million dollars for the National Loan, but Mr de Valera asked that the 'target' should be raised to five million. He toured the various cities in every part of the United States, and was everywhere received with great enthusiasm, not only by Irish-Americans, but by many other persons prominent in American public life. The great sum asked for the National Loan was subscribed, the Irish case was explained to the people of America and widespread sympathy was won for the cause of Irish freedom.

Already, before the establishment of Dáil Éireann, Volunteers and political prisoners tried before British courts, civil or military, had 'refused to recognise the court' and demanded to be treated as prisoners of war, and, when this was refused, gone on hunger strike. A number of hunger strikes by large bodies of Irish prisoners had resulted in general releases of those concerned. In some cases, bodies of prisoners had carried out active resistance to their custodians. A number of important prisoners escaped from various Irish and English prisons, usually with assistance from Volunteers outside. In fact the British prison system in Ireland was undermined and broken up, and a number of members of prison staffs were working in collusion with our men.

In October 1920, occurred the heroic death, on hunger strike in Brixton prison, of Terence MacSwiney, Lord Mayor of Cork, an event which attracted attention to, and evoked sympathy with, Ireland's fight all over the world.

Another blow against the British administration was the boycotting of the law courts and the setting up of 'republican courts', to which litigants flocked, sure of inexpensive justice, and before which solicitors and barristers appeared. At a later date many men refused to serve on juries and court sessions had to be abandoned. When the atrocities of British agents had aroused public opinion, a large number of 'justices of the peace' (then, as still in England, occupying an honorary position) resigned their commissions.

As the RIC ceased to function, some lawless men tried to take advantage of the situation, and Óglaigh na hÉireann found themselves called on to enforce justice and maintain order in the evacuated countrysides. Robbers and other offenders were seized and dealt with, and finally a body called 'republican police' was formed, which functioned until the Truce.

Dáil Éireann now declared the collection of income tax by British officials in Ireland illegal and ordered all to refuse to pay it. The British found it impossible to take effective action against a wholesale refusal of payment. In April 1920, income tax offices all over Dublin, and in every part of Ireland, were raided by armed men and all the papers and records destroyed. On the same night no fewer than 315 evacuated RIC barracks were destroyed by fire. Not many days later, thirty more income tax offices were similarly treated and ninety-five more evacuated barracks burned down.

The secret organ of Óglaigh na hÉireann, *An t-Óglach,* of which I was editor, first appeared in August 1918, and was published regularly from that time to the Truce, except for an interval of six months spent by me in an English prison (from which I at length escaped). Originally appearing twice a month, it later became a weekly publication. We had our secret printing office and printers, who were never discovered by the enemy. This paper helped the men of the army to keep in touch with GHQ, and gave them information, instruction and encouragement not otherwise available. An army publicity department was organised which regularly supplied information to friendly journalists, Irish and foreign, and supplied reports to the government publicity department.

The intelligence department was greatly helped by the work of members employed in the postal service in Ireland, in London and even on the mail boats. Among many other things, enemy correspondence and communications were systematically 'tapped'.

The work of the army received much useful assistance from the women's organisation, Cumann na mBan, and the boy's organisation,

Fianna Éireann, which latter proved a training ground for young recruits to the fighting forces as they reached military age.

At the end of 1919 the British government decided on a new plan of campaign to counter the progress of the struggle for independence. It was decided to adopt a secret policy of assassination against the leaders of the army of Ireland. The intelligence department of our army was able to obtain full proof of the machinations of English agents, the first result of whose conspiracy was the murder of Tomás MacCurtain, Lord Mayor of Cork, in March 1920. At the same time a reign of terror was instituted by the RIC of Thurles, who carried out a number of outrages on unarmed people and even murders. Another British policy was the system of unofficial 'reprisals'. Wherever members of the IRA effected a coup, outrages were carried out on civilians in the locality by 'crown forces'. The British government pretended that these were cases of their forces 'getting out of hand' under great provocation. It was not yet prepared to take full responsibility for actions which, however, it had not only authorised but instigated.

By this time a large number of barracks in various parts of the country had been taken by storm, in some cases after hours of siege, by bodies of Volunteers with rifles, shotguns and the aid of explosives. The object of these attacks, apart from the destruction of the buildings, was the acquiring of arms and ammunition, which were scarce enough in every area. The RIC who surrendered were only disarmed and released. Parties of British soldiers were also attacked and disarmed. In many towns in the south, after such occurrences, British troops were let loose on the place, carrying out looting and burnings – which, however, paled into insignificance compared with what was yet to come.

In the besieging of RIC barracks, those who did not possess weapons, and many whose age precluded active service, were able to give valuable assistance by intelligence work: scouting, carrying messages, trenching or blocking roads and cutting wires. It was fortunate that in those days no barracks possessed wireless installations.

The first permanent body of fighting men was formed in Dublin in the summer of 1919, being attached to the intelligence department, under the name of 'The Squad', and many important and dangerous tasks were carried out by this body. At general headquarters the functioning of the intelligence department had become of paramount importance. As all the plots of the enemy were hatched in Dublin, and the details were planned there, it became of immense value to get any inside information on this matter, and we already had agents in every branch of the enemy administration, civil and military. A number of members of the political branch of the detective force were working hard for the IRA, and even the Secret Service was undermined. Raid after raid, however secretly planned, proved futile, as our intelligence department had information in advance and was able to warn those who were to be arrested. Spies and informers were speedily unmasked and met a well-deserved fate.

Early in 1920 a number of typed 'death notices' on Dáil Éireann notepaper were sent to men prominently identified with the struggle for independence. Our intelligence department was able to ascertain that these notices were typed in Dublin Castle, and even the room in which they were typed and the machine with which it was done. The notepaper had been seized on the premises of Dáil Éireann in Harcourt Street at an earlier date.

The number of members of Óglaigh na hÉireann was its highest in 1918, in face of the menace of conscription, though only a small proportion of these was armed. It was at this time that the brigades were organised in separate brigade areas. After the war, when the danger of conscription had passed, the membership was smaller, but those who remained were the most earnest and enthusiastic, as later events were to prove.

Late in 1919, the first steps were taken to form permanent 'columns' in brigade areas, and this proved a move of immense importance. These columns, moving about their area and carrying out attacks, ambushes and raids, achieved many notable triumphs, and gradually conditions in some parts of Ireland assumed the character of guerrilla warfare, in which the columns, bravely and capably led, showed the greatest military skill and efficiency in that particular style of warfare.

The local Volunteers in each district co-operated with them in their various operations, and the civilian population gladly gave housing and hospitality to their members and facilitated their work in many ways.

The normal strength of the RIC was about 12,000 men, but owing to wholesale resignations and the difficulty of getting new recruits, the number had dwindled to fewer than 10,000. Hundreds of barracks had been evacuated, and had been destroyed by our forces, others had been captured by force, and still the retreat went on. The English government now began to advertise for recruits for the RIC in England, offering very exceptional terms of pay and advantages. By June 1920, the country was full of these recruits. As RIC uniforms were not yet available for them, they were dressed in khaki, with black RIC belts and caps. Hence arose the popular nickname for them: 'Black and Tans'. When this name began to be associated with robbery, murder and every kind of outrage, they adopted it themselves with enthusiasm. A large number of these men were drawn from the criminal classes and the dregs of the population of English cities. With their assistance the 'new policy' of murders, lootings, burnings of houses and 'reprisals' made striking progress – though the 'reprisals' were still supposed to be 'unofficial'.

A special journal, *The Weekly Summary*, published in Dublin Castle, was issued to these men, inciting them to murder and outrage. Its contents, as a responsible government organ, were almost unbelievable.

Another force formed at the same time was the 'Auxiliaries', men with higher pay and a distinctive uniform. They also wore khaki at first, with a Glengarry cap, but later acquired a blue uniform. They were more formidable than the ordinary 'Black and Tans' because of their superior intelligence and courage. They operated in various parts of the country, but particularly in Dublin, where they were a familiar sight whirling around in lorries, raiding and 'holding up'. Even some members of that body developed sympathy with the IRA and gave us information and assistance.

A British general, in a letter captured by our intelligence department, referred to 'the new policy – stamping out terrorism by secret murder'.

In 1920 a number of murders of Irish citizens in Dublin, and in the country, were carried out in pursuance of this 'new policy'. Our intelligence department obtained a complete list of those concerned in this murder plot who were living in Dublin, and on 21 November 1920, the day known as 'Bloody Sunday', they were visited in their homes and shot dead. By way of 'reprisal' the Auxiliaries rode to Croke Park that afternoon in lorries, where a huge crowd of men, women and children was watching a football match between Dublin and Tipperary, and fired on the crowd, killing fourteen and wounding about sixty. The capture and murder by the enemy of the Dublin brigadier and vice-brigadier, Dick McKee and Peadar Clancy, at this date was a great blow to our army. Oscar Traynor was chosen as the new brigadier.

An active service unit of the Dublin Brigade, originally consisting of fifty men, was now formed and operated effectively. Of course their methods and armament were quite different from those of the columns. They carried not rifles but revolvers and hand grenades, for the manufacture of which latter a factory was now working.

For a long time previously the people of Dublin had been accustomed to seeing lorries of soldiers and Auxiliaries in the streets, with their rifles pointed out at the populace. The IRA hesitated to attack them, owing to the danger to the civilian population. Ultimately, when circumstances became critical, street ambushes were decided on, and became a frequent, almost an everyday occurrence, in various parts of the city. Shortly before the Truce, 'The Squad' and the ASU were incorporated in one body known as the 'Guard'.

In 1921 the total number of British regular troops in Ireland exceeded 35,000, and the RIC had to contend with nearly 50,000 men, well armed and equipped, occupying cities and towns, fortified places and points of vantage throughout the country. This does not include the Dublin Metropolitan Police, nearly 1,200 strong.

The British authorities had no idea of our actual strength, and were inclined to exaggerate it greatly; and many of our own people shared this delusion. The English Prime Minister, Mr David Lloyd George, declared in a speech in the House of Commons that they had to contend with 'two hundred thousand armed men'. Had that indeed been the case, then we could have achieved wonders, considering what we did with our small numbers and poor armament.

Even taking all the actual members of the IRA into account, we were outnumbered by considerably more than two to one; but to reckon our effective strength in terms of numbers would be very misleading. In many areas the Volunteers, however zealous and courageous, were unable to do much owing to their shortage of arms and ammunition – and, sometimes, owing to local circumstances. In fact there was hardly an area in the country where shortage of ammunition was not felt – and it was one of the most important tasks of general headquarters, besides intelligence, to import and distribute arms, ammunition and explosives. Agents were sent to England and Scotland, and received valuable assistance from Irishmen there, and Irish sailors on the cross-channel steamers constituted a regular branch of the army, smuggling in arms and ammunition and other military supplies – and sometimes secretly transporting men backward and forward between the two countries.

The IRA and IRB in England and Scotland gave valuable assistance in many ways besides this, as when they organised prison escapes and rescues, carried out reprisals in England by burning the houses of Black and Tans, and destroyed by fire a number of warehouses at Liverpool docks.

In Belfast and other centres in north-east Ulster, the republican forces had a peculiarly difficult and dangerous task, since they had to contend with the hostility not only of British crown forces, but the larger portion of the surrounding population; and many of their activities were followed by 'reprisals' by Orange mobs, on a greater scale than, and just as savage as, the Black and Tans. When a murderer of Tomás MacCurtain, District Inspector Swanzy, was shot dead in Lisburn, a mob burned and looted the houses of Catholics; and later there was an Orange 'pogrom' in Derry, which ended in casualties to the attackers. Despite these difficulties, the IRA in Belfast – and other areas – continued their activities, and carried out many successful coups.

When partition was established by the Government of Ireland Act of 1920, a boycott of Belfast firms, and even banks, was declared and enforced in the rest of Ireland, with such success as to alarm the partitionists. Indeed Sir James Craig, the first Premier of the six-county government, came secretly to Dublin, and obtained an interview with Mr de Valera, in the hope of coming to an agreement; but Orange diehards, learning of this, took alarm, and the hopes of agreement ended.

The burning of Patrick Street, the city hall and other places in Cork city as a 'reprisal' for an IRA ambush, on 11 December 1920, and the outrages and lootings that accompanied it, was one of many such cases, but it created a sensation outside Ireland. The English chief secretary declared that the identity of the sackers of Cork was not known; but shortly after that 'unofficial' reprisals ceased and 'official' reprisals, carried out by the regular troops, were substituted as a policy.

It was at this time, December 1920, that the English Prime Minister, Mr Lloyd George, secretly offered to the IRA through the Most Rev. Dr Clune, Archbishop of Perth, Western Australia, a truce similar to that agreed to in July 1921. The offer was conveyed to Arthur Griffith, Acting President, then in Mountjoy prison, who reported it to Michael Collins whom, on his arrest, he had appointed as his substitute. Before an agreement was arrived at, the diehard element in the British Cabinet insisted on a surrender of arms by our men and the negotiations broke down. A new campaign of terrorism was started.

Many murders and outrages were committed by British agents during this period. One atrocity which excited widespread horror and indignation was the murder, in the presence of their wives, of George Clancy, Mayor, and Michael O'Callaghan, ex-Mayor of Limerick, in March 1921. According to the late General Crozier, Commanding Officer of the Auxiliaries, who resigned in protest over the abuses and irregularities in his forces, a plot was also hatched, and nearly succeeded, to murder the Most Rev. Dr Fogarty, Bishop of Killaloe, whose sympathy with our cause was fearlessly shown at all times.

Execution of prisoners tried by court-martial now became frequent.

In the south martial law was declared. It was never quite clear to me what difference this made, as the military were equally in complete control, and equally a law to themselves in other areas. In Dublin 'curfew' was introduced in the summer of 1920, following a shooting affray between police and Volunteers. In the summer of 1921 curfew in Dublin lasted from 8 p.m. till 6 a.m., during which time the streets were patrolled by lorries. This did not prevent members of the IRA carrying out some operations during the 'prohibited' hours. In Cork city the curfew regulations and hours were even more drastic.

All this time those members of Dáil Éireann who were available held secret sessions in various buildings in Dublin, and the different departments of the republican government functioned, each in its own 'underground' office. Communication between the various offices was carried out by messengers, usually youths mounted on bicycles, whose courage and presence of mind were often called for in the vital work they had to do. Late in December 1920, Mr de Valera returned secretly from the United States, to which he had gone in May 1919, and the president's department was again added to the list of secret offices.

The various departments of general headquarters of the IRA carried on their work in a similar manner. The highest officers and directors of departments had offices and staffs and messengers, and there were, besides, what were sometimes called 'republican post-offices', shops where letters might be safely left to be collected by the IRA orderlies and subordinate officers. We had besides, several bomb factories and a number of arsenals in various places in the cities. Workers employed at the railway stations and on the trains, who were in the IRA, were responsible for 'communications', conveying messages to and from every part of the country, and keeping headquarters in touch with the various active brigades. This work of 'communications' was, of course, of vital importance, and, apart from the regular railway system, motor transport was also employed in some cases.

Acknowledgement should also be made of the great assistance given by doctors and hospital nurses, particularly in tending the wounded, concealing their presence from the enemy and helping their escape.

Many Irish men and women, who could help in no other way, helped with their money by assisting the dependants of republican prisoners, and by contributing generously to the 'White Cross', a fund started to aid those who had suffered as the result of enemy outrages, burnings and lootings and the 'unofficial' and 'official' reprisals. By this time the outrages of the Black and Tans had aroused protests even from those who had been reared in the pro-British tradition; and many who would not be suspected of national sympathies took steps to convey to the British government their disapproval of its policy.

Many striking operations, too numerous to refer to, were carried out by the IRA in Dublin and in other parts of Ireland, despite the drastic action of a powerful enemy, the numerous executions and murders, and other atrocities. Finally, on 25 May 1921, occurred an operation which is often regarded as a landmark in the history of the Anglo-Irish war.

In 1918, when confronted with the menace of conscription, Brigadier Dick McKee laid before general headquarters a plan to seize and destroy the Custom House, worked out to the smallest detail. In Easter 1920, when the plan to raid income tax offices was being drafted, it was proposed to revive this plan and include the Custom House in the list of offices; but a strong military guard had been placed on it, which rendered this impracticable. In May 1921, this plan was revived and on 25 May the Custom House was raided and set on fire, and all financial and other records of a large number of British government departments were destroyed. As I wrote in *An t-Óglach* at the time: 'The burning of the Custom House symbolised the final collapse of English civil administration in this country.'

Apparently the British government realised this, and thought the time opportune for renewing their overtures of December 1920. The pressure of public opinion abroad, and particularly in the United States, was beginning to be felt, and a great many liberal-minded Englishmen were growing restive at the reports from Ireland. Furthermore, the bulk of the English people were still war weary after four years of life-and-death struggle in the First World War and its aftermath, and did not relish a war so close to their own borders, keeping so many of their young men in the army on a war footing.

The British parliament had passed a 'Government of Ireland Act', better known in Ireland as 'the Partition Act', setting up two subordinate parliaments with limited powers in Ireland, and an 'election' was declared. Republican candidates for Dáil Éireann were returned unopposed for every constituency outside Ulster, and many for the northern province. The new Dáil Éireann continued to meet secretly, ignoring British legislation. Despite this flouting, the British government attained one object by their Act, the setting up of a separate 'government' in six counties of Ulster, before opening negotiations with the Irish nation's representatives.

In June 1921, a British officer in charge of a patrol arrested Mr de Valera and brought him to Dublin Castle. He was shortly afterwards released, and the English Prime Minister, Mr David Lloyd George, addressed a public letter to him on 24 June, inviting him, with any colleagues he might select, to a conference 'to discuss the possibility of a settlement'. This was the beginning of a correspondence and meetings which resulted in the agreement of a truce between representatives of the Irish and English army at the English military general headquarters in Parkgate Street, Dublin. It was the end of the Anglo-Irish War, and the first formal recognition by the British of the Irish forces as belligerents since the Siege of Limerick in 1691. This fact alone renders the Truce of 11 July 1921, a memorable triumph.

In this severely summarised narrative I have endeavoured to make clear the background, atmosphere, developments and chain of events which constituted the history of Ireland during a vital period. It is a history of which the various exciting episodes narrated in this book are important and interesting chapters. Many of these dramatic episodes are recounted by those who acted a part in them, others on first-hand evidence. Taken together they form a series of pictures of a period which gives material not only for the historian, but the student of social science, the dramatist, novelist and poet.

THE CONSTITUTIONAL BASIS OF THE NATIONAL STRUGGLE

by General Seán MacEoin, TD

(formerly Vice-Brigadier and Director of Operations Longford Brigade IRA and O/C Longford Brigade flying column)

Few people realise today what was the constitutional basis on which the national struggle was waged in the period 1919 to the Truce. When the government of the Republic of Ireland issued its proclamation in 1916, the signatories gave just their names, without stating the offices or ministries which they held in the government of the Republic. Each signatory held a particular office and appointment. Amongst the signatories to the proclamation was the president of the Republic, ministers of the various offices of state, and a commander-in-chief of the army. Though they described themselves as a 'Provisional Government', there is no doubt whatever that each man held an appointment or office similar to those held today by the head of the state and by the various ministers.

When, in December 1918, the Irish people got an opportunity to elect an independent parliament, they did so by an overwhelming majority in practically all of Ireland, and though, when it assembled on 21 January 1919, some of the elected members of parliament refused to take their seats in the First Dáil, as that parliament was officially named, their absence did not lessen its validity. When the First Dáil met it carried out the same procedure which is followed today. The election of a ceann comhairle was proceeded with, and Cathal Brugha became the first holder of that office. Father O'Flanagan opened the session with a prayer invoking the divine blessing upon that first elected parliament of the Irish people. The roll was then called. All elected representatives, from Antrim to Cork and from Dublin to Galway, had already been summoned to attend and their names were called. The constitution for the Dáil was submitted and approved. The Declaration of Independence proclaimed in 1916 was confirmed and was published in a new form in Irish, French and English. Delegates representing the Irish nation were appointed to the peace conference in Paris, and a message of peace and goodwill was sent to all the free nations in the world. A democratic programme was enacted and in the report of that programme is the first official recognition of a president of the Republic. It is given on page 22 of the official report of that first session which contains the phrase: 'We declare, in the words of the Irish Republican Proclamation, the right of the people of Ireland to the ownership of Ireland, and to the unfettered control of Irish destinies, to be indefeasible, and, in the language of our first president, Pádraig Mac Piarais, we declare that the nation's sovereignty extends not only to all men and women of the nation, but to all its material possessions, the nation's soil and all its resources.' In this quotation it is clearly established that we had a symbolic and executive head of the state in its first president.

The second session of the Dáil was held on 22 January, when standing orders were approved and a government or ministry was appointed. Cathal Brugha was elected president of the Ministry *pro tempore,* as reported on page 26 of the official report. The following ministers were appointed: Finance, Eoin MacNeill; Home Affairs, Michael Collins; Foreign Affairs, Count Plunkett; National Defence, Richard Mulcahy. On the same date, Seán T. O'Kelly, our present president of Ireland, was appointed ceann comhairle in succession to Cathal Brugha.

The next meeting of the Dáil was held in private in the Mansion House, Dublin, on 1 April 1919. Seán T. O'Kelly was confirmed as ceann comhairle. The priomh-aire, or prime minister, was then nominated, and Éamon de Valera, member for East Clare, was elected. On the following day, as stated on page 36 of the official report, the Prime Minister submitted the names of his ministers for the approval of the Dáil. Each Minister was proposed and seconded by a deputy of the House and approved by vote of the House, as follows:

Secretary for Home Affairs, Art Ó Griobhtha. Proposed by Liam de Róiste (Cork city). Seconded by P. Ó Maille (Connemara). Approved.

Secretary for Defence, Cathal Brugha. Proposed by J. MacGuinness (Longford). Seconded by Piaras Béaslaí (East Kerry). Approved.

Secretary for Foreign Affairs, Count N.G. Plunkett. Proposed by A. Griffith (East Cavan). Seconded by P. Ó Maille (Connemara). Approved.

Secretary for Labour, Countess Markievicz. Proposed by Liam de Róiste (Cork city). Seconded by S. Etchingham (East Wicklow). Approved.

Secretary for Industries, Eoin MacNeill. Proposed by Cathal Brugha (County Waterford). Seconded by Seán MacEntee (South Monaghan). Approved.

Secretary for Finance, Micheal Ó Coileáin. Proposed by A. McCabe (South Sligo). Seconded by H. Boland (South Roscommon). Approved.

Secretary for Local Government, Liam MacCosgair. Proposed by John Mahony (South Fermanagh). Seconded by R.C. Barton (West Wicklow). Approved.

Heads of Departments: Propaganda, L. Ginnell; Agriculture, R.C. Barton.

On 4 April it was decided to publish the names of the ministers or secretaries of state.

There is in the foregoing a clear picture of a properly elected and democratic government established by the votes of the people to guard the interests and rights of the Irish nation and its citizens and to speak both internally and externally on their behalf. It is difficult to realise today that the situation was not fully appreciated at the time by a great number of people, including some who had taken a very prominent part in bringing it about. It was not realised by all that there was a symbolic head, or president, of the Republic at that time, just as definitely as there had been one who signed the proclamation of 1916. The fact that the head of that government was described as a priomh-aire, or prime minister, should have been a clear indication to all reasonable and intelligent people that he was Prime Minister to a President.

I do not propose to give that person's name in this article, but I wish to stress the fact that it was by his orders that I was directed, at the meeting of An Dáil in August 1921, to propose that Éamon de Valera be elected president of the Republic. This motion was seconded by Richard Mulcahy. From the date of the proclamation of the Republic in 1916 until the assembly of the First Dáil in January 1919, the government of the Republic was in the hands of the supreme council of the IRB, to whose president all members had sworn obedience and allegiance as the titular head of the Republic. Owing to the fact that the country was under enemy occupation at the time, the democratic election of a republican government was an impossibility and the IRB government was in fact a predecessor of the many patriot underground governments which functioned and received recognition during the recent war. During this period the armed forces of the Republic consisted of the Volunteers, under the control of their own elected executive, and the circles of the IRB, under their centres.

An entirely new situation arose with the assembly of the First Dáil and its re-affirmation of the declaration of the Republic and its acceptance of the social principles embodied therein. There was then in existence an established government appointed by the legally elected representatives of the people, and to that government the supreme council of the IRB at once voluntarily ceded all its powers except one. The president of the IRB continued to be regarded by the Brotherhood as the president of the Republic until 1921, when, as I have already stated, Éamon de Valera was nominated and elected to succeed him.

This prompt and voluntary cession of its powers, in the moment of triumph, by a secret revolutionary body, has few parallels in history, and nothing could demonstrate more clearly the high patriotic motives that inspired the supreme council. This voluntary abdication in favour of the new government has never been fully understood by the public.

Having voluntarily divested itself of its executive powers at the commencement of 1919, the supreme council of the Irish Republican Brotherhood, however, did not itself dissolve until five years later. As long as the struggle continued, there was danger that the elected government and Dáil might, at any moment, find themselves extinguished by enemy action, and, should this happen, the supreme council held itself in readiness to carry on the fight as a 'caretaker' government.

The British declared war upon the Irish people and their government by proclaiming the Dáil, forbidding it to meet or function, and by proceeding to arrest, intern and destroy, in so far as it lay in their power to do so, every prominent member of the Dáil or of the armed forces established under the Ministry of Defence. The IRB and the Irish Volunteers were already in being and constituted a ready-made army determined to support and defend the Irish people and their government against all enemies, whomsoever.

At various meetings of the Dáil, as reported in the first, second and third volumes of the *Dáil Debates,* each Minister made written reports on the administration of his department, with the exception of the Minister for Defence, who made oral reports. In one of those verbal reports he informed the Dáil that the enemy was attempting to draw the Irish army into a defensive action suitable to the British, but added that his department intended to use 'their own methods'.

It is true that it was not until the private session of August 1919 that the oath of allegiance to the Republic was decided upon, but it was agreed that it must be taken by: (1) all Dáil deputies; (2) the Volunteers; (3) the officials and clerks of the Dáil; (4) any other body or individual who, in the opinion of the Dáil, should take the same oath. These decisions are reported on page 151 of the *Dáil Debates* for 20 August 1919.

The oath of allegiance was taken by the deputies and officials in October 1919, and thereby was concluded the building of a parliamentary and governmental institution. At that meeting the British proclamation banning the Dáil was announced, and authority was given to the Minister for Defence to undertake the task of defending the nation from this aggression. The Volunteer army, which then became known as the Irish Republican Army, was organised throughout the thirty-two counties and had been formed into brigades, battalions and companies. Accordingly, not alone had we a properly constituted government, but we also had a properly constituted national army, all members of which had taken the oath of allegiance prescribed by the government and parliament of the people. Hereunder is given the personnel of the headquarters, brigade staffs as entered on the roll of the headquarters, brigade and battalion staffs as entered on the roll of the director of organisation from January 1919 onwards. This roll, which is still in my possession, dates from January 1919, and is in the handwriting of Eamonn Price and Diarmuid O'Hegarty. It is, to the best of my belief, the only written record of its date, and its authorship is a guarantee of its accuracy; but it must be remembered that promotions, removals, additions and other alterations were very numerous between the commencement of the year 1919 and the Truce. Blanks are entered where the records were not kept or where organisation was not complete by January 1919. The numerals before the names of the officers denote ranks as follows: (1) brigade O/C or battalion O/C; (2) vice O/C; (3) adjutant; (4) quartermaster.

Headquarters Staff: Chief of Staff, Richard Mulcahy; Adjutant General, Gearóid O'Sullivan; Quartermaster-General, Seán Mc-Mahon; Director of Intelligence, Michael Collins. Other members of the staff included: J.J. ('Ginger') O'Connell, Diarmuid O'Hegarty, Liam Mellows, Eamonn Price, Rory O'Connor, Seán Russell, Michael Staines, Piaras Béaslaí, Seamus Donovan and, *ex-officio,* the O/C Dublin Brigade.

Cork No. 1 Brigade: (1) Seán O'Hegarty, (2) M. Leahy, (3) Florence O'Donoghue, (4) ———. 1st Battalion (Cork city): (1) Dan Donovan, (2) Tom Crofts, (3) ———, (4) ———. 2nd Battalion (Cork city): (1) Michael Murphy, (2) ———, (3) ———, (4) ———. 3rd Battalions (Srelane): (1) ———, (2) ——— (3) ———, (4) ———. 4th Battalion (Cobh): (1) M. Leahy, (2) ———, (3) ———, (4) ———. 5th Battalion (Whitechurch): (1) —— MacNamara, (2) ———, (3)

———, (4) ———. 6th Battalion (Firmount): (1) J. O'Leary, (2) ——— —, (3) Jim Barrett, (4) P. Collins. 7th Battalion (Macroom): (1) ——— —, (2) ———, (3) ———, (4) ———. 8th Battalion (Kilnamartyra): (1) Pat Sullivan, (2) ——— (3) ———, (4) ———. 9th Battalion (Rochestown): (1) Richard O'Mahony, (2) Denis Lordan, (3) Henry O'Mahony, (4) J. Barrett.

Cork No. 2 Brigade: (1) Seán Moylan, (2) George Power, (3) ——— —, (4) ———. 1st Battalion (Fermoy): (1) ———, (2) M.S. Keane, (3) ———, (4) Cors Leddy. 2nd Battalion (Mallow): (1) ———, (2) ———, (3) ———, (4) ———. 3rd Battalion (Castletownroche): (1) ———, (2) Eamon Creed, (3) ———, (4) ———. 4th Battalion (Charleville): (1) ———, (2) ———, (3) ———, (4) ———. 5th Battalion (Kanturk): (1) Denis Lyons, (2) Denis Murphy, (3) ———, (4) M. Courtney. 6th Battalion (Newmarket): (1) ———, (2) ———, (2) ———, (3) ———, (4) ———. 7th Battalion (Millstreet): (1) ———, (2) ———, (3) ———, (4) ———.

Cork No. 3 Brigade: (1) Charles Hurley (acting for Tom Hales), (2) Ted Sullivan, (3) Liam Deiseach, (4) ———. 1st Battalion (Bandon): (1) John Hales, (2) M. O'Neill, (3) James O'Mahony, (4) Tady O'Sullivan. 2nd Battalion (Clonakilty): (1) Batt Murphy, (2) —— Murphy, (3) James Hurley, (4) Pat O'Keeffe. 3rd Battalion (Dunmanway): (1) John Murphy, (2) S. Crowley, (3) Pat O'Brien, (4) Dan Hourihan. 4th Battalion (Skibbereen): (1) ———, (2) Cornelius Connolly, (3) Florence O'Donoghue, (4) Patrick O'Sullivan. 5th Battalion (Bantry): (1) Maurice Donegan (Tom Ward), (2) Thomas Ward, (3) James Spillane, (4) Pat O'Sullivan. 6th Battalion (Castletownbere): (1) Peter O'Neill, (2) William O'Neill. (3) John O'Sullivan, (4) Daniel O'Sullivan. 7th Battalion (Schull): (1) John Lehane, (2) William Murphy, (3) Gibbs Ross, (4) John McCarthy.

Clare East Brigade: (1) A. Brennan, (2) Thomas McGrath, (3) Joe Brennan. (4) Seán Murnane (J. Hannon). 1st Battalion (Newmarket-on-Fergus): (1) M. Murray, (2) —— McInerney, (3) J.J. Hogan, (4) M. Brennan. 2nd Battalion (Cratloe): (1) J. McNamara, (2) J. McCormack, (3) —— Rochford, (4) F. Ryan. 3rd Battalion (Ogonelloe): (1) Jack

Ryan, (2) P. Donnellan, (3) Thomas Menaha, (4) James Scanlon. 4th Battalion (Scariff): (1) Seán O'Halloran, (2) ———, (3) Mick Mahon, (4) ———. 5th Battalion (Tulla): (1) Timothy Burns, (2) ———, (3) ———, (4) ———. 6th Battalion (Killenanagh): (1) H. O'Mara, (2) ———, (3) ———, (4) ———.

Clare Mid Brigade (1) Frank Barrett, (2) Peadar O'Loughlin, (3) Joe Barrett (4) Seán O'Keefe. 1st Battalion (Ennis): (1) Con McMahon, (2) Liam Stack, (3) Michael Foley, (4) Michael McGuan. 2nd Battalion (Darragh) (Ballyea): (1) Pat Costello, (2) Michael Barrett, (3) Vesty Barrett, (4) Michael McMahon. 3rd Battalion (Corofin): (1) Seán Casey, (2) Peadar O'Brien, (3) John Monihan, (4) Michael Hegarty. 4th Battalion (Ennistymon): (1) Ignatius O'Neill, (2) Pake Lehane, (3) Anthony Malone, (4) Stephen Gallagher. 5th Battalion (Kilshanny): (1) Andrew O'Donoghue, (2) Thomas Shalloo, (3) Peter O'Brien, (4) Peter Considine. 6th Battalion (Ballyvaughan): (1) Seán McNamara, (2) T. Dillon, (3) Pat Hurley, (4) John Nestor.

Clare West Brigade: (1) J. Liddy, (2) Pádraig Clancy, (3) J. O'Durfer, (4) Pádraig Burke. 1st Battalion (Cranny): (1) James O'Dea, (2) M.C. Falihee, (3) ———, (4) ———. 2nd Battalion (Tullycrine): (1) Jack Flannagan, (2) Jack O'Donnell, (3) James Lorigan, (4) P. McNamara. 3rd Battalion (Cooraclare): (1) Dan Sheedy, (2) Tom Martin, (3) Mick McGrath, (4) Connor Whelan. 4th Battalion (Mullagh): (1) Chris McCarthy, (2) H. McKenna, (3) Dan Montgomery, (4) Patrick O'Dea. 5th Battalion (Carrigaholt): (1) James Talty, (2) M. McMahon (P. McGrath), (3) D.S. Conroy, (4) ———.

Kerry No. 1 Brigade: (1) P.J. Cahill, (2) Joe Melinn, (3) D. O'Sullivan, (4) W. Mullins. 1st Battalion (Tralee): (1) Dan Healy, (2) M. Doyle, (3) M. Fleming, (4) P. Barry. 2nd Battalion (Dingle): (1) An Seabhac, (2) M. Moriarty, (3) —— Fitzgerald, (4) M. Keane. 3rd Battalion (Castlegregory): (1) T. Brosnan, (2) D. Rohan, (3) M. Duhig, (4) ———. 4th Battalion (Listowel): (1) P. Landers, (2) M. O'Brien, (3) J. Sugrue, (4) ———. 5th Battalion (Ardfert): (1) T. Clifford, (2) P. McKenna, (3) J. Carmody, (4) Batt MacElligott. 6th Battalion (Killorglin): (1) F. Doherty, (2) T. Connor, (3) B. Dwyer, (4)

—— Scully. 7th Battalion (Lixnaw): (1) S. O'Grady, (2) T. Kennedy (or Kennealy), (3) —— Shanahan, (4) —— Mangan.

Kerry No. 2 Brigade: (1) D. Mahony, (2) D. Dennehy, (3) R. Devane, (4) Humphrey Murphy. 1st Battalion (Castleisland): (1) T. O'Connor, (2) ———, (3) —— Sullivan, (4) J. Mahony. 2nd Battalion (Firies): (1) P. Riordan, (2) ———, (3) ———, (4) ———. 3rd Battalion (Killarney): (1) M. Spillane. (2) M.J. Sullivan, (3) Pat O'Shea, (4) Jim Coffey. 4th Battalion (Rathmore): (1) H. Sullivan, (2) J. Kennedy, (3) M. Dennehy, (4) Michael Daly. 5th Battalion (Kenmare): (1) J. Rice, (2) ———, (3) ———, (4) ———, J. Flynn (transport).

Kerry No. 3 Brigade: (Caherciveen Battalion) (1) D. O'Riordan, (2) Denis Daly, (3) S. O'Crian (acting), (Muiris O'Cleary), (4) D. Daly. The following companies were included in the brigade: Caherciveen, Killoe, Ballycarbery, Filemore, Glen, Ballinskelligs, Waterville, Mastergeeha, Portmagee, Caherdaniel, Valentia, Loher, Bahoo.

Limerick East Brigade: (1) Seán de Bhal, (2) D. O'Hannigan, (3) S. McCarthy, (4) ———. 1st Battalion (Galbally): (1) Seán Lynch, (2) ———, (3) ———, (4) ———. 2nd Battalion (Kilfinane): (1) Justin McCarthy, (2) ———, (3 ———, (4) ———. 3rd Battalion (Kilmallock): (1) Michael Clery, (2) —— Cleary, (3) ———, (4) ———. 4th Battalion (Bruff): (1) John O'Connor, (2) ——— (James Dwyer), (3) ———, (4) ———. 5th Battalion (Kilteely): (1) W. Hayes (Owen O'Keeffe), (2) ———, (3) ———, (4) ———. 6th Battalion (Doon): (1) Dan Allis (M. Ryan), (2) Jack Stapleton, (3) ———, (4) ———.

Limerick Mid Brigade: (1) Peadar Dunne, (2) Owen O'Brien, (3) P. Doyle, (4) Jim Gallagher. 1st Battalion: (1) ———, (2) ———, (3) ———, (4) ———. 2nd Battalion (Limerick city): (1) H. Meany (James O'Brien), (2) J. O'Brien, (3) P. Doyle, (4) —— Rahilly (Wallace). 3rd Battalion (Castleconnell): (1) Seán Carroll, (2) ———, (3) ———, (4) ———. 4th Battalion (Patrick's Well): (1) ———, (2) ———, (3) ———, (4) ———. 5th Battalion (Caherconlish): (1) R. O'Connell (Clifford), (2) —— Hennessy, (3) —— Tierney, (4) M. Cremins.

Limerick West Brigade: (1) Seán Finn, (2) Garrett McAuliffe, (3)

J. Roche, (4) P. O'Shaughnessy (J. Colbert). 1st Battalion (Newcastle): (1) J. Liston, (2) J. Keilly, (3) P. Mulcahy, (4) J. Kiely (Pat Hayes). 2nd Battalion (Tournafulla): (1) M. Hartnett, (2) —— Aherney, (3) T. Leahy, (4) P. Fitzgerald. 3rd Battalion (Feohanagh): (1) C. Foley, (2) B. Sullivan, (3) ———, (4) M. Sheehy. 4th Battalion (Rathkeale): (1) J. Halpin, (2) W. Fitzgerald, (3) L. Meade, (2) P. O'Shea, (3) J. O'Brien, (4) J. O'Brien.

Tipperary North Brigade: (1) Seán Gaynor, (2) Liam Hoolan, (3) E. O'Leary, (4) F. Flannery. 1st Battalion (Nenagh): (1) Austin McCurtin, (2) Con Spain, (3) Michael Hickey, (4) M. Spain. 2nd Battalion (Toomevara): (1) Jeremiah Collison, (2) Hugh Kelly, (3) P. Kennedy, (4) P. White. 3rd Battalion (Portroe): (1) —— McDonnell, (2) M. Kennedy, (3) —— McDonnell, (4) Dan Costelloe. 4th Battalion (Borrisokane): (1) —— Cronin, (2) ———, (3) ———, (4) ———. 5th Battalion (Templederry): (1) P. O'Doherty (S. Capless), (2) Patrick Cash, (3) William Hanley, (4) P. O'Brien. 6th Battalion (Newport): (1) William Gleeson, (2) —— O'Connell, (3) Michael Gantley, (4) E. Maher. 7th Battalion (Roscrea): (1) ———, (2) ———, (3) ———, (4) ———.

Tipperary Mid Brigade: (1) James Lahy, (2) E. McGrath, (3) M. Kennedy, (4) John McCormack. 1st Battalion (Thurles): (1) Jerh Ryan, (2) P. Lahy, (3) William Short, (4) Michael Eustace. 2nd Battalion (Drombane): (1) Pat Kinnane, (2) James Stapleton, (3) Jn Dunne, (4) ———. 3rd Battalion (Templemore): (1) J. Scott, (2) Michael Egan, (3) Michael Hynes, (4) J. Ryan.

Tipperary South Brigade: (1) Seamus Robinson, (2) ———, (3) Conn Ó Maoldomhnaigh (acting for M. Crowe), (4) ———. 1st Battalion (Tipperary): (1) Seán Duffy, (2) C. Moloney, (3) Tom Ryan, (4) Denis Lacy. 2nd Battalion (Dundrum): (1) T. Dwyer, (2) M. Shehan, (3) Phil Fitzgerald, (4) Jack Ryan (Laurence). 3rd Battalion (Cashel): (1) Seamus O'Neill, (2) J. Grogan, (3) P. Hogan, (4) Pat Casey. 4th Battalion (Clonmel): (1) Frank Drohen, (2) Bill Myles, (3) William Hanrahan, (4) Seamus Kennedy. 5th Battalion (Cahir): (1) —— McGrath, (2) Michael Ledrigan, (3) Will Casey, (4) ———. 6th

Battalion (Drangan): (1) T. Donovan, (2) ———, (3) ———, (4) ———. 7th Battalion (Carrick-on-Suir): (1) John O'Keeffe, (2) ———, (3) ———, (4) ———. 8th Battalion (Rosegreen): (1) J. Davin, (2) P. Quinn, (3) J. Delahunty, (4) J. Purcell.

Waterford East Brigade: (1) W. Walsh, (2) Liam Keane, (3) Michael O'Neill, (4) Seán Lane. 1st Battalion: (1) Patrick Paul, (2) James Morrissey, (3) Seán Power, (4) M. Knox. 2nd Battalion: (1) J. Power, (2) ———, (3) ———, (4) P. Hanley. 3rd Battalion: (1) Joseph Rickard, (2) Edward Power, (3) Nicholas Power, (4) Patrick Kennedy.

Waterford West Brigade: (1) P. Ó Faolain, (2) George Lennon, (3) Philip O'Donnell, (4) —— Mansfield. 1st Battalion (Dungarvan): (1) L. Condon, (2) T.E. Power, (3) —— O'Donnell, (4) P. Lynch. 2nd Battalion (Lismore): (1) P. Morrissey, (2) E. Murphy, (3) T. Duggan, (4) T. Burke. 3rd Battalion (Ardmore): (1) James Mansfield, (2) N. Doyle, (3) Declan Slattery, (4) Rd Mooney.

Carlow Brigade: (1) Eamonn Malone, (2) P. Cosgrave, (3) Seán Hayden, (4) Pat O'Toole. 1st Battalion (Carlow): (1) M. Lennon (L. O'Neill): (2) M. Doorley, (3) ———, (4) ———. 2nd Battalion. (Baltinglass): (1) E. Nolan, (2) ———, (3) ———, (4) ———. 3rd Battalion (Clonmore): (1) W. O'Donoghue, (2) ———, (3) ———, (4) ———. 4th Battalion (Borris) (1) ———, (2) Seán Murphy, (3) ———, (4) ———. 5th Battalion (Athy): (1) J. Kavanagh, (2) W. Brennan, (3) ———, (4) ———. 6th Battalion (Suncroft): (1) ———, (2) ———, (3) ———, (4) ——— .

Dublin City Brigade: (1) R. Mac Aoi (McKee), (2) O. Traynor, (3) Charles Suarin, (4) P. McQuirk. 1st Battalion (North West): (1) Thomas Byrne, (2) George Irvine, (3) Liam Ó Cearbhall, (4) P. Rooney. 2nd Battalion (North East): (1) Seán Russell, (2) Pádraig Ó Dálaigh (Seán Mooney acting), (3) Hy. Colley, (4) P.T. O'Reilly (acting for Michael McDonnell). 3rd Battalion (South East): (1) Seosamh Ó Conchubhair, (2) Simon Donnelly, (3) —— Guilfoyle, (4) ———. 4th Battalion (South West): (1) Eamon O'Kelly, (2) Chris Byrne (3) Peadar O'Brien, (4) ———. 5th Battalion (Sappers): (1) Liam Archer, (2) Jack Plunkett, (3) ———, (4) ———. 6th Battalion (South County):

(1) ———, (2) ———, (3) ———, (4) ———. Seventh Battalion: (1) Gerald Boland, (2) P. Kavanagh, (3) Jack Hall, (4) Thomas Byrne.

Fingal Brigade: (1) Michael Lynch, (2) Leo Henderson, (3) V. Purfield, (4) ———. 1st Battalion: (1) M. Rock, (2) R. Gaynor, (3) ———, (4) W. Rooney. 2nd Battalion: (1) J. Sheils, (2) ———, (3) ———, (4) ———. 3rd Battalion: (1) ———, (2) T. Mackey, (3) ———, (4) ———.

Kildare One: (1) P. Clogan, (2) P. Purcell, (3) —— Fay, (4) P. Dunne. Companies and Company Captains: Maynooth. T. McGee, Kilcock; M. Flynn; Leixlip, James Farrell; Cloncurry, Patrick Feeney; Celbridge, Alex Dwyer; Johnstown Bridge, Chris Ford; Carbery, L. Dempsey; Mainham, Patrick Dunn; Straffan, John Logan; Clougharide, Patrick Malone; Broadford, Patrick Cusack.

Kildare Two (Athgarvan): (1) Thomas Harris, (2) M. Smith, (3) Seán Corry, (4) ———. Companies and Company Captains: Athgarvan, M. Cardiff; Ballymore Eustace, Arthur Doran; Newbridge, P. Roche; Naas, J. Rafferty; Prosperous, R. Harris: Robertstown, M. Fitzgerald; Two Mile House, A. Byrne; Valley, J. Kavanagh; Battin, J. Purcell; Blessington, —— O'Connor; Allen, H. Herbert.

Kilkenny Brigade: (1) Thomas Treacy, (2) James Lalor, (3) L. Dardis, (4) E. Comerford. 1st Battalion (City): (1) Tim Hennessy, (2) James Cullen, (3) Thomas Furlong, (4) Patrick Bryan. 2nd Battalion (Castlecomer): (1) George O'Dwyer, (2) M. Delany, (3) Murty Brennan, (4) Michael Fleming. 3rd Battalion (Goresbridge): (1) Martin Kealy, (2) William Canigan, (3) John Cottrell, (4) John Morrisey. 4th Battalion (Mullinavat): (1) M. McGrath, (2) R. Morgan, (3) Denis McDonald, (4) R. Kinneally. 5th Battalion (Callan): (1) James Rowan, (2) J.J. Dunne, (3) John Myles, (4) Patrick Walsh.

Leix Brigade: (1) Michael Gray, (2) Thomas Brady, (3) Martin Lynch, (4) Frank Golding. 1st Battalion (Maryboro): (1) T. O'Neill, (2) P. Pingleton, (3) J. McEvers, (4) M. O'Neill. 2nd Battalion (Clonaslee): (1) J. Gorman, (2) ——— (3) ———, (4) R. McEvoy. 3rd Battalion (Durrow): (1) T. Fennelly, (2) E. McEvoy, (3) J. Campion, (4) J. Fitzpatrick. 4th Battalion (Knocklaide): (1) Lee Brady (also director of organisation), (2) J. Kelly, (3) J. Ramsbottom, (4) J. Hyland. 5th Battalion (Portarlington): (1) J. Scully, (2) ———, (3) D. Flynn, (4) D. Gleeson. 6th Battalion: (1) E. Brennan, (2) F. Morris, (3) ———, (4) ———.

Longford Brigade: (1) Tom Redington, (2) Seán Connolly, (3) James P. Flood, (4) E.J. Cooney. 1st Battalion (Ballinalee): (1) Seán MacEoin, (2) John Murphy, (3) John Duffy, (4) Frank Davis. 2nd Battalion (Longford): (1) James Keenan, (2) Michael Murphy, (3) Andrew Quinn, (4) Thomas Farrell. 3rd Battalion (Lanesboro): (1) Thomas Gibbins, (2) Peter Skelly, (3) Frank McGarry, (4) Patrick Farrell. 4th Battalion (Ardagh): (1) Patrick Ryan, (2) Leo Baxter, (3) Patrick Trott, (4) ———. 5th Battalion (Drumlish): (1) P. Kiernan, (2) J.J. Brady, (3) James Mulligan, (4) Frank Whitley.

Louth Brigade (Dundalk Battalion): (1) Seán Gormley, (2) Felix Daw, (3) Jim Kennedy, (4) Tom Rogers. Companies and Company Officers: Dundalk, Tom McGrane; Dundalk B. Owen Clifford; Omearth, P. Oakes; Cooley, James Boyle; Dromiske, P. McAleer; Ravensdale, J. Brennan; Blackrock, Joe Coffey; Ballsmill, Frank Donnelly; Doomisken, J. Kavanagh; Brycrisy, P. Thorne; Louth, P. McKenna. Drogheda Battalion: (1) Pat Murray, (2) George Hughes, (3) Brian Higgins. Grangebellew: (1) P. Byrne, (2) M. Butterly, (3) John Conlon. Termon Fecken: (1) Peter Mooney, (2) Pat Mooney, (3) John King. Duleek: N. Connell. Ardee: (1) Eugene Kavanagh, (2) John Halligan, (3) Owen Doherty. Donneycarney: (1) John McEvoy, (2) M. Kearney, (3) Michael Mehane. Tullyallen: (1) William Tuite, (2) Bernard Mohan, (3) Thomas Downey.

Meath Brigade: (1) Seán Boylan, (2) Seán Hayes, (3) Seamus Finn, (4) Seamus O'Higgins. 1st Battalion (Dunboyne): (1) Bernard Dunne, (2) P. Callaghan, (3) D. Hall, (4) M. Toole. 2nd Battalion (Trim): (1) P. Mooney, (2) Michael Hynes, (3) ———, (4) ———. 3rd Battalion (Athboy): (1) Michael Fox, (2) Patrick Corrigan, (3) ———, (4) Patrick Carey. 4th Battalion (Kells): (1) P. Farrelly, (2) T. Reilly, (3) M. Cahill, (4) M. Govern. 5th Battalion (Oldcastle): (1) D. Smith, (2) John Farrelly, (3) P. O'Connell, (4) B. Daly. 6th Battalion (Navan):

(1) Patrick Fitzsimons (acting), (2) Arthur Levins (acting), (3) Kieran O'Connell (acting), (4) Leo McKenna (acting).

Offaly I Brigade: (1) Seán Kelly (acting), (2) Seamus O'Doona, (3) Liam Fitzpatrick (acting), (4) Thos Dunne. 1st Battalion (Tullamore): (1) Seamus McGuinness, (2) Seamus McGuinness, (3) Seán Talbot, (4) P. Egan. 2nd Battalion (Dangan): (1) Thomas Dunne, (2) Patrick Quinn, (3) James Scully, (4) James O'Brien. 3rd Battalion (Tyrells Pass): (1) P. Byrne, (2) P. Geraghty. (3) P. Lynam, (4) Patrick Carey. 4th Battalion (Edenderry): (1) J. Ryan, (2) L. Powell, (3) G. Bell, (4) D. Murphy.

Offaly II West Brigade: (1) Seán Mahon (acting), (2) ———, (3) Joseph Reddan (acting), (4) Seán Robbins (acting). 1st Battalion (Clara): (1) J. Fleming, (2) R. Morris, (3) R. Wier. (4) J. Finlay. 2nd Battalion (Cloghan): (1) ———. (2) ———, (3) ———, (4) ———. 3rd Battalion (Birr): (1) P. Delahunty, (2) P. Riordan, (3) D. Duffy, (4) W. King. 4th Battalion (Kilcormack): (1) M. Kelly, (2) J. Mangan. (3) J. Connolly. (4) M. Cordeal.

Westmeath (Athlone Brigade): (1) Seamus O'Mara, (2) Con Costelloe, (3) J. Manning, (4) Hugh Murtagh. 1st Battalion (Athlone): (1) Bernard Gaffney, (2) Patrick Watson. (3) Michael Cunniffe. (4) Ed Cunniffe. 2nd Battalion (Drumraney): (1) George Bartles (2) —— Connolly, (3) ———, (4) ———. 3rd Battalion (Summerhill): (1) B. Gaffney, (2) ———, (3) E. Cunniffe, (4) ———.

Westmeath (Mullingar Brigade): (1) D. Burke (J. Maguire) (2) J. Murphy, (3) B. Bagnall, (4) J. Doyle (—— Dunne). 1st Battalion (Mullingar): (1) M. McCoy, (2) H. Killeavy. (3) P. Byrne. (4) ———. 2nd Battalion (Loughinvalley): (1) W. Fox. (2) —— Garry, (3) P. Mahon, (4) —— Connell. 3rd Battalion (Milltown Pass): (1) Jos Bagnall, (2) J. Lennon, (3) P. Bracken, (4) ———. 4th Battalion (Castlepollard): (1) P. McCabe, (2) O. Brady, (3) J. Maguire, (4) J. Brogan.

Wexford Brigade: (1) Pilib Ó Lionam, (2) ———, (3) Liam Ó Laoghaire, (4) ———. 1st Battalion (Enniscorthy): (1) M.N. Doyle, (2) ———, (3) N. Somers, (4) Ned Doyle. 2nd Battalion (Enniscorthy): (1) P. Murphy (Fitzharris), (2) M. Murphy, (3) P. Brien. (4) J. Daly.

3rd Battalion (Wexford): (1) Tom Cousins, (2) J. Byrne, (3) Thomas Rutherford, (4) Thomas Cadogan. 4th Battalion (Carnew): (1) Tom Brennan, (2) Jos Kavanagh, (3) Pat Brennan, (4) John McGrath. 5th Battalion (Ross): (1) M. Ward, (2) P. Cleary, (3) P. McGrath, (4) E. Roe. 6th Battalion (Ferns): (1) Myles Breen, (2) arrested, (3) —— Dunbar, (4) J. Kelly.

Wicklow ( ): (1) James Geran, (2) P. Byrne, (3) M. Carroll, (4) C.M. Byrne. Companies and Company Officers: Wicklow, T. Hollywood; Roundwood, M. Rooney; Ashford, O. Shortt; Rathdrum, M. Byrne; Laragh, P. Byrne; Gleneally, P. Byrne; Barndarrig, P. Doyle; Avoca, P. Treacy.

Galway I (Connemara West Brigade): P.J. McDonnell, (2) ———, (3) Martin Connolly, (4) ———. 1st Battalion (Lettermore): (1) ———, (2) ———, (3) ——— (4) ———. 2nd Battalion (Lenane): (1) ———, (2) ———, (3) ———, (4) ———. 3rd Battalion (Clifden): (1) ———, (2) ———, (3) ———, (4) ———.

Galway II (Connemara East Brigade): (1) Michael Thornton, (2) M. Davoran, (3) E. Walsh, (4) M. Flaherty. 1st Battalion (Spiddal): (1) P. Costelloe, (2) ———, (3) ———, (4) ———. 2nd Battalion (Inverin): (1) B. Dillane, (2) ———, (3) ———, (4) ———. 3rd Battalion (Moycullen): (1) L. Coyne, (2) ———, (3) ———, (4) ———.

Galway III (Galway Brigade): (1) M. Newell, (2) N. Niland, (3) J. Hosty, (4) J. Broderick (Athenry). 1st Battalion (Galway): (1) J. Broderick (city), (2) ———, (3) P. Lally, (4) ———. 2nd Battalion, (Athenry): (1) G. Morrisey (2) ———, (3) J. Barret, (4) S. Jordan. 3rd Battalion (Headford): (1) L. Darcy, (2) ———, (3) P. Dooley, (4) ———.

Galway IV (Gort Brigade): (1) J. McInerney, (2) P. Howley, (3) J. Coen, (4) P. Ruane.

Galway V (Tuam Brigade): (1) Con Fogarty, (2) ———, (3) T. O'Grady, (4) —— Conway. 1st Battalion (Tuam): (1) T. Dunleavy, (2) J. O'Neill, (3) ———, (4) T. Ryan. 2nd Battalion (Dunmore): (1) J. Moloney, (2) ———, (3) —— Glynn, (4) —— Knight.

Galway VI (Ballinasloe Brigade): (1) P. Fitzpatrick, (2) ——, (3) J. Murphy, (4) ———. 1st Battalion (Mount Bellew): (1) J. Haverty, (2) ———, (3) T. Higgins, (4) J. Coppinger. 2nd Battalion (Ballinasloe): (1) P. Byrne, (2) ———, (3) B. Moore, (4) J. Broderick (Aughrim).

Galway VII (Loughrea Brigade): (1) M. O'Keeffe, (2) ———, (3) J. Quinn, (4) P. Coy. 1st Battalion (Loughrea): (1) P. Burke, (2) ———, (3) M. Regan, (4) M. Nevin. 2nd Battalion (Portumna): (1) —— Grace, (2) ———, (3) P. Lahy, (4) ———. 3rd Battalion (Eyrecourt): (1) M. Kenny, (2) ———, (3) B. Connor, (4) ———.

Leitrim Brigade: (1) Seán Mitchel, (2) Jas Wrenn, (3) Jos O'Beirne, (4) Frank Sweeney. 1st Battalion (Carrigallen): (1) J.J. McGarry, (2) Patrick Doherty, (3) John J. Cooney, (4) Patrick McGovern. 2nd Battalion (Ballinamore): (1) Bernard McGowan, (2) M. Bohan, (3) Francis McGovern, (4) Terence Boyle. 3rd Battalion (Mohill): (1) Francis O'Rourke, (2) Patrick Keville, (3) Gerard Flynn, (4) James Maxwell. 4th Battalion (Drumkeeran): (1) Stephen Flynn, (2) Hugh Wrynne (Rynne), (3) Louis Ward, (4) P.J. McMorrow.

Mayo North Brigade (Ballina): (1) T. Ruane, (2) E. Gannon, (3) P. O'Connell, (4) D. Sheerin. 1st Battalion (Belmullett): (1) Enri Ua Gairín, (2) Martin Moran, (3) Seán Neary, (4) ———. 2nd Battalion (Ballycastle): (1) Dr Crowley, (2) Seán Ó Longáin, (3) A. Ó Feargaill, (4) John Deane. 3rd Battalion (Ballina): (1) George Delany, (2) Matt Delany, (3) Seán Concannon, (4) Patrick O'Beirne. 4th Battalion (Foxford): (1) Dr Ferris, (2) Dr Dunleavy, (3) Seán O'Moran, (4) M. Docartaig. 5th Battalion (Corbally): A. Cleirig, (2) M. Beirne, (3) Seamus Ó Caomanaig, (4) E. O'Hanrahan. 6th Battalion (Crossmolina): (1) Seán O'Flynn, (2) B. O'Hegarty, (3) Éamon Ó Baoghail, (4) ——. Seventh Battalion (Bangor): (1) Peadar Ó Maille, (2) ———, (3) ———, (4) Eamon O'Huston.

Mayo South Brigade (Cross): (1) T. Maguire, (2) C.H. Burke, (3) M. O'Brien. (4) Jos Brennan. 1st Battalion (Cross): (1) ———, (2) ——, (3) ———, (4) ———. 2nd Battalion (Ballinrobe): (1) ———, (2) ———, (3) ———, (4) ———. 3rd Battalion (Claremorris): (1)

———, (2) ———, (3) ———, (4) ———. 4th Battalion (Balla): (1) ———, (2) ———, (3) ———, (4) ———.

Mayo East Brigade (Kiltimagh): (1) J. Corcoran, (2) ———, (3) A. Flattery, (4) Jos Sheehy. 1st Battalion (Swinford): (1) Thomas Fitzgerald, (2) P. Finn, (3) Dan Caulfield, (4) M. Gallagher. 2nd Battalion (Ballaghadereen): (1) ———, (2) ———, (3) ———, (4) ———. 3rd Battalion (Kiltimagh): (1) John Walshe, (2) P. Grennan, (3) T. Sheehy, (4) V. Freyne. 4th Battalion (Ballyhaunis): (1) ———, (2) Dominick Byrne, (3) A. Kenny, (4) ———.

Mayo West Brigade: (1) Tom Derrig, (2) Michael McHugh, (3) E. Moane, (4) M. Kilroy. 1st Battalion (Castlebar): (1) Brod Chambers, (2) P. Jordan, (3) H. Merchant, (4) —— Prendergast. 2nd Battalion (Westport): (1) Jos Ring, (2) James Rushe, (3) M. Griffin, (4) P. Lavelle. 3rd Battalion (Newport): (1) P. Foherty, (2) P. Melchrone (3) P. Monaghan, (4) P. Kelly. 4th Battalion (Louisburg): (1) P. Kelly, (2) A. Harney. (3) —— Joyce. (4) —— Lammon.

Roscommon North Brigade: (1) Seamus Ryan, (2) —— Dockery, (3) A. Lavin, (4) M. Killilea. 1st Battalion (Boyle): (1) John Kelly, (2) ———, (3) ———, (4) ———. 2nd Battalion (Elphin): (1) —— Owens, (2) ———, (3) ———, (4) ———. 3rd Battalion (Strokestown): (1) Bill O'Doherty, (2) ———, (3) T. Mason, (4) ———. 4th Battalion (Crossna): (1) J.J. Doyle, (2) V. Ryan, (3) T. Moran, (4) J. Glynn. 5th Battalion (Carrick-on-Shannon): (1) J. MacCormack (S. Durr acting), (2) D. Meehan, (3) W. Ward, (4) M. Moore.

Roscommon South Brigade: (1) ———, (2) ———, (3) ———, (4) ———. 1st Battalion (Castlerea): (1) Richard Betagh, (2) ———, (3) ———, (4) Stephen McDermott. 2nd Battalion (Oran): (1) ———, (2) ———, (3) ———, (4) ———. 3rd Battalion (Roscommon): (1) ———, (2) ———, (3) ———, (4) ———. 4th Battalion (Knockcroghery): (1) ———, (2) ———, (3) ———, (4) ———.

Sligo Brigade: (1) W. Pilkington, (2) ———, (3) ———, (4) ———. 1st Battalion (Sligo): (1) ———, (2) ———, (3) ———, (4) ———. 2nd Battalion (Grange): (1) ———, (2) ———, (3) ———, (4) ———. 3rd Battalion (Ballymote): (1) ———, (2) ———, (3) ———,

(4) ———. 4th Battalion (Gurteen): (1) ———, (2) ———, (3) ———, (4) ———. 5th Battalion (Riverstown): (1) T. Duignan, (2) ———, (3) ———, (4) ———. 6th Battalion (Tobercurry): (1) ———, (2) ———, (3) ———, (4) ———. 7th Battalion (Ballintogher): (1) ———, (2) ———, (3) ———, (4) ———.

Belfast Brigade: (1) Seán O'Neill, (2) J. McKelvey, (3) Leo Murphy, (4) Arthur Agnew. 1st Battalion: (1) Roger McCurley (R. McCormac), (2) Jos Savage, (3) Hugh Corven, (4) Seamus Woods. 2nd Battalion: (1) R. Maxwell, (2) J. McFee, (3) ———, (4) Seamus Keating.

Antrim Areas Brigade: (1) ———, (2) ———, (3) ———, (4) ———. 1st Battalion (Ballycastle): (1) W. Lynn, (2) ———, (3) ———, (4) ———. 2nd Battalion (Cushendall): (1) Archie McSarrow, (2) ———, (3) ———, (4) ———. 3rd Battalion (Dunloy): (1) Bob Dillon, (2) ———, (3) ———, (4) ———. 4th Battalion (Ballymena): (1) Denis O'Neill, (2) ———, (3) ———, (4) ———. 5th Battalion (Larne): (1) H.M. Erlaine. (2) ———, (3) ———, (4) ———.

Cavan Brigade: (1) ———, (2) ———, (3) ———, (4) ———. 1st Battalion (Cootehill): (1) Seán McGorry (2) ———, (3) R. Reilly, (4) T. McGorry. 2nd Battalion (Carrickallen): (1) Eugene O'Reilly, (2) ———, (3) P. Shields, (4) M. Lynch. 3rd Battalion (Cavan): (1) Michael Gilheany, (2) M. Smith, (3) Michael Reilly, (4) —— Reilly. 4th Battalion (Belturbet): (1) Patrick Fitzpatrick, (2) ———, (3) E. McMurrough, (4) Hugh Curry. 5th Battalion (Curlough): (1) Patrick Woods, (2) Jos Robinson, (3) Dennis Maher, (4) Jas Donohue. 6th Battalion (Ballinagh): (1) C.P. Fitzpatrick, (2) —— Dowd, (3) J. Finnigan, (4) Jos McCaffery. 7th Battalion (Virginia): (1) Hugh O'Donoghue, (2) Jack Kinard (B. Brady), (3) Hy Fitzsimons, (4) T. Smith. 8th Battalion (Crosserlough): (1) Hugh Maguire, (2) ———, (3) Patrick McCahill, (4) Ed O'Reilly. 9th Battalion (Bailieboro): Frank Connell, (2) —— McCabe, (3) Ned McGovern, (4) M. King.

Derry Areas Brigade: (1) ———, (2) ———, (3) ———, (4) ———. Derry City Battalion: (1) Pádraig Shields, (2) —— MacGialla, (3) John Quinn, (4) —— Keenan. 1st Battalion South Derry (south of area): (1) Thomas Larkin (Ballyrowan), (2) James Grogan, (3) Patrick Mol, (4) ———. 2nd Battalion South Derry (north of area): (1) John Mooney (2) —— Haughy, (3) Pat Lynch (Maghera), (4) ———.

Donegal East Brigade: (1) Henry McGowan, (2) ———, (3) J.D. McLoughlin, (4) Daniel Doherty. 1st Battalion (Strabane): (1) Jas Curran, (2) —— McKee, (3) P. McGuire, (4) T. Scott. 2nd Battalion (Castlefin): E. McBreaty, (2) John O'Flaherty, (3) T. McGlyn, (4) J. Byrne.

Donegal West Brigade: (1) Joe Sweeney, (2) J. McCole, (3) ———, (4) G. Meehan. 1st Battalion (Dungloe): (1) F. McDonnell, (2) B. Sweeney, (3) P. Breslin, (4) P. O'Donnell. 2nd Battalion (Gweedore): (1) P. Coyle, (2) J. Corr, (3) J.J. Gallagher, (4) J. Kelly. 3rd Battalion (Creeslough): (1) Joe Cafferty, (2) C. McGinley, (3) P. McGinley, (4) W. McGinley.

Donegal South Brigade: (1) John Hueston, (2) Brian Monaghan, (3) S. McGroarty, (4) John McGinley. 1st Battalion (Ballyshannon): (1) Thomas McShea, (2) P. Doherty, (3) P. Givanny, (4) J. McFinn. 2nd Battalion (Donegal): (1) ———, (2) ———, (3) ———, (4) ———. 3rd Battalion (Inver): (1) P. McFinn, (2) James McGuire, (3) Thady Higgins, (4) Jas Boyle. 4th Battalion (Killybegs): (1) James Cunningham, (2) Ed Boyle, (3) ———, (4) ———. 5th Battalion (Ardara): (1) P.J. McHugh, (2) F. Gallagher, (3) Denis Hasken, (4) John Huesten.

Down East Areas Brigade: (1) ———, (2) ———, (3) ———, (4) ———. 1st Battalion (Castlewellan): (1) James Johnston, (2) M. Murray, (3) Samuel Rogers, (4) Thos Brannigan. 2nd Battalion (Loughenisland): (1) John Branife, (2) Seán Flannigan, (3) Patrick McVeigh, (4) P.J. Keilty. 3rd Battalion (Downpatrick): (1) Thos O'Connor, (2) John O'Donnell, (3) Willie Byrne, (4) Jas Crosskerry. 4th Battalion (Portaferry, Upr Ards): (1) ———, (2) ———, (3) ———, (4) ———.

Fermanagh Brigade: (1) F. Carney, (2) ———, (3) ———, (4) ———. 1st Battalion (Arney): (1) Terence Fitzpatrick, (2) —— Green, (3) J. McGuire (4) J. Brennan. 2nd Battalion (Lisnaskea): (1)

J. Reithy, (2) J. Smith, (3) ———, (4) ———. 3rd Battalion (Tempo): (1) Patrick Malarky, (2) J. Sleven, (3) Philip Murphy, (4) ———. 4th Battalion (Beleek): (1) Seán Carthy, (2) J.J. Stephens, (3) John James McGonigle, (4) ———.

Inishowen Brigade: (1) ———, (2) ———, (3) ———, (4) ———. 1st Battalion (Carndonagh): (1) Leo Lafferty, (2) James Devereux, (3) Patrick Lynch, (4) Dan Lynch. 2nd Battalion (Buncrana): (1) W. O'Doherty, (2) A. Cassidy, (3) Jos McLoughlin, (4) John McLoughlin. 3rd Battalion (Moville): (1) ———, (2) ———, (3) ———, (4) ———.

Letterkenny Brigade: (1) Jas Dawson (J. Delap), (2) Pat McMonagle, (3) W.J.P. McGintey, (4) J.P. McMonigal. 1st Battalion (Letterkenny): (1) Hugh McGrath, (2) ———, (3) ———, (4) ———. 2nd Battalion (Rosnatall): (1) H. Fullerster, (2) ———, (3) ———, (4) ———. 3rd Battalion (Churchill): (1) M. McCoy, (2) ———, (3) ———, (4) ———.

Monaghan Brigade: (1) ———, (2) ———, (3) ———, (4) ———. 1st Battalion (Clones): (1) Dan Horan, (2) Thos Coffey, (3) Jack McGrath, (4) Frank Sheridan. 2nd Battalion (Monaghan): (1) Thomas Donnelly, (2) Patrick McGrory, (3) Thos Gillanders, (4) Edward Connolly. 3rd Battalion (Scotstown): (1) James McKenna, (2) Thos Brennan, (3) John McCabe, (4) John McGough. 4th Battalion (Lattan): (1) Terence Magee, (2) Pat McDermott, (3) James Sullivan, (4) Anthony Daly. 5th Battalion (Carrickmacross): (1) P.J. O'Daly, (2) Frank Burns, (3) Tom O'Brien, (4) Patrick Kelly.

Newry Areas Brigade: (1) ———, (2) ———, (3) ———, (4) ———. 1st Battalion (Newry): (1) Jas Goodfellow (D. Doherty), (2) Hugh Crebben, (3) Charley Grant, (4) John Quin. 2nd Battalion (Banbridge): (1) J. Wright, (2) B. Grennan, (3) E. Hellan, (4) ———. 3rd Battalion (Kilkeel): (1) John O'Hogan, (2) Michael White, (3) Jos Cunningham, (4) ———. 4th Battalion (Camlough): (1) Chas McGenety, (2) Enndie Searon, (3) B. O'Hanlon, (4) ———. 5th Battalion (Newtownhamilton): (1) George Rushe, (2) Charles McGlennen, (3) John Shortt, (4) Henry McKenna. 6th Battalion

(Armagh): (1) Pat Hanway, (2) ———, (3) J. Mallon, (4) ———. Seventh Battalion (Lurgan): (1) Michael Murnly, (2) John McConville, (3) Bernard McCann, (4) Hugh McShanes.

Tyrone Brigade: (1) ———, (2) ———, (3) ———, (4) ———. 1st Battalion (Omagh): (1) P. Donnelly, (2) ———, (3) T. Holland, (4) Jas O'Neill. 2nd Battalion (Dungannon): (1) Thos Leonard, (2) —— Cush, (3) W.J. Kelly, junr, (4) ———. 3rd Battalion (Carrickmore): (1) P. McGuirk, (2) Seán Corr, (3) Frank Curran, (4) Eamonn Donnelly. 4th Barralion (Coalisland): (1) Jos Cavanagh, (2) P. Gates, (3) ———, (4) Thos McGowan. 5th Battalion (Dromore): (1) Frank Smith, (2) E. Gallagher, (3) J. Gallagher, (4) ———. 6th Battalion (Clogher): (1) Bernard Early, (2) ———, (3) ———, (4) ———. Seventh Battalion (Gortin): (1) Peter Clarke, (2) ———, (3) ———, (4) ———.

The following chiefs of republican police were also appointed to enforce the civil authority of the state, and to maintain order:

County Monaghan: W. McMahon. Clones: P. Carty. Monaghan: James McKenna, Scotstown; J. Smith, Lattan; Frank Morris, Carrickmacross. Roscommon: E. Hegarty (south); H. Keegan, J. Tanner (north). Clare: E. Waldron (mid); S. Scanlon, (east). Sligo: M. Silke. Westmeath: G. Carroll, Mullingar. Dublin: John Condron. County Tyrone: P. Curran, Omagh; Vincent Bradley, Coalisland; V. Quinn, Dungannon; J. Grogan, Carrickmore; Nicholas Smyth, Dromore; Pat Holywood, Gorten. Belfast: P. McFadden. County Cavan: P. Smyth, Carrickallen; —— Connolly, Cavan; T. McGee, Cootehill; Terence Reilly, Belturbet; John McCaffrey, Curlough; J. West, Crosserlough. County Donegal: Pat Lynch, Inishowen; Matt McKeefey, Maghera. Derry city: John Fox. Offaly: M. McDermott; M. Boland, Offaly No. 2. County Galway: Mark McDonogh, east Connemara; Stephen Coyne, west Connemara; Stephen Ream, Tuam. Athlone: E. Dowling; J.J. Elliott. Wexford: Loftus H. Smith (north); Richard Sinnott (south). Longford: Thomas Robinson. Kildare: Seán McKenna. Naas: ——— No. 1. Cork No. 3: Samuel Kingston; Cork No. 4: P. Healy; Cork No. 1: D. de Barra. Leitrim: P. McDonald; P. Lamph, Newtownhamilton. Limerick: Morgan Costelloe (mid); Ed

Ryan (east); Jas Roche (west). Tipperary No. 1: Frank McGrath; No. 2: Wm Shortt; No. 3: P. McDonagh. Kerry No. 1: ———; Kerry No. 3: P. O'Connor. Castleisland: Jim Reidy. Fermanagh: Terence Corrigan, Enniskillen; T. Corrigan, Arney. Carlow: E. Tracey. Kilkenny: Thomas Walsh. Louth (north): Thomas Clancy. County Down: Thomas McKivergan, Banbridge. Wicklow: James Gerrard.

Many vacancies in the government and parliament, and in the Irish Republican Army were caused by enemy action which included murder, arrest and deportation. Elements of our forces in enemy hands were continuing to fight by every means at their disposal, and the Irish Republican Army was attacking the enemy at many points throughout the country.

A judicial system of arbitration, parish and district courts, and a police system had been built up under the auspices of the Sinn Féin party. The majority of local government bodies such as county councils, district councils and corporations had declared their allegiance to the elected government of the nation. British administration, the courts included, had broken down over a great part of the country, and even the British military, Black and Tans and RIC were unable to maintain the authority of the imperial civil arm. Under the British system every county had a civil head in the person of His Majesty's lieutenant of the county, and deputy lieutenants; but they were unable to give effect to or carry out civil administration. In some areas, like my own in Ballinalee, County Longford, there were units of the Ulster Volunteers in existence. In a great number of cases the men who belonged to them were very decent Irishmen, but they felt bound to give their loyalty to the King of Great Britain and to their brothers in the north, who were opposed to self-government for Ireland.

The gallant prison struggle of Terence MacSwiney, Lord Mayor of Cork, who died in Brixton jail, having endured the long agony of a hunger strike that had lasted for seventy-four days, drew admiration from most parts of the world and, I am sure, even from some of our enemies. Following his death on 25 October 1920, and his funeral, a general order was issued by the Minister for Defence and by the headquarters staff, for an intensification of our defensive measures. It is arising from that order that I can tell the story of what has become known as the Battle of Ballinalee. My purpose is to show the extent to which the people had united against British aggression. It was the Sinn Féin party which had been given the mandate at the general election of 1918, to set up an independent Irish parliament. In that election Sinn Féin had wiped out the Irish Parliamentary Party, which would have continued to send MPs to the British parliament at Westminster. Yet, once the British had declared war on the independent Irish parliament, which had become known as the First Dáil, every nationalist element in the country rallied to its support. Side by side with Sinn Féin stood Labour, the Irish Parliamentary Party and the Ancient Order of Hibernians. In a word, priests and people stood shoulder to shoulder against the common enemy, united in their defence of Dáil Éireann.

THE DUBLIN SCENE: WAR AMID THE OUTWARD TRAPPINGS OF PEACE

by Donal O'Kelly

(editor Hibernia*)*

The opening of the year 1920 found Ireland in a state of war, with Dublin as the seat of two belligerent governments, and the headquarters of two belligerent armies. This state of war had actually been in existence since the suppression of Dáil Éireann in September 1919, but with the coming of the new year it became obvious that the British government had decided to 'pacify' Ireland by a policy of open terror. According to British propaganda, all the trouble in Ireland was the work of a 'murder gang' from whom the Irish people had to be protected; and the incontestable fact that the 'murder gang' was the lawfully constituted army of a lawful and freely elected government did not trouble the propagandists at all. What did gravely trouble them and their employers was the equally incontestable fact that the *de jure* government of the Republic was rapidly becoming the *de facto* government of Ireland. British civil administration was breaking down, and in most parts of the country the King's writ was giving way to that of Dáil Éireann. All that the police and military could do to restore British authority, in the way of raids, arrests, curfew, press censorship and deliberate terrorisation of the civilian population, had been done without success. The people stood firm and the most notable result of the policy of British government so far had been the extensive resignations from the RIC of those of its members who refused to wage war upon their own people. This rot had to be stopped at all costs, and to stop it there arrived two entirely new additions to all the armed forces of the crown – cross-channel recruits for the RIC known as 'Black and Tans', and the Auxiliary Division of the RIC, known as 'Auxiliary Cadets', or more commonly as 'Auxies'. The Black and Tans made their first appearance in March 1920, and the Auxiliaries followed them in July.

Of the Black and Tans – so called because of their uniform of khaki tunics and black trousers – nothing good can be said. They were recruited from the offscourings of English industrial populations; their individual fighting qualities were not remarkable, but they were past masters of the arts of murder, looting, arson and outrage. In the long run, their infamy recoiled on the heads of the people who had let them loose. The Auxiliaries were a very different proposition. Ex-officers of the British army, with considerable combat experience, they were mostly men of the type which war had unfitted for any normal occupation. To give them their due, they were men of reckless courage, who knew no fear, and they gave obedience to no one, neither to their own officers nor to the government which paid them. Their brief was to exterminate the IRA by any method they chose to use, and they were amenable neither to the civil courts nor to military law. They were licensed terrorists and murderers, sure of protection by the British government, whatever their crimes. In the early days, when the Dublin Castle authorities made some attempt to punish those guilty of particularly revolting outrages, the criminals secured immunity by the threat of the truth about the British government's terrorist policy in Ireland. This threat was invariably effective. The Auxiliaries were trained at the Curragh and organised in companies of a hundred men. In Dublin their HQ was Beggars Bush barracks, with companies at Ship Street barracks and the LNW Hotel, North Wall. Elsewhere they were stationed in the martial law area and wherever IRA activity was particularly strong. By autumn they had companies in Kilkenny, Limerick, Cork, Galway, Mayo, Clare, Meath and Kerry. The Black and Tans reinforced the regular RIC garrisons.

A study of the military disposition of the opposing forces reveals, in Dublin as elsewhere, a fantastic disparity. East of the city was the sea, controlled by the British navy and an ever-open gateway for reinforcements, while to the north, west and south was a ring of barracks, manned by some 15,000 military of all arms, including artillery, armour and cavalry. Portobello and Beggars Bush to the south, Richmond, Wellington, Islandbridge and the Royal barracks to the west, Marlborough and Arbour Hill to the north, all linked by a system of intermediate strongpoints, enclosed the city in a ring of military power. Twenty miles to the north lay Gormanstown camp and thirty miles to the west was the Curragh of Kildare, after Aldershot, the largest military establishment in islands. There were aerodromes at Tallaght, Baldonnell and Collinstown, troops under canvas in Phoenix Park, while Dublin Castle and the adjoining Ship Street barracks dominated the centre of the city.

To oppose this massive deployment of imperial power stood the Dublin Brigade, commanded by Dick McKee and, after his death, by Oscar Traynor. The brigade was composed of part-time, unpaid citizen-soldiers, organised into four line battalions and one engineering battalion, whose combined total fighting strength of all ranks never exceeded 1,200 men. IRA striking power was determined, not by the men, but by arms available, and these were always in pitifully short supply. The Dublin Brigade fought, and won, its battles mainly with revolvers and automatic pistols, most of them captured from the enemy, homemade grenades and landmines. Such rifles and light automatics as the IRA possessed were employed in rural areas. Due to shortage of weapons, the brigade could never deploy more than a fraction of its strength for armed action, but nonetheless, it kept up an unceasing offensive by means of ambushes, raids, offensive patrols, special missions and supporting actions for the GHQ Squad and the active service unit. By containing so many enemy effectives in Dublin, it helped to relieve the pressure on the rural brigade areas.

Such then was the military position when, as the spring of 1920 matured, the people of Dublin faced an ordeal that was to test their fortitude to the utmost. From April 1920 until the Truce in July 1921, the 400,000 people who constituted the population of Dublin, lived and went about their daily work in an atmosphere of unbroken tension and fear that never relaxed – an atmosphere the horror of which it is almost impossible to recapture after a lapse of over thirty years. It was an atmosphere of war, but of war conducted amid all the outward trappings of peace. Men and women went about their daily affairs to the accompaniment of grenade explosions and small arms fire. General Crozier, at that time commanding officer of the Auxiliaries, has stated that 'rifle, machine-gun and revolver fire was as normal in Dublin as night firing in trenches in France'; while, according to Piaras Béaslaí: 'The roar of bombs and the report of guns were familiar to the ears of all by day and night.' Through all this, the shops were open, business went on, men worked and played, made money and lost it, women went shopping, children played, young people made love and danced and went to the pictures, while terror walked beside them. Military in full war kit patrolled the streets; armoured cars and lorries, crammed with Auxiliaries and Black and Tans, prowled the town where every street crossing and lane held promise of a possible ambush. The unseen army of the Republic walked the streets too, and the first warning of its presence was the crash of bombs and revolver fire. When this happened it was *sauve qui peut* for the passers-by – their one hope of safety to get away from the scene before the vengeful lorries roared through the streets, mounting the footpaths deliberately, the occupants firing wildly in sheer fury. After such an ambush, whole blocks of buildings in the city would be cordoned off and every occupant searched. Trams would be held up by trigger-happy Auxiliaries and all male passengers taken off for questioning and searching. The gates of St Stephen's Green, or any other park in the city, would close, and everyone found inside would be subjected to interrogation and search. On such occasions, if there were no women searchers about, many a woman found herself the custodian of a revolver surreptitiously slipped to her by the stranger sitting beside her, and many a man, already searched, found himself the temporary possessor of highly dangerous documents. Such incidents were accepted as unavoidable aspects of a period of terror, when it was impossible to distinguish friend from foe, and people went about their business with closed lips and wary eyes.

If the days were bad in the Dublin of those days, the nights were infinitely worse. Curfew was in force always, although the period varied from as late as midnight to as early as 6 p.m. During the curfew hours the whole city was given over to the British forces, and the Auxiliaries could work their will without fear of hostile witnesses. The lorries kept up their unceasing patrol and it is significant that no sound roused more terror in those nights than that of a motor engine. In the locked houses conversation would die away as the growl of a heavy motor was heard – only to be resumed when the dreaded sound had receded. Sometimes the lorry did not pass, and then the terrified people knew that the worst had happened and that they were in for a raid. Rifle butts crashed on the door, and a stream of uniformed and armed blackguards, as often as not half or wholly drunk, would burst in and line up the inmates at the point of the gun. If an ambush had taken place the raiders in wanton temper might wreck the premises, looting what they fancied, abusing and terrorising the family, and as often as not carrying off the men 'on suspicion' or for no reason whatever. Arrest and detention without trial was, of course, the order of the day.

The prisons of Mountjoy and Kilmainham were packed, and the guardroom in Dublin Castle became the ante-room of the internment camp at Ballykinlar. The final note of tragedy was struck by the curt announcements of official executions – ten in Dublin, thirteen in Cork and one in Limerick. The hanging, after torture, of the seventeen-year-old Kevin Barry, taken prisoner in a fair fight, proclaimed very plainly to the people of Dublin the fact that, in this struggle, the British authorities considered themselves untrammelled by the rules of civilised warfare.

Fourteen months of this sort of existence would try the endurance of any civil population in the world, particularly when, as in the case of Dublin, the people had very little idea, owing to the rigid censorship, of what was happening or of the strategic purpose of it all. Actually every move by the IRA was part of an overall plan in which the Dublin Brigade had a definite and vital role, quite different from that of other brigade areas. In the country the IRA strategy was the time-honoured one of hitting the enemy hard and often, and of inflicting as many casualties as possible. In Dublin the presence on the streets of a dense civilian population would alone have prevented the implementation of this strategy but, apart from this, the Dublin Brigade had two main objectives – the defence of the civil administration of Dáil Éireann and the destruction of enemy administration. In fact, the attainment of both these objectives necessitated the paralysing of British police and military intelligence for, like all armies of occupation, the crown forces were blind and helpless unless guided by their spies. Most of the military action in Dublin therefore was directed against intelligence personnel, as in the case of the burning of the Custom House.

As far back as September 1919, Michael Collins, whose own intelligence service was a miracle of efficiency, had realised the necessity of eliminating enemy intelligence and had recruited from the Dublin Brigade a special force to undertake this mission. In Dublin the eyes and ears of the British administration were the plain clothes G-Division of the Dublin Metropolitan Police. Collins gave the G-men peremptory notice that those who continued their political work after a certain date would be shot on sight, and on the expiration of his ultimatum he ordered the GHQ Squad, as his special service group was called, to execute those who ignored it. At first 'The Squad' numbered only four, Paddy Ó Dálaigh, Joe Leonard, Ben Barrett, and Seán Doyle, but was soon reinforced by Jim Slattery, Vinnie Byrne, Mick O'Reilly and Tom Keogh. Later recruits included Frank Bolster, Eddie Byrne, Jimmy Conroy, Paddy Griffin, Bill Stapleton, Ned Breslin, Johnny Dunne, Seán Caffrey, Johnnie Wilson, Jackie Hanlon and Pat McCrea. Mention must also be made of Mick McDonnell, who, although not a member of 'The Squad', was associated with its formation and many of its actions. McDonnell's gallantry and ardour made him one of the outstanding figures of the Dublin Brigade. From the outset and throughout its whole period of operations, 'The Squad' was commanded by Paddy Ó Dálaigh, with Joe Leonard as second-in-command. Collins personally selected the members of 'The Squad' in order to make sure that it would only contain men who could be relied on to maintain rigid discipline and to operate scrupulously to orders. The men of 'The Squad' were true to their trust, and not one man was shot by them except on the direct orders of the Dáil Cabinet. Where doubt existed, Collins and Cathal Brugha saw to it that the suspect got the benefit of the doubt, and no man was executed by 'The Squad' whose guilt had not been proved.

'The Squad' worked in closed liaison with GHQ intelligence, and its operations against the G-Division were continuous and effective. Among the G-men executed were Detective Officers Barton, Brooks, Wharton, Revell, Talton and Constable Kells. Other executions included those of Captain Lee Wilson, Deputy Commissioner Redmond, the British spies Jameson, Pike, Brady, Halpin and Doran, night porter in the Wicklow Hotel; Alan Bell, a civil servant engaged in the task of locating and securing Dáil Éireann funds, was also executed. Other actions in which 'The Squad' participated included attempts to shoot Lord French and, most daring of all, the attempted rescue of Seán MacEoin from Mountjoy prison. In the latter operation, 'The Squad' was reinforced by three brigade gunners trained in the use of the Hotchkiss gun.

After the virtual collapse of police intelligence, 'The Squad' found itself called upon to deal with a new menace, for the cream of British military intelligence was then brought into the fight, quite independently of Dublin Castle. Picked men, under orders from Whitehall, and having no apparent connection with the British authorities in Ireland, made their unostentatious way into the country and took up residence as civilians in various houses in town. These men were masters of their craft, and very quickly established a formidable organisation of native spies and touts from whose isolated gleanings they were able to build a highly efficient espionage service. They reported directly to London in code and were ready for a decisive coup against the Dáil ministry and the IRA, when Collins, whose own intelligence rarely failed, struck first. This terrible menace was crushed once and for all on 'Bloody Sunday', when groups from the various battalions of the

Dublin Brigade, led by a Squad member as far as numbers permitted, or by a member of GHQ intelligence, accounted for fourteen enemy spies, all of them key men of British military intelligence.

While 'The Squad', reinforced, as occasion arose, by elements from the battalions, was carrying on its counter espionage campaign, an active service unit was organised within the Dublin Brigade. This unit, formed in November 1920, did not operate until early in 1921. It consisted of fifty men under the command of Captain Paddy Flanagan, with Mick White as second-in-command, and was a brigade organisation under the control of Oscar Traynor, the Brigade O/C. Like the members of 'The Squad', the members of the ASU were withdrawn from their jobs and employed as whole-time soldiers, being paid out of Dáil Éireann funds. To these two units, therefore, belongs the distinction of having been the first cadres of the regular army of today.

The coming into action of the ASU sped up still further the tempo of the war in Dublin. What little semblance of discipline had ever been maintained among the Auxiliaries had long since vanished, and they carried on their campaign of murder and outrage at their own sweet will. While the whole police force was organised as a terrorist body, there were certain elements in it with what might be described as a natural talent for murder, and these formed the notorious Castle Murder Gang, which raided and shot on the principle that it didn't matter how many civilians died if there was any chance of an IRA man being among them. The leader of this gang was an RIC officer who had originally come from the west of Ireland to identify a prisoner, and who had evidently found the atmosphere of Dublin Castle and the depot in Phoenix Park congenial, for he remained in Dublin. He gathered round him a gang of kindred spirits, English, Scottish, Welsh and not a few renegade Irishmen like himself, and conducted his own private campaign against the IRA. The full tale of the infamies committed under cover of curfew by the Castle Gang will probably never be told, but we do know that murder, after torture, of unarmed prisoners, was one of its specialities. Brigadier McKee and

Peadar Clancy, with a chance associate named Clune, were among its victims, as were John Lynch of Kilmallock and two young men shot under revolting circumstances in an hotel in Parliament Street.

A number of Volunteers, some of them prominent officers, fell victims to the Castle Murder Gang, but during the dark hours of curfew numerous civilians also were murdered for no apparent reason at all. One can only assume that these onlookers to the fray, who were certainly neither Volunteers nor connected with the republican government, were the unhappy victims of false information, private vengeance or just lust to kill on the part of an organisation described by Piaras Béaslaí as 'a gang of RIC bravos, drawn from various parts of the country, its numbers organised for the purpose of assassinations and outrages'.

The members of the gang, armed and in civilian clothes, moved round the city in a body too strong to be engaged in the crowded streets of the city, so the ASU and the battalions of the brigade struck back by increasing the intensity of their ambushes of Auxiliary and Black and Tan lorries. As Paddy Ó Dálaigh put it to the writer: 'With this unit carrying out ambushes and 'The Squad' picking off spies, the city was certainly a hot spot.'

The Squad and the ASU mustered their full strength to join with the 2nd Battalion of the Dublin Brigade in the most important single engagement of the whole war in the Dublin Brigade area – the burning of the Custom House. The action was entirely successful, but the cost in casualties was heavy – seven killed, twelve wounded and about seventy captured out of a total force of some 120. As a result of these losses, 'The Squad' and the ASU were amalgamated to form one unit, which from then on was known as the Guard and was commanded by Paddy Ó Dálaigh.

In June plans were completed for the shooting, on a fixed date, of every Tan visible on the streets of Dublin, in public houses and in hotel bars. Luckily for the Tans they were confined to barracks that night, except for two who were shot dead the moment they appeared in Grafton Street. The unit remained active until the coming of the

Truce, which was agreed on 9 July and became operative on 11 July. Ambushes planned for that day had to be hurriedly called off.

Since March 1920, for fifteen seemingly interminable months, the people of the Irish metropolis had walked under a dark cloud of fear, danger and suspicion. Now the cloud had lifted, and though the IRA grimly prepared for a resumption of hostilities, the people, in their vast relief, refused to look closely into the future, and made merry in the atmosphere of relaxed tension. Mercifully, in those halcyon summer nights, when no lorry rumbled and no gunfire sounded, none foresaw that this Truce was but a lull before the agonising storm of Civil War.

ORDEAL BY FIRE: HOW CORK CITY FACED THE TERROR

by Donal O'Kelly

(editor Hibernia*)*

While the War of Independence was in every sense a national struggle, embracing the thirty-two counties of Ireland and controlled by a national parliament in Dublin, its conduct, strategy and development inevitably varied a great deal in different theatres of active war. As befitted the metropolis of Ireland, Dublin was the focal point throughout the eventful years. To it attached the splendour and prestige and pain of 1916 and in the ensuing phases of the struggle it was the seat of both the British and republican administrations. It paid the price of leadership in the holocaust that destroyed its finest thoroughfares in 1916 and the trials of its people were many and grievous in the campaign of 1920 and 1921.

In this final phase of the war Dublin was, however, but one of many centres of resistance to the enemy. By this time all Ireland was on the march. The intensity of the struggle depended on many local factors, natural and human, but it is an incontestable fact that at a very early date the southern counties, and Cork in particular, took the lead in military activity and remained in the forefront until the bitter end. Cork put more men in the field than any other county, undertook the biggest and most costly engagements in the war, maintained an unbroken offensive against the enemy and suffered more intensively than any other area at his hands. During the long months from the death of Terence MacSwiney until the Truce, Cork was a theatre of active warfare and when fighting ceased there was hardly a town of importance in the entire county that had not suffered some damage.

It is worthwhile, therefore, to consider the development of events in Cork and to try to analyse the factors that enabled it to contribute so much in moral and material things to the successful outcome of the war.

In this article we are concerned primarily with the progress of events in the city of Cork, and the first difficulty confronting us is the impossibility of drawing any sharp line of distinction between the roles of city and county. The story of Dublin is the story of the Dublin Brigade and the special GHQ units, but in Cork the position was quite different. At the commencement of serious hostilities there was one brigade of Volunteers covering the whole county with headquarters in the city, but as early as January 1918, this formation had become unwieldy. The county was, therefore, sub-divided into three brigade areas and henceforth Cork city was an integral part of the Cork No. 1 Brigade area, which extended from Youghal in the east, north to Donoughmore and Macroom, and west to the borders of Kerry. The brigade consisted of ten line battalions, plus special services and of these the 1st and 2nd Battalions were recruited from and operated mainly in the city and immediate suburbs. At the height of the struggle, in February 1921, a separate city command was formed, consisting of the two city battalions and the active service unit drawn from their ranks, but this was a formation within the brigade and subordinate to the brigade O/C. It frequently happened that members of the city battalions took part in operations outside the city; brigade headquarters was always situated in the city; so that for all practical purposes the stories of Cork city and of Cork No. 1 Brigade cannot be segregated from each other. The city battalions supplied from twenty to twenty-five members to the brigade active service unit, in addition to supplying the entire personnel of their own ASU. Within the city, the 1st Battalion covered the whole built-up area north of the south channel of the River Lee, while the 2nd Battalion operated south of the river.

We are not primarily concerned here with the period of reconstruction and organisation that followed the 1916 Rebellion. It was, however, significant of coming events, and typical of the spirit that animated the Volunteers in Cork, that a highly successful raid for arms took place at the Grammar School as early as September 1917. Twenty service rifles, used for the instruction of the School OTC were secured in this raid and formed the nucleus of the brigade's armament. It was not the least boast of the brigade that throughout the struggle it found its armaments for itself. It had to do so, for the slender resources of GHQ were incapable of meeting more than a fraction of the demands made on them.

In Cork, as elsewhere, 1918 and 1919 were devoted to preparations for the coming struggle, punctuated by raids for arms and occasional clashes with police and military. The conscription crisis found the Volunteers in Cork organised into regular battalions with a numerical strength then, as all through the fight, far in excess of the armaments available. Drilling and training went on uninterrupted, and gradually the tempo quickened. Soldiers were attacked in the streets of the city as early as January 1918, and in September of that year other soldiers were disarmed at Richmond Hill. In November came the shooting of Head Constable Clarke in Leitrim Street and the arrest and rescue of Captain MacNeilis. The Volunteer spirit was being moulded by a master hand and the pattern of events to come was taking shape. If there is one clear conclusion to be drawn from the experience of that time, it is that the waging of guerrilla warfare depends on the quality of local leadership and here we find the secret of Cork's military success. Tomás MacCurtain, first O/C of the Cork Brigade was, in the most exacting sense of the word, a true leader of men. A patriot and a language enthusiast, he was also a public administrator of the first rank, but above all he was a soldier, with the soldier's gift of firing his subordinates with his own energy, enthusiasm and courage. It was natural for men to follow where MacCurtain led and to give that utter confidence and loyalty that only a true leader can inspire. He made the Cork Brigade the fighting machine that it was and attracted to himself subordinate officers of outstanding quality.

The year 1919 was devoted by MacCurtain and his staff to training, organisation of special services, raids for arms and sporadic attacks on military and police personnel. Above all it was the period in which the military situation was assessed and future strategy decided. Judged by ordinary military standards, the picture presented was not a rosy one. On the one side were the Volunteers, ardent, disciplined and enthusiastic, but untrained in combat and pitifully short of arms. Opposed to them was the British governmental and military machine, with immense resources of personnel, arms and money. British military headquarters was Victoria barracks, Cork, with a permanent garrison of two infantry battalions, divisional headquarters, and special services. Ringing the city were the great military garrison towns of Buttevant, Fermoy, Bandon, Cobh and Kinsale. There were also the camps at Ballincollig, Moorepark, Spike Island and Kilworth. Mallow was another military post, and armed police garrisons were numerous; with headquarters at Union Quay and barracks in Barracks Street, Elizabeth Port, Douglas, Blackrock, South Infirmary Road, King Street, Togher, Tuckey Street, Bridewell, Sundays Well, Abbey barracks, Northgate Street, Watercourse Road, St Luke's, Commons Road and every town and village beyond the city's perimeter. As elsewhere in Ireland the RIC men were the eyes and ears of the British administration, and so their elimination became a primary objective of IRA strategy.

In the opening days of 1920 the storm broke in real earnest. It was going to be a fight to a finish this time and the IRA went all out for its objectives – the crippling of enemy intelligence, the destruction of local RIC posts, the smashing of British civil administration and the infliction of the maximum damage and casualties on enemy forces. From now on Cork No. 1 Brigade was in action almost continuously and the newspaper files of the time reveal an unbroken series of attacks on police barracks and police intelligence personnel, ambushes of military and police, raids on mails, captures of enemy military stores and attacks on military patrols. The enemy retaliated by raids, arrests and terror tactics against civilians. The culminating point of the terror campaign was the murder on 20 March of Brigadier Tomás

MacCurtain. MacCurtain had been unanimously elected lord mayor of the city on 31 January, thus uniting in his person the offices of chief magistrate and of officer commanding the republican forces in the city. It is true, of course, that in Cork, as elsewhere, there was a unionist minority and a considerable 'garrison clique' which, through sentiment and interest, was loyal to the crown. Some members of this section of the community carried their loyalty to the point of forming a civilian branch of British intelligence, but they were so far out of touch with the popular movement that their value to the enemy was slight. Those who showed signs of becoming dangerous were quickly eliminated. There had also been in Cork, as in every garrison town, a noisy group of ladies, dependants of men serving in the British army, who, thanks to a generous 'separation allowance' were enjoying a prosperity they had never known previously. They rightly considered the Volunteers to be a threat to their economic welfare and manifested their displeasure by jeering and throwing stones at Volunteer parades. The end of the war in 1918 and the consequent cessation of separation allowances, terminated abruptly the activities of these pests.

Apart from these elements, the solidarity of civil support for the Irish Republican Army was remarkable.

Cork is a small city, where many people are known to one another. The IRA leaders were known by name and appearance to thousands, but they were never betrayed. In 1921 for a whole fortnight an IRA squad waited on the same street to ambush General Strickland, and their names and business were well known to very many passers-by, but no information about them ever reached the enemy. Brigade headquarters from 1916 to May 1921, remained at the premises of the Wallace sisters in St Augustine's Street, and other brigade offices were in Princes Street, Cook Street, Marlborough Street and Patrick Street, but, though their location was an open secret to many, enemy intelligence never found them.

The murder of Tomás MacCurtain was a grievous blow to the brigade and indeed to the whole independence movement, but before his death he had perfected a military machine that functioned independently of individuals. His vice-commandant, Terence MacSwiney, took over command of the brigade and on 31 March Brigadier MacSwiney became the second republican lord mayor of Cork. The story of MacSwiney's arrest on 12 August 1920, and of his long, drawn-out agony and death in Brixton prison needs no retelling here. It may, however, be noted that by the time he succumbed to his incredibly prolonged hunger strike of seventy-four days, he had drawn the eyes of the whole civilised world upon him and the cause for which he died. Terence MacSwiney was Cork city's greatest, noblest and most effective contribution to the cause of national independence.

The fight went on. Terence MacSwiney remained in command of the brigade until his arrest, with Seán O'Hegarty as vice-brigadier and ultimate successor. Florence O'Donoghue was brigade adjutant, which post he held until, on the formation of the 1st Southern Division in April 1921, he transferred to the divisional staff. Other brigade staff officers were Joe O'Connor (QM), Bill Mahony (signals), James Grey (transport), Eugene O'Neill (engineering), Seán Culhane (IO – succeeded on his arrest by H. O'Mahony), Roger O'Connor and Tadhg Donovan (medical), and Sheila Wallace (communications). The 1st Battalion was commanded successively by Terence MacSwiney, Fred Murray, Dan Donovan (Sandow), Tom Crofts, Patrick (Pa) Murray and Seán O'Donoghue, and the 2nd Battalion by Seán Sullivan, Mick Murphy, Con Neenan, Peter Donovan and Tadhg Sullivan. The brigade activities made the defence of isolated RIC barracks impossible and one after another these were evacuated by the enemy and burned by the IRA. Income tax officers were destroyed and intelligence officers ruthlessly hunted down. Early spring saw the coming of the Black and Tans to reinforce the RIC garrisons in such barracks as were still standing and the intensification of the British government's policy of calculated terrorisation. Cork was by midsummer a city of belligerents and from this period on the civilian population had to call on all its fortitude. British civil administration was breaking down; throughout the south of Ireland the King's Writ no longer ran and King's Counsel pleaded in the Sinn Féin courts or not at all.

Mr Justice Samuels, opening the Summer Assizes and finding himself faced with a list of 477 indictable offences committed in the previous three months, declared the position to be 'unspeakably grave'. The learned judge did not exaggerate, for this was the last King's Assizes held in Cork. On 17 July, Col Smyth, Divisional Commissioner of the RIC, was shot dead in the County Club and on 28 August, District Inspector Swanzy paid in Lisburn the price of his participation in the murder of Tomás MacCurtain. His executioners, two members of the Cork Brigade, were back in Cork the following morning, before the Lisburn police had started looking for them. Togher, Commons Road, Blackrock, King Street, Victoria Cross and St Luke's barracks were destroyed and the police fell back on their Union Quay headquarters. The Auxiliaries arrived at Victoria barracks and soon made their presence felt. IRA casualties from death and capture were heavy, but all time the intensity of IRA attacks increased. Curfew patrols were sniped nightly and attacks on military transport were increasing. In June a military car was captured at Glanmire, and in July two military lorries were captured and burned at Dennehy's Cross. Ambushes increased in number and magnitude and by day and night the plain people of Cork went their way in an atmosphere of terror and sudden death. They faced the dangers and humiliations of hold-ups, searches, raids, arrests, confinement to their homes, and the ever-present risk of being caught by rifle and revolver fire.

Things seemed to be about as bad they could be as the autumn of 1920 darkened into winter. The of death Terence MacSwiney had redoubled the fury of the IRA offensive and the kidnapping in November of four military intelligence officers at Waterfall, followed by the ambush at Dillon's Cross, saw the coming of Cork's darkest hour; the burning of the city and the imposition of martial law. The wanton and deliberate destruction of Patrick Street and the City Hall by crown forces in December was a numbing blow, but the people stood up to it without a whimper and the stricken shopkeepers, anticipating the technique of bomb victims of the Second World War, made it a point of pride to clear some corner of their ruined premises where they could carry on their trade.

Martial law had been proclaimed on 10 December by the viceroy and came into effect in Cork, Kerry, Limerick and Tipperary on 4 January 1921. Its imposition mattered little to the IRA, against whom the enemy had for long employed every weapon in his armoury, and the chief difference noticeable was that under it prisoners were shot instead of being hanged as heretofore. It was very different for the civilian population, who now lived under the perpetual menace of summary trial by military courts. By the terms of General Strickland's three proclamations it became the duty of every householder, lodging housekeeper and hotelier to display inside the door of his establishment a list showing the name, age, sex and occupation of every occupant. Separate lists were to be kept for each flat or tenement, and changes had to be reported to the police within three hours. Landlords were held responsible for the conduct of their tenants and for arms or explosives found on their premises. Written reports on all occupants had to be furnished daily to the police. Everyone, under pain of military trial, was bound to report the possession by others of arms of ammunition, and to reveal immediately any knowledge of rebel activities, of houses frequented by rebels, or of relatives of his whom he suspected of being rebels. 'Any attitude of neutrality,' said the proclamation, 'is quite inconsistent with loyalty, and will render those adopting it liable to trial by military courts.' In brief, failure on the part of any citizen to become a spy on his fellow countrymen was a military offence. The imposition of martial law involved many other humiliations and restrictions, but the above extracts will give some idea of what life meant for the civilian population of Cork city for the six weary months from 4 January 1921 to the Truce. To their eternal credit, the people bore their added burden without flinching, and the fight went on, the main brunt of it being borne by the city ASU, a full-time force drawn from the two city battalions and formed in September 1920, under the command of 'Pa' Murray. In February 1921, Tom Crofts was appointed O/C of the city, and on his arrest in March, he was succeeded by Mick Murphy.

Murphy in his turn was arrested early in May and his place as O/C of the city was filled by Dan Donovan, who had been in command of the brigade column since the previous January.

By this time enemy intelligence had almost completely broken down. Although the military and police had been greatly reinforced at the end of 1920, they made no attempt to re-occupy positions from which they had been driven and large areas were now completely clear of enemy troops. The remnants of the old RIC were unwilling or afraid to give information and intelligence officers, spies and informers had been ruthlessly hunted down and exterminated. The Chief of British Intelligence, Captain Kelly, was a good IO, but could make little progress because he could never find agents who were able to penetrate even the fringe of the IRA organisation. Plain clothes officers of his staff, in despair at their department's lack of success, took action on their own, but these unfortunates never had a chance and were duly wiped out by the IRA, whose own intelligence squad, consisting of Jeremiah O'Brien, Denis Hegarty, Frank Mahony, Jim Fitzgerald, Bob Aherne and Mick Kenny, was well informed of the activities of enemy intelligence personnel. With one exception, civilian spies constituted no real danger to the IRA, but this exception nearly cost the brigade dearly. He was a retired army officer, and one day he sent a message by hand 'in clear' to Captain Kelly, giving accurate information of the movements of the brigade staff officers to their billets outside the city. The message fell into the hands of the brigade intelligence organisation, and that night the writer of it was executed; but to this day no one knows how he obtained his accurate and deadly information.

By the beginning of 1921, the brigade was self-supporting in the matter of munitions. Each battalion had its own armourer and bomb manufacturing squad, and a central bomb factory was established in Connolly's Yard, on the Ballinlough Road. Grenades were cast here and the necks were screwed in at the Technical School and in the laboratories of University College Cork. 'Warflour' and other explosives were manufactured in premises in Cook Street that now form part of the Victoria Hotel. This important activity was under the control of the brigade quartermaster and brigade chemist, Joe O'Connor and Raymond Kennedy, with the help of Jimmie Mehigan, Willie Nenan and a man named Connolly, who was a metal-moulder by trade. So successful were the city munition factories that they became the main source of supply of grenades and mines, not merely for the brigade, but for most of the 1st Southern Division.

From fairly early in 1921, it became obvious that the IRA in the south was steadily attaining its objectives and that the whole British position was becoming untenable. British administration had collapsed and large areas were completely free of enemy occupation. With their intelligence service in ruins, the British were drawn back to their large cantonments and their last weapon, the terrorisation of the populace by outrage, arson and martial law had also failed. The Tans and Auxiliaries continued to do their worst, and undoubtedly the strain on both the IRA and the civilian population was terrific. Both were near the limit of their endurance, but that limit was reached. The British will to fight failed before the people's will to endure, and in July 1921, peace, for a while at least, came to the war-torn city of Cork. The centre of the city lay in ruins and in almost every street the blackened shells of burned-out houses and RIC barracks told their own grim story. Cork mourned the long list of her gallant dead, her trade was shattered and the material damage suffered enormous; but her people had fought the good fight, and in July 1921, that seemed all that mattered. In the ranks of Cork No. 1 Brigade, then about 7,500 strong, all was well.

APPENDIX

1. List of brigade staff at time of Truce: Seán O'Hegarty, O/C; Michael Leahy, vice-O/C; Dominick O'Sullivan, adjutant; George Buckley, asst adjutant; Seán MacSwiney, quartermaster; Seán Lucey, asst quartermaster; Herbert O'Mahony, intelligence officer; Eugene O'Neill, engineer; Corny O'Sullivan, asst engineer; James Grey,

transport; Wm O'Mahony, signals; Peadar Ryan, records; Sheila Wallace, communications; Raymond Kennedy, chemist.

2. Casualty List. Brigade staff – Tomás MacCurtain assassinated by British 20/3/1920; Terence MacSwiney died hunger strike 25/10/1920; Denny Barry died hunger strike 20/10/1923.

1st Battalion – Christopher Lucey, 10/11/1920; Willie Murphy, 14/12/1918; Daniel Crowley, 23/3/1921; Thomas Dennehy, 23/3/1921; Jeremiah Mullane, 23/3/1921; Daniel Murphy, 23/3/1921; Michael O'Sullivan, 23/3/1921; Denis Spriggs, 28/7/1921; Tadhg Barry, 23/11/1921; J. O'Brien, ———; L. Mulcahy, 26/11/1920; C. Morrissey, 26/11/1920; Con Delaney, 10/12/1920; Jerh Delaney, 10/12/1920; M. Tobin, 20/5/1919; D. McCarthy, ———, P. Hanley, 1920.

2nd Battalion – P. O'Donoghue, 23/11/1920; Seamus Quirke, 9/9/1920; Tadhg Sullivan 19/4/1921; Charlie Daly, 28/6/1921; P. Trahey, 23/11/1920; James Mehigan, 23/11/1920; Stephen Dorman, 23/11/1921; C. Daly, 1920; J. Murphy (died on hunger strike), 25/10/1920.

ARMS AND AMMUNITION TAKEN FROM NAVAL SLOOP LYING IN BANTRY BAY

CORK NO. 3 (WEST) BRIGADE, 17 NOVEMBER 1919

As told by participants to Flor Crowley

The breeze which had freshened with the flow of the tide had faded to a whisper at the ebb. The lap of the waves as they licked at the pier-wall, the doubtful melody of the youths who sauntered aimlessly across the square whistling 'Wrap the Green Flag Round Me', the sudden doleful yelping of a dog, the occasional outburst of song from the men below deck in the sloop moored to the pier – these only disturbed the hush that night had brought down upon the town of Bantry and upon its bay. The moon, full and pleasant as a fat man's face, hung a ball-hop above the hill behind the town, blinding the street lamps with her brilliance. It was a night for pleasure and for peace.

It was Sunday night, 17 November 1919, a night on which a handful of Bantry youths, few of them more than mere boys, by an act of calm and calculated courage, which would have done credit to seasoned military veterans, made a daring haul of arms and ammunition, that considerably improved the IRA position in west Cork. For months before, the 5th Battalion at Bantry, like every other battalion in the West Cork Brigade area, had been organised and ready. This state of organisation and preparedness in every town and village and ploughland between Innishannon and Muintervara was mainly due to the untiring and unrelenting efforts of one man, a man whose genius for organisation, whose contagious enthusiasm for the cause, whose compelling charm and unmistakable honesty made him, in sober fact, the father of the fight which followed in west Cork. To others may have fallen the greater glory of leadership on the field of battle, but the glory is his of having made possible that battle, the many battles for which west Cork was to become famous. There can be no struggle without sacrifice, no victory without bloodshed. In every company in each battalion of the 3rd Cork Brigade there were men, some young, others no longer young, who did not fear the sacrifice, who did not dread the bloodshed, for there had gone among them a man whose word and whose example had inspired and fired them, whose fervour and deep patriotism had stirred them as Pearse had stirred the men of 1916.

That man, the man who moulded the men of west Cork into the best organised fighting unit in Ireland, was Liam Deasy, Adjutant of the 3rd Brigade. With unerring knowledge Deasy realised that the greatest fight of all was soon to be staged in Ireland. As adjutant at that period, he was responsible to the brigade O/C, Tom Hales, for the organising of his brigade area, for bringing the young men into the Volunteers, and for winning over the people of west Cork to his side. First he secured the men to fight when the fight was necessary. Then he secured the people to stand loyally behind the fighting men, as they did in all the months of guerrilla war that followed. With a patience that was unwavering and a knowledge of people and places that was almost phenomenal, he journeyed to every townland, almost to every household, in west Cork, often finding apathy awaiting him, always leaving enthusiasm behind him, for it was an attribute of the man that his honesty never failed to impress those he met. So, when the call to arms came, the men of west Cork responded nobly and the people of west Cork no less nobly. The leaders who directed the struggle had but to say 'we want men to fight', and the men were at their service. Those leaders had but to say 'we want food and shelter for our fighting men', and the people of west Cork were there to afford them food, shelter and genuine welcome at any time of the day or night, so well and so thoroughly had the man Liam Deasy done his work of preparing, organising, inspiring; so well had this modern Rory O'Moore succeeded in welding his brigade area into a solid phalanx behind the cause of freedom.

But even in 1919, with all the months of work which Liam Deasy and his fellow-leaders had put into its formation, the IRA in west Cork was still little more than a nominal force. No force of men can wage war without arms, and up to that date in November 1919, the 3rd Brigade was still practically an unarmed unit. A few revolvers, an occasional badly scored shotgun, indifferent supplies of ammunition even for these – that was the extent of the armament of the west Cork IRA. Britain feared their fervour not at all. Words never pierced the hide of a British politician. Impressive displays of unarmed manpower amused Britain's military leaders. Let the Irish talk, let them drill and march and hold meetings. As long as they possess no arms they can do no more than talk and march and hold meetings. So, even in 1919 England could still sit back and smile smugly at Ireland's efforts to effect independence.

The 5th Battalion, taking in Bantry and the western seaboard of the county, was then commanded by Maurice Donegan. Ralph Keyes was captain of the Bantry Company, a worthy captain of a worthwhile command. At the Keyes home in the centre of the town of Bantry, the battalion had its unofficial town headquarters, and not many homes in Ireland played so unselfish a part in the struggle as did that house of the Keyes family of Bantry. Mrs Keyes, heart and soul behind her sons of the IRA, regarded every Volunteer as her own son, and treated each of them as such. Her home was always their home, her hospitality was unbounded where each man of them was concerned. This was a woman of the calibre of Anne Devlin, one who never reckoned cost or danger as long as the cause was served, and served well.

To this staunch headquarters word was brought on Tuesday night, 12 November 1919, that with careful planning and rapid execution, a certain quantity of British arms could be captured – and on that night there began a series of plans, a testing and a re-testing of schemes which were not to be without influence in the eighteen months of war which were to follow.

A familiar sight in Bantry in those days was a British patrol boat, a fast submarine chaser of the First World War, which at varying intervals called at the port of Bantry for supplies. This boat of the sloop variety was well manned and well armed. Her custom was to anchor well out from the pier where her officers deemed her safe from the possible attentions of the IRA. Her captain had, in fact, been strongly advised by the local RIC and by the local military leaders that his boat should never come too close to the pier, for those were the days when the IRA was beginning to do desperate things to secure arms, and as long as it did not secure those arms the police and military had little to fear. Not a single rifle existed in the battalion area up to that time, and the British wished to keep the position so.

Week after week this sloop anchored out in Bantry Bay. Week after week nothing happened. A feeling of security must have settled upon her captain, for despite the warning of the police and military, he finally abandoned the custom of casting anchor out in the bay and decided to tie his boat up close to the New Pier, 180 yards from the main square at Bantry. Twice this had been done, and nothing had happened. A third Sunday morning he tethered his boat to that pier, and in twenty-four hours almost his entire complement of arms and ammunition had fallen into the hands of the Irish enemy.

The town of Bantry sits cushioned into a background of hills, facing out over its historic bay. A prong of slob, dried-out at low water, stabs deep into the town square, one of the largest squares in the county. To the south of the slob, running close to the water's edge, is the main Cork road. At this side the Old Pier stands. At the far side, on the north, is the railway terminus and station, the most southerly railway point in Ireland. The Great Southern line, sweeping in a horse-shoe arc, encircles the town, with its station close to the water side. Less than 100 yards from the station is the New Pier, a rectangular jetty built out over the water of the bay and pointing, finger-post fashion, over at Whiddy, a mile or more across the water.

In those days of 1919 and up to the Treaty, Bantry workhouse, standing 300 yards above the square, at the south of the town, was battalion headquarters of the King's Liverpool Regiment. A garrison of 200 men occupied it, under the command of Colonel Jones, a fair and humane officer who would tolerate no excesses among his men. It was this British officer who, a year later, protected four IRA prisoners, Maurice Donegan, Ralph Keyes, Seán Cotter and Con Sullivan – all of whom had taken part in the events of 17 November 1919 – from assassination by the RIC. In November 1920, the four had been captured unarmed after attending Mass and receiving Holy Communion at Durris, and taken to Bantry. Knowing the part these men had been playing in the fight, which had gone on since 1919, the RIC determined to shoot them as a reprisal; but Colonel Jones intervened to save the prisoners – an Englishman intervening to save Irishmen from being murdered in cold blood by Irishmen! Such was the temper of the times.

In addition to the military garrison in Bantry in 1919 there was, as well, an RIC garrison of sixty men. These had their barracks at the south side of the square, within sight of the railway station and the pier. It was a nightly routine that a strong combined patrol of military and police should parade the town of Bantry from sunset to sunrise, a fact which made IRA activities in the town extremely hazardous. The patrol used to visit the railway station (within hailing distance of the pier) on its tour of duty. Notwithstanding this patrol, the Bantry IRA was never long inactive, seriously impeded though it was through lack of adequate arms and ammunition. This, then, was the general position in and around Bantry on the eventful evening of 17 November 1919. It had been a day of bleak winter sunshine. The night was bright with brilliant moonlight, by no means an ideal condition for the project which the IRA contemplated.

The British sloop had been tied up at the New Pier by the railway station for hours. The entire routine of its crew was known to the local IRA through Volunteer McCarthy, who was employed as mate in the Bantry steamboat, *Princess Beara,* which plied between Bantry and Castletownbere. McCarthy, through his position on this craft, was able to note and mark down the movements of the crew, while the sloop was in port. He had been able to ascertain the position of the arms on board the boat, how they were stored and guarded, the disposition of the crew at given times, and the fact that the officers invariably went ashore at a certain time each Sunday to make merry at one of the local hotels. These facts McCarthy conveyed to IRA headquarters at Keyes' house. With all the information available, 'Mossie' Donegan, Ralph Keyes, Seán Cotter, Michael O'Callaghan, and six members of the local company, set about planning ways and means of capturing the arms aboard the gun-boat. Plans were made, reconsidered, abandoned. Other plans were made, and in their turn they, too, were abandoned. These youths – not one of them except, perhaps, Ralph Keyes, had yet reached the age of twenty – knew that their task was a dangerous one, that it had to be executed with the most accurate precision in timing, that there could be no hitch in their plans, no blundering in the carrying out of the operation, for one untimely shot from one of the crew, one warning shout, an incautious word or movement on the part of their own men, and the entire operation would have failed. Worse than that, they knew that failure would inevitably mean death or capture for the night patrol on the square, a couple of hundred yards from the pier, could not fail to hem them in a sealed corner with the sea at one flank, unscalable cliffs on the other and a heavily armed enemy in front. It was, then, success, complete success, or failure, which meant either death or capture.

With this sobering thought in mind Donegan, the senior officer in the operation, made his final decisions, momentous decisions for a boy of fewer than twenty years of age, but worthy of the man who later made so enduring a name for himself as a soldier in two Irish wars, as camp commandant of prisoners in the internment camp at ill-famed Ballykinlar, as an escapee who coolly walked in disguise through the main gate of Ballykinlar, as the convicted felon in Belfast jail, as Major commanding our own 31st Battalion during the years of the Emergency, and as principal teacher of the model schools in Cork city. At nineteen the boy was already a man in judgement, in courage and in determination. So too were his friends on that historic occasion,

Ralph Keyes, Seán Cotter, and Michael O'Callaghan, all of whom played honourable parts in the wars that were to follow. And when the call to arms came again in 1940, Keyes and Cotter served as captains in the 31st Battalion, under Donegan, its O/C, and O'Callaghan became Judge Advocate General of the army.

A normal sight on any fine night in Bantry was people strolling casually along by the railway station and out upon the pier. This fact was a valuable aid to Donegan and his friends when they came to approach their objective by the pier. There was nothing suspicious in a few pedestrians walking along towards the station in no apparent haste. Therefore, their plans were that they should proceed towards the pier, walking in pairs and at irregular intervals. Their numbers could not be big, for too many could easily defeat their plans by attracting the attention of the enemy patrol. It was, therefore, decided that four men should constitute the initial boarding party – Donegan, Keyes, O'Callaghan and Cotter – and that six others, to help in the ultimate removal of the arms, should wait by the railway station entrance until they were signalled forward after the boat's crew had been overpowered. In addition to these, two scouts were posted on the square to keep the military patrol under observation and to signal its possible approach. Two further scouts were positioned by the railway station to see that no enemy could approach that way.

At 8.30 p.m., with all those arrangements finally perfected, the four men who made up the boarding party approached the pier. They had between them two .38 revolvers and a few rounds of ammunition for each, a very inadequate stock of arms with which to undertake the capture of a British naval sloop. But they depended more on surprise and slickness of execution than on strength, to bring them success, that element of surprise which so often decides big issues in warfare.

Luck was with them that night, for as the advance party strolled with a very unnatural assumption of casualness towards the pier, the sailor who had stood the watch by the wheel-house suddenly abandoned his post and went below to join his comrades, whom they could hear singing and laughing below-deck. It was a providential

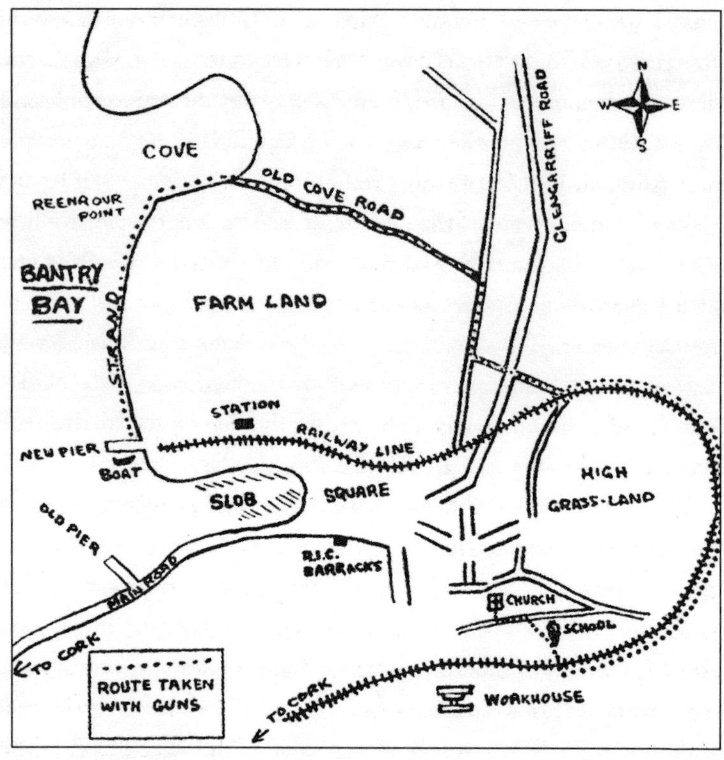

development for the men whose purpose it was to overpower this man without causing any commotion. Now the necessity for silencing him was removed, and they could see him descending the hatch as they approached the vessel.

No sooner had his head disappeared below deck than the four IRA men leaped aboard. Drawing his gun, Donegan pulled open the hatchway to the cabin below and menaced the sailors there, who were now cornered and helpless. The boat was already at the mercy of the IRA. The element of surprise had indeed favoured them, in even greater measure than they had dared to hope. Taken entirely by surprise, completely unarmed, the British sailors were totally helpless. Sharply they were told that they were to remain as they were, that at the first sound of alarm from them a bomb would be dropped among them. This was a bluff, but it worked well, for the sailors could not know that there was no such thing as a bomb in the armament of the Bantry IRA in those days. So, assuming that the threat was a very real one, the sailors abandoned valour for discretion, and in the minutes that followed they were a very docile ship's company, subdued and submissive. A signal from the four on board the gunboat brought their six comrades out of their hiding by the station house. Swiftly but silently they swarmed aboard the boat. Two of them were placed on guard over the sailors below, while Donegan and the others tackled the door leading into the boat's arsenal. Foreseeing possible difficulty with this door, a sledgehammer had been brought along by the IRA – that sledgehammer and two .38 revolvers constituted the entire complement of weapons among them for the occasion.

A hefty blow from the sledge, wielded by very willing arms, and the armoury door was burst open to reveal an unforgettable sight to the men who swarmed anxiously around. There neatly arrayed in their racks, like pins in a paper, were ten carefully oiled, perfectly preserved rifles. It was a sight that some of those Bantry youths will never forget. Ten excellent Ross-Canadian rifles, the first of their kind they had seen – they looked to those young IRA men what the manna in the desert must have looked to Moses. These weapons were of the ordinary .303 calibre, but heavier than the British army Lee Enfield rifle. With long range and with great accuracy, these Ross-Canadian weapons were specially suited for purposes of sniping, and their particular brand had been used by snipers in France during the 1914-1918 war years. These ten weapons appeared like treasures from Ali Baba's cave to Donegan and his comrades that night at Bantry.

But there was little time for pause. Serious work was still ahead. Rifles were swiftly handed out, boxes of ammunition grabbed and passed along to the pier. Bags specially provided for the purpose were rapidly filled with ammunition. Ten revolvers were packed into side-pockets. Everything that could be stored away was forced into the bags; equipment, Verey light pistols, ammunition of all kinds, and in five minutes that little arsenal was completely cleaned out of warlike material.

The first and most difficult phase of the night's work was now accomplished, but much more remained to be done. There was little use in capturing valuable guns and ammunition if they were to be lost again before they could be safely stored away. A storage place had been already decided upon before the raid had been undertaken, but it was a long and dangerous trek from the pier to that selected spot, a long and wearying trek for the heavily laden dozen men. Impossible for them to pass through the town from the pier. At any moment the enemy patrol might be upon them, and heavily burdened as they were, their chances of escape would then be negligible. Foreseeing this contingency, they had already planned out their line of retreat from the pier, a long, circuitous route, but it was the only one for them.

Back of the pier and due north of it lay the strand, stretching along for 500 yards by the foot of the cliffs. This, they decided, was the first leg of their line of retreat. Thrusting a gun down the hatchway at the imprisoned sailors below, Donegan issued the warning that they were not to move or raise any alarm for at least an hour. Then onto the strand he and his party plunged, each man staggering under the weight of British guns and ammunition.

The bright moon was now a good deal of a mixed blessing. It lighted their way sufficiently to enable them to pick their steps with care along the beach; but it also showed up their bodies in relief against the background so that the enemy could scarcely miss them should the alarm be given too soon, and, even then, they knew that their final word of warning to the sailors would not be heeded in full. As they rounded Reenrour Point, a quarter-mile from the pier, the cove lay before them. Then along the Old Cove Road they laboured the difficult 500 yards to the junction, where it joins the main Glengarriff road. A scout, sent ahead to see that the way was clear, waved them on beyond this dangerous point. Over the railway bank they climbed and onto the line as it swings away around the town, towards the south and west. Six hundred yards ahead was the point they hoped to reach.

The less robust among them were tiring now, for the journey had been a killing one at an almost non-stop double, labouring under a heavy load. It was with genuine relief that they swung off the railway line at the south and approached the boy's school, where they had hoped to store away their captured guns in the ceiling above the schoolroom. Two monitors of the school, Jack Mahony and his brother Jim had been given the key by the principal, Jeremiah McCarthy. But even then their difficulties were not at an end, for the ladder that had been procured was too short to reach the hole in the ceiling, and so the school had to be abandoned as a dumping place for the guns. It was a difficult situation. But with so many obstacles already surmounted that night, that one other obstacle, difficult though it was, did not dishearten them.

One other possible safe storage position remained to them – the parish church! The sexton there was Mr Keyes, father of Ralph, who had played so prominent a part in the night's work. Unknown to the clergy of the parish, Mr Keyes guided 'Mossie' Donegan and his men up the ladder that led through the church ceiling up to the roof. There they laid the captured guns, and there they remained in safety for months to come.

But the alarm was then abroad, had been abroad for some time, for the sailors aboard the gunboat had not remained silent for the full time given them. After a half-hour one of them poked his head through the porthole of the cabin and shouted for assistance. The night patrol had been on the square, no more than a couple of hundred yards from the pier, during all the events aboard the boat. It now heard the first shout for help and the alarm was up. The IRA men with their captured arms had just reached the school when the bugle from the military post a few hundred yards away sounded the alarm. In a moment the town was in an uproar, with army lorries rushing here and there, and army and police patrols scouring street by street. But neither the military nor the police ever dreamt that the captured guns might be hidden in the church, no more than a good hurley puck from their own base at the Old Workhouse.

It was a futile night for the British garrison in Bantry. They made widespread searches, but no arrests, and they found no trace of the guns they had lost. The men who had planned and executed the raid went their different ways from the church. Some, to divert suspicion, went to a dance which was being held that night in the town. Their commanding officer went directly home and was in bed before eleven o'clock, a fact which shows the speed with which the whole exploit was carried through. Not many minutes later the Donegan home was raided by the RIC, who had obvious suspicions regarding the men who had carried out the raid, but had no proof to substantiate their suspicions. The sergeant in charge of that particular party swore bitter oaths against the ship's company and officers who had ignored the police warning and tied their boat at the pier, and so in their culpable carelessness had played directly into the hands of the IRA. And well he might, for with good rifles and a large supply of ammunition in IRA hands the struggle had taken on a new phase and the threat to British security had become a real one in west Cork.

LORD FRENCH WAS NOT DESTINED TO DIE BY AN IRISH BULLET

DUBLIN BRIGADE AND TIPPERARY VOLUNTEERS, 9 DECEMBER 1919

by Dan Breen, TD

(formerly QM 2nd Southern Division IRA)

The year 1919 was drawing towards its close as the four of us, Seán Treacy, Seamus Robinson, Seán Hogan and myself, set out for Dublin for discussions with GHQ regarding further activities in our Tipperary Brigade area. Treacy and myself were then fully recovered from wounds we had received at Knocklong where we had assisted in the rescue of Seán Hogan from his RIC captors.

Our existence in the capital was a rather precarious one during the next few weeks. We had, of course, plenty of friends there, including our own county-man, Phil Shanahan, the Fleming family at Drumcondra, and later Professor Carolan of 'Fernside', all of whom were delighted to help and harbour us whenever we cared to call upon them. We did not, however, feel inclined to impose upon the hospitality and generosity of those good friends, and so we often found ourselves short of ready funds, though Treacy's uncle, Mr George Allis, frequently managed to secure money for us from his friends back in Tipperary.

Our reputations were already well known to GHQ and we were sometimes invited to assist the city Volunteers in their exploits against the common enemy. The biggest and most important of these exploits came about some weeks after our arrival in Dublin in an entirely unexpected fashion.

The four of us were then staying at the house of yet another of our friends, Mrs Boland of Clontarf. We were awakened one night by Michael Collins, who told us that we had been selected to take part in an attack upon then British Lord Lieutenant in Ireland, Lord French, who was to drive from Kingstown (now Dún Laoghaire) to the viceregal lodge at five o'clock the following morning. So Collins, head of our intelligence department, had been informed.

I wish to make it clear at this juncture that neither then nor later did we or any of our comrades entertain any feeling of animosity for Lord French as a man or as a soldier. We tried hard to kill him, it is true, but it was not so much the man himself we wished to wipe out as that of which he was a corporate symbol, British rule in Ireland. Lord French to us that night and for many nights to follow was not merely a man but an institution, the evil institution of England's dominance in our land. He was the figurehead representing British tyranny in Ireland and as such we wished to destroy him.

In truth, Lord French was not a man whom one could think of with hatred. He was a soldier, and presumably a good one, for at one period in the early days of the First World War he commanded the British forces in France. In Ireland, as the tool of the British government, his task was to subdue the Irish, by any means he might employ, but to subdue them. His was not the prerogative to argue with his masters or to question their policy. His was to obey orders – and his orders were to humiliate Ireland and if possible to destroy her!

So it was that while we bore no malice against the man himself, we hated with our very souls the things he stood for in Ireland. We believed that in removing the man we would help appreciably in removing that which he represented. We believed, too, that in shooting Lord French we would help to focus the eyes of the entire world upon Ireland's unhappy lot, upon her gallant fight against the might of a great empire, upon the truth that though a bloody war had been fought in Europe 'that small nations might be free', Ireland, one of the smallest and the weakest nations of them all, was still captive in the spider-web of Britain's Empire.

Quickly, but quietly, we pulled on our clothes on that late November night while Collins explained to us the plans for the proposed attack. Moving off in the darkness, we set out for College Green and took up pre-arranged positions in Church Lane off Dame Street – only to be informed later that Lord French must have changed his plans and that the attack was off.

That was the first of at least a dozen abortive attempts to ambush Lord French and his escort, but always, either by blind luck or good intelligence work, the Lord Lieutenant seemed to avoid being where we had expected him to be at a given time, and the task of shooting him seemed to be a hopeless one.

But luck seemed to be with us in the end, for we finally received positive information that French would be in a certain place at a certain time the forenoon of 19 December.

The place was Ashtown station in Dublin, two miles from the city. Lord French was due to arrive at this small station on the 11.40 a.m. train on the forenoon of 19 December, leave the train at that point, and travel the remaining couple of miles to the viceregal lodge by car. This was the information conveyed to IRA intelligence, and on that information we were ordered to act. Accordingly, eleven of us, Treacy, Hogan, Robinson and myself; the Dublin Volunteers, Mick McDonnell, Tom Keogh, Martin Savage, Joe Leonard, Vincent Byrne, Tom Kilcoyne and our leader for the occasion, Paddy Daly, set out for Ashtown along the Cabra Road route towards Ashtown Cross.

Two hundred yards from the station at which the Lord Lieutenant was due to arrive was Kelly's public house, then a plain country pub, but since replaced by a more up-to-date structure. Then, as now, it was known as 'The Half-Way House'.

In pairs we approached this house, and in pairs we entered and mingled with those who occupied the bar. We ordered drinks and proceeded to make ourselves agreeable to other customers. But all the while we were having the station closely watched, and we already had laid our plans for the proposed attack, which was to be directed from behind a hedge at the right-hand side of the road. Some of our men had been told to occupy a position at the crossroads, so that no passers-by should walk inadvertently into the line of fire. Three of us, Martin Savage, Tom Keogh and myself, were selected to push a horse-cart across the road in front of the oncoming cars of the Lord Lieutenant and his escort, so as to delay their passage through the ambush lines.

Meanwhile, we had been giving the impression to the other occupants of the public house that we were merely casual cyclists passing through and that we had no more than a haphazard acquaintance with each other – and all the while every man of us was keyed up to a concert-pitch of nervous tension, for I have yet to meet the man who will not show signs of strain while he is waiting for action.

Looking down the ladder of thirty years, I can now see clearly the errors into which we fell that day at Ashtown. A few of those errors were due in part to a certain immaturity of judgement in our own plans, for, remember, these were early days in the struggle and neither our men nor our officers had yet reached the standard of efficiency which they were to achieve later in the War of Independence. The main error of the day was, however, due to a change of programme on the part of Lord French, a change which was directly responsible for his escape at Ashtown that day. It was a variation of plan that we could not have anticipated.

Lord French's usual bodyguard and escort consisted of, first, a motorcycle scout, followed in close order by three cars. The first car normally contained a strongly armed party of specially picked guards. With the third car it was the same as with the first one, while French himself invariably travelled in the second car. This morning, however, whether acting under the influence of some premonition, or acting merely on an impulse of the moment, he elected to travel in the leading car of the party rather than in the second – and, premonition or accident, his change of plan saved Lord French's life that day!

Directly the train drew into the station the word was passed along to us. Immediately we rushed to our appointed positions. Savage, Keogh and myself began to push our cart across towards the centre of the road – and with the more sober judgement which one gains with the advance of years, I can now see how hopelessly futile was that task of ours, fraught as it was with the gravest danger, for in doing it we had to expose ourselves to the certain fire of the enemy. The cart was just a plain, rather fragile country horse cart, and I realise now that a plank of plywood or a sheet of tissue paper would be almost as effective against the impact of those steel-bodied cars of the viceregal party.

Immediately that we started to push our cart onto the road, the first unpredictable hitch of the day occurred. A policeman from the lodge had just appeared upon the scene to keep the road clear for the Lord Lieutenant's passage, and he forthwith set about trying to push us and our cart off the road. We argued with him, assuming a pose of blank stupidity in the hope of deceiving him, but he still insisted upon impeding us and in forcing us to get clear off the highway.

The position had grown precarious, for the cars were expected on the scene at any second. Vincent Byrne had already signalled their departure from the station, so that the situation was critical. We tried hard to get him to move away without showing actual violence to him, but he took no heed of either our air of simulated stupidity or our requests to him to mind his own business. We swore at him with no more success – and then there occurred an incident which placed in jeopardy the entire work of the day. Seeing the dogged intervention of the policeman with our plan to block the roadway, one of our men behind the hedge must have lost control of his nerves for the moment, for he hurled a grenade at the policeman's head and knocked him flat in full view of the motorcycle scout and of the leading car of the Lord Lieutenant's party which had swept into full view fifty yards away.

Our instructions had been to allow the first car to pass through unimpeded, and to concentrate our attack upon the second car. Obviously suspicious that something unusual was afoot, the driver of the first car accelerated and flashed through our lines untouched, though Seamus Robinson, setting aside instructions for once, hurled an ineffective grenade after it. In it Lord French sped to safety all unknown to us.

The brunt of our attack was directed upon the second vehicle in which we had expected the Lord Lieutenant to travel. With grenade and bullet we assailed it, and it staggered across the road into the far ditch. Out of it stumbled the driver, the only man in it – and we suspected immediately that our attack had been in vain as far as shooting Lord French was concerned.

Meanwhile the third car, containing four soldiers armed with rifles and a fifth armed with a light machine gun, had gone into action. The main force of their fire was directed against the three of us on the centre of the road. Our shelter was of little advantage to us, consisting only of the light timbers of the cart we had tried to push onto the road. We returned their fire with our revolvers, while our comrades behind the hedge poured grenades and bullets upon them.

But these men were soldiers by profession, and one of them was a marksman of merit. This man set deliberately about his task of picking us off. His rifle resting on the high back of one of the front seats of the car, he took cool and unhurried aim. His first shot caught young Martin Savage through the throat, killing him outright. The second bullet from his rifle blew my hat away, and the third took me in the left leg above the knee, and left me almost helpless, and then with a final burst of fire, the car tore away towards Phoenix Park and through the gate leading to the viceregal lodge.

The fight was over, and we had gained nothing by the day's work beyond wrecking one of Lord French's motor cars. We had lost a valued comrade, for Martin Savage had died where he fell. I, myself, did not feel too happy, for my leg gave me considerable pain.

Lord French bore a charmed life, or else he was not destined to die by an Irish bullet.

MONAGHAN MEN'S BAPTISM OF FIRE AT CAPTURE OF BALLYTRAIN RIC POST

MONAGHAN BRIGADE, 14 FEBRUARY 1920

by P.J. O'Daly

(formerly Vice-Brigadier, Monaghan No. 2 Brigade IRA)

IN THE YEARS between 1916 and 1920 there was little IRA activity in County Monaghan, other than of a routine kind such as organising Sinn Féin clubs. The IRA had a twofold object in building up the clubs. The idea was to get all the young men of military age enrolled as members first of all, so that they would be available when called upon for such tasks as to assist at elections and to raise funds for national purposes. It was felt that when the first object had been attained, the older members would automatically fall into line behind these young men in the movement that was slowly but surely leading to militant action. Such was the position at the end of 1919.

As 1920 dawned it was apparent that there was a need for an intensive drive to form more IRA companies throughout the county, and Eoin O'Duffy set about organising the various districts. Though lack of arms and ammunition was a crippling drawback, the work of organising and training the men went ahead. At the beginning of February, officers from the County Monaghan battalions met regularly and examined plans for an early stroke against the enemy. About the same time Ernie O'Malley, a staff captain from GHQ, arrived in the county, and he immediately proceeded to collect information and to prepare for an attack on Ballytrain RIC barracks. Ballytrain was decided upon because it was the most isolated police post in the county, and probably the easiest to capture. When the preparations had been completed and a plan of the barracks and details of the armament kept in it had been obtained, through Volunteer Barney Marron of Ardragh, a tradesman who had been carrying out repairs in the building, it was decided to make the attack on the night of 13 February. Some time previously the police had strengthened the defences of their post with sandbags filled with breaker chippings.

On the night of the attack, IRA contingents, drawn from units that were eventually to form parts of the five battalions of the later-established Monaghan No. 2 Brigade, converged on the enemy outpost, which guarded the traffic routes leading from Carrickmacross to Cootehill and from Castleblayney to Shercock, where two important roads intersect. IRA elements of the same units also stood by to fell trees at chosen points and to block the roads leading to the barracks, a semi-detached, two-storey building. In all about 120 IRA men had been mobilised, but little more than half of them armed, for the available armament amounted to no more than about a dozen rifles, twenty revolvers and automatics, and about thirty shotguns. Gelignite was also available. The unarmed men were required to trench roads, fell trees, demolish bridges and erect barricades, to impede enemy reinforcements. For these purposes they brought along 'cross-cuts', hatchets, sledgehammers and pickaxes. It was considered important that as many men as possible should be used in this, the first militant operation in the area, not because so many were needed, but to ensure that largest number possible would be given the chance to experience active service conditions.

Abutting the barracks and under the one roof with it, was a store which had an important part in the plans of the attackers. Both barracks and store belonged to David Mitchell, whose own house across the road from them was seized and occupied by about thirty attackers who took up position there some time after midnight. It was the only building that gave cover and a view of the front of the RIC post, and was the only point from which IRA riflemen and shotgun men engaged the defenders. Command of the IRA forces was held jointly by Eoin O'Duffy and Ernie O'Malley, and the other officers who participated in the operation were Dan Hogan, Seamus McKenna, Terry Magee, Charles Emerson, John McCann, James Flynn, Phil Marron and P.J. O'Daly. The command post was in David Mitchell's house, and O'Duffy and O'Malley directed operations from there.

It had been decided that the attack would commence at midnight, but it was 1 a.m. when the first shot rang out. A brief interval followed that first sharp crack of a rifle, and it remained unbroken till further shooting was directed against the barracks. Some time elapsed before reply was made by the garrison, which consisted of Sergeants Lawton and Graham and Constables Gallagher, Murtagh, McDonnell and another. The line of fire against the post was at an angle of some thirty degrees from what would have been a direct line, and apart from this weakness in the position of the attackers posted in Mitchell's house, it soon became evident that the defenders could not be dislodged by rifle and shotgun fire alone, at least not unless they had spent their ammunition. Desultory firing continued for about two hours, during which period occasional rapid bursts of fire by the defenders would draw a similar reply from the attackers. The IRA riflemen, however, were in the main merely providing cover for a demolition group which consisted of four of their comrades who, from the beginning of the attack, had been engaged mining the gable wall that separated the barracks from Mitchell's store. The four were John Donnelly and his son Thomas, Patrick McDonnell and Patrick McCabe, all of whom had silently entered the store before the attack began. For their purpose they used gelignite that had been purloined from the Monaghan County Council during quarry blasting, in the years 1918 and 1919. Taken from under the very eyes of RIC guards by council workmen at the instigation of Eoin O'Duffy and P.J. O'Daly, then employed by the council as assistant county surveyors, the gelignite was known to the IRA as 'Bás gan sagart' or 'Death without the priest!'

Their first attempt to take a police barracks was, indeed, a weird experience for the attackers, none of whom, with the exception of

O'Malley, had previously been under fire, with the noise of battle about them, and the flashes of gunfire from both sides of the road stabbing the winter darkness. From time to time O'Duffy, with the aid of a megaphone, called upon the RIC to surrender, but they made no reply that could be heard above the din.

At last the explosive had been packed into the gable wall of the barracks by the demolitions group operating under cover of the adjoining store, and everything was in readiness to set off the mine. The police were warned to stand clear, and, in a few moments there was a terrific boom, the vibration of which was felt a quarter of a mile away. The echo resounded for fully two minutes, and immediately after it had died away, the police agreed to surrender in response to a fresh summons to do so by O'Duffy. They were ordered to pass their weapons out through a window to waiting IRA men, and when that had been done, they filed out, led by the grizzled old Sergeant Lawton who was carrying his Rosary beads in his hands and reciting his *Paters* and *Aves* in Gaelic. It was a strange scene. Lawton pleaded for mercy and asked the attackers to spare his life, saying, 'We are all Catholics like yourselves.'

'How do you know what we are?' came back the stern response. In his previous station, Lawton had been very active, besetting members of the IRA, and he had succeeded in having some men sent to jail. These misdeeds and the prosecutions for which he had been responsible were enumerated for him at the surrender, and old Lawton was, indeed, a most despondent and miserable person. His comrades were in little better shape. Their uniforms were white with the dust that had been caused by the explosion, and all six looked more like flour millers than policemen, as they filed their ghostly way out of the ruins of their barracks. It was learned later that some of the RIC wanted to surrender earlier in the attack, but that Lawton had insisted on holding out, as he felt that if captured he would be executed because of his activities against the IRA. The police surrendered six carbines, one Verey light pistol (which they did not use during the attack and which, years later, was presented to the National Museum), a quantity of rifle ammunition and police equipment. It was about 4 a.m. when the IRA men withdrew, their task successfully accomplished. Behind them they left six very frightened RIC men.

With the IRA gone from the scene and daylight on the way, the RIC decided to send word to Carrickmacross of the disaster that had befallen the Ballytrain post. In addition to the surrender of the garrison, and the loss of all armament and equipment, the building had suffered extensive damage. There was a gaping hole in the mined gable end, the walls were cracked and part of the roof was damaged. Sergeant Graham, apparently the only member of the garrison who had emerged unscathed from the engagement, was chosen to take the bad news to Carrickmacross, and he had tramped about six miles of the road in the carrying out of that mission, when he was picked up and given a lift by a man driving a pony and car, on his way to the town to attend the 8.30 Mass.

I had barely time to get ready for early Mass myself, after returning from the attack, and it so happened that two of the Carrickmacross police occupied a seat behind me in the church. It was with great difficulty that I was able to avoid falling asleep during Mass, and I was concerned that my state of fatigue and sleepiness might be observed by the police who would quickly associate it with the events at Ballytrain barracks, when they heard of them. A commotion occurred during Mass, and the two RIC men rushed out of the church. I immediately realised that the disturbance probably indicated that word of the Ballytrain attack had been received at the Carrickmacross RIC barracks. After Mass, a local man approached me in town, and enquired: 'Did you hear about Ballytrain?' Having replied that I had not heard anything, I was given the astonishing piece of news that 'all the police were killed last night at Ballytrain'. 'A bad job,' my information added, and I agreed!

The police of the Ballytrain garrison were brought into Carrickmacross Union Hospital and were placed under the care of the late Dr Peter McKenna. On the following Friday I was visited by some of their brothers-in arms from the Carrickmacross RIC post, and my place was searched without anything of an incriminating nature being discovered. Some arrests were made in the county, but the police seemed to have nothing to work upon and to be merely acting upon their suspicions alone. A report was whispered around the neighbourhood that at least one IRA man had been killed during the attack, but that was not correct. None of the attackers were hit.

One of the barricades thrown up on the night of the attack was at a point opposite a manse, and the crash of falling trees disturbed the slumbers of the clergyman who resided there. Having gone out to investigate the cause, and having come upon a number of men sawing and felling his trees, he proceeded to reprimand them for stealing his property. He was in full blast, venting his righteous indignation, when it suddenly seemed to strike him that there was something very odd about those nocturnal wood-cutters. For one thing they were armed, and he had barely realised that fact when he was peremptorily ordered back to his house where, it is hoped, he found comfort and solace even though his slumbers may have been disturbed and fitful.

A man who had been sauntering along towards another of the barricades was greatly surprised when he was made prisoner. He protested that he was a law-abiding citizen, and always loyal to the British government. A search of his person brought to light two bottles of poitín. His profession of loyalty to Britain could be attributed to the fact that he had mistaken the men at the barricade for members of the RIC in mufti, and that he was ready to profess anything likely to keep their hands off his precious bottles of 'mountain dew'. He was trussed up and thrown into a shed from which he managed to escape after some time, minus his poitín!

The effects of the Ballytrain attack were immediate. The civilian population, especially those nationalist sections which had been hostile to Sinn Féin – and these included the members and supporters of the Old Nationalist Party and, more especially, of the Ancient Order of Hibernians – began to show themselves as being favourably disposed towards the movement for complete independence. The operation had made these people realise that they were no longer fighting a purely political issue solely against a political party; that a military body had entered the lists, pledged to fight for that freedom which was desired by the great majority of the people. All opposition to Sinn Féin, at least from what might be termed nationalist elements, soon disappeared. A further effect of Ballytrain was to bring home to the people of Monaghan the fact that the war with Britain had started in earnest. The winning of the first round against the British enemy resulted in a big influx of young men of the county to the ranks of the IRA. The enemy forthwith evacuated his posts in the rural areas and the garrisons that were withdrawn from them were used to strengthen those in the larger towns. Although the fact was not immediately apparent to everybody, the IRA was then aware that the RIC intelligence had practically broken down. Its contacts with the people had been largely severed and nobody could be found who would carry information to the British. The King of England's Writ no longer ran, particularly outside of the towns, and even inside them the people had little further recourse to that British institution which in former times, they had called 'the Law.' For the further, the majority of them were to take their litigation to the Irish republican courts.

From a purely military point of view the attack on Ballytrain RIC barracks might not be considered a great achievement, but the moral effects that it produced were of tremendous importance. On the day after the attack the surrounding countryside was scoured for information by British military, who even resorted to questioning the children from the schools in the area in the hope that they might pick up a lead to the men who had reduced Ballytrain barracks; but nobody could be found who had any information to give them. One old man, who was being questioned about the affair, was overheard to say that old men were not given information about such matters. With one of his sons in the movement, it was obvious where his sympathies lay, and, once he had got beyond earshot of his inquisitors, he exclaimed with gusto, 'That's the stuff to give them!' Another old man made a twenty-mile journey by jennet and cart, just to see the demolished RIC post and to bring home a souvenir from the wreckage. When John O'Donovan visited Carrickmacross in 1835, he stated that he found the people there as Irish as they must have been in the days of Owen Roe O'Neill, and so, Monaghan, which is proud to be in Ulster, was never brought 'to heel' by the British invader.

In June 1921, one of the many IRA seizures of mails in the area brought to light a letter to which was attached a bill for fees by the doctor who had attended the policemen wounded at Ballytrain. It was for sixty guineas, and had been submitted by the accountant general's office to the district inspector in Carrickmacross, a man named Maunsell, for his observations. Maunsell's memorandum on the subject of the doctor's fees was as follows:

> I would recommend that this account be paid, because doctors do not care to have anything to do with policeman in these times.
>
> Signed,
> MAUNSELL, D.I. Carrickmacross

One of the Irish-American papers published an account of the attack on Ballytrain barracks, and illustrated it with what purported to be an artist's impression of the building in the actual process of being blown up. The policemen were shown as having been shot through the roof of their post, and grabbing their helmets as they sailed through space!

Ballytrain was the first police barracks in Ulster to be captured by the IRA, and the third in Ireland. Twelve companies participated in the operation, viz., Monaghan, Wattle Brigade (Fermanagh border), Clones, Newbliss, Greenan's Cross, Killanny, Mile River, Magheracloone Lower, Tyholland, Donagh (north Monaghan), Carrickmacross and Corduff (south Monaghan). Some of the men had to travel long distances to take part in the attack, and they were conveyed by motor car to and from the area. All returned to their homes immediately after it, though serious consideration had first been given to a suggestion that they should proceed to Shercock, four miles away, in County Cavan, to attack the RIC barracks there. It was eventually decided that a second project of the kind in the one night might be too big an undertaking, especially as no plans had been prepared for it. The rifles and ammunition captured from the police at Ballytrain were later used in operations against British forces. Charles Walton of Carrickmacross, who had driven a car in which numbers of the attackers were conveyed to and from Ballytrain, did not complete his task until 8 a.m. He was subsequently questioned and threatened by the police, in a vain attempt to force him to divulge information.

Of the officers who participated in the attack, the rank of Battalion Commandant was held by Dan Hogan, Terry Magee, James Flynn, Seamus McKenna and P.J. O'Daly. Barney Marron, of whom there was no braver man in the county, was shot dead in a raid for arms on the morning of 1 September 1920. He is buried in Corcreeagh graveyard, about six miles from Carrickmacross, on the Monaghan-Cavan border. A Celtic cross was unveiled in his memory, and that of his brother Patrick, in 1939, by the 5th Battalion, Monaghan No. 2 Brigade. It is one of the finest monuments in the county, and the inscription is completely in Gaelic.

What had been the Ballytrain RIC barracks was subsequently rebuilt, and is now the Garda Síochána station. Actually, it is in the townland of Shantonagh, about a quarter of a mile from Ballytrain, a place of about half-a-dozen houses, two of them public houses. Around the time of 1798 about 300 people lived there, but today it puts one in mind of Goldsmith's 'Deserted Village'. The stranger who stops there on his way through is noted by its few inhabitants, and local gossipers will surmise about his business

From an archaeological point of view, Ballytrain is interesting. On an adjacent hill is a cromlech that occupies about a rood, and is known as Trean-More's Grave. This Trean-More is said to have been a grandfather of Finn McCool, and to have given his name to the place as Baile Tréin.

And so, as the old song has it, 'Everything has but a time'. The 'battle of Ballytrain' has become but a memory, even for those who took part in it. It is hoped that this short account of the operation will perpetuate that memory of an eventful night, 13–14 February 1920, when, appropriately, the IRA password was '303'. The occasion went into a ballad much in favour at the time as:

That day of renown
When the rebels of Monaghan they all gathered around
The leaders addressed them and men of great fame
When an order was issued to attack Ballytrain.

ROOF FIRE TECHNIQUE WAS EXPLOITED IN CAPTURE OF BALLYLANDERS BARRACKS

EAST LIMERICK BRIGADE, 27 APRIL 1920

by Lieut-Colonel J.M. McCarthy

(formerly Adjutant, East Limerick Brigade, IRA)

HIGH INTO THE night sky, there to outshine the bright moonlight and bathe the ground below in sun-like radiance, the Verey light signals rose and fell. These fingers of flame, sent skyward as symbols of alarm and calls for aid by the police garrison of Ballylanders RIC barracks, marked the opening of the IRA attack on that post on 27 April 1920. It was probably the first time that these firework signals, originally designed for the trench combats in the European war, had illuminated the County Limerick countryside; it was also the first barracks attack by the IRA in that county, and the initiating move in a campaign that was to unfold in widening scope and intensity over the succeeding months.

As befitted such an occasion, one designed to be their baptism of fire, the operation had been carefully planned by the IRA leaders in east Limerick. But first of all, the decision to undertake it had, of course, to be made. Necessarily, this had to be made at brigade level, as no single battalion or company unit at that time would have sufficient arms at its disposal for the purpose. Neither would it have been in a position to ensure the very essential co-operation of adjoining units in the way of erecting road blocks and so on, to impede hostile reinforcements.

Thus, while the attack was primarily an operation conducted by the Galtee Battalion, the oldest and principal battalion unit of the brigade, it was carried out under the auspices of, and with the co-operation of, brigade headquarters. Indeed, it might also be said to have been under the auspices of GHQ in Dublin. This came about through the presence in the area of Tomás Malone, then known under the name of 'Seán Forde'. He had been sent to County Limerick nominally as an organiser of the Republican Loan campaign, but actually in practice his duties assumed an increasingly military character. Nor was this to be wondered at, for apart from his inherent military aptitude, his final instructions, as received from Michael Collins, were: 'Get those Limerick men into the fight!'

It was not that the Limerick men needed much urging. In fact, the Irish Republican Brotherhood members of the Galtee Battalion had for some time been working for a more pronounced and enterprising military policy in their area. As elsewhere, the IRB members were a small select body in the Volunteers and the spearhead of the organisation at that period. With this policy as the real issue, there had arisen a local dispute among the Volunteers, causing not inconsiderable disorganisation. This was largely because, for the great bulk of the Volunteers, the dispute appeared to be a mere conflict of personalities and they took sides or remained neutral on that basis and in ignorance of the real point at stake.

In the outcome, the decision to attack Ballylanders RIC barracks vindicated the IRB standpoint twice over. For not only was the decision largely inspired by the IRB, but it was planned and led almost entirely by its principal local members and that notwithstanding the fact that not all of them then ranked as Volunteer officers. The decision having been taken and approved by the Brigade Commander, Seán Wall of Bruff, who attended some of the initial meetings of the planners, these then resolved themselves into a small staff for the detailed planning and execution of the operation.

This small planning staff comprised Tomás Malone ('Forde'), Tadhg Crowley of Ballylanders, Edmond Tobin of Glenbrohane and Jack MacCarthy of Kilfinane, who was also vice-commandant of the battalion at this period. Others attending the staff conferences from time to time included Seán Meade, members of the Crowley family (brothers of Tadhg Crowley) and Thomas Murphy, all of Ballylanders. As the occasion required, other Volunteers from the locality were called in for consultation or assignment of tasks.

Most of the conferences to plan the attack were held at Edmond Tobin's house at Glenbrohane, near Ballylanders. The post to be assaulted was a strong stone structure, steel-shuttered, dominating the village street from its site at the corner of a crossroads. But it had one weakness, unrealised in all probability by the police garrison. That was the semi-detached character of the building, a second house of a similar type being alongside, gable-to-gable. On the other side, the gable of the barracks was an open one, abutting on the road to Kilfinane. The front of the building faced the fairly wide open space of the square and the long village street. At the rear little or no field of fire existed for the defence, and it only required to be kept under observation by an attacker.

The defenders' weak point – the second building in the block, which served as the local dispensary – was made the pivot on which centred the whole scheme of attack. This scheme was one which the police could hardly have anticipated, at that period at any rate, as it employed what was then a new technique in barracks attacks. This was to break through the roof of the second house from inside, and through the opening thus made to break through the roof of the barracks. The bombing and igniting of the barracks' top floor would then follow.

Tomás Malone took charge of this critical task and of the assault as a whole. At the other gable – the open one – the firing position fixed upon was O'Grady's house, with J. MacCarthy, the battalion vice-commandant, in charge. From O'Grady's premises, which was separated from the barracks by some fifteen yards of roadway, a semi-circle of other firing points was selected to cover the front of the barracks, these positions being located in Upton's, Burke's, Condon's and Crowley's premises, with Tadhg Crowley, Seán Lynch and Pat Hannigan supervising in this sector. The main framework of the assault plan being thus settled, there remained innumerable lesser, but essential details to be perfected, such as timing of occupation of positions, the hour of attack, collection of equipment, erection of barricades, arrangements about the signals, and so on.

In due course these matters, and the awkward problems some of them presented, were satisfactorily settled. The details arranged extended even to the provision of a stretcher, a first-aid station manned by the local Cumann na mBan and – further afield – the co-operation of neighbouring brigades was secured in the way of impeding road traffic from Fermoy, Buttevant and Tipperary, the British military centres whence reinforcements might be dispatched to Ballylanders. An inner ring of road blocks, at a mile or so on all sides of the village, was also established and manned. Counting the parties on these inner road blocks, at a small observation post set up in stables at the rear of the barracks, and those manning the main firing points, the number of Volunteers participating numbered sixty, being comprised – apart from the Ballylanders Company – of parties from Galbally, Kilfinane, Bruff and Kilmallock. The Kilmallock contingent included the then Battalion O/C, Seán O'Riordan. The number in the actual attack, that is those manning the firing positions, was, of course, much smaller, amounting to some twenty-five, each of the firing posts having an average strength of four Volunteers.

In the event all these preparations worked out as planned, and down to the smallest detail, if the workmanship put into the construction of the stretcher be excepted. This appliance was a piece of amateur carpentry, hastily knocked together and fated to let down – in every sense of the term – one of its amateur constructors before the night was out. Initially, however, it fulfilled satisfactorily its first task – the removal of a seriously ill lady to a place of greater safety than that of her residence, which was in the line of fire. This transfer was effected immediately prior to the hour fixed for opening the attack, and not without considerable difficulty, due to the need for quietness, exact timing and having to surmount an eight-foot high fence of barbed wire with the loaded stretcher.

Concurrently, the attacking party proper was assembling at a crossroads less than a mile from the village, receiving final instructions and, where needed, the men were assigned local guides to their various firing points. At the last moment an incident occurred which threatened ruin to the project. Suddenly, in the still night, a shot rang out from the midst of the assembly. To the keyed-up Volunteers it sounded louder than a thunder-clap, and it seemed almost certain it would give the alarm to the nearby police garrison. No such effect was produced, however, the final reconnaissance reports as they came in showing that the police were all within their barracks and evidently unaware anything unusual was afoot. What might have been a very unlucky shot for the Volunteers had, it transpired, been discharged accidentally in the course of some last-minute instruction in rifle manipulation, which was being imparted to one of the Volunteers, Peter Steepe of Kilfinane. Incidentally, this member of the attacking party, who was in no way responsible for the accident, calls for special mention in that he was a Protestant, a member of that community in the Kilfinane locality, which has branches here and there in County Limerick, known as 'Palatines', a name derived from the place of their ancestors – the Palatinate in Germany.

The Volunteers had moved quietly to their position around 11 p.m. and had occupied them without incident. After a hurried erection of some protection against the volume of fire expected to be directed on them by the police garrison, all eyes were turned expectantly on the dispensary post, the house adjoining the barracks. From that post was to be given the signal to open fire. After a short, but tense, wait, a green pinpoint of light flashed out. It was the signal. From the semicircle of firing positions stabbed the rifle flashes of the opening volley, swiftly intermingled with the swish of the Verey rockets and the answering fire of the defenders. For the half-hour that followed, the quiet village street became a focus of concentrated light and sound.

Simultaneously with the opening volley, the break through the dispensary roof was started and quickly accomplished. From the point of vantage thus gained, the roof of the barracks was within reach. Soon the dull thud of heavy stones crashing on the slate roof was added to the volume of sound. A gaping hole appeared in the roof, but the reaction of the defenders was swift. They brought rifle fire to bear on the gap. For a while this fire threatened to prevent the attackers exploiting their initial success. In the end a grenade was dropped through the opening and silenced this defensive effort. The grenade was followed by quantities of paraffin oil and a lighted torch. Almost at once the flaming torch spread a rapidly growing circle of fire through the top storey of this wing of the barracks.

Meanwhile, at the opposite gable, a hot exchange of rifle fire was taking place between the post in O'Grady's and the defenders firing from their gable-end windows. This was a point-blank duel in which the flashing rifles of defence and attack seemed almost muzzle to muzzle. The police, behind their steel shutters, had the advantage of position, being practically immune behind this solid, loopholed protective screen, as against a hastily thrown up breastwork of bedding at the windows through which the Volunteers fired. Of the two upper-storey windows in the Volunteer post, one was manned by D. O'Hannigan and the other by the officer in charge of the post, with Seán Meade of the local Volunteer company, standing in between under cover of the room wall where he awaited his chance to fire. This he could get only by one of the firers yielding position and weapon to him, no more than two rifles and two firing points being available there. Eventually his turn came. For some time the volume of fire from the barracks against this post had been intense and well-directed. It was afterwards noted that the woodwork of the windows was deeply scored from the passage of bullets entering there to impinge on the barricade of bedding or on the opposite wall of the room. This well-aimed fire soon found its mark; a bullet struck Seán Meade at his firing point at one of the windows. It was evidently a serious, and possibly fatal, wound.

His companions, coming to his aid, found him completely collapsed and proceeded to get him downstairs out of the line of fire. That was accomplished with difficulty, owing to his collapsed condition and the impossibility of his helpers adopting other than a crouching posture under the quick succession of bullets still penetrating the windows. On reaching the comparative safety of a ground floor room, his wound was examined and found to be a clear-through penetration of the chest, one obviously needing skilled and swift attention. The stretcher, of which he was one of the constructors, was again brought into use to take him to the first-aid station. On the way it broke under the strain and deposited its burden heavily on the ground. The wounded man was given preliminary aid at the station until the arrival of the local dispensary medical officer, Dr Hennessy.

Throughout these events the defensive firing of the police from the front face of the barracks remained intense, though less concentrated, as it had to be distributed against a number of separated positions. At the same time it was seen that the flames, which had blazed up at one end of the barracks roof, were gaining a grip on the whole top storey. Clearly, the attackers saw that the exercise of patience and maintenance of their rifle fire against the barracks to prevent the garrison fighting the flames could only have one result. The police evidently came to realise that too, for with the top floor well alight, they gave indications of surrendering by slackening their rate of fire, and finally by a complete cessation of fire and the display of a white flag through one of the windows.

The ground floor of the barracks was still intact as the Volunteers entered to take the surrender. The police, all unwounded, numbered five – a small garrison, but one which, instead of offering a defence of half-an-hour's duration, could have held out indefinitely behind their steel shutters were it not for the exploitation by the attackers of the single weak point in the defensive layout. In the circumstances, the Galtee Battalion had every reason to be satisfied with its first serious operation and its results – the complete destruction of the post, the capture of the rifles, grenades and miscellaneous equipment of the garrison, and all at the cost of a single casualty.

Happily, that casualty did not prove a fatal one. Having been medically attended, the wounded man's condition was such that it appeared the most humane decision to leave him undisturbed at the first-aid station, despite the inevitable capture this involved. However, a chance was taken to save him from the enemy, and in a motor car provided and driven by Jack Crowley, the wounded Volunteer was hurriedly moved by devious routes to the residence of Mrs Burke, Laurencetown, Kilfinane, some five miles distant. There, under the care of Dr Maurice Fitzgerald and two nurses, the Misses O'Sullivan, he remained a considerable time before being fit for removal to the County Hospital in Limerick city. Prolonged treatment followed there until the patient was sufficiently strong to complete his recovery at Mount Melleray Abbey, where he filled an appointment under an assumed name. A year later he was able to report for duty and assume office as intelligence officer of East Limerick Brigade, which by then had recorded a long list of engagements since that initial and successful effort at Ballylanders.

HISTORY REPEATED ITSELF IN THE ATTACK ON KILMALLOCK BARRACKS IN 1920

EAST LIMERICK BRIGADE, 28 MAY 1920

by Lieut-Colonel J.M. MacCARTHY

(formerly Adjutant, East Limerick Brigade, IRA)

Long before the fashion of erecting memorials to the 'Unknown Soldier' came into being in countries abroad after the First World War, Kilmallock boasted such a monument. It was the memorial to the 'Unknown Fenian' who fell in the attack on Kilmallock police barracks in 1867. That event was to be re-enacted fifty-three years later – and history to repeat itself in more ways than one – when the East Limerick Brigade IRA decided to lay siege to the same barracks on the night of 28 May 1920.

In that attack the Volunteers were attempting a task bristling with difficulties that seem insurmountable, but they had the satisfaction of successfully concluding an effort which had proved too much for their predecessors in 1867. As in the 1867 Rising, the attackers on this occasion also suffered one fatal casualty. Curiously enough, the parallel was further continued in that the Volunteer killed, Liam Scully, like the 'Unknown Fenian' of 1867, was a stranger in the locality, being a native of County Kerry, who, but a short time previously, had taken up a Gaelic League teachership in the neighbourhood.

Looking over old papers dealing with the Rising of '67, another notable circumstance comes to light. The roll of the participants in the Kilmallock attack in '67, who were tried and sentenced to transportation or imprisoned for – as the charge had it – 'most wickedly, maliciously and traitorously making open war against our said Lady the Queen,' was repeated almost name for name, and, in many cases, in blood relationship, by the attackers of 1920.

New expedients were used by the Volunteers to overcome the difficult obstacles in the way of this attack. One was the improvisation of what would now be called 'Molotov Cocktails', and to these missiles the destruction of the barracks was largely due. Their use ensured that a fire, started by a bomb in a wing of the building, was steadily expanded to embrace the whole barracks, and defeat all efforts by the garrison to extinguish the blaze.

That outcome was brought about, however, only by much planning, good tactics and a prolonged fight. Fronted by a lawn, the barracks was set back from the street, its front face being in line with the rear of a business premises, Carroll's, a slight gap intervening between the two buildings at their nearest points, that is, between the left rear corner of Carroll's house and the right front corner of the barracks. As in the case of Ballylanders police barracks, attacked successfully just a month previously, this proximity of another building was seen to be capable of exploitation by an attacker. In this instance, the gap between the corners of the two buildings, though only a few yards in width, and the different alignment of the two premises, did not afford quite the same facilities as in the earlier operation where the buildings concerned were joined to one another, gable to gable. A counterbalancing feature in the Kilmallock lay-out was, however, the fact that the roof of Carroll's house rose much higher than the nearby roof of the barracks and, once securely attained by an attacker, would facilitate an assault on the barracks rooftop despite the intervening gap. In all other respects the barracks was defensively a very strong post, a solid masonry structure, steel-shuttered, loopholed and thickly surrounded by barbed wire entanglements.

With Carroll's premises fixed on as the pivotal attacking position, three other main combat posts were selected. These were the houses directly fronting the barracks on the opposite side of the street, Clery's

Hotel, the Provincial Bank, and O'Herlihy's shop. The left-hand gable of the barracks offered no point of vantage to either defence or attack, while the rear, containing the usual out-offices, was covered by a party detailed for that purpose.

The scheme of attack was worked out at a series of conferences presided over by Brigadier Wall and held at the farmhouse of Thomas Sheedy of Ballingaddy, midway between Kilfinane and Kilmallock. Generally the tactics decided upon followed those adopted so successfully in the preceding attack at Ballylanders – the central feature being again an assault on the roof. In this instance, however, a stronger defence of a more elaborately fortified position was to be anticipated. Indeed, subsequent to the destruction of the Ballylanders post, questions asked in the British parliament had indicated that an attempt to take Kilmallock barracks was expected and had been prepared for by a strengthening of the garrison and its fortifications. All this meant special care and meticulous planning by the Volunteers. Coming so soon after the assault on Ballylanders, the local store of munitions was low and had to be replenished from far afield, not only the neighbouring brigades in Cork and Tipperary being called on for the purpose, but Dublin as well. The movement of these supplies, and their assembly at two special dumps near Kilmallock, in face of an alert enemy expecting such preparations, was successfully accomplished, though some of the carrying parties narrowly escaped disaster.

The material side of the project, including arrangements for providing extensive quantities of petrol and paraffin oil, having been completed, the concentration of the Volunteers required for the attack was planned. To avoid detection and to ensure exact timing of arrival of the various parties, this had to be worked out precisely, especially as representatives of Cork, Tipperary and even East Clare units were to participate. An assembly point in a field close to the town eventually saw the punctual arrival of the various contingents close on midnight. They totalled approximately sixty Volunteers, of which number some thirty were to take part in the actual attack and the remainder to man various close-in barricades and outposts. Simultaneously the creation of a circle of more distant barricades and demolitions was in progress at the hands of the local units on all routes leading to Kilmallock, especially on those from the hostile military centres at Buttevant, Tipperary and Limerick.

Approaching midnight, the assembled Volunteers were assigned to sections, tasks detailed and leaders designated for each section and its combat post. Carroll's house, the post giving access to the barracks roof, was allotted to Tomás Malone ('Seán Forde') with Edmond Tobin and P. Hannigan, both of Ballylanders, among others in his section. Facing the barracks, Clery's Hotel had Tim Crowley in control, the Provincial Bank being assigned to D. O'Hannigan and a garrison which included Tadhg Crowley, Ballylanders; D.P. MacCarthy of Kilfinane; J. Lynch and J. O'Brien, both of Tankardstown; and Michael O'Keeffe. Herlihy's premises fell to the lot of J. MacCarthy of Kilfinane, and its garrison included the East Clare leader, Michael Brennan.

These posts and that at the back of the barracks' yard were occupied on time and without incident, each party being directed to its destination by guides from the local Volunteer company. In the case of the Provincial Bank and O'Herlihy's shop, entry was gained from the rear. In the other three posts there was more direct access by the normally used entrances, that at Clery's being opened to the attacking party by a Volunteer who had booked into the hotel earlier in the day in the guise of a commercial traveller. In all the occupied premises, the Volunteer parties took special pains to cause the minimum damage and disturbance, and appreciation of their care and courtesy in those respects was afterwards freely expressed, in particular by the bank authorities. In some instances sandbags, already filled, were laboriously brought into the posts to avoid the necessity to make use of household effects as barricading material for the windows.

To the occupying parties in the three houses facing the barracks, as they hastily barricaded the lower portions of the large windows as firing points, the dark, rather squat enemy post looked grim, forbidding and seemingly impregnable. From this front face of the barracks – the 'broadside' of the defence, as it were – would come the greatest volume of defensive fire. Thoughts, too, turned on the numerical strength of the police garrison. On this point there had been some conjecture, as the numbers of the RIC in the post had varied almost daily over a long period. The final and probably accurate estimate for this particular date had put the strength at one sergeant and seventeen constables. But there was little time for these last-minute reflections. Shortly after midnight the previously agreed on light-flash signals winked out from the skylight on Carroll's roof where Malone and his aides perched precariously.

This flanking position, as is so often the case in combat was the decisive one, so far, at least, as the chances of destroying the barracks were concerned. At the same time it was recognised that the brunt of the conflict, so far as concerned the return fire of the police, would be borne by the three attacking posts facing the barracks. While events followed expectations in these two respects, it turned out that the fate of the actual garrison of the barracks was decided not by any of these main positions, but by the seemingly minor post at the rear.

The thud of the first missile – a heavy iron weight, numbers of which had been brought to the scene – as it hit the slate roof of the barracks, partly thrown, partly dropped from Carroll's skylight, was lost in the opening crash of musketry. The crunch of similar missiles that followed could be heard more clearly as the initial wave of sound from the opening rifle volley gave way to a brief silence of the rifles, which was succeeded by separate groups of shots as each post fell into its own rate of fire. The working space at the skylight was cramped and awkward, and for a time this gave rise to doubt as to whether the number and weight of the missiles it permitted the attackers to launch at any one time, would suffice to breach the barracks' roof. But this doubt was short-lived; the slates began to give way under the repeated impact. Soon a gaping hole appeared, laying bare a small portion of a top-floor room at that side of the police building. Confidence restored by this success, the way was clear for the next stage in the attack plan – bombs, petrol and paraffin would be propelled through the breach until the final objective was secured.

Meanwhile, from the posts fronting the barracks poured a steady rain of rifle fire and quite as heavy a volume of answering shots came from the police garrison. This return fire of the defenders had been slow in starting – thus denoting they had been taken by surprise – but gradually it built up to a regularity of stabbing flashes from the double row of steel-shuttered windows. It was finding its targets in the opposite windows across the roadway. Soon these were mere gaping apertures, the glass from which had been showered in fragments on the attacking riflemen firing over the window sills from kneeling or lying position on the floors of the front rooms. In the bank post a Volunteer was hit, apparently by a direct shot, but on examination the wound was found to be from flying glass. In the post at O'Herlihy's a police bullet dislodged a massive curtain pole, bringing it down heavily on the head of the post commander who, curiously enough, was the only Volunteer wearing a steel helmet on the occasion, and so escaped injury. In this duel the police had the advantage of position. From the security of their loop-holed steel shutters they could seek their targets with deliberate, aimed fire. The attackers on the other hand, had to fire over the top of low and improvised barricades. Even if a lucky shot of theirs found its way through one of the barely discernable loopholes of the barracks, it would be unlikely to strike a defender. But mere maintenance of a steady fusillade amply fulfilled the mission of these three posts. Irrespective of its finding a human target, it kept the police pinned down in their firing positions and prevented effective counter-action against the point of main threat – the attackers' flank position.

There, a road oil tank wagon had been moved to the front of Carroll's shop. It was just out of the line of fire, being covered, in relation to the barracks, by the gable of Carroll's premises. From this tank car a chain of buckets conveyed the oil to the roof-top post. Quantities of empty bottles had also been provided, and these – an early form of the missile later used in the Second World War under the name of 'Molotov Cocktail' – were filled with petrol, and some with paraffin, for use as fire-spreading missiles. Thrown from buckets or in the filled bottles, oil began to pour through the broken roof. A flaming torch followed, but failed to ignite the oil-soaked rafters until a grenade was thrown, the explosion from which spread the flame of the burning torch. Soon the fire took a strong grip. It seemed only a matter of time before the whole building would be ablaze, provided the police garrison was kept pinned down. But just then an unlooked-for development occurred – the attackers' flanking position, Carroll's house itself, took fire!

Quickly the fire-raisers had to reverse their role, for a while it looked like a losing fight to curb the unwanted fire, especially when a bucket of paraffin that had been mistaken for water, was thrown into the blaze and added fuel to the flames. In the confusion and heat of battle a parched Volunteer mistakenly drank paraffin instead of water! He became painfully sick and, while able to resume duty after a while, it was only with difficulty he later completed a long journey home at the conclusion of the engagement. In the end, the fire was got under control and the task of spreading the flames in the adjoining building resumed.

By 2 a.m. most of the upper part of the barracks was well alight, and part of it was beginning to collapse. It was, therefore, deemed opportune to give the police garrison a chance to surrender. Cessation of fire was ordered, and demands to surrender were shouted. Some muffled shouts in reply were heard, point being given to them by a volley of police fire from some part of the barracks. Accordingly, the attack was resumed. For the next few hours it followed the earlier pattern, except that rifle fire from the barracks dwindled to scattered shots. Some of the attackers were then operating from street level, alternately appearing around the corner of Carroll's house, throwing a filled bottle of oil against the front of the barracks, withdrawing and again reappearing to repeat the process.

With the dawn, the rifle fire from the police had died away entirely. The main barracks building was then all but completely in ruins, with the roof and most of the upper floor collapsed to ground level. It looked like the end. But it was at this stage that the attackers suffered their single casualty. Liam Scully was one of the attacking party, as also he had been in the assault at Ballylanders the previous month. Taking his stand in the centre of the open street in front of the barracks, he opened fire, and was answered by a single shot from the ruins. He fell where he stood. Brought under cover by a few of his comrades who rushed to his aid, he was attended to by Nurse O'Sullivan and Miss Maura Sheehy, both of whom were available in readiness for such emergencies – one of many sterling services these ladies rendered to Volunteers. But the fallen Volunteer was beyond human aid; his death must have been almost instantaneous.

It was now discovered that the police garrison, or rather its survivors to a number then unknown, had succeeded in retiring from the barracks proper to one of the small out-offices in the rear. This retreat had been effected out of view of the attackers' post at the back of the barracks, and it was probably the rearguard of this withdrawal who had fired the final and fatal shot of the defence.

If the surviving police were to be captured, a new attack on an entirely separate building would have to be mounted. Time did not permit this, with the hour close on 7 a.m. and heavy military and police reinforcements momentarily expected to close in on the town. Leaving a barracks completely demolished with all its store of munitions, the Volunteers began their withdrawal which was effected without any sign of life from the remnants of the police garrison. It was never properly established what losses that garrison had suffered. Estimates ranged from very large figures to the more conservative – and probably accurate – figure of one constable killed and two wounded.

So ended the second occasion that Kilmallock barracks was the centre of military conflict. To the attackers of the Fenian Brotherhood and the Irish Republican Army the cost in blood had been similar; in 1867, the 'Unknown Fenian'; in 1920, the all-but unknown Volunteer from distant Glencar, County Kerry.

A CLEVER RUSE LEADS TO DISARMING OF HIGHLANDERS NEAR MIDLETON

CORK NO. 1 BRIGADE, 5 JUNE 1920

by Patrick Cashman

(formerly of Fianna Éireann; attached to 'B' Company, 4th Battalion, Cork No. 1 Brigade IRA)

MIDLETON, APPROXIMATELY MIDWAY between Cork and Youghal, is the most centrally situated town in east Cork. In the early years of the present century it was reckoned as one of the leading provincial towns of Munster. Its long-established industries, the Distillery and the Avoncore Flour Mills, provided a reasonable percentage of the working population with steady employment. The adjacent limestone country, with its fertile soil, was availed of to the fullest by the hard-working, industrious farmers of the area, who found in their hometown a ready market for their produce. The monthly fair was then a regular feature in the life of the district, and is still one of the best patronised in the southern counties.

While many of our provincial towns have suffered under modern changing conditions, Midleton has retained its erstwhile importance. Its industrial potential has been increased in recent years by the establishment of the worsted industry under the aegis of the late Mr William Dwyer. This latter industry has added materially to the prosperity of the locality, which can today boast of a progress comparable with the best developed areas in the country, a tribute to the genius and enterprise of the townspeople and the inhabitants of the hinterland.

The contentment begotten of this prosperity did not deflect the people's interests in the past from their national obligations. They were ever a people truly national, always proud of the fact that east Cork produced an O'Neill Crowley and a 'Manchester Martyr'. It was natural, then, to expect that the new spirit engendered in 1916 would find an echo amongst the peace-loving, warm-hearted, kindly people of this district.

Midleton formed its Volunteer unit shortly after 1916, and some of these pioneer Volunteers soon earned the attention of the British authorities and were subjected to periods of imprisonment. Their places in the Volunteers were promptly taken by other ardent spirits. Not until the Volunteers had become really militant, and adopted the role and name of the IRA, did the Midleton Company begin to assert itself, and once the die was cast, the men of Midleton pursued their activities with a thoroughness, an aggressiveness and a relentlessness that taxed to the fullest the ingenuity, the numbers and the endurance of the RIC and British soldiers operating in the area. In fairness, it is only right to state that the Midleton men were captained by a man of very high ideals, of fearless calibre and a strategist second to none, for such was Diarmuid Hurley of happy memory, from the Bandon area, who was shot near Midleton in May 1921. It must be recorded too, that some of the Midleton Volunteers hailed from the adjacent rural areas, and meshed in, and worked in harmony with their town confederates, demonstrating a spirit of friendship, responsibility and comradeship that ultimately secured triumph for the IRA.

This spirit was gradually imbibed by the other companies in the 4th Battalion, Cork No. 1 Brigade, and when the flying column was eventually formed it embraced men from almost every company in the battalion area. Simultaneously with other areas, the routine organisation of the Irish Volunteers went on apace in the 4th Battalion area during the years 1917–1919. The dawn of 1920 saw the first major operation, the siege and capture of Carrigtwohill RIC barracks on 3 January. This siege, prolonged and fierce, was a shock to the British authorities who, so far in this district, had not reckoned with the training, the equipment, the discipline and the resoluteness of the Irish forces as typified by those men from Midleton and Cobh engaged in the attack. The operation was carefully planned and its success, without the loss of a single life, caused jubilation amongst the revolutionaries, not alone throughout County Cork, but throughout the whole country.

Castlemartyr RIC barracks, without any preconceived plan, fell before the Midleton Company in the following month. The battalion had the responsibility for the assault and capture of Cloyne RIC barracks in May. These successes were remarkable for the fact that no life was lost, an enduring compliment to the genius, care and judgement of those in charge of the engagements. As well, the successes raised the confidence of the men in their officers and in the cause for which they fought.

To counteract this sharp offensive, the enemy was forced to locate British soldiers in Midleton, never a garrison town like Cobh and Youghal, respectively twelve and sixteen miles distant. The presence of regular military in the town would be a deterrent, minimising the opportunities that the 'boys', as the active IRA men were known, hitherto had been using to the fullest. So the British thought. This deployment of British troops had the opposite effect, for the IRA interpreted it as a real challenge, which they were determined to meet. Thenceforward Midleton became the focal centre for the whole 4th Battalion area, which area was subsequently reorganised into two battalions, namely, the 4th and 10th.

With the British military at their door, the men of the Midleton Company felt that for them the red tocsin of war had at last sounded. They eagerly sought the opportunity of measuring their strength and prowess with the enemy. The Essex Regiment was the first to occupy the town. Its stay was uneventful. The troops were mostly confined to their quarters – a disused factory in the town. A cycle patrol of these soldiers passing through the town one day revealed to one of the local leaders, the possibility of an ambush. Before such a possibility could eventuate, however, the Essex were replaced by the Cameron Highlanders, on Saturday 5 June 1920. The Midleton men had thoughts on the morrow as they enjoyed their customary weekend relaxation and pondered on the reason for the change in the personnel at the military post. They were aware that they were being called on in the morning, for a lightning raid on the RIC barracks at Ballycotton, that well-known summer resort on the coast, nine miles from Midleton.

At 7.30 on that eventful Saturday evening, a patrol of the Camerons, composed of twelve men, including two lance-corporals, fully armed, and piloted by a policeman, left their quarters and went by a back road in the direction of Carrigtwohill. A vigilant Volunteer immediately informed Diarmuid Hurley, who happened at that time to be chatting to some people in the Main Street. Hurley secured two scouts, Paddy Daly and Dan Walsh, to trail the enemy, observe his movements and bring back word immediately the soldiers commenced their return journey. Hurley then took counsel with his closest associate, who had previously conceived the feasibility of such an ambush. Hurley and his friend procured their revolvers and proceeded casually towards the northern end of the town, where the military were located. On their way they instructed any Volunteers whom they saw on the street to follow after them. They had brought with them two bowls which they meant to throw along the road for the purpose of diverting the attention of those who might suspect their movements.*

It was past 8.30 p.m. and just then the two scouts returned, breathless, with the news that the soldiers had gone into Carrigtwohill, which meant that they would likely return by the main Carrigtwohill-Midleton road. Hurley and his men proceeded towards Carrigtwohill in the hope of encountering the patrol, and they travelled in twos to give the impression that they were just having a walk. When they congregated 200 yards out, there were only nine in all. True, one man who went to procure his revolver arrived just in the nick of time for the actual ambush, making the full complement ten. Not more than three of the number were armed. This can readily be understood, when one realises that the men assembled were just having a casual Saturday evening stroll on the street when called on, and, not being aware of the design afoot, had not gone to secure any firearms. Hurley and another

Volunteer threw a score of bowls. This necessitated the scattering of the little party, so vital a consideration in this instance. Some went about 150 yards ahead to 'watch' the bowls for fear of their getting lost. The remainder stayed back with the competitors.

When about a mile from Midleton, the advance men of the party reached the turn that brought the Mile Bush into view. They observed the soldiers returning on their bicycles, cycling two abreast and in scattered formation, and then almost 400 yards distant. They passed back word to the men in the rear, namely, the bowling competitors, and the few others. In order to decoy the enemy, the score continued, but in a very half-hearted way. The 'boys' were ordered to stretch out a distance equal to that dividing the front and rear cyclists in the patrol. As the front cyclists came abreast of the advance party of the IRA the latter stepped back to give way, as had been arranged, and stood with their backs to the northern fence. Naturally they carefully scrutinised the soldiers, but most of all were their eager eyes attracted towards the rifles hitched onto the bicycles, as the main purpose of the ambush was to secure the firearms the soldiers carried. The 'boys' looked so unconcerned and so innocent that no suspicion entered the minds of the members of the patrol.

By the time the foremost cyclists had come abreast of the men in the rear of the IRA party the furthest back cyclists were within a few yards of the forward units of the IRA. Hurley and his fellow competitor stood coatless with folded arms, awaiting the front cyclists to come abreast of them. They held their loaded revolvers in their right hands, completely concealed because of their folded arms. They fired simultaneously without releasing their folded arms, the bullets, of course, entering the fence behind them. The shots were the signal, and in the twinkle of an eye eleven soldiers and the RIC man were lying on the road, having been thrown from their bicycles, some coming into violent contact with the road. They presented a pitiable and helpless picture, bewildered, disconcerted, angry and vanquished. Accurate timing was the telling factor in this as in most ambushes. One or two IRA men had each to deal with two cyclists, as the latter outnumbered their attackers. Resistance by the soldiers was out of the question. The RIC man pleaded for mercy. Eleven rifles fully loaded, with bayonets attached, became at once the property of the assailants.

But what of the twelfth soldier? He had trouble with his bicycle and was delayed further back. Hearing the shots and seeing the hold up 200 yards ahead, he dismounted and opened fire. His companions were quickly ordered to get on their feet and to put their hands up. The missing soldier ceased fire, took to the fields, threw his rifle into a hedge, and succeeded in reaching his base in approximately an hour. Unacquainted with the terrain he must have had difficulty in getting back, or perhaps it was that he did not wish to be the first to bear the gloomy news.

The soldiers were marched back along the main road and then down a side road where, after an interval of half-an-hour, they were dismissed. A motor car on its way from Cork was held up and used to convey the captured guns to the house of Mr Fitzgerald, Ballinbrittig. The car was later handed over to its driver occupant, who seemed to have been quite pleased that he was afforded the privilege of helping the IRA.

The IRA, in jovial mood, returned to the town, while the Camerons, dejected and despondent, went back by a circuitous route to their quarters to report. They must have been ordered to return to the scene of the ambush at once, for in a few minutes a lorry, packed with heavily armed soldiers, issued from the barracks and careered at a rapid speed to the scene of the encounter. It was then almost dark. The residents in a cottage nearby were roused, interrogated, threatened and abused in words found in no dictionary. The soldiers later procured the gun deposited in the hedge by the escaping member of the patrol. They returned to the town and began to fire indiscriminately, questioning and making prisoners of any pedestrians they met. Some of these were later brutally handled at the military quarters. The police, well barricaded in their bastion 100 yards from the military base, hearing the firing and aware of the ambush which had taken place about 9 p.m. returned the fire, convinced that their barracks was being attacked.

This fire lasted for almost an hour. Some animals in the line of fire were discovered dead in the morning, but there was no human life lost, though the residents suffered a few hours of real terror.

Such, in brief, is the account of what is known locally as the Mile Bush ambush, which for its neatness, the strategy employed, and its complete success, will always be remembered as a typical engagement of Irishmen pledged to the cause of freedom. The Midleton men, enthused by their success, went on the next morning as had been arranged to storm Ballycotton RIC barracks. They found to their dismay that a detachment of military had been posted in the village during the night, and held guard near the barracks, the assault on which had then to be called off.

* * *

So FAR AS can be determined now, the following is the list of the names of the men who participated in the Mile Bush 'ambush': Diarmuid Hurley, O/C: Tadhg Manley, Joseph Ahern, M. Desmond, D. Desmond, Jerry Aherne, M. Hallahan, T. Hourihan, M. Casey and M. Barry. Diarmuid Hurley, as already stated, was killed in May 1921; Jeremiah Aherne, the brothers Desmond and Michael Hallahan fell at Clonmult, 20 February 1921; Joe Aherne, later Commandant Aherne, died suddenly in 1951; Tom Hourihan died in January 1953.

Almost a fortnight after the ambush, Tadhg Manley, who played a leading part in it, was arrested and sentenced by military court. He served a long term of penal servitude and was subjected to severe and humiliating treatment for refusing to wear the convict's uniform.

Cornelius Murray, a British ex-serviceman who was not a member of the IRA, and who was not associated in any way with the ambush, was also arrested and tried by military court. He was sentenced to three years' penal servitude, but was released after some months. It was well known amongst the Volunteers that he was arrested in mistake for David Desmond, whom he resembled in stature and build.

In the summary of evidence handed to the accused men at their court martial there was the most staggering exaggeration and the most glaring perjuries by the British witnesses. One soldier swore that he had been held down by ten armed men; another that thirty men, all armed, came across a field after the patrol had been held up. These assertions are typical of the stories that were 'framed up' in those days to save the 'faith and honour' of the British administration in Ireland.

* Road-bowling is a game almost exclusive to Cork city and county, though a kindred game has been popular in Counties Mayo, Armagh and Antrim for some generations past. The bowl, made of iron and weighing 28 ozs, is perfectly round. It is thrown with a rapid under-hand swing as distinct from the over-arm delivery used in cricket bowling. 'Scores', as bowling matches are usually called, are played over distances varying from one to over two miles, from a certain starting point to a pre-arranged finishing post. The winner is the man who covers the distance in the least number of throws, or shots, of the bowl, making each subsequent throw from the 'tip' or mark at which the bowl stopped in the foregoing throw.

Corners or bends on the road are 'lofted' – that is, the bowl is pitched across the corner, and must land on the road off the 'loft', otherwise the player is penalised a 'bowl of odds' for throwing a 'dead bowl'.

A familiar sight almost everywhere in Cork county is to see crowds of men, a few when the 'score' is small, as many as 2,000–3,000 at a big contest, lining a bowling road on a Sunday afternoon, or even a week evening when practice scores are usually played. These crowds are invariably spread out over a length of 200–300 yards of road, some standing back at the point from which the throws are being made, others congregating well ahead where the bowl is expected to stop.

HORSE FAIR WAS BACKGROUND TO WELL-REHEARSED COUP IN ENNIS

MID-CLARE BRIGADE, 23 JUNE 1920

by Joe Barrett

(formerly QM, Mid-Clare Brigade, IRA, and O/C Mid-Clare Brigade flying column)

PROPAGANDA, ONE OF the most powerful weapons in the waging of war, is an art in which the British have excelled for centuries. Seldom did they ply it more diligently than during the period of the fight for freedom waged by the Irish Republican Army. Their propagandists were at work in the county town of Ennis, as the June days lengthened in the year 1920, and sedulously they endeavoured to foster among the people a belief that the men of the IRA struck only in the darkness of the night; that they were, in effect, assassins who had neither the inspiration of a cause, nor the courage that comes from that inspiration.

As is ever the case with official propagandists, excuses had to be found to discredit the achievements of the opposing forces and to bring them into disrepute. The creation and maintenance of prestige is a primary purpose of propaganda. In 1920, the prestige of the British was at a low ebb throughout the area of the Mid-Clare Brigade. In almost every district their well-armed and strongly posted police force was becoming very seriously demoralised as a result of attacks made upon it, and because of other operations carried out against it by IRA units. It was in these circumstances that disparaging observations alleging lack of courage on the part of the IRA were hawked and bandied about by the enemy wherever listeners could be found.

Over a period of eleven months, RIC barracks situated in country districts had been experiencing attacks by members of our different units. On 19 July 1919, the police stations at Inch and at Connolly were surrounded and bombed. At Inch the back wall was blown out of the barracks and later the post at Tiermaclane, between Ennis and Kildysart, was attacked on a couple of occasions. Clarecastle RIC barracks was also the objective of an IRA operation, and in May 1920, a lorry-borne detachment of military was attacked on the Ennis-Kilrush road by a force under Vice-Commandant Michael Barrett.

The coming of June found the police sheltering behind their steel-shuttered and sand-bagged windows, watchful, but for the most part, immobile in the rural localities. On the other hand, our men were drilling and organising, but they urgently needed arms and ammunition in order to press home the fight with greater vigour. Our brigade officers were examining ways and means to repair this want. As a result of observations maintained by our intelligence agents, we turned our attention to the enemy garrisons in Ennis, where a successful operation would achieve the two-fold purpose of defeating his propaganda and, at the same time, making a valuable addition to the all-too-slender armaments of the brigade.

Stationed in the town at the time were some thirty members of the RIC and in addition to these there was a company of infantry belonging to a Scottish regiment. This company occupied the old jail adjacent to the junction of Carmody Street, O'Connell Street and the Limerick road. In the Butter Market, about half a mile from the old jail, was an army transport park over which the jail garrison maintained a twenty-four hour guard of one corporal and six men. We noted that the guard was relieved each evening between five and six o'clock, and that the men coming off duty marched back from the Butter Market to the jail by a route that was never varied. It lay along Carmody Street as far as the junction of O'Connell Street and the Limerick road, at which point the military turned to the left into O'Connell Street. We also observed that they marched in double file carrying their rifles with fixed bayonets at 'the slope', and that approximately twenty-five paces separated each file of two men, with the corporal in charge marching between the second and third files. It appeared to us that this patrol could be captured and disarmed, and following careful study of its routine movements and of other factors, we decided upon a rather original plan of operations, and fixed the evening of 23 June as the date to carry it out. It was the day of the annual Spancil Hill horse fair, and on the evening of the fair the streets of Ennis were always crowded with dealers and horses from all parts of Clare and adjoining counties.

During the early weeks of June we selected twenty-one men for the job, from the 1st, 2nd and 3rd Battalions of the brigade. Each night, under the trees of Drumconora Wood, three miles from Ennis and on the road to Galway, these men were exercised in the tactics to be followed in the streets of the town on the evening of 23 June. In the wood a route was mapped out which roughly corresponded to that over which the British patrol marched each evening in Ennis. Along that route seven men representing the enemy patrol marched, night after night, and their capture was carefully rehearsed and explained until each member of our attacking party understood perfectly his own particular role. In brief, the plan amounted to a division of twenty-one attackers into seven sections of three men, with a section detailed to deal with each member of the British patrol. At a given signal, they were to spring upon the patrol, each section taking on its allotted man. One member of each section was to cover the soldier with a revolver. It was the task of the second man to seize the rifle and equipment, while the third member of the section was to ensure the silence of the soldier by gentle throttling.

It was a plan that depended for its success upon split-second timing and a complete absence of anything that resembled fumbling. Speed and silence were essential, for the operation would be carried out within the very shadow of the old jail in which the company to which the patrol belonged was billeted. When added to that hazard was the fact that the attempt would take place in the streets of a county town on the evening of a great annual horse fair, its nature can be fully understood. After a week of the nightly rehearsals in Drumconora Wood, every man of the attacking party was considered capable of carrying out his given task and each man felt confident of his own ability to discharge it.

But the architects of the plan were determined to leave nothing to chance. Amongst the precautions taken by them was one that provided against the possibility of the members of the patrol or of other enemy forces in the town becoming suspicious that something out of the ordinary was afoot, especially when the attackers had taken up their positions. It amounted to taking the fullest advantage of the fair day scene. In addition to the actual attacking groups, seven members of the IRA were given instruction to bring horses to the junction of O'Connell Street, the Limerick road and Carmody Street, and to hold them there at intervals of twenty-two yards, on the evening of the operation, so that the attackers could pose as horse dealers while waiting for the enemy patrol. Everything would then be in keeping with a normal street scene in the town of Ennis on the evening of the Spancil Hill fair. Marked on the accompanying sketch-map are the positions at which the horses were held and at which the attackers also gathered in groups at half-past five on the evening of 23 June. They thus occupied the best possible striking positions without giving any cause for suspicion on the part of either the military or RIC.

About the middle of the crossroads, at the point marked 'A' on the map, I took up a position and pretended to be interested in the horse dealing. From that point I was able to see the approach of the enemy for more than 200 yards. When I sighted the patrol the time was about five minutes to six, and as the soldiers marched nearer, the horse-dealing mounted to a crescendo, excited 'buyers' wrangling and disputing noisily with indignant and recalcitrant 'owners'. It was a piece of by-play well calculated to deceive even the most sceptical, for the men were enacting part of their own civilian lives; all were taking part in something well known to them from childhood, so that the parts in which they were cast did not present them with the slightest

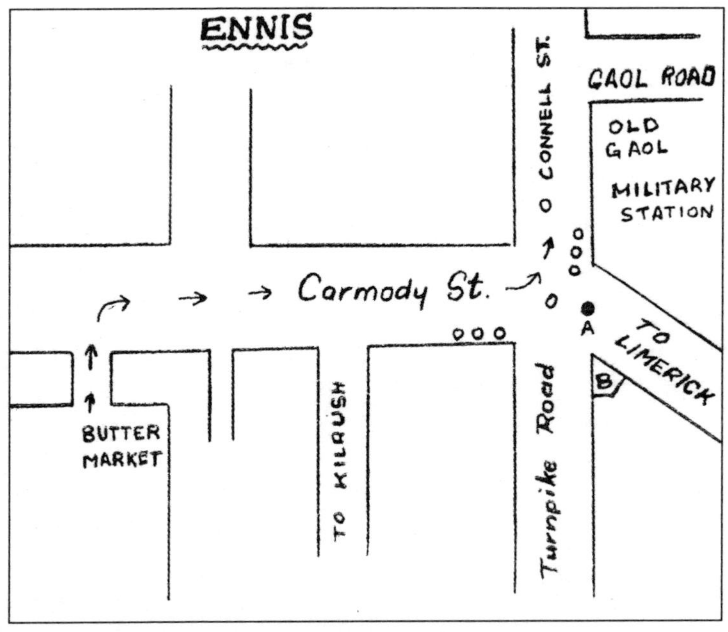

difficulty. Steadily the military marched towards the spot where the merits of horses were being extolled with vehemence and decried with acid and sarcastic comment.

From my strategic position I saw the patrol reach the crossroads, and the leading file of two men wheel left into O'Connell Street. They were followed by the second file of two. At that stage the line of my vision of the patrol had been cut, with four of its members out of sight in O'Connell Street. In Carmody Street still, but approaching the corner, were the corporal and the last two men. They had no view of the four men in O'Connell Street. At that moment I blew my whistle, our pre-arranged signal for the attack to begin. Panther-like, the attackers sprang to action. Each soldier was held up, gripped by the throttle and disarmed in a series of movements carried out almost simultaneously. The corporal, alone, showed fight, but his resistance was quickly overcome with a few well-directed punches by Seán O'Keeffe.

Within the space of two minutes the operation was over, and the members of the patrol were being marched speedily into D'Arcy's Yard, marked 'B' on the map, where their web equipment, steel helmets and ammunition, totalling 350 rounds, were gathered in without delay. It was a neat piece of work, carried out efficiently and expeditiously under the very noses of the garrison in the old jail.

The seven British soldiers were safely locked up in one of D'Arcy's stables, and the captured equipment and arms were loaded into three waiting motor cars, which immediately pulled out for Kilmorane, some miles outside the town. The cars were driven by John Joe Egan, Jack Mellett and Mick Kennedy. Travelling in them also, to guard the booty, were Seán O'Keeffe, Micko Foley, Con MacMahon and Mick Hegarty. In the meantime, the other members of the column had dispersed in ones and twos. The equipment was taken over by the officers of the 2nd Battalion.

The following participated in the task: Joe Barrett, O/C; Seán O'Keeffe, Peter O'Loughlin, Jerry O'Dwyer, P.J. O'Doherty, Paddy Considine, Paddy McNamara, John Joe Egan, Frank Keane, Michael Nugent, Con McMahon, Liam Stack, Michael Hegarty, Thomas Baker, Paddy Casey, J.J. Clohessy, Michael Foley, Jack Mellett, Paddy Brody, Dan McNamara, Sammy Moroney, Jack Darcy, Patrick Davis.

The manner in which the operation had been conducted, and its complete success, greatly enhanced the prestige of the IRA in the area. It had been witnessed by many people from the town and district, and though several of the attackers were well known to the onlookers, not one of them was betrayed. The effect of the operation on the enemy propagandists in Ennis is best left to the imagination.

A FIGHTING REARGUARD SAVED IRA IN THE RETREAT AFTER THE AMBUSH AT RINEEN

MID-CLARE BRIGADE, 20 SEPTEMBER 1920

As told to Patrick Lynch

In the preparation of this account of the ambush at Rineen the author was fortunate to have the assistance of Mr Joe Barrett of Kilrush, formerly QM Mid-Clare Brigade and O/C Mid-Clare Brigade flying column; and also the assistance of Messrs Seamus Hennessy, Anthony Malone, John Joe Neylon and John Minihan, formerly of the 4th Battalion, Mid-Clare Brigade. He wishes to thank them for having made it possible for him to describe this fine action. His thanks are due again to Mr Seamus Hennessy (who commanded a shotgun section in the ambush), and to P.J. Hurley of Miltown-Malbay, for having read and checked the proofs; and to the proprietors of The Cork Examiner *for having placed their newspaper files at his disposal.*

A FEW MILES in from the rugged west Clare coastline, at a point south-east of the wide curve of the bay of Liscannor is the town of Miltown-Malbay. The road that connects it with Lahinch on the coast, about seven miles further north, extends over low, rolling country of the kind that skirts the Atlantic all the way up from the mouth of the Shannon. For about two miles out of Miltown it falls with a steady gradient, to the place that is known as Rineen Cross. There a sunken by-road branches south-west and rises sharply to cross the West Clare Railway line which, at that point, hugs the brink of an eminence high above, and practically parallel with, the Miltown-Lahinch road. A little to the north-east is Ennistymon, about two-and-a-half miles on the far side of Lahinch and about ten miles from Miltown. Around Rineen are little hillocks, the small green hills of Clare. Through them runs the West Clare Railway line. Looking north-west from that part of the railway line, when visibility is good, it is possible to discern what appears to be the shapes of gigantic whales, aloof against the Atlantic horizon, their enormous elongated bodies low in the water. In summertime they are often enveloped in the transparent fabric of a light sea mist, and, unless there happens to be a Dalcassian guide on hand to explain the objects, it is difficult for the stranger to realise that he is looking on the distant outlines of the Aran Islands. Immediately south of the railway line at Rineen are small fields bounded by low ditches, and beyond them is mainly bogland that stretches to distant Mount Callan. North of the main road the land falls away appreciably and slopes over a quarter of a mile of marsh and shingle, to the sea.

Before dawn on the morning of 22 September 1920, elements of the 4th Battalion of the Mid-Clare Brigade, IRA, had moved into battle position at Rineen, in preparation for an encounter with the enemy that was destined to be of surprising scope and classic in the execution of its later phases. The officers had felt for some time previously that the battalion had reached a stage in its training and discipline when, despite severe limitation in armament, it could send an active service unit to carry the fight to the enemy, at least on a moderate scale, with reasonable hope of success. The 4th Battalion, in common with other units in the brigade, maintained a close watch on the enemy in the battalion area, and the movements of his convoys and patrols had been noted. The attention of the battalion officers had been attracted in particular by the movements of a small Crossley tender in which a number of RIC were observed to make routine journeys over the ten-mile stretch of road between Miltown-Malbay and Ennistymon. The journeys were invariably made on Wednesday mornings, when the patrol would set out from Ennistymon at about half-past ten and arrive back there shortly after noon. In the circumstances, the tender was a suitable objective, to give the battalion its first taste of active service. It was decided to ambush it. The place chosen for the operation was Rineen, where the sunken by-road rises above and dominates the main road and offered concealment and protection to the attackers. At no point would men in position along the by-road be more than thirty-two yards distant from the main road before them. It was an ideal position from which to attack a limited force, such as that which the battalion officers had chosen for their objective. With the location decided upon, Ignatius O'Neill, the battalion commandant, set about making preparations calculated to achieve the maximum degree of success with the operation.

Before proceeding to describe the action at Rineen it is necessary to say something about the character of the man in charge of the operation, for it can be stated truthfully that it was O'Neill's bold and resolute leadership and military training which extricated the column from what should have been certain disaster. What manner of man was this Ignatius O'Neill, of whose personality and achievements, in the days when he and the men who served under him were 'on their keeping', so much is heard in Clare? The memory of this gay, gallant and fine soldier is still fresh in his native country, where his name is a household word and his deeds have almost become legendary. Of stock long associated with the national struggle, he was born in Miltown-Malbay in 1896, son of Patrick Hugh O'Neill, an extensive merchant in the town, and of Mrs Ethel O'Neill. His forebears, both on the paternal and maternal sides were in the Land League fight, in which his mother's brother, a member of the patriotic Hynes family of Toureen, Spancil Hill, Ennis, gave his life on the scaffold. Tall and with a flaming thatch of red hair, Ignatius was of athletic build and was decidedly an adventurous type. He had his primary schooling in Miltown-Malbay and subsequently he went to Blackrock College, Dublin, where he made a name for himself on the field of sport. His secondary education completed, an urge to travel and the adventurous streak in him asserted themselves, and he made up his mind to emigrate to the United States where he expected to find a fruitful field for bold endeavour. With him went two childhood and college comrades, a son of Dr Hill of Miltown-Malbay, and young Healy, son of Dr Healy of Mullagh. The outbreak of the First World War, in August 1914, found the trio in New York and ready marks for the propagandists who were busy upholding the Allied cause as a sacred fight for 'the freedom of small nations'. It was hardly likely that any of them needed much urging to get into the fight. They made hurried tracks for the Canadian border, and were soon in the ranks of the Irish Guards with whom they saw active service in France. Tragedy struck quickly at the comradeship of the three young Claremen. Within a short time of their arrival in France, Hill had fallen in battle. O'Neill was wounded later and was sent back to an English hospital for treatment and to recuperate. It was probably during his period of convalescence in England, when he had ample time to reflect and take stock of things, that he first heard the call of Ireland, and that there was borne in on him the realisation that, if small nations were really in need of his help, his own native land had the prior claim. Once he had begun to think about Ireland and her long struggle against foreign domination, it was inevitable that he would become a factor in her latest fight for freedom.

Thus, it came about that on that September dawn of 1920, the active service unit of the 4th Battalion of the Mid-Clare Brigade, IRA, which had just moved into position from which to engage the British enemy, was commanded by the tall, red-haired ex-Guardsman, Ignatius O'Neill, who already had a reputation for his soldierly qualities, his chivalry and daring. Mobilisation of the force under his command had been completed in the early hours of the morning. Before midnight the Ennistymon, Innagh, Lahinch and Moy Companies had reported outside Moy Chapel, every man with twenty-four hours' rations in his haversack. Earlier in the night the Lahinch and Ennistymon Companies had assembled at Dan Lehane's of Cragg, Lahinch, and then moved on to Moy Chapel. While on the march from Moy to Rineen, the four companies were joined by the Miltown-Malbay, Glendine and Letterkelly Companies, near Ballyvaskin. It will be seen how very fortunate it was that the IRA force was that day under the command of such an experienced and valiant soldier as O'Neill.

The IRA active service unit, which numbered about sixty officers and men, all told, had arrived at Rineen under cover of darkness and, having posted sentries, settled down to rest, concealed in the sunken by-road. The two oldest men in the unit were Owen Nestor and Ned Hynes of the Ennistymon Company, both married and having young families. They had also participated in the disarming of a party of military at Ennistymon, in July 1920. With the coming of daylight, O'Neill took his officers over the ground and finally explained to them in detail the purpose and plan of the operation. When that had been done and he was satisfied that each section leader understood his task, he made a close inspection of all arms and rejected a number that he did not consider to be serviceable. Of nine service rifles at his disposal, six had been captured from the British at Ennistymon in the previous July and were found to have been maintained in excellent condition. He kept a rifle for himself and issued the remaining eight to John Joe Neylon, Dave Kennelly, Dan Lehane, Michael O'Dwyer, Seán Burke, Steve Gallagher, Patso Kerin and Anthony Malone – all good marksmen. Two grenades were given to Peter Vaughan, a former member of the American army, who had experience of grenade throwing whilst on active service in France. Vaughan, a Clareman, had thrown in his lot with the IRA when he had come home on leave. The other members of O'Neill's force were armed with shotguns. He had mobilised many more men than were necessary for the success of the limited task, because of the uplift to battalion morale that would inevitably follow as a result of so many of the officers and men having had combat experience.

There were about eighty-five yards between the opening of the sunken by-road and where it met the railway line, high above the main road. Extended in line from a point near the top of the by-road were placed forty shotgun men, commanded by Patrick Lehane, the battalion vice-commandant. To their right and considerably nearer the entrance, was a section commanded by O'Neill in person, which comprised five riflemen, seven shotgun men and the grenadier. The task of these two sections was to cover the main road along which the enemy was expected to travel. None of Lehane's men had been posted further than thirty-two yards from the main road which, at no

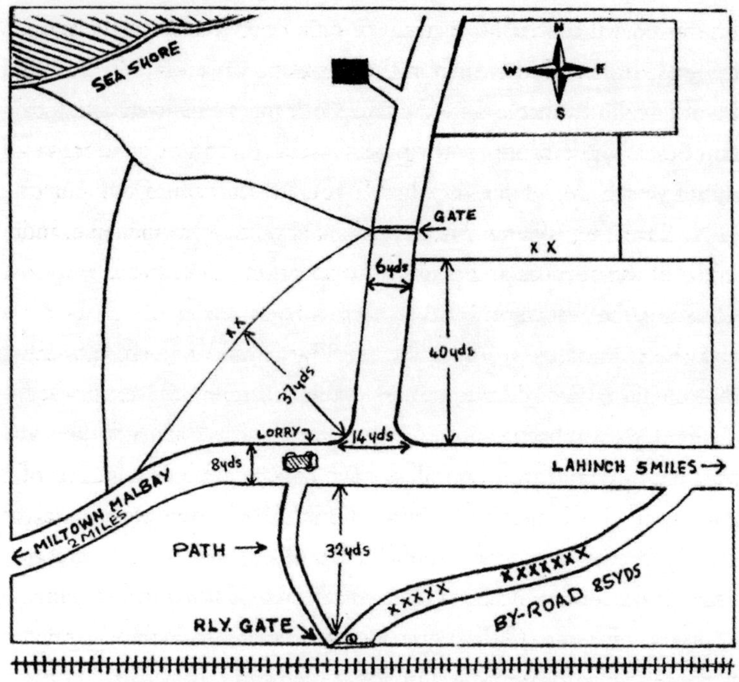

point, was more than twenty yards from the furthest man in O'Neill's section. The entrance to the by-road was hidden by bushes, and bushes and fern were used to camouflage and conceal the men inside from the view both of users of the main road and travellers on the railway. Riflemen were also posted behind cover in the fields on the opposite side of the road, so that fire could be concentrated on both sides of the lorry, and to deal with any of the enemy who might attempt to break out of the ambush on that side. The position was a veritable death trap for a small force like the expected tender of RIC.

From concealed positions atop the hillocks about the ambush site, IRA scouts had a wide sweep of country in view, and nothing could get close to Rineen unknown to them. Thomas Moroney was in charge of them, and, from their vantage points, they scanned the approaches for signs of the enemy, particularly the Ennistymon road along which the RIC patrol would come. An enemy advance would be signalled promptly to the Volunteers who waited below, sitting with their backs to the walls of the by-road, or lying about in their concealed positions, their weapons beside them. It was an anxious time for officers and men, as few of the unit had combat experience. Watches were in hands many times as the morning dragged on slowly and the autumn sun climbed into a sky of perfect blue. It could have been a day out of mid-summer, that autumn day, cloudless and with warm sunshine, and nothing to suggest that the peaceful rural countryside was shortly to become a place of turmoil and sudden death. On the stroke of noon a message was signalled from a hilltop nearby. 'Three cars coming,' read the astonished IRA officers who were thus unexpectedly confronted with the necessity of making an instantaneous decision whether to attack such a large force. O'Neill did not hesitate. The dispositions of his men were inadequate for the task. He would withhold fire and, when the enemy had passed, would seek new positions better suited to dealing with three vehicles, in the hope that the enemy would return over the same route. Only a brief, decisive attack, like that planned for the single RIC tender, could be successfully launched from the Rineen site. It would be bad ground on which to engage three lorries of well-armed enemy forces with untried Volunteers, and the further disadvantages of having but nine long-range weapons available, no adequate cover in case of a pressed withdrawal and the close proximity to sources of enemy reinforcements.

Behind the men who manned the sunken by-road was a steep hillock, rising to open country that stretched southwards for miles. Enemy troops from Miltown-Malbay, no more than two miles distant, could easily cut off a retreat in that direction. North and west was the sea. Withdrawal from Rineen, under pressure of superior enemy forces, could prove a hazardous, if not altogether disastrous, undertaking for the poorly armed and inexperienced active service unit. Under the circumstances, O'Neill's rapid decision to allow the enemy through unmolested on his outward journey, was the only one compatible with the safety of the IRA force. He had scarcely made it when the sound of an approaching lorry could be heard clearly. Along the road that curved into the ambush position swept a Crossley tender. As it was driven past the guns of the concealed IRA men, the first stroke of the Angelus rang out, and the bell was still being tolled when it had passed out of sight. That the enemy had noticed nothing suspicious while on the way through the ambush position spoke well for the concealment and camouflage of the IRA. The discipline of O'Neill's 'raw' force had been good. What damage one nervous shot could have done! No time to think about that, then, with two more lorries to come. No sound of their approach yet. What could be keeping them? In a flash the realisation came on O'Neill that a mistake had been made, that the signaller's message had been 'Police car coming', and not 'Three cars coming'. Too late then to do anything about it; nothing but to remain in the positions, in the hope that the RIC patrol, for such it was, would return shortly.

O'Neill ordered John Clune of Innagh, to cycle into Miltown-Malbay and find out what he could about the tender and the plans of the patrol. The scout was not long about his mission, and the news which he brought back indicated that the time for action was almost at hand. The tender was parked outside the RIC barracks in Miltown, facing towards Ennistymon, and apparently in a state of readiness for an almost immediate return. The sound of its engine was heard within a short time of Clune's arrival back at Rineen, and its advance was signalled by scouts posted on high ground. Weapons were firmly gripped at the ready. Only seconds to wait. A rifle shot fired by John Joe Neylon was to be the signal for the attack to commence, and it was the task of the riflemen to make certain of hitting the driver to prevent the tender being driven through and out of range of the shotguns. Around the bend and into the trap came the tender. The signal shot was fired and its echo was lost in the overwhelming crash of rifles, shotguns and grenades. The tender careered wildly for some yards and then came to an abrupt stop, the driver slumped dead over the wheel and all but one of the other occupants literally blasted to death by the devastating concentration of musketry. It seemed impossible that any of the RIC could have survived the opening volley. Yet one of them made a flying leap out of the tender, and so surprised the attackers by being able to do so, that he was past the rifle positions north of the road and racing in the direction of the sea, before fire was opened on him. He had covered a good 500 yards when he fell to the rifle shooting of Dan Lehane, Tom Burke, John Joe Neylon and Michael O'Dwyer.

The IRA men were quickly out on the main road to gather up the weapons, ammunition and equipment of the dead RIC. First to reach the tender was Ignatius O'Neill's brother, Alphonsus, who dragged out the driver and immediately began to smash the engine. The extent of the capture, especially the ammunition, was found to be greater than what had been expected. Six rifles with 3,000 rounds of .303 ammunition, and one revolver with fifty rounds of .45 calibre ammunition, comprised the booty. The bodywork of the tender had been cut to pieces by the concentration of close-range fire, though both grenades had overshot their mark and exploded harmlessly in a field north of the road. The dead RIC men were a gruesome and bloody sight. Steve Gallagher set out to get the rifle and equipment of the constable who had been killed when running towards the sea. O'Neill himself distributed the captured rifles and ammunition and was preparing to withdraw with the spoils, when the scouts frantically signalled an enemy approach in force from the direction of Lahinch. It would appear that the scouts, their vigilance temporarily distracted by the events of the action just concluded, had failed to observe the second enemy force, which consisted of ten or twelve lorries of military, until it was almost on top of the active service unit. To say that the IRA was surprised by the unexpectedness of this development would be a miracle of understatement. O'Neill's concern for the safety of his inexperienced and badly armed men was back with interest. There was not a moment to be lost if they were to be extricated from the difficult situation which had developed and a calamitous rout avoided. They would be no match for about 150 regular military, certain to have machine guns and rifle grenades.

That was the position when Steve Gallagher, leisurely returning with the rifle and equipment of the sixth constable, heard a warning of danger shouted to him by Seamus Hennessy and saw his comrades doubling up the rising ground towards the railway line. He promptly raced after them, across the road, up the slope of the eminence and over the tracks. Below, on the road, the enemy transport was being hastily pulled up and, above the engine sounds and the screech of brakes being urgently applied, could be heard the excited English accents, the shouting of orders and the metallic clank of equipment and weapons as the soldiers jumped down from the trucks. It subsequently transpired that this enemy force had come out in response to a call for help from west Clare, and was bound for a point about fifteen miles further south of Rineen, where a resident magistrate named Ledrum had been captured and executed. Knowing nothing of what had happened at Rineen, the thought of action nearer at hand could hardly have occurred to the military as their transport rolled along towards Rineen. The situation there had taken them completely unawares in the same way that their arrival on the scene had surprised the IRA. Be that as it may, they lost no time about sizing up the position and were quickly pressing forward in the wake of the retreating Mid-Claremen. Up the rise they doubled, hastily firing their rifles as they advanced. On the heels of the first wave of them were rushed three machine guns and these were soon drumming away in support of the riflemen. Targets were hard to hit, as the IRA were making good use of the available cover, and it was apparent that their withdrawal was being ably directed.

Immediately that the scouts had signalled the approach of the second enemy force, O'Neill ordered his main body to break up into small groups and retreat southwards towards the boglands, whilst he covered them with a small group of riflemen who included Michael O'Dwyer, Dave Kennelly and Michael Curtin. The riflemen, who conducted themselves like veterans in the rearguard action that followed, were divided into two sections, and each section in turn covered the withdrawal of the other in the classical manner, making the most skilled use of every scrap of cover available on a stretch of country that could scarcely be less suited to the purpose. The captured rifle ammunition proved invaluable during this phase of the engagement, which could not have been sustained without it. The riflemen of the rearguard alone stood between the entire IRA force and a staggering defeat, as the shotguns with which most of the men were armed, would have been useless at the range. Besides, the shotgun men had but a few cartridges apiece. The steadiness of the rearguard under heavy fire and the skill with which it was handled baffled the British, who were reluctant to push forward over open country, following one determined charge that had cost them casualties. Machine-gun fire cut up the earth about O'Neill and his riflemen, and bullets sang as they ricocheted off stones in the low ditches that gave some cover. But these Mid-Claremen remained cool and steady, taking advantage of the cover afforded by ditch, drain, watercourse and tram of hay, and giving back an accurate return of lead that kept the enemy to ground, while the withdrawal towards the bogland continued. It was considered unlikely that the British would attempt to follow the retreat through the bogs and the opinion turned out to be correct.

The action was broken off at about 2,000 yards, by which time the men of the main body had scattered to safe hiding places, though not before some of them had narrowly escaped being hit, especially by the machine-gun fire. Peter Vaughan was with them and his battle experience had contributed a great deal to the success of the general withdrawal. O'Neill had been wounded in the thigh, and Curtin, who now lives in New York, had also been wounded. Dr M.T. Hillary, Dr D. McClancy, Dr T. Curran and Nurse May Davitt were brought out to tend to their wounds. O'Neill and Curtin were then borne on stretchers, across the mountain, to a house in the Moy Company area, and the other wounded men were able to continue on foot. It was difficult to assess what the enemy casualties had been, but it was believed that the day had cost him fourteen killed. The IRA men who had been posted north of the road at the ambush position had been able to retreat towards the sea and to disperse without having been seriously engaged. Along both withdrawal routes the men were met by the people and given encouragement and assistance. Cans of tea and stacks of buttered bread were handed to them as they moved past.

The British admitted that three soldiers had been killed. An official announcement gave the names of the police dead as: Sergeant Hynes, Athlone; Constables J. Hodnett, County Cork; J. Harmon (late of the Royal Artillery), London; Michael Kelly, Roscommon; J. Maguire, Mayo; and J. Harte of Sligo. On the evening of the ambush the British held a military court of inquiry at Ennistymon, which issued the following finding:

> The Court, having carefully examined the bodies and the ground where the ambush was laid, and also considered the evidence, are of opinion that the six members of the RIC were brutally murdered by unknown persons with flat-nosed rifle bullets, and shots fired from rifles and shotguns at close range from a carefully prepared ambush.

West Clare people were to pay dearly in loss of life and destruction of property for their support of the armed forces of the nation. The first blows fell on the Honan and O'Gorman families, whose homes stood nearby the scene of the ambush. Parties of enraged soldiers descended upon these defenceless people and shouted with savage exultation as they applied the torch to their dwelling places. Soon flames were stabbing viciously through the roofs, and smoke rising skywards indicated to the withdrawing IRA men that forces of the British crown were again following that pattern of cowardly and infamous behaviour they had made peculiarly their own, namely, that of wreaking vengeance upon helpless civilian populations for reverses suffered by British arms.

In the carrying out of reprisals, the British brought death and desolation to many parts of Ireland, but few places experienced the horror and brutality of the enemy punitive measures more than did the towns and districts of Ennistymon, Lahinch and Miltown-Malbay, following the fighting at Rineen. It was close to midnight on 22 September when the police turned ferociously upon Miltown-Malbay. Most of the town's inhabitants were already abed by that hour, but they were quickly brought to their feet by fusillades of shots in the streets, the crash of shattered plate-glass windows and the sound of splintering woodwork, all to the accompaniment of shouted jeers and curses. Townspeople who had the temerity to peep furtively through their windows for the authors of this nocturnal visitation saw groups of yelling RIC men moving along the sidewalks, firing their weapons and smashing doors and windows with their rifle butts as they passed. British law, as employed to hold a small nation in bondage, was about to be administered with such object in view, and in a manner that was to have the approval of the British government and parliament.

A gang of RIC hoodlums smashed their way into the hardware shop of Mr P.H. O'Neill, father of Ignatius and Alphonsus, and gave it to the flames. They dealt likewise with the licensed premises of Mr Edward Roche, the drapery and bar of Mr P. Collins, and the residence of Mr Michael Hayes on the Ennis road. Flames from the burning buildings lit up the town, and the streets resounded to the reports of rifles and revolvers discharged at random by the police with the object of terrorising the people. More police were seen to arrive in lorries, and with the advent of these additional preservers of public order, who immediately began a house-to-house search for 'much wanted men', the townspeople fled Miltown-Malbay and sought safety in the surrounding countryside. With the town entirely to themselves the police put aside the torch and their other objectives for some hours, during which they devoted themselves to the more profitable task of spoliation. They helped themselves liberally to drink from the casks and the bottles in the public houses, and to money, valuables and general goods which they robbed from shops and private houses. When they had looted all that they could carry away they turned again to arson, resuming with the residence of Mr Michael Marinan, and continuing with the licensed premises of Mr Austin Jones and the drapery shop of Mr Michael Casey. By that time the police, crazed by the liquor they had been drinking for hours, rushed about the blazing streets, whooping and firing their weapons, and they lacked but war-paint to compete for savagery with North American Indians on the warpath during America's Indian wars. It was a spectacle of barbarism, a primitive and fantastic instance of a state of lawlessness and disorder achieved by police. By about five o'clock in the morning they had exhausted their energies in pillage and destruction, and their gigantic act of terrorism tapered off with the burning of a Ford car that belonged to Dr Hillary, who had resigned his Justiceship of the Peace a short time previously.

When the legalised looters had withdrawn from the streets of ruined and pillaged Miltown-Malbay, it was seen that eight houses had been burned to the ground, and daylight revealed that not more than ten houses in the entire town had escaped damage and despoliation in some degree. The sidewalks were piled with debris. Slate fragments from the burned-out houses, heaps of broken and blackened glass, liquor bottles and an assortment of goods littered the streets. Apparently, the drunken police had been unable to carry away all that they had stolen from the homes of the people. Smoke from the still-smouldering ruins hung like a pall over Miltown-Malbay on the following morning as the townspeople straggled back to find out how much of their property had escaped the vengeance of the police. Despite the distress caused by the scenes of desolation that confronted them, the people found consolation in the fact that no lives had been lost, a happy circumstance that probably owed more to their prudence in clearing out of the town than to police consideration for their lives.

The sacking of Miltown-Malbay by the RIC was no haphazard affair, but a calculated act, in the perpetration of which the members of that force stationed in the town probably sought, and certainly received, assistance from other members of the force stationed elsewhere, who arrived in the town in lorries after the work of destruction had commenced. Plentiful supplies of petrol were at their disposal and they set about the fire-raising so thoroughly that all of the eight houses they burned down collapsed within less than half-an-hour of being set on fire.

It will be recalled that before the unbridled fury of the RIC had been unleashed on Miltown-Malbay, regular troops had commenced the British reprisals for the ambush at Rineen by burning the homes of the Honan and O'Gorman families. Unfortunately, the measures of retaliation carried out near the scene of the ambush were to embrace more than the burning of two houses of rural Irish families. Later the same evening the soldiers shot an old man named John Keane, who, with a horse and hay cart, was bringing home hay from his meadow. They fired on him and killed him in cold blood.

But the most appalling of the horrors that marked the British reprisals for Rineen were committed in Ennistymon and Lahinch, on the same night that Miltown-Malbay was destroyed. The RIC reported that an article of clothing bearing the name of Tom Connole, a young married man of Ennistymon, had been found at Rineen following the IRA withdrawal. The report was not true. It had been invented by the police as an attempt to justify a dreadful act they had planned to carry out that night; for these RIC men had decided that Tom Connole should die as a reprisal for Rineen, even though they had no proof that he had taken part in the ambush or that he was even a member of the IRA. They did not have to worry about providing proof. With the British government authorising reprisals the police could, with impunity, take unto themselves the functions of judge, jury and executioner in such circumstances. That night they surrounded the Connole home. Some of them broke into it and dragged out Tom and his wife and their children, and then sent the house up in flames. In the presence of his family they bound Connole, hand and foot, and shot him to death in the street. One would think that with the perpetration of those awful deeds the RIC would have left the distracted family with their dead. But they had not finished yet. These fiends in uniform seized the bound and bullet-riddled body of Tom Connole, feet and shoulders, and swung it into the flames. His blazing home had become his funeral pyre. It mattered not to the British that Tom Connole had not been with O'Neill at Rineen. They had to have blood. The circumstances under which they murdered Connole are the more horrible when it is realised that, at the time, they had not yet looted the drink by which they were inflamed when they carried out further atrocious acts that night.

Leaving the flames to consume the mortal remains of the man they had just murdered with such ferocity, the police moved on to achieve further distinction in the campaign of frightfulness on which the British government had pinned its hopes to break the spirit of the Irish people. Through the town they went, burning and looting. Flames darted skywards from the homes of the Whelan, Cleare, Callinan and Davitt families. The course of devastation set by the police next led to the drapery establishment of the Davitts and to the licensed premises of the Madigans. In Mr Madigan's place they came upon liquor so much to their liking that they laid aside the torch to fill themselves with looted drink. Back in the street later, a number of these ruffians intercepted twelve-year-old P.J. Linane as he was carrying a bucket of water to help extinguish the flames that were shooting from a neighbour's house. They shot him dead.

The people of Lahinch, less than three miles away, had already been given a grim forewarning of the wrath to come. That evening British raiders had burst in upon Dan Lehane of Cragg, near the town, whose sons were known to be members of the IRA. When they moved on British justice had been done. Dan Lehane, fatally wounded in the throat, was left for dead by the British, near his burning home. The raiders warned of what was in store for Lahinch. Had they not done so the red glow over Ennistymon that night would, in itself, have left the people of Lahinch under no doubt about what to expect from the occupants of the lorries that lumbered towards their town in the early hours of the morning of 23 September. The police who came to Lahinch in these lorries were bent on vengeance, their passions inflamed by the events of the day, by the looted drink they had consumed and by the devilish crimes they had just committed.

Soon Lahinch was on fire at many points. The Town Hall was a blazing inferno, and burning also were business places and houses that belonged to the O'Dwyer, Howard, Flanagan, Vaughan, Halpin, Walsh and Reynolds families. Most of the inhabitants had cleared out to the sandhills nearby when they heard the approach of the police. All had not been able to get away in time. A young east Clare farmer named Sammon, in Lahinch for a holiday after the harvest, fell to RIC bullets whilst he was helping a woman out of a house threatened by flames that were ravaging an adjoining building. Burned alive in a blazing house was Patrick Lehane, the battalion vice-commandant, who had commanded the shotgun men in the ambush. He was the son of Dan Lehane of Cragg, who was then at death's door and whose home had already been destroyed.

Since about midday on 22 September, police and soldiers had been searching the countryside for Captain Ledrum, a resident magistrate who lived in Kilkee and who had been arrested early that morning by the West Clare IRA at a place between Doonbeg and Craggaknock, and subsequently executed. The British knew that it was unlikely that they would find him alive, so in the course of their search they burned almost every rick of hay between Ennistymon and Miltown-Malbay, and houses and hay along the road by Doonbeg, Bealaha and Kilkee.

Not since the time of Cromwell and Murrough the Burner had so many parts of Ireland been laid waste and pillaged. Within the space of days farmstead and hayricks had been burned over large tracts of Clare and south County Galway. Amongst the towns sacked in the same period were Miltown-Malbay, Ennistymon, Lahinch, Mallow, Balbriggan and Newcastle West, with many houses burned in villages in Tipperary and Roscommon. Referring to the mass destruction carried out by the British, Mr Arthur Griffith told a group of journalists that what were described as reprisals were not reprisals at all, but a calculated political policy not connected with any events in the country and directly organised by the British government. In another statement, issued soon after the reprisals that followed the ambush at Rineen, Mr Griffith said that the reply of the British government to the lawful and peaceful expression of the nation's will for freedom as expressed at the general election in December 1918, had been:

> Since New Year's Day 1919, 38,720 armed raids on private houses of Irish citizens, 4,982 arrests and imprisonments, 1,604 armed assaults, 102 sackings and shootings-up of towns, and 77 murders of unarmed, inoffensive citizens, including women, and children from ten years of age.

In the British House of Commons, Mr Arthur Henderson moved:

> That this House regrets the present state of lawlessness in Ireland, and the lack of discipline in the armed forces of the crown, resulting in the death or injury of innocent citizens and the destruction of property; and is of the opinion that an independent inquiry should at once be instituted into the causes, nature and extent of the reprisals on the part of those whose duty is the maintenance of law and order.

As might be expected, one of the principal opponents of the resolution was Sir Hamar Greenwood, the British government's Chief Secretary for Ireland, who, as was his custom when endeavouring to defend the horrible conduct of crown forces in Ireland, had recourse to distortion, falsehood and misrepresentation. Greenwood had this to say of the ambush at Rineen, to bolster up that defence:

> The fifth (man) though badly wounded, managed to crawl away from the car, four hundred yards. He was pursued. Shotguns were used within a foot of him to blow his body to pieces. The car was on the road with these men mutilated beyond recognition when, within ten minutes, another car containing police and soldiers came along. They lost their heads. They went to the villages of Ennistymon and Lahinch. I am sure that the House, whatever its opinion may be as to this resolution will, at any rate, give me its sympathy in trying to bring peace out of chaos in Ireland. It is true that reprisals followed the murder of those gallant men. Sixteen houses and shops were destroyed; houses that were considered to be owned or occupied by notorious Sinn Féiners.

Greenwood made significant use of the word 'villages' to describe the towns that had been devastated, thereby aiming to leave an impression of remote places inhabited by primitive people, much in need of the civilising influence of British bombs and bullets so generously spent in like missions in India, the North-West Frontier and elsewhere within the Empire. Even *The Times* of London felt constrained to make this pointed comment on the subterfuge, when referring to the sacking of Mallow, which followed within six days of the havoc caused the west Clare towns: 'We shall, doubtless, be told by the leading ministerial organ, that Irish towns are not really towns, but only villages.'

Greenwood wound up his explanation of the Clare reprisals:

> Here, again, I am convinced that the people of these two villages [Ennistymon and Lahinch] knew of this ambush. The place of the ambush covered a long stretch on both sides of the road, and from the evidence of bandoliers, hay-beds, haversacks, coats, blankets, meat tins, and so on, it was clear that the bivouac was within sight of many houses. I am putting to you the provocation that comes to brave men.

The House gave Greenwood its 'sympathy'. The resolution was thrown out by an overwhelming majority, 346 votes to 79.

On 1 October a coffin was seen on the railway line at Kilmurry, County Clare. Police who went out to investigate found that it bore a label 'to Kilkee'. Inside was the body of Captain Ledrum.

THE ONLY BRITISH MILITARY BARRACKS CAPTURED BY THE IRA WAS AT MALLOW

CORK NO. 2 (NORTH) BRIGADE, 28 SEPTEMBER 1920

As told to Pat Lynch

THEY WILL TELL you in many parts of Ireland that it is unlucky to turn in your tracks. The superstitious would have it that one should not go back into a building on the impulse of an afterthought, once the threshold is crossed on an express mission. Yet take the case of Constable Keane of the Royal Irish Constabulary. The constable would appear to have been a man who did not hold with 'old wives' tales'. At any rate, whilst stationed in Mallow he owed his life to the afterthought which caused him to return to the RIC barracks from which he had emerged but minutes previously. It happened on a fine morning in the late autumn of 1920. He had been barracks' orderly over the preceding twenty-four hours and, having handed over duties, he walked out into 'the new street', as Mallow people were wont to call the steep, broad thoroughfare to which they have given the name of William O'Brien Street.

Facing up the hill was the Town Hall. The building dominated the street down which Constable Keane was walking on his way to his home and his breakfast. The town looked tranquil in the morning sunlight. In the sunlight too, the S-hook buckle of the policeman's waist-belt glinted on his ample stomach, and the gleam of the burnished metal stood out against the dark cloth of his tunic, as he walked slowly along the sloping side-walk. From the inside of an upper window of the Town Hall, the tip of the foresight of a service rifle was trained on the glinting belt buckle of the constable's belt. As he descended the gradient, the rifle muzzle was depressed while the mark shone back to the engaged eye of the weapon, the rifleman observed tensely to a comrade: 'I must get him before he comes to the corner.'

The glinting buckle advanced. Then the constable turned abruptly and retracted his steps up the hill. The sniper lifted his head and spoke again: 'It was a near thing,' he said with obvious relief. 'The order was to let nobody leave the barracks.' Unaware that he had walked cheek by jowl with death, Constable Keane re-entered the barracks' day-room to deal with a suddenly remembered detail. Unaware he was, too, as were his comrades-in-arms in the RIC barracks that, less than a quarter of a mile away, an eventful chapter of history was being fashioned at that very moment. The date was 28 September, and the first and only British military barracks in Ireland to be completely captured was in the hands of a daring detachment of the 2nd Cork Brigade of the Irish Republican Army, at the time of Constable Keane's escape. Of that detachment the riflemen in the Town Hall comprised an outpost whose function it was to pin down the local RIC garrison in its barracks on 'the new street'.

Writing more than a generation after the event, in an era of native government and full national status, it is difficult to convey the elements of courage, tenacity, intelligence; of efficient planning and administration that went to make the capture of Mallow military barracks by the IRA the most successful operation of its kind. It must be realised that it was undertaken when the national territory teemed with British troops and armed police whose duties were military duties, and not police duties. Mallow was then a garrison town and had been for several hundred years. Eight miles north of it lay Buttevant, where one of the largest military barracks in the country was located. Not far from Buttevant were the great military training camps of Ballyvonaire, while nineteen miles to the north-east was Fermoy, with its large permanent military garrisons and huge barracks adjacent to the big training centres of Kilworth and Moorepark. Twenty miles to the south-east was the city of Cork with its many thousands of troops, both in the posts within the city and at Ballincollig, about six miles west of it, on the Macroom road. Thirteen miles westward a detachment from a British machine-gun corps held Kanturk. And every town and village had its post of RIC men, armed to the teeth.

28 September will always mark a notable double anniversary for the venture of the War of Independence in north and north-east Cork. For the capture of the first and only military barracks to be taken, with its entire store of arms and equipment, was also the first operation of a newly organised flying column of the Cork No. 2 Brigade. 'The Mallow Raid', as it came to be known, marked the beginning of a series of stern engagements carried out under the leadership of General Liam Lynch or his staff officers, from the bounds of Waterford and Limerick to the borders of Kerry. These engagements were to rank for pride of place with the best and most valiant efforts of resistance by oppressed people in any age, and were to add further lustre to the bright tradition of Irish soldiering.

For the success of the Mallow operation, credit of no ordinary kind must go to two members of the Mallow IRA Battalion, who were mere youths at the time. The idea of capturing the barracks was theirs and they were the key men who made the operation a success. Today, Dick Willis of Mallow is a painter and Jack Bolster is a carpenter. On that far-off morning of 1920 they followed the same trades as now. They were then employed on the civilian maintenance staff of the barracks which was occupied at the time by the 17th Lancers. It is because they were watchful and alert, and made good use of their intelligence, that this important chapter of our struggle for freedom can be written.

In the first week of August 1920, the leaders of the republican army in north Cork laid plans for the establishment of a brigade flying column. On the night of Saturday, 7 or 8 August, a brigade meeting was held in the vicinity of Mourneabbey, about five miles from Mallow. Its purpose, the formation of a column, had been previously decided upon partly because of the increasing number of battalion and company officers who were being forced 'on the run' throughout the brigade area. Banded together, they would be more than capable of meeting the enemy's attempts to crush the national forces. As a co-ordinated fighting unit, a flying column would be mobile, well-trained and disciplined, and capable of striking fast, frequently and with good effect.

As a result of the discussions at Mourneabbey, it was decided that each of the seven battalions in the area would supply two or three officers towards the nucleus of the column. The seven battalions concerned were: Fermoy, Castletownroche, Charleville, Kanturk, Mallow, Newmarket and Millstreet. Commanding the 2nd Brigade at the time was General Liam Lynch. Whilst he was willing to take on the duties of column leader, it was the opinion of the meeting that his exceptional qualities of heart and mind would be of greater value to the movement in the position of Brigade O/C. A tireless organiser and inspiring leader in whom there was rare combination of thinker and man of action, Liam Lynch was of no ordinary calibre. When the history of his time comes to be objectively written, few men are likely to emerge with the same distinction as the brave and chivalrous chief of the 2nd Brigade.

When it was agreed that General Lynch would continue as Brigade O/C, the choice for column leader was Paddy Clancy of Kilfinane, County Limerick, who was a creamery manager employed at Allen's Bridge between Newmarket and Kanturk. The decision was also taken to mobilise the column during the following fortnight. Matters were to turn out differently, for Paddy Clancy's leadership of the column was not to be. One morning, some few days after the Mourneabbey meeting, he died the soldier he was beneath a hail of British bullets at Derrygallon, scarcely three miles from Kanturk. Two nights previously the Kanturk Company of the IRA had attacked the military guard on a grounded aeroplane at Drominagh, near Clonbanin. Paddy Clancy and his friend, Jack O'Connell, were in the attacking party and the following morning they rested at O'Callaghan's farmhouse, Upper Bluepool, Kanturk. The next night they spent at Jack O'Connell's home, at Derrygallon. An informer gave news of their whereabouts to the machine-gun corps detachment in Kanturk police barracks. While the two IRA men slept, the house was surrounded by men from the British machine-gun corps, led by a sergeant of the RIC garrison at Kanturk. Both fell riddled to death when attempting to escape. When the British came up to the dying IRA men, one of the soldiers offered to go for a priest but was forbidden to do so by the RIC sergeant.

The loss of the newly appointed leader, and the arrest of about four other officers nominated for the column, delayed its mobilisation. It was not until the middle of September that the unit was got together. Assembled at Glenville, between Killavullen and Cork, its headquarters was the house of Mrs Hickey of Badger's Hill. Representatives of the Newmarket, Fermoy, Castletownroche, Charleville, Kanturk and Millstreet battalions participated in a full course of training by the unit, at headquarters, as also did Brigadier Liam Lynch and Brigade Adjutant George Power of Fermoy. Men of the Mallow Battalion reported for training at headquarters each evening and at the weekends. Rifles that had been captured from the British in an operation at Fermoy twelve months previously provided most of the column's armament.

The members of the column were: Newmarket Battalion: Patrick McCarthy, Michael O'Sullivan, Dan Browne; Fermoy Battalion: Larry Condon, John O'Mahony, Daniel Daly, Matt Flood; Castletownroche Battalion: Daniel Shinnick, Jeremiah Donovan, James O'Neill, Michael O'Halloran; Charleville Battalion: Patrick O'Brien, Thomas Coughlan; Kanturk Battalion: Daniel Vaughan; Millstreet Battalion: Patrick Healy, John Healy; Mallow Battalion: Tadhg Byrnes, Jack Cunningham, Paddy McCarthy (Mourneabbey), Owen Harold, Jeremiah Daly. At the end of the first week, Ernie O'Malley, a staff officer from Dublin, arrived and took over the training. About ten days later the column moved from Glenville to Island, Burnfort, with the intention of laying an ambush at Mourneabbey, on the Cork-Mallow road. While Liam Lynch, Paddy O'Brien of Liscarroll and Ernie O'Malley were surveying a proposed ambush position on the main road at Mourneabbey, the idea of the Mallow raid was put forward.

Tadhg Byrnes, an officer of the Mallow Battalion and member of the column, arrived at headquarters with a message from Dick Willis and Jack Bolster to the effect that the capture of the military barracks in the town appeared to be possible.

Because of their position in the barracks, Willis and Bolster were able to observe the daily routine of the garrison and they decided that the capture of the place would not be difficult. Having conveyed that opinion to their local battalion officers, they were instructed to make a sketch map of the barracks. When that was prepared they were called to the column headquarters at Island, Burnfort, for questioning by Liam Lynch, Paddy O'Brien, Ernie O'Malley, George Power and the staff. The same night, Lynch and O'Malley went with Dick Willis into Mallow to study the lay-out of the surrounding district. Among the details of the garrison's routine that Willis and Bolster reported to the column leaders, was the important information that each morning the officer in charge, accompanied by two-thirds of the men, took the horses for exercise outside the town. The bulk of their arms and ammunition was left behind. According to the two Mallow Volunteers, the barracks was ripe for the picking during the absence of the party exercising the horses.

Mallow barracks differed from other buildings of its type in many towns throughout Ireland. Military barracks usually comprised a large collection of buildings occupying more or less isolated and generally elevated positions on the outskirts of the towns or cities in which they were placed. Situated at the end of a short, narrow street, and on the western verge of the Town Park, Mallow barracks stood on an unusually low-lying location and, comparatively speaking, it was small in size. Surrounded by a high stone wall, its southern limit touched the park and its entrance gate and wicket opened on to Barrack Street, which thoroughfare connects with the main street at the point where the roads from Cork, Limerick and Kerry form an intersection. Virtually in the town, the place could be approached from the Town Park as well as from the main street. These and other details were carefully studied by Liam Lynch and O'Malley. Dick Willis and Jack Bolster knew the ground from childhood, as did Jack Cunningham and Owen Harold, other officers of the Mallow Battalion. So did Tadhg Byrnes. All five gave invaluable assistance in the preparations. Owen Harold was billeted in a house in Barrack Street from which he was able to observe all comings and goings of the military. Dick Willis and Jack Bolster were allotted tasks within the walls of the barracks. Tadhg Byrnes and Jack Cunningham were chosen to attack with the main body of the column, which included Commandant Denny Murphy of Kanturk.

It was an intrepid, yet eminently feasible plan on which the column acted. On the morning of 27 September, in their Burnfort headquarters, the men were ordered to prepare for action. Under cover of darkness they moved into the town that night and entered the Town Hall by way of the park at the rear. The eighteen men of the column were strengthened by members of the Mallow Battalion, and as morning approached a number of men were posted in the upper storey of the Town Hall, from which they could command the approaches to the RIC barracks, on the 'new street'. Their task was to prevent the RIC from going to the assistance of the military. An important feature of the plan was that Willis and Bolster would enter the military barracks that morning in the normal way, but accompanying them would be an officer of the column who, if questioned, would represent himself as a contractor's overseer working under the Board of Works. The officer was Paddy McCarthy of Newmarket. Earlier in the year he had escaped with President de Valera from Lincoln jail, in England, and a few months after the Mallow raid he died bravely in the town of Millstreet, in a gun battle with Black and Tans.

Most things went according to plan. McCarthy, Willis and Bolster entered the barracks without mishap and the 'contractor's overseer' duly set about making entries in his notebook, to justify the role he was playing. The garrison followed its well-known routine. Into the country for the morning canter went the officer in charge, taking with him the main body of troops. In the barracks remained about fifteen men under the command of a senior NCO, Sergeant Gibbs.

The Lancers passed through the streets under the watchful eyes of the men high up in the Town Hall, each soldier riding a horse and leading another. They had with them but two rifles and five revolvers, having left the bulk of their arms in the barracks.

Immediately that the military had passed, the attackers advanced by the rear of the Town Hall to the park along the northern edge of which they moved towards the bottom of Barrack Street. In the Town Hall behind the attackers were six men to cover the RIC barracks. The attackers numbered about twenty men. All were armed with revolvers, which were considered the most convenient and suitable weapons for the operation. They were led by Liam Lynch. As they moved through the park, the men took an urgent decision to alter one aspect of the plan of attack, without Lynch's knowledge. The reason for the change was the concern of the men for the safety of their chief. It had been part of the original plan, decided on by Lynch himself, that on arrival at the wicket, Ernie O'Malley would attempt to induce the sentry to open it, by presenting a letter addressed to the barracks' warden. Once the wicket was open, Lynch would lead the attacking party through it; this was the part of the plan that the column changed. Knowing his tremendous value to the army in the south, it was felt that he should not be exposed to the unnecessary danger of leading in the attackers, for if he should be killed or captured the national cause would be seriously injured.

Meanwhile, certain that he would be first through the wicket gate, and completely unaware that he was to be pushed aside at the last moment, Liam Lynch led the little band into Barrack Street. He had issued strict instructions that there was to be no shooting by the attackers, save as a last resort. Inside the walls, and in the vicinity of the gate since the exercising party had departed, were Paddy McCarthy, Dick Willis and Jack Bolster, their revolvers concealed. In due course Ernie O'Malley presented himself at the wicket with a letter in his hand. Behind him, and out of sight of the sentry, were the other members of the main attacking party, led by Liam Lynch, Paddy O'Brien and George Power. Sergeant Gibbs, then in charge of the barracks, was supervising the shoeing of a horse, at a point to the left of the gates, when the sentry answered O'Malley's knock at the wicket. When it was opened sufficiently to permit the bogus letter for the barracks' warden to be passed in, Ernie said he wanted to hand it personally to that official. At that the sentry attempted to close the door again, but O'Malley prevented this by wedging his foot between it and the frame, and in a second the soldier was over-powered.

In rushed the attackers, two or three of whom jumped ahead of General Lynch. McCarthy, Bolster and Willis immediately went into action at the guardroom where they held up the guard. Realising what was happening, Sergeant Gibbs rushed towards the guardroom in which rifles were kept. Called on to halt, he continued determinedly though one of the IRA officers at the gate fired a warning shot over his head. As he reached the guardroom door, the IRA officer fired again and, simultaneously, one of the IRA men in the guardroom fired also. Mortally wounded, the sergeant fell at the guardroom door.

By that time the majority of the attacking party was inside the gate, and each man had immediately gone about his allotted task. Stray military personnel in different parts of the barracks were rounded up; arms were collected. Straw and petrol were distributed throughout the buildings with the intention of setting them on fire. Three waiting motor cars pulled up to the gate and into them were piled all the rifles and other arms and equipment found in the barracks. In all some twenty-seven rifles, two Hotchkiss light machine guns, boxes of ammunition, Verey light pistols, a revolver, and bayonets, were taken away. The prisoners were put under lock and key in one of the stables, with the exception of a man left to care for Sergeant Gibbs.

The whole operation worked with clock-like precision and according to plan, save for the shooting of the sergeant. Twenty minutes after the sentry had been overpowered the pre-arranged signal of a whistle blast was sounded and the attackers withdrew through the Town Park and safely reached their headquarters at Burnfort, along the mountain road out of Mallow. Before the withdrawal, the petrol-soaked straw was set alight in the buildings, but they did not take fire, due to the fact that the stairs and passageways were constructed of stone flagging.

Expecting reprisals, the column moved along the roads south of the Blackwater to Lombardstown that night, and positions were taken up around the Lombardstown Co-Operative Creamery. Following successful operations by the IRA it was the custom of the British to wreak their vengeance on isolated co-operative creameries, in a vindictive effort to destroy the economy of the community, and to discourage the people from billeting and feeding the men of the columns. The Mallow raid, however, was to have greater repercussions than the destruction of a mere creamery and co-operative stores and the brigade officers had erred in their appreciation of the British reaction to the success of the daring attack. Into the town of Mallow, on the following night, came large detachments of troops from Buttevant and Fermoy, released from any form of discipline. They literally scoured the town, burning and looting, firing and pillaging at will. High over the rambling streets the night sky was red with the flames of many burning buildings.

True to the pattern for reprisals already set in so many other parts of the country by the British, the raiders first descended upon the Town Hall in which were housed the offices of the Urban Council, the Labour Exchange, the Surveyor's offices, the Social and Commercial Club rooms, the archives of the town and a large hall that was used for such functions as concerts and dances. As in the majority of towns, the building was the centre of the administrative and social life of the district. A lorry of uniformed hooligans, frenzied and officerless, detrucked in front of it. Above the clamour which they caused, an English voice was heard to call out for 'the petrol', which was quickly forthcoming. Applied by means of a pump, petrol was liberally sprayed all over the large building. Within a short space of time the Town Hall was a mass of flames. The soldiers then swooped upon the drapery establishment of Mr J.J. Forde, not far away, on the opposite side of the street, and soon it too was belching flame and smoke. Warming to their task, the British next set fire to the Bank Place residence of Mr Wrixon, the town clerk, and with it the pharmacy of his son, which was in the same building. Both men had barely time to escape into the street, with no more than the clothes they were wearing. Yelling like savages, and firing their weapons wildly, the British continued their orgy of destruction with complete abandon. They sent up in the flames of the great holocaust the private hotel of Mr George Hanover, the boot and shoe establishment of Mr Thomas Quinn, the merchant tailor's shop and residence of Mr R.M. Quaile, the drapery shop of Mrs Cronin, the residence of Mr Stephen Dwyer at West End, the garage and premises of Mr W.J. Thompson and the great creamery of Cleeve which gave employment to 300 of the bread-winners of Mallow. Stricken townspeople, men, women and children, ran through the blazing streets, in search of refuge, their cries of anguish accentuating the terror created by the awful scene of destruction. On every side were the hiss and roar of flames, the crash of masonry as the doomed buildings collapsed, and the aimless discharge of weapons by the inflamed troops. Up the steep hill to the Parochial House rushed a crowd of women and children who sought the protection of their parish priest, Very Rev. Canon Corbett. These were accorded asylum in the nearby convent schools. Another group of terrified women, some with children in arms, sought refuge in the cemetery at the rear of St Mary's church, where they knelt or lay above the graves. It was a night of terror, the like of which had never previously been endured by the people of Mallow.

The character and extent of the wanton and senseless reprisals outraged fair-minded people all over the world. Details of the havoc that had been wrought and pictures of these scenes of destruction were given in many newspapers. *The Times* of London, had the following editorial:

> Day by day the tidings from Ireland grow worse. The accounts of arson and destruction by military at Mallow as revenge for the Sinn Féin raid which caught the 17th Lancers napping must fill English readers with a sense of shame.
>
> The authorities would have been fully entitled, after the raid, to arrest on suspicion of complicity any townsfolk against whom a *prima*

> *facie* case could be established. No complaint could have been made had they dealt summarily with any insurgent caught in possession of arms. They were not entitled to reduce to ruins the chief building of the township and to destroy the property of the inhabitants merely as an act of terrorism.
>
> The name of England is being sullied throughout the Empire and throughout the world by this savagery, for which the Government can no longer escape, however much they may seek to disclaim, responsibility. We shall, doubtless, be told by the leading ministerial organ that the Irish towns are not really towns, but only villages …

On the Sunday morning following the wholesale destruction of property in Mallow and the terrorism perpetrated on the people of the town by the British, St Mary's parish church was crowded for eight o'clock Mass. Slowly, the grief-stricken and beloved Canon Corbett, parish priest of Mallow, mounted the steps of the pulpit to address his people. He had seen all the havoc and misery wrought in their town by the forces of the crown. He had come to his church that morning along a route flanked by the blackened ruins of tall and dignified buildings. Hundreds of his flock had been deprived of their livelihood as a result of the burning of Cleeve's Creamery. With a heavy heart he spoke that morning, ironically referring to the 'great victory' over women and children achieved by the British army in Mallow. In a voice that shook with emotion he described the scenes and incidents he had witnessed on Mallow's night of terror:

> … the rush of frantic women and children to my door at midnight asking, for God's sake, to provide them with some place of safety or refuge; bullets hissing over our heads as I tried to stow them into the Convent Schools; another crowd in St Mary's cemetery – mothers with infants at their breasts sitting on the family burying ground, as if they thought their dead could aid them. Splendid business premises burned to the ground and a winter of unemployment made sure for hundreds by the burning of Cleeve's factory. These are amongst the signs of victory, won not by Zulus or Sioux Indians, but by Englishmen; the great victory of Mallow at midnight of the 28 September 1920.
>
> 'Reprisals,' they said, by the civil and military authorities. They are not reprisals. They are, as Mr Arthur Griffith points out, a calculated policy to goad our people into insurrection now as in 1798, an excuse for drenching

> the country in blood. I have only to repeat the advice of our good Bishop: 'Be patient.' God sees all and in His own good time, will deliver His people who trust in Him.

With these words, Canon Corbett, standing before his congregation, utterly broke down and left the pulpit.

There can be few instances of official vandalism perpetrated on such a scale except it be the burning of Cork city by the troops of the same imperial aggressor. Barbarous treatment of terrified women and children and old people by drunken troops was the answer of the British army to a bold and successful operation carried out against it. Chivalry and honourable behaviour the British met with vile conduct that besmirched the noble calling of the soldier. Little wonder it was that the arms captured from them at Mallow were used with such deadly effect in many an encounter in which the men of the republican army personified and symbolised that dictum of the great Mallowman, Davis: 'disciplined habits and military accomplishments are the pillars of independence'.

INSIDE INFORMATION ACTED ON EFFICIENTLY LED TO FALL OF TRIM BARRACKS

MEATH BRIGADE, 30 SEPTEMBER 1920

by Seamus Finn

(formerly Vice-O/C 1st Eastern Division, IRA)

TRIM, THE CAPITAL of County Meath, had an RIC barracks and a police force in keeping with its importance. The barracks, a miniature fortress of stone walls and barred windows, stood in the centre of a plot of ground two acres in extent on the south side of the Fair Green which opened on two sides of it. Facing to the east, it stood 150 yards from the Summerhill road, and was surrounded by a wall fifteen feet high. Strong iron gates barred the approach.

In the summer of 1920 this police stronghold held a garrison of twenty-five constables, two sergeants, one head constable and one district inspector, a fact which, in addition to the solidity of its structure, made it a very formidable enemy post.

In 1920 too, the Trim area held a strong Volunteer battalion, an IRA unit which had already proved its worth six months earlier in the fight for Ballivor barracks, when its members had shown that they possessed both determination and daring. Since then they had been given a special course of training so that now they were efficient as well as determined and daring fighters. A series of police swoops during the preceding months had deprived the brigade area of some of its best officers, but others had been trained to fill the vacancies, and by the summer of 1920 the area was in a solid position.

Towards the end of 1919 and in the early months of 1920, attacks on several police barracks had been planned, but each time there had to be last-minute change of plans resulting in repeated disappointments – except, of course, at Ballivor, where one policeman was shot and where our men seized all the arms and ammunition kept in that barracks.

A boast made by one of the Trim police regarding the impregnability of the barracks there caused us to consider the possibility of attacking the Trim stronghold. The suggestion was discussed with the men of the Trim Battalion, and they unhesitatingly agreed that the attack should be carried out. So our decision was made, and our next step was to devise ways and means, and to lay efficient plans of attack.

In this respect we were afforded very fortunate assistance by an ex-RIC sergeant named T.J. McElligott, who had earlier resigned from the police force as a protest against Britain's conscription plans for Ireland during the First World War. This man gave us the names of constables who were reliable from our point of view, and one of these in turn gave us valuable information regarding the layout of the barracks itself and regarding the movements of its garrison. He told us, for one thing, that the district inspector was to be absent during a certain weekend, and this item of information decided us upon the date of our contemplated attack, Sunday 30 September 1920!

The undertaking was a big one, requiring careful planning and perfect timing on the part of the brigade staff whose task it was to plan the attack, and superb pluck and fighting ability on the part of the men who were to carry it out.

The Meath Brigade area at that time took in the entire county, and the Delvin district in County Westmeath as well. Its officers were Seán Boylan, Dunboyne, brigade O/C, Seán Hayes, Drumbarragh, brigade vice-O/C, Seamus Finn, Athboy, brigade adjutant, and Seamus O'Higgins, Trim, brigade quartermaster.

The brigade was composed of six battalions. The 1st Battalion was centred on Dunboyne, and led by Commandant Kit Lynam; the 2nd was centred on Trim, led by Commandant Pat Mooney; the 3rd was centred on Athboy, led by Commandant Seán O'Grady, and later by

Commandant Michael Fox when O'Grady returned to his native County Clare; the 4th Battalion took in Kells and the surrounding areas, and was led by Commandant P. de Burca, who later went to Dublin and was replaced by Commandant Pat Farrelly of Moynalty; the 5th Battalion took in the Oldcastle area and was led by Commandant Seán Keogh until his arrest, then by Commandant Seamus Cogan until he was killed in action in June 1920, then by Commandant Pat McDonald until he too was killed, fighting his way through a British cordon, and finally by Commandant Davie Smith of Whitegate; the 6th Battalion covered the Navan area and was commanded by Commandant Pat Loughran until his arrest, and then by Commandant Paddy Kelly of Johnstown.

With the information which we had been given by the constable to guide us, we set our scouts to note carefully the movements of the police on each successive Sunday prior to the date fixed for the attack. Their report was a detailed and comprehensive one, which gave us exact information on the activities of the police garrison at the particular time which interested us.

The report said that the bigger portion of the garrison left the barracks at 7.55 a.m. each Sunday morning for eight o'clock Mass, leaving, therefore, less than half their force behind on barracks duty. One sergeant, and occasionally the head constable, would remain in the barracks, and in all, we estimated that the manpower of the garrison at that time each Sunday morning would be about eight men. On Sunday morning, 30 September, we knew that the district inspector would be absent and his quarters vacant.

With these details at our disposal, we arranged a meeting with the officers of the Trim Battalion with whom we went over carefully all phases of our plans, for it was upon these officers and their men that the brunt of the fighting was to fall. When we were satisfied that these men knew all that was expected of them, our next task was to organise all possible protection for them during the fight, in the event of police reinforcements attempting to break through to the rescue of the Trim garrison. With this in view, we held a conference with the battalion officers of other areas in the county and issued orders that all roads leading to Trim should be systematically blocked. This matter arranged to our satisfaction, we made elaborate arrangements for the dumping of the arms we hoped to capture, and also for the provision of transport.

The business of procuring oil and the other inflammable substances to be used against the barracks was delegated to the brigade adjutant. The vital job of capturing the police who had gone to Mass, as they emerged from the church, was entrusted to the men of the 1st Battalion under Brigade O/C Boylan, and Commandants Lynam and Dunne.

A final joint meeting of the brigade council and the officers of the Trim Battalion was held on Tuesday night, 25 September, at Trim. All details of the attack were gone over, and when each man felt perfectly satisfied that he knew the entire plan of the action minutely, a further serious consideration was then discussed – that of affording protection to our well-wishers and friends in Trim against possible reprisals on the part of the enemy following the attack. We surmised that the homes of our most prominent local supporters, the O'Higgins family, O'Hagans, Mooneys, Allens and Plunketts of Navan Gate, might be attacked by the police. Therefore we arranged that O'Hagan's house should be occupied by twelve men drawn from the Trim Battalion, with eight others in Kelly's, and four in Barney Reilly's to cover Market Street where the O'Hagans, the O'Higgins family and the Mooney family lived. Ten men from Athboy and eight from Kilmessan were to be positioned at Navan Gate to cover Plunkett's and Allen's. All of these men were to be armed with rifles, revolvers, shotguns and hand grenades.

On Friday 28 September, the brigade adjutant again met the principal men of the Trim Battalion who were to carry out the operation. Once again every phase of the plans was gone into in detail. It was further decided that the men should mobilise on the Saturday night at O'Hagan's and would billet there for that night in a big room upstairs. A certain point on the wall surrounding the barracks was selected as the point over which the attackers were to climb – this was the point directly opposite the absent district inspector's quarters, where, we felt, the initial moves of our men were most likely to escape detection from the occupants of the barracks. This point was at the side gate leading on to the Fair Green. The time taken to reach this part of the wall from O'Hagan's in Market Street was carefully checked, for it was an important factor that our men should not reach the point from which the attack was to be initiated too soon after the first section of the police had left on their way to Mass. Our intention was to give those who had remained behind sufficient time in which to settle down to their normal barrack duties, so that they might be fully occupied with their morning chores. As well as that, we wanted to give the Mass-going section of the garrison ample time to reach and enter the church. We would then be sure of being able to capture and overpower them should they attempt to leave when the sounds of the attack began.

Feeling confident that everything was clear to the men of Trim and that every man understood his own individual part of the morning's work perfectly, the brigade adjutant then set off for Athboy to arrange for men there to go to Trim on Sunday to help meet the enemy reprisals. From there he travelled to Kells where he met Bob Mullen with whom he arranged for road blocks to be erected in that area. There also he arranged for transport to take him to Trim in time for the attack, and also to convey back the oil which the local company captain, Willie Doyle, had seized at Athboy to be used in setting fire to the barracks.

He was fortunate in meeting Nick Gaynor of Ballinlough Company in Kells. This Volunteer promptly suggested that he should drive the brigade adjutant back in his own car. Having collected the oil at Athboy on their way back, they arrived at Trim at 8 p.m. on Saturday, and garaged their car at Plunkett's of Navan Gate. From there they went to O'Hagan's where they met the Trim officers who had already arrived.

The men had all reported present by the pre-arranged time, 9 p.m. Two revolvers loaned for the operation by the Navan Company were handed over by Volunteers Keating and Byrne, both of whom pressed hard to be allowed to participate. Their services could not be availed of, however, as we had but sufficient weapons to arm the men already detailed for the job. The plans for the attack on the following morning were once again gone over, and when the tea and sandwiches which Mrs O'Hagan had kindly sent up to us had been duly sampled, we sent out two scouts to keep check upon the possible movements of the police that night, posted guards at the front and rear doors of our billet, and then settled down to get what sleep we could.

The night passed uneventfully, and by 6.30 on Sunday morning we were all astir and had begun our final arrangements. At 7.30 the men fell in, in three sections. Section No. 1 consisted of Commandants Mick Hynes and Paddy Mooney, who were in actual charge of the attack; Lieutenants Mick Giles and Harry O'Hagan; Volunteers Joe Lawlor, Pat Fay, Stephen Sherry, Joe Kelly from the Trim Company; Volunteers C. Caffrey, P. Quinn and J. O'Brien from the Kilmessan Company; Captain Pat Giles and Volunteer Larry Giles from the Longwood Company. All belonged to the 2nd Battalion. Section No. 2 were: P. Duigenan, John Higgins, Pat O'Hagan, J. Healy, Joe Nolan, Phil Doggett, Pat Hynes, P. O'Hara, Matty Mathews, Pat Lawlor and L. Sheary. Section No. 3 were: Pat Proctor, J. Andrews, P. Andrews, Dick Harmon, C. Reid and M. Plunkett. The brigade adjutant and Volunteer Nick Gaynor were to cover the front of the barracks with rifles once the attack began.

The men of No. 1 Section were all armed with revolvers, ranging from .45s to .32s. Their instructions were to climb the wall at the point selected, rush the back door of the barracks directly opposite that point, and so gain admittance to the barracks and, if possible, to overpower and capture the police. No. 2 Section was to follow closely upon the heels of No. 1, help in the work of overpowering the police, and then to gather up and remove all arms, ammunition, grenades, and other war materials that the barracks contained. No. 3 Section was set the task of bringing along the tins of oil and petrol with which the barracks was to be set afire. Its task was to sprinkle the building liberally with both oil and petrol and then touch off fires where they were likely to do most harm in the shortest possible time.

Our plans worked like magic. The men of No. 1 Section were over the back wall and through the door before the police knew anything of what was afoot. Taken so completely by surprise, they were overcome almost immediately, all, that is, except Head Constable White who rushed towards a box of grenades but was shot through the lung before he could do any harm to our men. He alone showed any heart for struggle, and so the reputedly impregnable Trim RIC barracks fell into our hands without even a semblance of resistance, thanks entirely to the elaborate planning of the brigade and local officers in conjunction with the information given by our contacts among the RIC, to the perfect timing with which the operation was carried out, to the cool and efficient way the men had set to work, and to the excellence of our intelligence men.

Gathering all the arms and other war materials we could find, and having helped the captured police to remove their personal belongings and those of their friends at Mass, we set fire to the barracks which soon was a blazing holocaust and before noon was no more than a smouldering ruin.

Head Constable White had been shot through the lung and badly wounded. We got him attended to by Dr T.J. Lynch who had him removed to the hospital section of the local workhouse – where, incidentally, we had had arrangements made for the treatment of any of our own men who might happen to be wounded in the attack. Fortunately, however, we did not require attention, for our men had carried out their morning's work without suffering as much as a scratch.

Meanwhile, at the church, our friends had been equally successful. Under the leadership of Brigade O/C Boylan, Battalion Commandant Lynam and Vice-Commandant Frank Carolan, those men, mainly drawn from the 1st Battalion, captured the police as they left the church. One policeman, hearing the confusion outside, hid in a confessional, but he too was taken when the numbers had been checked and he was missed from the company. In this part of the action, together with the three officers, were Barney Dunne, James Maguire and M. Phoenix, all from the Dunboyne area.

With the barracks well aflame, we checked our capture of arms and ammunition – twenty rifles and carbines, twenty shotguns, of which some were no longer serviceable, and six revolvers, was our capture of arms; ammunition for all arms, a box of grenades and some bayonets constituted the remainder of our capture, altogether a very satisfactory morning's work!

At a hastily summoned conference it was decided that the men should all get out of town as quickly as possible, rest during the remainder of the day, and then reassemble at O'Hagan's at nine o'clock that evening to await possible enemy activities.

The brigade adjutant, with Volunteers Sherry and Lalor of Trim, and Volunteer Gaynor to drive, securely dumped the captured arms, then set off to Athboy to meet the company officers there, and having arranged for the return journey to Trim that night, they settled down to a well-earned sleep.

But events did not work out so happily in Trim. A convey of the enemy arrived there about 4 p.m. in the afternoon, and in a spirit of reprisal they fired indiscriminately through the town, wounding some youths who were playing hurling. In alarm, some of the more prominent men of the town approached the officers in charge of the British forces, and were assured that no further reprisals would be taken for the destruction of the barracks. These townsmen met our officers and men when they arrived to take up positions from which they could prevent reprisals, and told them that such precautions were no longer necessary. Our men were actually hampered when making preliminary arrangements to occupy their positions, and consequently they had no choice but to withdraw. The following morning brought a shock when we learned that the Tans had broken loose during the night and burned down houses in the town, contrary to the assurances of their officers.

At an inquiry held at IRA headquarters in Dublin, the officers constituting the court declared that, in view of the interference of the townspeople of Trim in the matter, little or no responsibility rested with our men for their failure to guard against the possibility of British reprisals in Trim.

It was not until later that we were able to remove the captured arms and ammunition from the dump in which we had placed them, for our movements were hampered by a particularly active company of Auxiliaries who had been drafted into Trim immediately following the fall of the RIC barracks. Eventually, the booty was distributed safely over various areas of the brigade, with the exception of the box of grenades which was re-captured by the enemy. This was seized by a hold-up patrol, between Trim and Ballivor, when it was being conveyed to Ballivor by Tom Byrne of Raharney Company. Byrne was badly beaten up by Black and Tans and was later sentenced to ten years' penal servitude which he was serving in an English jail until released under the terms of the Truce.

The worst of the British official reprisals for the destruction of Trim RIC barracks was not launched until approximately four o'clock on Monday morning, when about 200 Auxiliaries and Black and Tans from Drogheda descended upon the town and began an orgy of terror and destruction. The O'Higgins home was their first objective and they smashed their way into it, to find that only Mrs O'Higgins and her daughter were inside. Brigade Quartermaster Seamus O'Higgins and his brother Seán were still with the active service unit. The two ladies were given but a few minutes to get out of the house, which was then sent up in flames. It was but the first of many fired during a night that will never be forgotten by those who witnessed the scenes of plunder and brutality that followed. Fully a quarter of the town was completely gutted. Amongst the places burned by the British, in addition to the O'Higgins house and shop, was the residence and drapery shop of Harry and Bob Allen, in High Street. Bob Allen was chairman of the Sinn Féin Comhairle Ceanntair, but Harry took no part in politics. The bakery and mineral water works of J. & E. Smyth & Co. of Market Street, also went up in flames, together with a residence attached. Smyth's employed about a hundred persons and the object of the burning was to create unemployment. The home of Commandant Mooney's parents was also smashed up and both were brutally ill-treated. The parents and sister of Volunteers P. O'Hagan and Harry

O'Hagan were similarly abused, and their home wrecked and furniture and effects smashed. Lalor's house in Castle Street was destroyed by fire and the parents of Paddy and Joe Lalor were beaten up. Many other houses were broken into and looted. Few public houses escaped. On the same morning some of the RIC who had garrisoned the barracks raided the home of our contact, Constable Patrick Meehan, of the Trim RIC, who had resigned a few days previously. He had been in contact with us since the resignation of Sergeant McElligott, and had kept us very well informed of enemy activities. Fortunately he was not at home at the time of the police raid and consequently he escaped certain death and mutilation. Following the raid he contacted some of our men, and a car was commandeered to drive him to safety. The car was driven by Denis Maher, now Rev. Father Denis Maher of the Welsh Mission. Meehan was much sought after by Tans and British agents, but was successful in evading their attention. He is now a superintendent in the Garda Síochána, and is stationed in County Longford.

A garrison of Auxiliaries and Black and Tans subsequently posted in Trim gave real hell to the townsfolk. As a result of the conduct of that particular group of Auxiliaries, Brigadier-General Crozier, who was head of the force, resigned his command following the looting and burning of Chandler's public house in the hamlet of Robinstown, which is about five miles from Trim, on the main Trim-Navan road. Chandler's place was a rendezvous of the Meath Hunt in its palmiest days, and consequently its owner was not without influence in official circles. That situation, however, cut no ice with a party of Auxiliaries who arrived in Robinstown on the night of 9 February 1921. They were in no mood for pleasantries. Having questioned Bob Chandler as to whether he had any arms and ammunition, and having been informed that he had none, they beat him and kicked him down the stairs. They then set about looting his hostelry, a task that was after their own hearts and for which they were well equipped. Necks were broken off bottles and drink was consumed to the value of more than a hundred pounds. Fittings and stock were wantonly smashed and destroyed. They ill-treated Chandler's invalid mother, a very old lady, stole many valuables and made a bonfire of clothing and furniture before they left the place. Bob Chandler gave details of the damage to the IRA and subsequently he had to go on the run from the British.

Two Auxiliaries who had been in the looting of Chandler's went urgently to Dublin and reported what had taken place to General Crozier, 'at the peril of their lives,' wrote the General, 'as their comrades would undoubtedly have killed them had they known.' A number of the Auxiliaries were immediately suspended. 'By the middle of February 1921,' continued Crozier, 'conditions had become so impossible that I resigned. The "occasion" of my resignation was the "Trim incident" connected with the dismissal of the policemen, their reinstatement and the condonation of their offences by the government. In reality there were dozens of "occasions", many more grave than the Trim incident. I returned to Dublin after I had resigned, at the request of the chief secretary, in order to help to solve the Trim question. The inquiry which was held by the police was a pure farce. The court martial department of GHQ told them so and told me so also.'

When divisions were formed in the Irish Republican Army in April 1921, Meath became the kernel of the 1st Eastern Division. The following appointments were made: Divisional O/C: Commandant-General Seán Boylan; Divisional Vice-O/C: Colonel-Commandant Seamus Finn; Divisional Adjutant: Colonel-Commandant Patrick Clinton; Divisional Quartermaster: Colonel-Commandant Seamus Higgins; Divisional Director of Engineering: Colonel-Commandant E. Cullen; other officers on the divisional staff were: Commandant Paddy Mooney, Assistant Training Officer; Captain Arthur Levins, Captain Martin Finn and Captain Donal Landers. The divisional area included the following brigades: Dunboyne and part of north Kildare; Navan, which included all the original Trim and Navan Battalions; Kells, which included the original 4th and 5th Battalions, and part of east Cavan as far north as Kilbride East; Athboy, including part of Westmeath; Mullingar and the surrounding areas; Edenderry, north Offaly and part of south Meath; Naas and central Kildare as far as old Kilcullen and the Curragh; Fingal; Drogheda and all south Louth.

THE RUAN RIC LET THEIR DEFENCES DOWN SLIGHTLY AND IN CAME THE IRA

MID-CLARE BRIGADE, 14 OCTOBER 1920

by Joe Barrett

(formerly QM Mid-Clare Brigade IRA and O/C Mid-Clare Brigade flying column)

It has been said that nothing is too hard for a search to uncover. The taking of RIC barracks by an active service unit of the Mid-Clare Brigade IRA early on an October morning in 1920 could be pointed to as proof of the assertion. For a long time the brigade officers had vainly sought a means of getting men inside the barracks with the object of effecting its capture by overpowering the garrison. It was the only way we could contemplate taking the place, as our poorly equipped units could have no hope of carrying it by assault. In fact, it was doubtful whether anything short of artillery would be capable of reducing the building.

Situated in the centre of the Mid-Clare Brigade area, the formidably fortified and strongly garrisoned RIC barracks at Ruan was regarded as a pivotal point in the British system of defence posts in the county. Standing some six or seven miles from Ennis, it commanded one of the approaches to the capital town, and hampered the free movement of battalion and brigade elements. The barracks was a valuable observation post too, and as a receiving and clearing house for information it was a very considerable asset to the enemy intelligence system. It was important to the effectiveness of the brigade that the enemy should be forced to withdraw the garrison, and the IRA officers considered plans to achieve that end. The most satisfactory way to bring it about would be by the capture of the place with its large complement of rifles and revolvers, and stores of ammunition and warlike equipment in general. We in Mid-Clare were in urgent need of military equipment, as, indeed, was every IRA unit in the country. Arms were to be had mostly by wresting them from the enemy, as spoils of war. It was determined by the Mid-Clare officers that, in the process of ridding the area of the Ruan RIC garrison, the police arms and ammunition would be taken as well. How was that purpose to be achieved? That was the problem.

The RIC barracks at Ruan was a three-storey building in which were stationed two sergeants and eleven constables. Built of solid masonry it had been made into a veritable fortress by the garrison with the assistance of military sappers. It was surrounded by an almost impenetrable barrier of barbed wire entanglements, up to a height of five or six feet. All the windows were steel-shuttered and were further protected against attack by bags filled with stones and gravel. Barbed wire screens dropped to the ground from its upper storeys. Altogether, it looked a tough nut to crack, with its appearance of impregnability. It was spoken of as a place that the IRA could never succeed in taking, a point of view that was assiduously encouraged by the police.

Having decided that it should be captured and destroyed the brigade lost no time in grappling with the problem. A constant watch on the movements of the garrison was set up. Their official routine as well as their individual and collective habits were closely observed, day after day and night after night. Within a reasonably short time our intelligence had established contacts within the post and had uncovered a weak chink in the enemy's armour; his Achilles heel had been laid bare. A simple way to overcome the difficulty of getting men inside the building had been found in one of the routine tasks of the garrison.

It was the duty of the constables to collect the milk supply for the barracks from a house that stood 300–400 yards to its rear. The

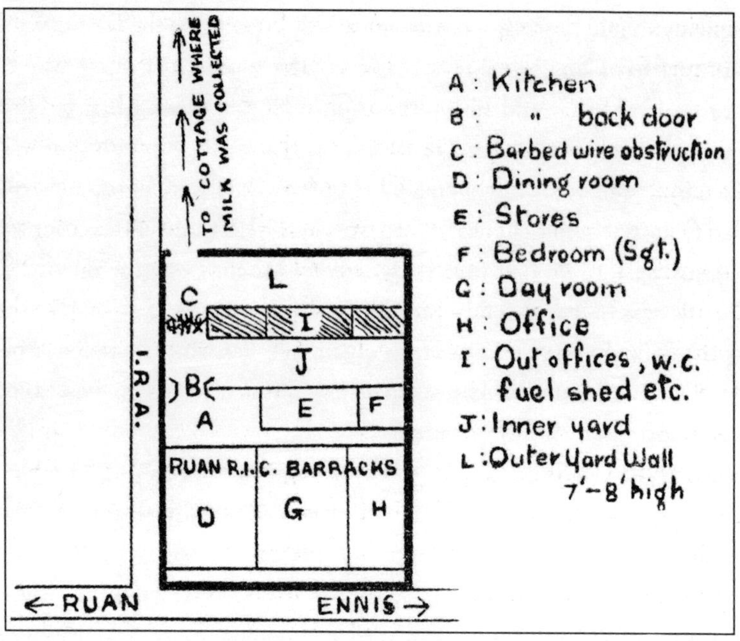

man detailed for the task always left the building by the back door, between seven and eight o'clock in the morning, and proceeded along a passageway between the out-offices and a high wall that enclosed the barrack yard. The passage was about six feet wide and was completely blocked to a height of six or seven feet by a barbed wire entanglement which the constable opened and pushed aside when going for the milk. It was noted that it remained open until he returned, and, what was even more important, our intelligence had discovered that the back door to the barracks itself was left on the latch until he got back with the milk. The discovery of these almost incredible pieces of carelessness by an otherwise watchful garrison provided us with the means of getting men past the defence and into the building. With the barbed wire defences of the passage down, the attacking party would move quickly to the back door and enter. The chances of taking the garrison by surprise at that hour of the morning were considered good, and plans were laid for an almost immediate attempt.

Though the plan was basically simple, its successful implementation depended upon careful attention to detail. Some nights prior to the morning fixed for the operation the ground about the barracks was reconnoitred by Seán Casey, O/C 3rd Battalion, and myself. Though we moved cautiously, dogs barked their objection to the nocturnal intrusion; yet the din they created appeared to have held no special significance for the police, who may not have noticed it at all. Nevertheless, we decided that there should be no barking dogs when the attempt would be made, and that their silence should be ensured by the lying down of a suitable supply of bait and poison beforehand. As a result of the reconnaissance, it was decided that the attackers would approach the barracks on bare feet to avoid the noise which nailed boots would make, particularly along the concrete passageway, in the stillness of the morning. There would be two parties engaged on the job, an assault party proper and a covering force. The group to enter the building would consist of two officers and twenty-nine men, picked from all the units in the brigade for their coolness, courage and resourcefulness.

An elaborate and widespread series of road blocks was made an integral part of the plan of attack, for there was danger that our men engaged would be discovered and encircled by superior enemy forces which could be rushed by lorry from Ennis to Ruan in little more than a quarter of an hour. The road blocks were in two rings, an outer and an inner circle. The inner one, which blocked all the immediate approaches to the barracks, consisted of felled trees and hundreds of tons of heavy stones. Each such barricade was covered by eight shotgun men. The outer protective circle was more far flung and comprised twenty barricades erected at intervals along all roads radiating from Ruan. Some of these blocks were as many as ten miles removed from the barracks. The task of building and manning these networks of obstruction was delegated to the 3rd Battalion, which was assisted by two companies from the 1st Battalion and two from the 5th.

Everything was in readiness for the attack by the evening of 13 October, and the men participating had assembled at various centres. By nightfall we had mobilised at a vacant house about four miles from our objective, and there the nature of the operation was clearly explained to the men. Nothing had been left to chance. A sketch map of the inside of the barracks secured by our intelligence was used to brief the assault party, and this showed that the ground floor consisted of a kitchen, a sergeant's bedroom, a pantry and a hall. It was known that two constables armed with rifles and revolvers kept guard in the kitchen, and to deal with them an officer and four men were detailed. To a section leader and two men was assigned the task of overpowering the sergeant. The subjection of six constables in a large bedroom on the first floor was the objective of a section leader and seven men. To cope with three constables who occupied a medium-sized bedroom on the second floor, a section leader and four men were numbered off, and a section leader and two men were given the job of overpowering a sergeant whose single bedroom was on the same floor. An officer and three men were to act as a general utility group, to give assistance to any section that might need it inside the barracks. Outside, a section leader and two men were to attend to the constable who would go for the milk. When the instruction had been given each section clearly understood what was expected of it. The outside covering force was divided into three sections of seven men, each section under the command of an officer, and instructed to operate in conjunction with ten scouts and five guides.

In the early hours of the morning of 14 October, we advanced towards the barracks. On arrival at a wood on the Dromore estate, about half a mile from our objective, the assault party removed their boots and moved in under the high wall at the rear of the building. Out of sight of the exit they waited noiselessly for the constable to emerge, and once they had seen him clear of the building, they would pad silently on bare feet up the passage that led to the back door of the tall fortress. Not a sound broke the stillness; the dogs of Ruan would bark no more, for the regrettable but unavoidable expedient of spreading poisoned bait had been completely effective. There was an air of tension as the men awaited the appearance of a constable who, all unknowingly, was the key to the situation in every sense of the phrase. Should he fail for some reason to go for the milk that morning, then we would be playing Hamlet with the Prince of Denmark in the wings. Time dragged and minutes seemed like hours. At last there was sound of movement inside the barracks yard. A door had been opened and shut, and there was the noise of the barbed wire entanglement being pushed aside. Footsteps were heard on the passage and out came the constable. He was given a couple of minutes to get clear of the building and to reach the point where a section leader and two men were waiting to pounce on him. Then the signal for the assault was given. Up the passage dashed the Volunteers and in matter of seconds the startled constables who were on guard in the kitchen had been disarmed. Each IRA group moved on to its task with clock-like precision. The sergeant in the ground floor bedroom was a prisoner before he had realised what was taking place. The police who slept on the top floor surrendered without a struggle, so great was their astonishment at finding armed IRA men amongst them, in the imagined security of their fortified post. The only fighting was in the large bedroom in which a gun battle took place between the six constables who occupied it, and eight IRA men. Three of the police had been wounded, one of them fatally, before they surrendered. It was all over within a couple of minutes, and the IRA were masters of Ruan RIC barracks. The enemy wounded were immediately given first aid by our men, and a priest and doctor were hastily summoned. No time was lost in collecting the surrendered arms and ammunition, and the general equipment which included a number of bicycles. The whole was piled into a waiting char-a-banc which then moved off to a pre-arranged destination, under escort. By that time the wounded constables had been moved to a nearby dwelling house and everything possible had been done to make them comfortable. Whilst preparations to demolish the captured barracks were afoot, the members of the garrison were paraded on the road outside by Commandant Ignatius O'Neill. A dishevelled lot they looked, and the story of their complete surprise and utter discomfiture was evident in their unwashed appearance, partly buttoned tunics and unlaced boots.

Sharply O'Neill gave them an order to fall in for foot drill. All complied with alacrity, with the exception of the senior sergeant who obstinately refused to be drilled by an IRA officer. O'Neill, a former Irish Guardsman who had learned his trade the hard way in the 'School of the Soldier "A"' was not the type who would readily tolerate disobedience to a military command that he might utter. The recalcitrant sergeant was apparently possessed of some rudiment of wisdom, however, for he did not persist in his attitude, and sulkily 'fell-in' with the others before it had become necessary for O'Neill to apply some persuasion. Up and down the narrow road marched the bewildered police, the noise their nailed boots made on the road re-echoing in the crisp October air. Half the village watched in astonishment as the peelers 'jumped-to' in response to orders bawled out by O'Neill in a parade ground voice that would have been the envy of any sergeant-major who could have heard it. 'A-bout-turn!' 'Halt!' 'Stand-at-ease!' rang out the familiar foot-drill commands. It was an occasion that will be long remembered in Ruan.

When the demolition of the barracks had been completed by fire, the police were escorted to some houses in which they were given breakfast. They were warned to remain in the houses for at least an hour, and under pressure, an undertaking was forced from them to the effect that they would neither encourage nor participate in any form of reprisal. Local unionists were warned also that their mansions would be given to the flames in the event of people friendly to the IRA being burned as a reprisal for the destruction of the barracks. The warning had the desired effect.

The captured stores were sufficient to equip a fairly strong active service unit, for they comprised fifteen rifles, fourteen revolvers, one automatic pistol, two Verey light pistols, 1,000 rounds of .303 ammunition, 700 rounds of .45 ammunition, fifty rounds of automatic ammunition, 200 rounds of buckshot, a number of Verey light cartridges, a box of assorted ammunition, three boxes of Mills hand grenades and thirteen bicycles. It was a magnificent haul. Well satisfied with the morning's work, the different units that had participated in it set out for their respective areas. One of them, drawn from the 2nd Battalion, narrowly avoided walking into an ambush that had been laid for them by British military at a place called Shallee on the road between Ennis and Ennistymon. Local scouts, however, had learned of the enemy move in good time and warned the IRA men who easily avoided the trap that had been set for them.

A TIPPERARY COLUMN LAYING FOR RIC HAD TO FIGHT MILITARY AT THOMASTOWN

TIPPERARY NO. 3 (SOUTH) BRIGADE, 28 OCTOBER 1920

As told by participants to Edward. J. Delaney

THE THOMASTOWN AMBUSH took place on Thursday morning, 18 October 1920. It had for its unusual feature the surprise of the ambushers themselves, who, busy preparing for their first venture, an attack on a police lorry expected from Thurles, were run into by a lorry load of British soldiers from Templemore. At this time the British reign of terror was mounting to its peak. The newly recruited Black and Tans and Auxiliaries, many of them convicted criminals released from English jails for their fell work in Ireland, were let loose throughout the land, with official incitement to murder. Raids, lootings, sackings, burnings, outrages and shootings were the order of the day. Houses and creameries, villages and towns were pillaged and burned; civilians, young and old, were dragged from their beds in the dead hour of night, and brutally beaten or murdered in presence of their mothers, sisters or wives. Tipperary county came in for its share, and in that year, as early as July, *The Irish Bulletin* reported that Kilcommon (twice), Thurles, Templemore, Emly and Rearcross had been shot-up and partially or wholly wrecked. But intense though the terror was, it did not cow the people, nor did it daunt the IRA or the men of Tipperary, who struck back with vigour.

The 3rd (or South) Tipperary Brigade had for its field of operations the southern portion of the county, an area stretching from the western end of the Glen of Aherlow to the boundary of County Waterford on the south, and extending on its other sides to Tipperary, Hollyford, Rossmore, Dulla, Killenaule and Drangan. In a wide area around Tipperary town operated the 4th Battalion of the brigade and this was the unit responsible for the Thomastown ambush.

The battalion had just organised the No. 1 flying column, composed of two Volunteers from each company, with a few men from East Limerick. Dinny Lacy was in command, with Michael Fitzpatrick from Tipperary as adjutant. Since the column was only in its infancy (and hardy infants they were) no further regular officers had yet been appointed. The column had not yet carried out an engagement on its own, and so its leaders were eager to 'blood' its members, and prove its worth in a clash with the enemy. A suitable opportunity soon offered. Its efficient intelligence officer, Paddy Horan, had reported that a small covered lorry carrying armed police or Black and Tans travelled a few times every week, and regularly every Thursday morning, from Cashel to Tipperary. It was believed that this lorry was on its way from Thurles to Limerick, these two places being strongly held military centres of the time; and that it carried important dispatches which it would be well worthwhile to capture. The battalion too would welcome any opportunity to increase their supply of arms and ammunition, of which they stood in urgent need. Accordingly, at a meeting held at O'Sullivan's farmhouse, Grantstown, a regular rendezvous of the battalion, it was decided, a day or two before 28 October, to ambush this lorry on the Cashel-Tipperary road.

The little village of Thomastown, once an ornament of the Thomastown Estate, stands on this road, half-way between Cashel and Tipperary. About 400 yards on the western or Tipperary side of the village, the site for the ambush was chosen. This site was probably selected by a man with local knowledge, Brian Shanahan of Grantstown, a cool and experienced fighter, who was later to become battalion commandant. At the selected place the road is straight, with dips to east and west. Its southern boundary is the high wall of Thomastown demesne. This wall provided excellent cover, with gaps at intervals through which the ambushers could shoot. It also provided a covered retreat for a considerable distance to east or west inside the wall, after which the ambushers could choose their direction across the undulating countryside.

On the opposite or northern side of the road there is a deep quarry, roughly rectangular in shape, its edge, almost seventy yards long, running right by the road, from which it was separated by a thirty inch high wall, then clean of bushes or trees. On the opposite or inner edge of the quarry there was a bank of clay, the stripping of the rock ledge, which made a rampart. The ambushers behind this rampart could fire across the quarry (a distance of only about sixty yards) at the enemy on the road, without danger to their opposite numbers inside the demesne wall. The ambushed British, therefore, would be exposed to fire from both sides of the road, and they would have no cover. Their nearest mobile reinforcements were at Cashel or Tipperary, six miles off. There were sixteen men in the barracks at Golden, two miles away, but they had no lorry. There were no road blocks to delay other lorries which might happen to come – in fact, the ambush appears to have been decided upon and attempted at short notice, with little if any preliminary planning in detail.

The ambush party consisted of the No. 1 flying column, with the exception of two, who were sent on important duty elsewhere. The column was reinforced by men of the 4th Battalion from the area of Donaskeigh and Donohill, and a small group of experienced fighters from the 3rd Battalion, which operated in the area of Dundrum. The party consisted in the main of sturdy farmers and farm-workers, and a few equally determined men from Tipperary town. They were led by the intrepid Dinny Lacy, a man of high ideals and unflinching courage whose guiding principle was: 'Never ask a man to do anything you would not do yourself.' Lacy had long since left his position as foreman at Dalton's Coal Stores, Tipperary, to devote his whole time and energy to the fight for independence.

The party had spent the night of 27 October a short distance to the north of Thomastown, being quartered in friendly houses in

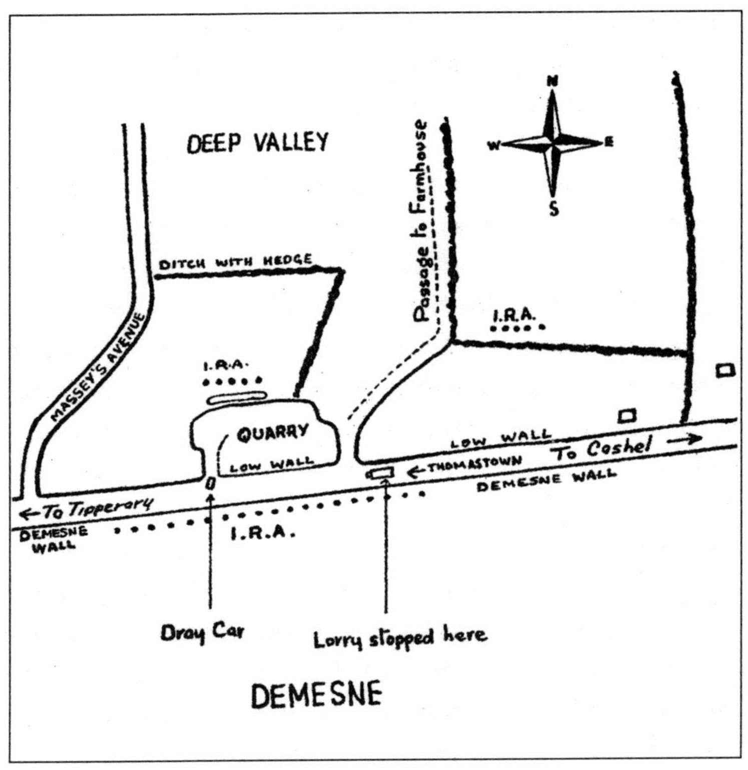

Grantstown and Ballinard. On the morning of 28 October they left their headquarters at O'Sullivan's, Grantstown, and crossed the fields south to the Thomastown road. It was perfect weather, almost like a summer morning. Many of these men were about to receive their baptism of fire, but it seemed to worry them none at all. Many of them, too, were but ill-equipped for the business in hand. There were, perhaps, fifteen service rifles and a few revolvers among them. Others were armed with shotguns, or perhaps single-shot Martini rifles which were of little use. Some few had fifty rounds of ammunition – there were many who had not more than ten. One East Limerick man had but a single-barrelled shotgun and six cartridges. There was one solitary bomb, carried by a 3rd Battalion man, Jim Gorman, and this later proved to be a dud.

The ambushers had allowed themselves time to be in position before the lorry was due. Scouts with bicycles were posted to the east and west, the man to the east being the important one. When he saw the enemy he was to cycle post-haste to the ambush position and pass through, raising his cap once for one lorry, and twice if there were two, so that the hidden ambushers would know what to expect. For the ambush barricade a common dray car was pushed by two Volunteers from a neighbouring farmer's yard and concealed in the entrance to the quarry. A wire was attached to the car by which at the appropriate moment, it was to be pulled across the road by a man inside the wall. It would then, it was hoped, halt the enemy lorry opposite the quarry.

Passers-by were turned back for safety, though children had gone through to the village school. The movements of the column had been observed, rumours spread. Trouble was expected and tension was high in the village. The ambushers were taking up their positions, riflemen behind the quarry, a few men behind the hedge on their eastern flank and the others inside the demesne wall. Dispositions had not been completed, and there were still a few men on the road, when the scout from the village or eastern side arrived at breakneck speed on his bicycle. And almost on his heel came, not the expected police, but a lorry load of the Northamptons from Templemore.

Thereafter everything seemed to happen in an instant, Jack Tierney partly pulled out the dray car (he had to retreat under fire), the enemy stopped short of the ambush position, lining the sides of the lorry with rifles at the ready. Jim Gorman inside the wall coolly pulled out the pin and threw his bomb, which failed to explode, Dinny Lacy shouted 'Hands Up' and fired his revolver, Brian Shanahan and one or two others leaped from the road for the wall and cover as rifles and revolvers on every side spoke their grim message of death. Many of men inside the wall were at a disadvantage, since the lorry had not come into the ambush position, and they had to fire in a direction opposite to what they expected. They soon moved along towards the lorry, however, and improved their positions. The men behind the quarry also moved east as far as cover permitted.

The fight was fast and furious, and lead flew in all directions. People working in the field heard bullets zip through the trees, or saw them cut holes in turnip leaves in the gardens, and they crawled to cover. Children in the village school crouched on the floor and prayed. The Northamptons, said to be on their way to the rifle range for practice at Ballyglass near Tipperary, were getting practice sooner than they expected. They leaped from the lorry, took what cover they could beneath it and between it and the demesne wall and vigorously returned the attackers' fire. The officer moved about it in the open roadway, recklessly urging his men and firing continuously himself. Men inside the wall who fired at him at such close range that they could scarcely miss, saw their bullets take no effect. It afterwards transpired, when his claim for compensation was heard, that he had been wounded in several places. His escape with his life was believed to be due to his wearing chain mail beneath his tunic, as many British officers were then suspected of doing.

Half an hour passed, perhaps more, with the British still stubbornly resisting. There was now the possibility of the police lorry or other lorries arriving, in which case the ambushers, with their depleted ammunition, would possibly be outnumbered and outflanked. Lacy, mindful of this danger, blew his whistle for his men to break off the engagement, and this they did, firing as they went. A few of the men inside the wall went east and then south. The others crossed the main road at the dip to the west of the quarry, and retreated north by Massey's Avenue in the direction of Grantstown and Ballinard; and the men behind the quarry went with them. The avenue runs across a deep valley through which they could escape unseen.

In the withdrawal Lacy had a narrow escape. Just as he leaned back to reload his rifle, a hail of bullets riddled the bushes where his head had been. He and his men, expecting reprisals that night in Grantstown and Ballinard, spent the night on watch there and the 3rd Battalion men returned to their own area. When the firing stopped, the ambushed lorry, with a few soldiers in it, turned and made for Cashel. It returned later with reinforcements from Cashel and Golden, but the ambush party was then clean away. During the shooting, too, a military lorry from Tipperary stopped short of Kilfeacle, over two miles away. Some of its occupants took up positions inside the road ditch and some advanced a short distance through the fields towards Kilfeacle – but they came no further.

The British had by far the worst of the Thomastown engagement. Three soldiers were killed outright and several wounded, and it was believed at the time that the fatal casualties could have been ten or eleven. The only casualty on the IRA side was Michael Fitzpatrick, adjutant of the column, who, early in the fight, was hit three times. His first wound was in the head, probably from a bullet glancing off a stone in the wall. This knocked him back into a partly exposed position. A second bullet went clean through his side, not deeply, and a third entered his thigh, and striking a bone, took a downward direction. This was the bullet which was eventually to give him serious trouble.

Two of his comrades, Jim Bishop and Rody Hanley, helped Fitzpatrick along inside the wall to the west, and thence to the farmyard of Jerry O'Dwyer, which stands far in from the road. Jerry directed them to keep moving south through his farm and out a back way, while he caught and harnessed his pony to the trap, to follow and take them out of the area before the hue and cry would begin. Jerry was soon on his way south, out on the Bansha road and down to Kennedy's, the house deep in the fields to which he had directed them. They had missed their way, but Jerry soon found them at Arthur O'Brien's and brought the wounded man on his back to the trap which he had left at Kennedy's. All through his ordeal Fitzpatrick bore himself with admirable fortitude and courage, never once yielding to pain or showing the slightest sign of fear in his dangerous predicament. At Arthur O'Brien's he had coolly examined the hole in his thigh, and plugged it with cotton wool soaked in iodine from the small first aid kit which he carried.

One of Fitzpatrick's comrades now went to look for Bill Quinlan who was in the neighbourhood, and who would know a safe hide-out. Jerry, with the wounded man and the other, drove by a disused passage through Kennedy's farm towards the Brownbog road, until Devereux's house was reached. Here Fitzpatrick, now almost exhausted, was put to bed. A trusty neighbour was sent to Bansha for Dr Russell, with instructions to cross the fields, avoid the barracks and approach the doctor's house from the rear; and this he achieved without being observed.

Bill Quinlan now arrived and declared Devereux's house unsafe since it was too close to the Brownbog road on which British lorries had been during the previous few days. The wounded man had to endure being dressed again and put into the trap, a severe trial, but he bore it with grit, and he was driven by quiet by-roads to Chris Barron's house in Kilmoyler, where bed was a blessed relief. The doctor who had promptly come out on receiving the call, was brought on from Devereux's to Barron's, where he rendered all the medical aid possible. Probing, however, failed to find the bullet in the patient's thigh, and it was clear to the doctor that Fitzpatrick was a case for hospital and an operation.

With the wounded man in bed at Barron's, Jerry now had to get home, not knowing what had transpired in Thomastown in his absence. Only when he started back did he observe that his two sheep dogs had followed the trap all the way. This suggested the story, if he were held up and questioned, that he had been driving cattle. His pony, 'Irish Eyes', well-known to racing folk, made short work of the return journey, and he reached the southern end of his farm without incident. Leaving the pony and trap by a hedge in the field he cautiously reconnoitred the house. All was quiet so far, so taking a bucket he hurried back to the trap, which he quickly washed at a pond in the field, to remove all possible trace or scent of blood.

That evening, early, after the dead and wounded had been removed to the military hospital in Tipperary, three lorry-loads of Black and Tans arrived at the ambush scene festooned with weapons, and leading a bloodhound, which helped them none at all. (Bloodhounds had already been used in other places in the attempt to trail ambushers, but the Volunteers used pepper to spoil their scents.) It was believed by the military that some of the ambushers were wounded, and the surrounding district was scoured. Houses and farmyards were thoroughly ransacked, gaps and other soft places examined for footprints, people questioned, abused, and threatened at the point of rifle or revolver, and their statements regarding their movements of the morning checked in detail. The local sergeant of the RIC vouched for the good faith of the people – and secretly advised them to look out for trouble, because later in the evening, when the Black and Tans would be drunk he would have no restraining influence – in fact he would probably be in danger himself.

Practically all the people in the village and district left their homes, expecting the worst. The teacher's residence (close by the ambush scene) which the occupants had temporarily vacated three weeks before, was forcibly entered. Portable household articles were loaded on the lorries, and the house and remaining furniture completely burned. Two cocks of hay in a field nearby were burned. Two other houses had their contents partially wrecked. A fire started in one of these died out after burning a hole in the floor. Intense military activity continued in the district for the next few days. One woman returning to her partially wrecked home was refused admission by an armed soldier stationed at the open door. When those who suffered damage claimed compensation from the British they were summoned before a military court in Tipperary barracks, questioned on oath regarding their connections or sympathy with or assistance to 'Sinn Féin' and then informed that the destruction was probably the work of a roving band of Black and Tans, for whom the military disclaimed all responsibility!

We have now to return to the wounded man, who was helpless in bed at Barron's with a bullet in his thigh. Arrangements were being made as quickly as possible for his removal, and on the second Sunday after the ambush Seán Allen, Patrick Deere, and Seán Fitzpatrick, the wounded man's brother (who succeeded him as adjutant) arrived with a hired car and driver to take Michael to Limerick, over thirty miles away. Driving by devious by-roads, they avoided Tipperary town and emerged on the main Limerick road at Monard. They passed through Oola without question, though they overlooked the fact that Michael was still wearing a blood-stained bandage on his head.

They removed the bandage and they continued their journey in a mist to Pallas, there to be halted by a British barricade across the road manned by an armed sentry. Their driver, Tom Behan, himself a British ex-serviceman – and a man of resource – jumped out of the car, ostensibly to put up the hood. As a sergeant came forward from the nearby post, Behan, ignoring the sentry, approached the sergeant, greeted him cheerily as an army comrade, showed his ex-serviceman's badge, produced his army discharge papers and explained that he was driving friends. The sentry had only got as far as looking into the car when the unsuspecting sergeant gave Behan the word to proceed, which he promptly did, with his ambush casualty and three other wanted men, all of whom, doubtless, had been keeping their finger (and toes) crossed!

Fifteen miles more, and Dr Robert's house in Limerick was safely reached. There the good doctor X-rayed the damaged leg. An operation was needed, and the doctor put the patient in his car, to take him to St John's Hospital. They had gone but a short way when the military held them up, but Michael's luck held. The doctor impatiently declared that he had a critical operation case in his car and could not be delayed, and he was allowed to go through. Michael was soon deposited in the hospital, where his chart informed the observer that he was Martin Fitzgerald, who suffered from bone disease. Next morning an operation failed to find the bullet which, owing to movement of the leg, had shifted since the X-ray. Michael had to be taken to the doctor's house for a second X-ray and thence back again to the hospital. Both journeys were safely accomplished, and the second operation located the elusive bullet. The leg, then apparently poisoned, swelled and became painful, and resisted all efforts to heal it. To add to Michael's difficulties, a message came in that he would have to be removed, as the hospital, which was believed to have come under suspicion, was expected to be raided for the wounded man. The leg was now so bad, however, that

Dr Roberts was firm in his opinion that removal would be the end of his patient. So in the hospital Michael had to remain, and the expected raid luckily did not take place.

The weary months dragged on, with the leg apparently a hopeless case – and then, perhaps in answer to prayer, it suddenly took a turn for the better. It continued to improve, and the day came when Michael could stand. Soon he could walk, and one day he ventured abroad for exercise with a friendly fellow-patient, Michael Dore of Newcastle West. On their way back they were held up by Black and Tans, but they bluffed their way through, and they were dismissed as a pair of cripples, with a present of a cigarette each!

Eventually, one day early in May, Michael was discharged. He travelled by train to Limerick Junction, and made his way home from there through the fields. With his leg almost as good as ever, he was soon back on active service, subsequently becoming quartermaster to the 2nd Southern Division.

GRENADE BURSTS HERALDED ATTACK ON ELEVEN LORRIES AT BALLINALEE

LONGFORD BRIGADE, 1–8 NOVEMBER 1920

by General Seán MacEoin, TD

(formerly Vice-Brigadier and Director of Operations, Longford Brigade, IRA, and O/C Longford Brigade flying column)

In September 1920 I was appointed vice-brigadier and director of operations for Longford and a portion of Leitrim and Cavan. The fact that I was then County Centre of the IRB may have led to these appointments. Later on I was elected Provincial Centre. The Longford Brigade, both Volunteers and Cumann na mBan, was fully organised for active service by 1 November, on which date my column was divided into three parts, with my headquarters at Ballinalee, a section at Granard and another at Longford town. An engagement had taken place between the Granard section and the RIC, and the Black and Tans had arrived in Longford and Granard, both of which places were strongly held by the enemy. In Longford town the upper military barracks was occupied by a company of the 18th Lancers, and a battalion of the East Yorks held the lower barracks. The RIC headquarters for the county was also there, and there were posted to it a county inspector and his staff, and a force that comprised a district inspector, two head constables and about fifty constables. Granard was occupied by a district inspector of the RIC, a head constable and about thirty constables. The RIC was grouped under the command of the divisional commissioner, stationed at Kildare.

My headquarters in Ballinalee was connected by telephone to a point outside Longford town. The only method of communication I had with Granard was by runner or dispatch rider, and I was kept informed of events there through the reports of Seán Murphy, commander of the local section. All three sections were organised for the defence of Longford, Ballinalee and Granard, which the enemy was hourly expected to attack, on 1 and 2 November. The British had given towns and villages to the flames in several brigade areas, and we had orders to defend our towns and villages at all costs.

It was difficult to get information about the enemy's plans. On 1 November I was informed that his forces in Longford had been increased and that large reinforcements had also been sent to Granard. I decided to send a reliable officer named Frank Davis into Granard for the purpose of getting first-hand information of the enemy's strength and dispositions. No sooner had I taken that decision than a report came in which stated that a constable in mufti had been to Ballinalee and was on his way back to Granard. Orders to follow him were immediately issued to Davis, who succeeded in overtaking him about a few hundred yards from the parish priest's house on the Granard side of Clonbroney parish church. Fire was opened and the constable was fatally wounded. The shooting was heard by the parish priest, Father Markey. He hurried to the scene and administered the Last Sacrament to the constable, who died a few minutes afterwards. Davis returned to my headquarters accompanied by Father Markey. He made his report and handed over to me the notebook and diary of the constable. The parish priest then put to me the question: 'What am I to do?' In reply I suggested that he should return to the scene of the shooting, have the body removed to a farmhouse and then send his servant boy to Granard, with word that the constable was dead on the road. To that the parish priest replied: 'No, I will not do that. I am not prepared to tell a lie for you or for anyone else, and I can't tell the truth, for I know that it would mean trouble for Davis. I am satisfied that the man is in heaven. If I send a messenger in I am bound to be interrogated and that would create an impossible situation for me.' In consequence of Father Markey's attitude I had to send in word myself to Granard that the constable was dead. The British refused to act on the information, believing it to be a ruse on my part to draw them into difficult country. They would not come out. I next sent word to some people in Ballinalee, who went to the scene of the shooting and took the body into Longford. It had lain on the road over twenty-four hours.

Two lorries of police, which included the district inspector and Black and Tans, went to Father Markey's house on 2 November and arrested him outside his hall door. They interrogated him, and, as we generally called the process, they gave him the 'once over' in violent manner. He refused to make a statement concerning the shooting of the constable near his house, and, in fact, refused to answer any question beyond replying in the affirmative that his name was Patrick Markey, PP. His attitude enraged the police, who insisted that he knew all about the shooting of the constable, whose name was Cooney. When he made no response to the charge, they sentenced him to death. The district inspector gave him permission to retire into the house. When Father Markey had re-entered it he made for the kitchen and escaped by the kitchen door that gave onto a hidden laneway. Despite his sixty-one years he lost no time in covering the approximate four miles that lay between his house and my headquarters on France Road. He sought protection, and the only means that I had of taking care of him were to attach him to the column and place him under orders. He accepted that situation and remained a while at my headquarters, which were about 400 yards from Father Montford's house. As we were likely to come under fire, I decided to move Father Markey to Hargadon's, a very quiet place, about four miles away, and to put a small guard over him. He remained there for some days and I kept in almost continuous contact with him. As the various battles took place, however, we had to move him about a great deal and he suffered considerable hardship, for the weather was severe with frost and snow.

Prior to the events described, the police had been very active in Granard. A district inspector named Daniel O'Keeffe, who was a native of Dungarvan, had issued car permits to some IRA officers, including one to J.J. Brady of the 5th Battalion. It had been observed by the enemy that Brady's car was used by the IRA during attacks upon the upper military barracks in Longford and on the police barracks at Ballymahon and Arva. O'Keeffe was dismissed from the force as a result, and was replaced by a young ex-army officer, who was given orders to take action against the IRA and clean up the area. The new district inspector was fatally wounded in the Greville Arms Hotel in Longford, on the night of 31 October 1920. The IRA, under Vice-Commandant Seán Murphy, occupied positions in the street the same night and an engagement took place during which the police were forced to retreat to their barracks. On 2 November we received information that Granard was likely to be burned. Some slight enemy reinforcements, which consisted of Black and Tans and old RIC, had already arrived there. I proceeded to Granard, taking a section of the column with me, and leaving behind adequate protection for Ballinalee. With Vice-Commandant Murphy's force we took up position at the Catholic church end of Granard and on both flanks. It was then about nine o'clock. Contact was made with the local scouts and they reported that everything was quiet and that there were no enemy patrols on the streets. About eleven o'clock a force sallied forth from the RIC barracks and made straight for the old home of Father Markey. It was a big business premises, owned by his brother James, and situated at the corner of the main street and the Edgeworthstown road. It was unoccupied that night, as, like many other buildings in the town of Granard, it had been vacated by staff and family. We awaited events. The police called for the house to be opened up, and when there was no response they broke in the door, and, having sprinkled the inside of the shop with paraffin, they proceeded to set it alight. Some of them were still in the shop and others were outside on the street when I gave the order to fire. Thirty-five rifles barked at 150 yards' range. Several of the enemy were wounded, and those who had escaped being hit immediately rushed back towards the barracks, dragging their wounded with them. Following their precipitate retreat we put out the fire they had started in Markey's. We remained in Granard until the following morning, and no further action was taken by the enemy. Well satisfied with our work, we then drew up a new plan for the defence of Granard, in conjunction with our previously arranged defence of Ballinalee.

The first report of action by the British in Longford town was received on 3 November. I learned that they were about the town in substantial numbers, drinking heavily, but apart from having arrested a prominent citizen named Francis McGuinness, and having paraded him through the streets with the Union Jack, no other incident occurred until the evening. Then a large convoy of eleven lorries pulled into the town from the Mullingar direction. They searched and damaged St Joseph's Temperance Hall, and were loud in their boasting that Ballinalee was about to suffer.

Ballinalee is built on crossroads and extends from north to south with the main Granard-Longford road forming an intersection in the centre of the village. At its southern end stands the Protestant church and the Catholic church is at the northern end, near a bridge which spans the River Camlin. To the east lies Granard, nine statute miles away, with Longford a similar distance to the west. Outside the village, on the Granard road, stands the national school and the curate's house, marked 6 and 15 respectively on the map. As we could not find out what movement of troops was likely to attack us, my Ballinalee forces were divided into five parts. One was stationed to the west of Doherty's crossroads, one to the east at the school and overlooking the Granard road, one at the Protestant church (2), one on the east side of the village, covering the church and the bridge, and my own headquarters at Rose Cottage (1) on the crossroads. The object was to let the enemy come into the village. Should he divide himself north and south, our forces were to open fire from each end, at the signal of a whistle blast and the explosion of two grenades, and those from the east and west were to close in, so that we would hold all exits from the village. About five o'clock in the evening information was received that the enemy was very turbulent in Longford, and about an hour later news came in that eleven lorries of RIC and Black and Tans had left Longford in the direction of Dublin.

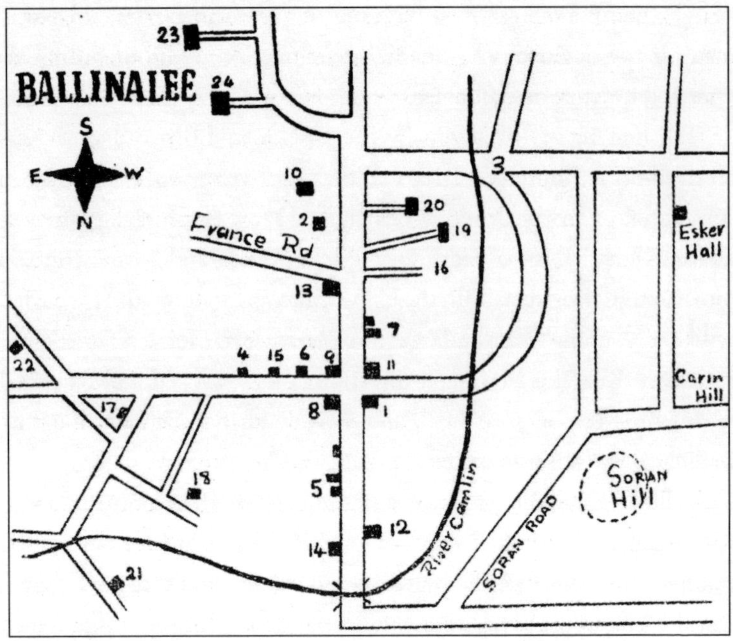

A Novena was being made in the Catholic church at the time, conducted by the local curate, Father Montford, and he had received information that Ballinalee stood in grave danger. He was highly strung, though possessed of great courage, and he advised the people who had assembled in the church to disperse and to clear away from their homes as quickly as possible. I had to countermand his instruction and direct that the people would return to their homes. The Novena was completed, but it was impossible to persuade the people to remain in the village of Ballinalee, with the exception of three families: P.J. Heraty and his family; the sub-postmistress and her family; and Patrick Murtagh and his family. All the others evacuated the town, notwithstanding my efforts to prevent them. The curate even decided he would go with them. I insisted that he should remain, for we were likely to go into action at any time, and, as we were by no means saints, his services would be needed in the event of any of us being seriously wounded. He thereupon ordered me to mobilise my total force, which

I did, falling the men into two lines, with each man carrying his arms and equipment. Addressing them, Father Montford told them that he wished to prepare them spiritually in anticipation of their going into action, but, that as time was short, he would ask them if they all had the intention of going to confession. Having replied in the affirmative, they were told to say a confiteor and then to make an act of contrition aloud. When the prayers had been said Father Montford gave the men general absolution and then asked me if he could leave. In reply I told him that he must either join the parish priest at Hardagon's, or remain in his own house. He refused to do either. I then ordered him to go to the house of James Hosey, about a statute mile from the village, and to remain there until I would relieve him. This he agreed to do.

My officers were then instructed to take up their posts, and the time was about 9 p.m. Food had been distributed and the defence of Ballinalee was ready. I made contact with Longford and found that everything was quiet. Vice-Commandant Murphy was holding Granard in accordance with the defence plans decided upon on the night of 2 November. No report had come in from him and there was no indication that anything was wrong in Granard.

About 11 p.m. a car was signalled approaching from Longford. It had been permitted to pass through by the section at Doherty's crossroads, but on arrival in Ballinalee it was signalled to stop. The only occupant of the car was Rev. Father Clancy, now PP of Cloone in County Leitrim, who had been a British army chaplain. He had been decorated some time previously for bravery during the 1914–1918 war, and had been given an honorary rank. We did not know what his national feelings might be. Just then one of the officers of the column reported that he had been absent from the parade when general absolution was given, and he sought permission to go out to Hosey's to Father Montford. I inquired of Father Clancy whether he had faculties, and, as he replied that he had, I informed him that a young man wished to go to confession. 'Very well,' he said, and drove his car to the foot of the hill near Farrell's shop, where the officer awaited him. He put his stole round his neck and heard the confession. When he had finished and was about to move off the officer greeted him with a friendly 'Goodnight, uncle!' It turned out that Father Clancy had heard the confession of a nephew of his own, and seeing that the young man carried a revolver and a kitbag, his interest rose immediately. 'What's all this about?' he asked urgently, and without giving the young man time to reply he went on to provide the answer to the question himself by observing, 'So you're in this too!' I then decided to inform Father Clancy that we were expecting an enemy force to attack the village and to attempt to burn it. He greatly doubted the likelihood that this would happen and said that he thought it was not possible. I then directed him to proceed to a certain house and to remain there. He thought it inconvenient and suggested Denis Kerrigan's place as an alternative. I agreed, and he went there immediately. Kerrigan was sub-sheriff of Longford and it was he who had revealed the enemy's intentions to Father Montford. The young officer whom Father Clancy had just shrived was attached to my own staff and returned to his post jubilantly. Every man of the column was then prepared, and if needs be, ready and willing to lay down his life.

Just as we had settled down at our positions a report was received from Hart's (4) that there was a red grow visible in the sky over Granard. A dispatch rider was about to be sent to Granard to ascertain the reason for it when information came in that a large number of lorries was approaching Ballinalee from the Granard side of the village, their heavy headlamps lighting up a long stretch of the road. Within a few minutes we learned further that my home and forge, about 600 yards from Hart's had been surrounded. The forge (17) is in a diamond on the right-hand side of the main Granard-Longford road through Ballinalee, and three good roads were available to the British for the purpose of surrounding it. Needless to relate, they found no one at home, and, for some strange reason, they did no damage beyond forcing the door of the house. Almost immediately afterwards they restarted their lorries and drove straight to the village of Ballinalee. All of our posts were alerted and told to prepare for action. Ten lorries swung to the right, down the main street towards the Catholic church

(12), and the leading lorry drew up near the bridge. Another lorry had stopped on the crossroads at the end of the courthouse (9). The British were given an order to dismount approximately midway down the street. We waited patiently, for I had ordered that action was not to begin until the signal was given. The enemy commander blew a single blast of a whistle, and the eleventh lorry turned and fell into line with the other ten. That was grand, as the entire enemy force was then in one compact body in front of my post.

I ordered my section onto the road and to lie over on the roadway at the rear of the lorries. At the same time Seamus Conway, Father Clancy's nephew, moved rapidly down to about centre-ways in the line of lorries, and from his haversack he extracted two Mills No. 4 grenades. Whilst he was doing so the enemy commander ordered some of his force to move to the crossroads where we were in position. When they were within fifty yards of us I called on them to halt and to surrender, and at the same time I gave three blasts on the whistle. Conway promptly delivered his grenades one after the other into the centre of the halted lorries, and we opened fire on the advancing party. Hell then broke loose. The enemy cut out his lights and opened up with a Maxim machine gun. A Lewis gun joined in, firing wildly and even causing casualties amongst enemy troops. When this had gone on for five minutes I again blew my whistle, this time for a ceasefire, and I called upon the enemy to surrender. There was also a ceasefire by the British and they asked for our terms. I demanded an unconditional surrender which they refused to give. 'What then?' they asked, and I replied, 'A fight to the finish.' By that time Conway had rejoined us following his bomb throwing.

As we had but sixty rounds of ammunition per man, it was essential that the other units of the column should join us, and, as they had not appeared, I sent Thomas Early to the church to bring down Captain Hugh Hourican's party. We had to conserve our fire, while the enemy fired in all directions and continued to do so for at least two hours; people who were listening to the sound of firing thought that it went on for about four hours. No reinforcements reached me. A ceasefire was ordered for we had noted that there was a great deal of activity by the enemy under cover of darkness. We were unable to determine what he was up to, until, about five a.m., a lorry engine was started down near the bridge. It was immediately followed by another and one by one the enemy lorries moved off in the darkness. Over the bridge they went and up the Soran road, a very bad by-road which eventually reaches Longford following various turns and twists. They did not arrive back in Longford until 2.30 p.m. on the following day.

Meanwhile, we were in the awful position of having been reduced to five rounds per man, and we could neither waste those precious rounds nor withdraw. So we held our positions and the coming of daylight revealed a remarkable scene. About the area in which the lorries had been drawn up were pools of blood, and strewn all over it were items of military equipment, revolvers and thousands of rounds of .303 ammunition. There were also boxes of chocolates, boxes of boot polish and every conceivable commodity, all of which apparently had been looted from the shops in Granard. Thus, it happened that my men, who had commenced the engagement with sixty rounds apiece, ended up with 500 or more rounds each.

About 9 p.m. Johnny Collumb arrived from Granard with the information that many houses had been burned in the village, and that practically every house had been looted and robbed; that Vice-Commandant Murphy, having noted the extent of the enemy forces, and having come to the conclusion that his own force was inadequate for the defence of the town, had withdrawn about five miles in the direction of the Cavan border. He failed to report to me at Ballinalee or bring his force in that direction. A charge was subsequently made against him, but he was acquitted on the grounds that his force was inadequate and that the orders were not written or sufficiently detailed to enable him to carry them out.

Father Clancy had barely arrived at Kerrigan's when he saw the advance of the enemy forces. He counted the lorries, as I did, and we later agreed about the number of them. The military commander in Longford, in his report of the operation, stated that a number of RIC, led by a senior officer, the divisional commissioner from Kildare, had asked him for a military escort, and he gave them one lorry which carried an officer and twenty men. On his return to Longford on the afternoon of 4 November, the officer, who had been in charge of the military escort reported that they had been ambushed at Ballinalee by a huge force which numbered several hundreds. According to him, numbers of the enemy were seen to fall in the course of an engagement which lasted for several hours. He said that they succeeded in beating off the ambushers eventually and returned to barracks with one killed and some others slightly wounded.

At Hosey's, Father Montford listening to the explosions, the rifle and machine-gun fire in the distance, came to the conclusion that we were all killed and said so. With two others for an escort, he left Hosey's and, having crossed the River Camlin, sought refuge in St Mary's Seminary in Moyne. The pastor, Father Markey, remained at Hargadon's, quite jubilant and confident that none of our forces had been killed.

About four o'clock on the afternoon of 4 November all the various units of the column reported for duty. A new defence of Ballinalee was prepared, for I was of opinion that the enemy would not leave us undisturbed. I moved my headquarters south of the Protestant church to a position on the France Road to Cavan through Gurteen. I commandeered the rectory, which was occupied by the Rector, the Rev. H.J. Johnston, and I also took over O'Farrell's, Gurteen; Gilshenan's, and James Archibald's house and forge on the France Road. My colleague, Seán Connolly, who had been sent to Roscommon by GHQ, sent word that, if required, he was prepared to bring a force from Roscommon to help me with the defence of Ballinalee. I replied asking him to come at once.

On the night of 1 November I had started writing my report for the chief of staff and the director of intelligence. I had it finished by the morning of 3 November, and it included, for the information of the chief of staff, my new plans for the defence of Ballinalee, which had been hurriedly drawn up. In accordance with the plan, the Granard and

Longford units were brought into Ballinalee, so that a full mobilisation of all our arms, ammunition and equipment was made for the defence of the village, Seán Connolly arrived on the morning of 5 November, and was accompanied by Commandant Bill O'Doherty, Strokestown, of the Roscommon Brigade, and by a number of riflemen from the same brigade. Having outlined to Seán Connolly, my proposed defence of the village, and having explained our responsibility and duty to protect Father Markey, I then told him that I was going to bed, to get my first sleep in seventy-two hours. Connolly checked the defence posts and decided to alter one of them from Croppy's Hill (16) back to Rose Cottage (1). He placed Lieut M. Kenny in charge of that post. I had been about two hours in bed when a dispatch was brought to Glishenan's where I was sleeping. There was considerable commotion amongst the guards, but the dispatch bearer insisted upon seeing me. The dispatch was from Lieut Kenny who commanded the Rose Cottage post, and it simply amounted to mutiny. He claimed that the original position in which he had been placed was the proper one, and that Rose Cottage would be untenable. I upheld the authority of Seán Connolly and, having ordered Lieut Kenny to maintain the post at Rose Cottage, I issued a stern order that any attempt at disobedience or neglect of duty would be drastically dealt with in the future. I then went back to bed and slept for two more hours. Seán Connolly had returned to Gilshenan's at the end of that period and together we discussed the question of the Rose Cottage post. It was decided to evacuate it and to re-occupy the original position at Croppy's Hill. Seán Connolly issued the necessary order himself. We were determined to hold Ballinalee, and to defend it at all costs. The enemy's set-back on the night of 3 November and morning of 4 November had been his first defeat in an attempt to burn a village.

The people of Ballinalee, including Father Montford, did not return before 7 November. In the meantime, the curate's house had remained unoccupied. Word was sent to us that a small enemy force would come to Ballinalee, to remove the widow and the family of the constable who had been shot near Father Markey's house, together with their furniture and effects, and that it had no other duty to perform. It was decided that no action would be taken against the enemy unit. An officer of the column named Barney Kilbride, who had been finding difficulty in sleeping on the hard ground round by the Protestant church, decided that Father Montford's bed was much better suited to the purpose. On his next break from duty he gaily retired to rest in the priest's house and was there when the enemy force arrived in Ballinalee for the purpose of removing the dead constable's family and effects. Two lorries drew up at Father Montford's house. It was open, and the military went in and upstairs where they found our friend in bed. The British officer inquired if he was the priest. Kilbride replied that he was not. He said that he was the priest's boy and told the officer to get to hell out of that. He was fully dressed in bed, but had the bedclothes pulled over himself, and had his revolver by his side underneath the clothes. The British officer apologised and withdrew. Barney Kilbride, feeling that in certain circumstances the hard ground by the Protestant church might have more to commend it as a resting place than the curate's bed, promptly rejoined his unit.

The family of Constable Cooney having been removed to Longford together with their effects, tension grew in Ballinalee. The night of 5 November was one made forever memorable as the result of a weird experience. All along our defence line one half of the column had been resting in the fields and in the graveyard whilst the other half remained on duty and on the alert. About midnight a series of lights started up on our right front, about two miles distant in the direction of Granard. Individual points of light were visible over a three-mile stretch, which extended almost to Doherty's crossroads, from which point we had telephonic contact with Longford. We contacted scouts who had been placed on all the outlying roads in the Granard direction, but none of them had anything to report. Nevertheless, it appeared that a large encircling force was approaching the village of Ballinalee. We calculated that there must be more than 2,000 men participating in the operation, but we wondered why they were making their advance so obvious by displaying so many lights. The only explanation of the lights that we could think of was that the nature of the country was making it difficult for the different enemy groups to maintain contact with one another in the darkness. We also came to the conclusion that our position had been given away to the enemy. It was a distinct possibility. For one thing, we had allowed enemy elements to enter Ballinalee to remove Constable Cooney's family and possessions. There was also the question of an intelligence agent whom I had employed and who was a prominent Freemason. He had been sent into Longford to get first-hand information of the enemy's plans and had returned with his report. As far as he could find out it had been determined to give Ballinalee a wide berth for a few days until reinforcements had been secured. He also brought back details of the losses suffered by the enemy in the battle of Ballinalee, and the advice that no movement was contemplated by the British other than the removal of the dead constable's family and effects. I had absolute confidence in this intelligence officer, notwithstanding his association with the enemy and the Masonic Brotherhood, and I was certain that I could trust him. Still, Seán Connolly and the other senior officers were uneasy. They were of the opinion that there was a very large enemy force advancing against us, that if we remained in our positions we would be encircled and that daylight would find us in serious difficulty. Longford was checked again and they assured us that there had been no enemy movement from that point. The scouts on the approaches were checked again and they too reported no enemy movement. It was puzzling and, following long argument and conference, I decided to withdraw the column to positions that would be outside an encircling ring. When we had travelled about three miles in the darkness, and had reached Early's, which overlooked McEoin's forge, I ordered a halt. There we found that what we had thought was an encircling army was nothing other than 'will-o'-the-wisp' over that three-mile stretch of moor and bogland. It was my first experience of this extraordinary phenomenon and, having regard to the circumstances, it was both disconcerting and terrifying. We returned to the France Road wiser men, dejected because we had made such fools of ourselves. Mr and

Mrs John Mullen set out to compensate us by preparing a breakfast of bacon and eggs for the entire force. We were very grateful to them though they had no cause to be thankful to us for, when the column had finished breakfast, little remained of a very fine pig which had been hanging as bacon from the kitchen ceiling. After breakfast we returned to our posts. Father Markey said Mass for us, and, following a long discussion with me, he returned to Hargadon's where he remained for some days.

We continued to hold Ballinalee. It is not my intention to give details of our day-to-day activities in this article, but mention should be made of some things of note which occurred during our first week in occupation of the village. One morning a signal was received that a lorry and a car were approaching Ballinalee. They were allowed in, for, as the village was firmly held, they could not get out again unless permitted by us.

The vehicles were drawn up at Rose Cottage, and I sent down Captain Seán Duffy to question the occupants. It transpired that they were pressmen, and he gave them a short account of the engagement of the night of 3 November. They then interviewed Mr and Mrs Heraty, who had remained in their house throughout the whole of the fighting in the village and who had observed much of the battle and the retreat of the lorries without lights and in disorder. The pressmen then left Ballinalee. About midnight the approach of a lone car was signalled. It stopped near Father Markey's house and the occupant, who inquired for me, said that he had an urgent message from the 'Big Fellow', as Michael Collins was known to all of us. No chances were taken with the midnight motorist. He was driven round in circles before being brought to my headquarters on the France Road. There he handed me a calling card belonging to the 'Big Fellow', and written on it in ink were the well-known initials, 'M.O.C.'. He informed me that he was Patrick Quinn of the *Irish Independent* and that he had accompanied the pressmen to Ballinalee earlier in the day. Whilst on the way back to Dublin he had discovered that one of the party was in reality a prominent Scotland Yard detective. He reported this to Collins immediately that he arrived in Dublin, and Collins had ordered him to return to Ballinalee at once, find me and inform me of his discovery. I then gave him a message for the 'Big Fellow', to the effect that I was satisfied that it did not matter if there had been twenty or a hundred Scotland Yard detectives with the pressmen; that it would have made no difference to my defence measures and that we were ready for any emergency. I gave Quinn a second report for Collins concerning the latest situation in Ballinalee. We were then full of confidence and, perhaps flushed with our success in the previous engagement; we felt that we could take on any army, notwithstanding the fact that a short time previously we had been shaken to our finger tips by the will-o'-the-wisp!

Father Montford had returned to his house, and I slept there some nights, adopting the idea of Barney Kilbride. One morning Father Markey came down to Father Montford's, and they both went into conference in the dining-room while I lay in a small room overhead. There was a knock at the hall door. Maggie McDowell, the curate's housekeeper, who was a member of Cumann na mBan, opened it to admit the Most Reverend Dr Hoare, Bishop of Ardagh and Clonmacnoise. He was admitted to the dining-room where pastor and curate had been in conference, and he immediately challenged Father Markey with being absent from his house while no one could tell where he was to be found. To this Father Markey made no reply, and he was then challenged to state why he had left the body of a Catholic lying on the road for twenty-four hours. His Lordship demanded to know the history of the case, and in a loud voice he condemned Father Markey's action. As the parish priest made no reply to all this, his Lordship inquired whether he was dumb, and then informed him that he was suspending him. Father Markey interjected: 'My Lord, you are not aware of the facts.'

'Then what are the facts?' the Bishop demanded again; but the parish priest made no reply. Turning to Father Montford, the Bishop asked: 'What did you do in all this?'

'Nothing, my Lord,' he replied, 'it was in the upper part of the parish.' His Lordship then told Father Markey that all who had taken part in the incident would be condemned from the altar on the following Sunday. Father Markey said that he could not and would not do that, and repeated that his Lordship was not aware of the facts. The Bishop then left and slammed the hall door as he went. When he had gone I appeared on the scene and enquired of Father Markey why he had not given him the facts. Father Markey replied that it would only be an embarrassment to him and that what he did not know would not trouble him. I then referred to the suspension, and he said: 'That's all right.'

On the following Sunday, his Lordship, having spoken sternly from the pulpit and condemned us, I decided to go myself to Longford to give him the facts of the situation. He received me at the Bishop's Palace, and I explained to him that I was a properly appointed officer, serving a lawful government through its Minister for Defence and his headquarters staff; that the government had been voted into office by the elected parliament of the Irish people; that I was fighting a defensive battle against the enemy; that this was a mother country and that the Irish bishops had declared that it was entitled to its freedom. I showed him that every operation of ours was carried out in accordance with the usages of war and that we took life only in self-defence and in defence of the nation and its parliament. His Lordship then said: 'As a loyal son of the Church, do you not think that you should have informed me of all this before now? How did you expect that we were to know of the organisation of the armed forces? There has been no declaration by the government or parliament to the effect that you are acting under their control, but now that I see that you are a properly constituted force my words of condemnation do not apply to you. You are not privateers, but the armed forces of the state. I wish you success.' He then gave me his blessing and I took my leave having, for the future, a real friend in the Bishop of Ardagh and Clonmacnoise. His attitude following my explanation of the facts did not surprise me, for as a young priest he had served three months in jail for his support of the Irish tenant farmers during the Land War.

We remained in undisputed possession of Ballinalee and district. Breastworks had been thrown up, trenches cut and communication lines established. Still the enemy did not interfere with us, though every day a large number of his lorries left Longford and passed through Edgeworthstown which is on the way to Granard. They followed the same road from Longford to Granard that they had used on the night of 3 November.

When the enemy did not come to us, I decided that we should take the initiative and go to him. Accordingly, I withdrew my forces from Ballinalee and proceeded to Ardagullin which is on the main road from Edgeworthstown to Granard. There we mined the roads and took up positions. Snow had fallen and there was hard frost. When we had held the positions for two nights and a day we received the astonishing information that the enemy had entered Ballinalee in force. He had ejected from their houses Pat Farrell and his family (7) and Father Montford (15), and had occupied both places and the schoolhouse (6). Soberly we took up our mines and carried them to a new headquarters which I set up at James Kiernan's of Drumeel, on the France Road. James was a prominent supporter of the Irish Parliamentary Party. Nellie Kenny, a member of the Cumann na mBan, was sent to Ballinalee to scout the position there and to find out the defence posts put up by the enemy. She reported back with a map which showed the defences at Farrell's, and with the information that both Father Montford's house and the schoolhouse had been vacated. I then prepared plans for an immediate attack on Farrell's. In accordance with these the column moved from Drumeel to Ballinalee, on 8 November, and we took up positions on all roads leading to the village. An attack was launched in force against the front and rear of Farrell's. Before it began Seán Duffy and I had succeeded in placing a mine on the end window of the building. We crawled on our stomachs in the frost, pushing the 56 lb mine in front of us and carrying with us the detonator and cable. We cut through the strands of barbed wire at the gable end of Farrell's and placed the mine on a windowsill. We attached the cable to our electric detonator and withdrew with the cable to Keenan's out-offices, facing the end of Farrell's and then attached our exploder. All was then ready for the attack, and we called upon the enemy to surrender. He refused to do so. We then exploded the mine and it blew the ceiling, shutters and the end of the house high in the air. Of the police whose posts had been at that end of the house, three were killed and several wounded. The engagement continued from midnight until 7 a.m., when we withdrew to Drumeel, on the France Road. We had no casualties, but the whole force was greatly fatigued following the Ardgullion episode and the night-long attack. About midday, when we had barely rested, an enemy force several hundred strong, re-entered the village and re-occupied the schoolhouse and Father Montford's house. When the British had settled in, they burned Duffy's of Cavan and the forge. Moving out to the France Road they also sent up in flames the house of Commandant Seán Connolly, who had by that time returned to Roscommon. Back in the village again they burned Hannigan's, Bracken's, Heraty's, Fox's, Early's and my own forge and house. We went immediately to Connolly's, but it was beyond aid when we got there, so we proceeded without delay to McGrath's Corner (13). It was still broad daylight and there was snow on the ground. Farrell's had been evacuated by the enemy and that end of the village was completely clear of his forces. We pushed down the village and had got as far as Farrell's (7) when a howling mob of Blank and Tans, RIC and military appeared at the top of the hill, at Rose Cottage (1). We promptly opened fire upon them and gave them ten rounds rapid. They broke immediately and fled to the schoolhouse and to Father Montford's house. Rockets and flares were sent up by them, calling for reinforcements, and they remained within the relative safety of their new posts, all the approaches to which had been blocked by extensive barbed-wire entanglements.

James Mackey Wilson, HM Deputy Lieutenant, brother of Field Marshal Sir Henry Wilson, lived in Currygranne House, about a mile and a quarter from Rose Cottage. I approached Currygranne with the intention of burning the place as a reprisal, as I had been authorised to do by GHQ. Whilst on the way to the house I thought the matter over. There were not in the brigade area more than a dozen houses that could be burned as reprisals for British outrages, and there was only one Wilson connected with the chief of the imperial staff of Great Britain. On that account I came to the conclusion that it would be wiser to adopt different tactics. I called upon Wilson, brought him out and showed him Duffy's and Connolly's on fire. I reminded him that the destruction had been carried out by forces acting under his brother's orders, and I insisted that he should write to Sir Henry and inform him that, if the British burned another house in County Longford, Currygranne would follow it up in flames, and, not only that, but he, James Wilson, would very probably die with it. He said that the field marshal would pay no heed to such a request. 'Well,' I replied, 'in that case it will be too bad for Currygranne and for you.' I added that, should he attempt to leave Currygranne, I would have him executed before he had reached Edgeworthstown or Longford. Before I left him I said that if the battle was left to the military forces of both sides to fight it out, I would, in the name of the government of the Republic, guarantee protection of life and property to him and all others of his sort in the county, on condition that they remained strictly neutral.

Next to receive a formal call from me was the Reverend H.J. Johnston, the Rector of Ballinalee, whose house I had previously occupied. I informed him that I was aware that he was an honorary colonel of the Ulster Volunteers, a member of the Orange Order and chaplain to the British forces then in occupation of the village. I pointed out his close association with the enemy forces, which he knew to have burned and destroyed the houses of innocent people, and said that his connection with the enemy was of a much more intimate kind than Father Markey's association with us. I explained to Mr Johnston that Father Markey had been sentenced to death by the British, and told him to inform them that Father Markey would be at home on the following day and every day afterwards, and that should they impose any hardship, indignity, injury or penalty upon the parish priest, I would be reluctantly compelled to deal likewise with himself. Mr Johnston replied that such would be an outrage. I agreed but added that it would also be an outrage if Father Markey was murdered; that by taking this step I was preventing two outrages. Mr Johnston went to the troops in Ballinalee. What he told them I do not know. I ordered Father Markey to be returned to his house and at 11 a.m. on the following day, a lorry load of RIC, and Black and Tans, and a lorry load of military drew up in front of it. We closely watched developments as the enemy officers left the lorries and proceeded to Father Markey's hall door. Later we learned the details of what passed between them and the parish priest. The officer in charge first enquired whether he was Father Markey, and having received a replay in the affirmative, he asked further whether he required any protection. Father Markey said: 'Protection from whom? You are the only people I require to be protected against.' The officer then blandly informed him that he was in no danger whatever from His Majesty's forces, and assured him that he would remain unmolested for the future.

I am glad to say that, with one exception, no house was burned in County Longford after that evening of 9 November 1920. The exception referred to, took place after the Clonfin ambush on 2 February 1921, when Commandant Finnegan, having expended all the ammunition for his short carbine, threw the rifle away and picked up a new one from a wounded Auxiliary, together with its ammunition. He failed, however, to remember that he had, with great care, engraved his name, rank and address on the discarded rifle. The following day, his home was raided and the enemy found a large number of old shotguns, partially constructed grenades, etc., in the house, which they promptly set on fire. They defended this action on the ground that the house was not private property, but an enemy post. Smith's house at Rathmore suffered a like fate for a similar stated reason.

Father Markey returned from the column to his parochial duties, and lived in Ballinalee until the Truce. I like to remember that, until their deaths, which occurred in the same year, he and the Reverend H.J. Johnston regularly signed my nomination papers for Dáil Éireann.

FOURTEEN BRITISH OFFICERS AND AGENTS EXECUTED IN DUBLIN ON 'BLOODY SUNDAY'

DUBLIN BRIGADE, 21 NOVEMBER 1920

by Piaras Béaslaí

(member of GHQ, 1918 to the Truce; formerly editor An t-Óglach, *Director of IRA Publicity and member of Dáil Éireann)*

In order to understand the chain of events which led to the grim happenings in Dublin on the day popularly known as 'Bloody Sunday' – 21 November 1920 – it is necessary to go back a number of years, and to grasp some aspects of British administration in Ireland.

One of the principal methods by which English governments had kept Ireland in subjection, particularly in modern times, was a highly organised and efficient system of espionage. Even, in the times of the first Elizabeth and James of England, Secret Service money was spent lavishly on spies, informers and traitorous Gaels, and on the hiring of assassins and poisoners. In later times the British system of espionage again and again nullified the efforts of patriots, and contributed more than anything else to defeat the attempts at insurrection in 1798, 1848 and 1867. Large sums of money were expended on this work, and particular use was made of such Irishmen as could be purchased, whose knowledge of their country and countrymen rendered them invaluable to the enemy. It was commonly said, and not altogether without justification, that the secret organisations of the United Irishmen in 1798 and the Fenians (or 'IRB') in 1865 were 'honeycombed with spies and traitors'; and this situation created a natural suspicion and mistrust among potential revolutionaries, and caused many sincere and patriotic Irishmen to fight shy of secret organisations aimed at attaining national independence.

After the debacle of 1867 the IRB continued in existence, but its numbers were few, and, owing to the widespread 'intelligence' system possessed by the British government, all those who held separatist, or what were then called 'extreme' nationalist opinions were well known to the agents of that government.

In the period of so called 'constitutional agitation' which followed 1867, the British administration relied chiefly on the Royal Irish Constabulary as their eyes and ears, as far as the country outside Dublin was concerned, and in the capital, the obvious centre of all kinds of national organisation, upon their detective force, of which a special branch had been formed for what was called 'political work' – besides the expenditure of a great deal of Secret Service money. The detective force knew all the men of revolutionary views and associations. They watched and reported all their movements and activities, all those in whose company they were seen, what houses and other places they frequented, and a variety of other matters, which enabled the authorities to feel that they knew exactly how far these men were a danger, and how to arrest them all simultaneously if at any time it was found expedient to do so.

These tactics had proved effective in 1865, when James Stephens and other members of the supreme council of the IRB were surprised and arrested in their houses without any difficulty. In those days the membership of the IRB was very great, but in later times the British government was satisfied that it was not numerous enough to be a menace, and was, perhaps, lulled into a false sense of security by the reports of agents. For the first time in 150 years British intelligence in Ireland was completely baffled when the insurrection of 1916 was organised without arousing suspicion, and took the British authorities entirely by surprise. The generation of 1916 was a better educated one and native spies and informers were not so easy to find as in earlier years. However the 'political' detectives of Dublin showed little compunction when they swooped on the disarmed prisoners of the Rising in Richmond barracks, and picked out some 200 of these – men known to them – for court martial and the prospect of facing a firing squad. Some of them showed themselves particularly zealous and officious in this dirty work, and, when called to give evidence at courts martial, did all in their power to secure the conviction of prisoners. Those of us who may not have realised the importance and danger of enemy intelligence work learned a lesson on the floor of the great gymnasium in Richmond barracks on Sunday 30 April 1916. One man there was Michael Collins who, fortunately, was not long enough in Dublin to be known to them, and the lesson was not lost on him.

The chain of events leading to 'Bloody Sunday' may be considered to have begun in the summer of 1918, when England was at war with Germany, and the Irish people with most of their leaders imprisoned and deported, found themselves faced with the threat of conscription, compulsory military service in the forces of England. At that time some young members of the 'political' section of the 'G' Division (the detective force), having thought for themselves and read and studied the course of events, found themselves in secret sympathy with the fight for Irish freedom. They decided to assist the work, not by resigning, but by staying in the force and secretly helping the cause of Ireland. Eamonn Broy, Joe Kavanagh, James MacNamara, and later David Neligan, through various intermediaries, got in touch with Michael Collins, and this was the beginning of a counter-intelligence system, organised by Collins, which was to undermine all the enemy's plans and machinery, and nullify his efforts again and again. The enemy's greatest and most formidable weapon was turned against himself, and no work was a greater factor in the successes achieved in the fight for Irish freedom than the intelligence system so efficiently organised by Michael Collins.

By 1920 the 'political section' of the detective force had ceased to be a danger to the leaders of the Irish army. Some who had shown excessive zeal in the service of the enemy had met sudden deaths, others were unable, even if willing, to function effectively; but every movement or plan of the enemy was known to our intelligence department. Again and again, an attempt at a 'round-up', a series of sudden, simultaneous raids, brought no results, as we had prior knowledge of the enemy's intentions.

The British government had now flooded Dublin with intelligence officers who moved among the people in the guise of civilians. These men were for the most part English, and lacked the necessary knowledge of Ireland and Irish conditions to do their work effectively, and reports sent in by them and intercepted by us showed a ludicrous ignorance of what it was their business to know. Some Secret Service men wisely drew their money and did nothing. One of these actually stayed in Vaughan's Hotel, at a time when it was frequented daily by Collins and other heads of the army, and even met and conversed with some of them, without showing any curiosity as to who or what they were. Others, however, were very active, and even, in a few cases, dangerous. One English agent named Jameson, who had previously posed in labour circles in England as a 'red' revolutionary, came to Ireland and actually got in touch with Collins, and at first even won his confidence. This man was ultimately unmasked and met the fate of a spy. After his death the English authorities frankly admitted that he was a Secret Service agent, an admission which caused much indignation in English labour circles, where he had acted the part of an agent provocateur.

But – as Mr Gladstone said of Ireland when he was carrying out a policy of coercion – the British government had not 'exhausted the resources of civilisation' in dealing with Ireland. A new policy had been secretly decided on early in 1920, and March of that year was to see its first results. At the beginning of the month a letter from a British intelligence officer who had just arrived in Dublin, to another, was intercepted by Collins. It referred to 'our little stunt' and stated that he had been 'given a free hand'. On 16 March, Lord Mayor Tomás MacCurtain of Cork received by post a note bidding him 'prepare for death'. Four days later he was murdered in his house by a party of men with blackened faces, one of whom bore a striking resemblance to the officer to whom the intercepted letter was addressed. This outrage was followed by other murders in different parts of the country. The new British policy was simply the assassination of Irish leaders and active Volunteers. A letter intercepted by Collins written by a divisional commissioner of the RIC referred to 'the new policy and plan – the stamping out of terrorism by secret murder'.

In May 1920, a number of members of Dáil Éireann and prominent Sinn Féiners received through the post sheets of Dáil Éireann notepaper on which was typed the words: 'an eye for an eye, a tooth for a tooth, therefore a life for a life'. These were intended to prepare the way for a series of assassinations, and the use of Dáil Éireann notepaper was obviously intended to cause mystification as to the authors of the murders. The Dáil notepaper had been seized by police during a raid on the Sinn Féin offices in Harcourt Street, Dublin, some months before and was actually being used by detectives of the political section for the writing of their reports.

Some reports typed in the Dublin district intelligence office in Dublin Castle had been intercepted by agents of Michael Collins. It occurred to him to ask a typewriting expert to compare the typescript in these documents with the 'death notices'. The expert was satisfied that the 'notices' were typed on the same machine. One of the intercepted letters contained a reference to a typist in the intelligence office which enabled us, through a new source of information, to identify the room in which the 'death notices' had been typed and the officer responsible. The new source of information was a young lady employed as a shorthand typist in Dublin district command in the Castle. I knew her well and knew that her sympathies were with the cause of Ireland. I approached her and brought her into contact with Michael Collins and she became a most useful and important intelligence agent. Through her we learned all the personnel of the English intelligence staff, their appearance, hours, haunts and habits. A list was made of all the civilians employed in connection with the military staff at Dublin Castle, and other military posts, and some of these were got in touch with. A list was made out of all serving officers living outside barracks, and, through various agencies, a number of Secret Service men living as civilians in Dublin were traced. Some of these were later identified as having been concerned in murders of civilians which occurred in Dublin and elsewhere.

One notable murder was that of John Lynch of Kilmallock, who was shot in his bed in the Exchange Hotel, Dublin, on 22 September 1920, by a party of officers and RIC, some in uniform and some in mufti. It seems probable that the murderers had confused him with Liam Lynch. Some of the assassins on this occasion were positively identified and paid the penalty on 21 November. One of them was living in a lodging-house in Mount Street under the assumed name of Patrick MacMahon. He was really an English intelligence officer named Angliss, but was able to assume an Irish accent and pass himself off as an Irishman. When 'in his cups' he avowed his crime to a trusted girlfriend, who imprudently gossiped about it, and thus the news reached our ears. When I told Collins what I had heard, I found he knew more of 'MacMahon' than I did myself.

It is not necessary to go into further details. Our headquarters staff accumulated unmistakable evidence that there was a conspiracy to murder Irish citizens, planned, engineered and carried out by the intelligence department of the English forces in Ireland, with the sanction and approval of their general headquarters' staff. We knew that a number of these men, who were involved in the conspiracy, were living among the people, disguised as civilians and acting as spies. As such they were liable to the death penalty, apart from the fact that they were known to be implicated in the murders of Irish citizens. In fact, it would have been impossible for some of these murders to be carried out without the connivance of all the military authorities.

These were the considerations which caused the Minister for Defence and the headquarters staff to come to the stern determination to break up this murder gang, punish the murderers and baffle their conspiracy by simultaneous action against all who could be reached on the morning of Sunday, 21 November 1920. A list of names and addresses was carefully compiled in which only those whose guilt was certain were included. It was arranged that armed parties selected from the intelligence squad and the Dublin Brigade should visit these various houses on the Sunday morning and execute justice on the malefactors.

On the Saturday night preceding the fatal day, a number of officers of GHQ and some brigade officers assembled upstairs in the smoke-room of Vaughan's Hotel. Collins was there, Dick McKee and Peadar Clancy, on which latter two, as brigadier and vice-brigadier, the lion's share of the responsibility for the arrangements for the morning had fallen. I was there for a time, having business with Dick McKee, but was called away from the room to meet Conor Clune of Quin, County Clare, who had arrived on a visit to Dublin and was anxious to see me. He had been brought to the place by Seán O'Connell. I stayed downstairs chatting with the two. (Clune was a fluent Irish speaker and an ardent Gael.) Meanwhile, the meeting upstairs broke up and those present left the hotel. They were only just gone when the place was raided by a party of Auxiliaries who had surrounded the hotel. They seemed to have good information and rushed upstairs with drawn guns to the smoke-room. In the confusion caused by their inrush I succeeded in slipping out into the back garden and scaling the wall which divided the place from the garden next door. I took refuge in a ruined stable, just in time to escape the searchlight. Seán O'Connell also escaped out the back, but poor Clune, not knowing his danger (he had, of course, no knowledge of what was planned for the morning) stayed behind, was duly arrested and brought to Dublin Castle. Later that night, the enemy effected a more important capture – perhaps their most important success in all their struggle with us. About an hour after midnight a house in Lower Gloucester Street where Dick McKee and Peadar Clancy were staying (both men being 'on the run') was raided, and the two men were arrested. A number of armoured cars and lorries were employed on the raid and shots were fired, though no resistance was offered – evidence of the enemy's nervousness. From the statement issued by the Castle authorities with regard to the prisoners, after they had been cruelly put to death, it was obvious that the captors had no idea of the importance of their capture; but the fact that they were not placed in any prison but kept in a very unusual place of detention – a room of the detective branch in Exchange Court, adjoining the Castle – has an ugly significance. The officer who carried out the raid and arrests has already been mentioned as taking part in the murder of Tomás MacCurtain.

Although the Dublin brigadier and vice-brigadier were arrested, the plans worked out by them were carried into operation on Sunday morning. Parties drawn from GHQ intelligence squad and the Dublin Brigade raided houses in various parts of Dublin, but nearly all on the south side of the Liffey. In one case they found that the person sought for had ceased to live at the address given. In all, fourteen English officers and agents were shot dead and five wounded, some mortally.

Angliss, or 'MacMahon' was shot dead in his bed, in a lodging house in Lower Mount Street. An officer who shared his room with him was not molested, not being 'on the list'. Another British spy who went by the name of 'Peel' occupied a bedroom in the same house. He saved himself by barricading the door of the room, so that the raiders were unable to gain access to him.

It happened that a party of Auxiliaries were passing the house at the time and heard the sound of the firing. They surrounded the house, fired on it and commenced to lay siege to it. But they kept a safe distance from the door. The IRA men inside, seeing themselves attacked, divided into two parties. One party of six made a dash out from the front door, exchanged a number of shots with the Auxiliaries, and got off safely, after a running fight. The rest attempted to get away by the back. This necessitated climbing a wall, during which one of their number, Frank Teeling, was wounded and captured by the Auxiliaries. This was the only capture made by the British forces in connection with the shootings of 21 November – and they did not hold Teeling long.

There was an important Gaelic football match between Dublin and Tipperary fixed for that evening in Croke Park, and it had been suggested beforehand that the GAA authorities should be warned to postpone the date of this match; but it was felt that such a postponement would implicate the GAA, in the eyes of the British authorities, in the doings of the morning, and give them a pretext for its suppression. The match was attended by a crowd of spectators estimated in newspaper reports as about 15,000. A large number of Auxiliaries and military arrived in lorries, surrounded the grounds and opened fire on players and spectators. Fourteen persons were killed, and about eighty were wounded, some of whom afterwards died of their wounds. The victims included a number of women and children, and Hogan, one of the players was shot dead. This cowardly massacre of innocent and unarmed Irish citizens was evidently intended as a 'reprisal' for the shootings of the morning.

Apparently, by way of explaining the raid on Croke Park, an official statement issued by the Castle authorities stated that they were satisfied that the shootings of the morning had been carried out by men from the provinces, who had come up to Dublin under the pretext of attending the match. It is difficult to say whether the enemy really believed this, but if they did they must have been very bad judges. To entrust such difficult and dangerous tasks to men not well acquainted with Dublin would obviously have been the height of folly. Needless to say, all those who took part in the operations were residents of Dublin, with a good knowledge of the city.

Dick McKee, Peadar Clancy and Conor Clune were murdered in the guardroom of the old detective office at Exchange Court, and the Castle authorities, who had now established a Press Bureau for the publication of their propaganda in the guise of official statements, issued a fantastic story to explain how the three men had met their deaths. The story was that the men in charge of them treated them with great kindness and allowed them full liberty of movement in a large room where a number of bombs were lying. They were sitting beside the fire chatting with their guards when they suddenly made a concerted rush, seized the bombs and flung them at the guards, but the bombs, not having been detonated, did not explode. They then tried to escape and in the struggle were accidentally shot. Such was the sort of fiction which the Castle Press Bureau expected the public to swallow. When the bodies were handed over to relatives a medical examination showed that McKee had received a bayonet thrust which pierced his liver, had broken ribs, and had a mass of abrasions on his face, besides bullet wounds, showing that he had been cruelly ill-treated. Clancy had not one, but a large number of bullet wounds in different parts of his body. No medical examination was made of the body of Clune, which was brought back to his home in Quin, County Clare, for burial. The bodies of McKee and Clancy were clad by their comrades in their Volunteer uniforms and were buried in Glasnevin after Mass in the Pro-Cathedral. Despite the risk, Michael Collins, the man most sought after by the enemy, attended the Mass.

Frank Teeling, who had been captured in the Mount Street fight, was tried by court martial and sentenced to death. In February 1921, he escaped from Kilmainham jail, along with two other important prisoners, Ernest O'Malley and Simon Donnelly. Another prisoner, Patrick Moran, accused of taking part in the Mount Street shootings (in which he had no share) was so confident of being able to prove an alibi that he declined the opportunity of escaping with the other three. He was subsequently tried, sentenced and executed, all evidence in his favour being ignored. A number of other prisoners were sentenced and executed on charges connected with the shootings of 'Bloody Sunday', but in no single case was the charge or verdict correct, though the victims were undoubtedly members of the IRA. The British authorities were not concerned with the evidence offered for the defence. They were only out to find victims, in the spirit of the reprisals at Croke Park.

On the Saturday before the fatal day, when I was conversing with Dick McKee, he remarked: 'I wonder what will be the effect of tomorrow's doings.' Ostensibly, it seemed to lead to an increase in enemy activity, wholesale raids and arrests, and fresh restrictions on the public, but behind the scenes it seems to have decided the British Prime Minister, Lloyd George, that his plans had failed, and that other methods must be resorted to. Immediately after 'Bloody Sunday' Mr

Lloyd George entered into secret parleys with various persons with a view to opening negotiations with the Irish leaders, and in less than a month he offered, through the instrumentality of Archbishop Clune of Perth, a truce similar to that agreed on in July 1921. The negotiations later broke down owing to the imprudence, or worse, of certain Irish public men, whose utterances and demands for peace led him to believe that his policy of 'frightfulness' was at last succeeding in breaking up the national solidarity. Another six months of warfare followed, but it is quite certain that it was not the doings of 'Bloody Sunday' or any other stern and drastic action by the IRA which caused this postponement. It was the utterances of the timid and cautious which caused a prolongation of the struggle, and it was the determined resistance of the IRA which caused the enemy later again to seek to come to terms with the forces of Irish freedom.

AUXILIARIES WIPED OUT AT KILMICHAEL IN THEIR FIRST CLASH WITH THE IRA

CORK NO. 3 (WEST) BRIGADE, 28 NOVEMBER 1920

by Tom Barry

(formerly O/C 3rd Cork Brigade flying column)

SIR HAMAR GREENWOOD, British Chief Secretary for Ireland, announced in the House of Commons in August 1920, that the RIC continued to resign and that in addition to those already departed 560 others had walked out in the months of June and July. He also stated that his Black and Tans, made up of British ex-servicemen, were now not only filling the gaps created by RIC resignations, but were actually doubling the 1918 strength of the RIC Black and Tans, and a new force called the Auxiliaries, would wipe out in Ireland all resistance to British rule. One hundred and fifty of this new force of Auxiliaries arrived in Macroom in August 1920, and commandeered Macroom Castle as their barracks.

Of all the ruthless forces that occupied Ireland through the centuries, those Auxiliaries were surely the worst. They were recruited from ex-British officers who had held commissioned rank and had had active service on one or more fronts during the 1914–18 war. They were openly established as a terrorist body, with the avowed object of breaking by armed force Ireland's continued resistance to British rule. Their war ranks ranged from lieutenant to brigadier-general, and they were publicised as the very pick of Britain's best fighters. Highly paid and with no bothersome discipline, they were habitual looters.

They were even dressed in a special uniform calculated to cow their opponents. Each carried a rifle, two revolvers, one strapped to each thigh, and two Mills bombs hung at the waist from their Sam Browne belts. It should be said in all fairness to the better type of British officers that they had refused to join this force.

Macroom was outside the West Cork IRA Brigade area, but the company of Auxiliaries stationed there seemed to concentrate, from the time of their arrival, on raiding south, in our brigade area. Day after day they travelled in to Coppeen, Castletownkenneigh, Dunmanway and even south of the Bandon river. By 1 November it seemed to me they were working on a plan to eliminate IRA resistance by terrorism, concentrating on one district at a time and then moving on to repeat their activities in some other area. They had a special technique. Fast lorries of them would come roaring into a village, the occupants would jump out, firing shots, and would order all the inhabitants out of doors. No exceptions were allowed. Men and women, old and young, the sick and decrepit, were lined up against the walls with their hands up, questioned and searched. No raid was ever carried out by these ex-officers without their beating up with the butt ends of their revolvers at least a half-dozen people. They were no respecters of persons, and seemed particularly to dislike Catholic priests. Actually in cold blood they murdered the aged Very Rev. Canon Magnier, PP, Dunmanway, on one of their expeditions. For hours they would hold the little community prisoners, and on more than one occasion, in different villages, they stripped all the men naked in the presence of the assembled people of both sexes, and beat them mercilessly with belts and rifles. They commandeered, without payment, food and drink, and they seldom returned sober to their barracks. Observing some man working at his bog or small field a few hundred yards from the road, they would stop their lorries and start their pleasant game. Laughing and shouting, four or five would take aim, not to hit him, but to spatter the earth or bog round him. The man would run wildly with the Auxies' bullets clipping the sods all about him. He would stumble and fall, rise again and continue to run for safety. But sometimes he would not rise, as an Auxiliary bullet was sent through him to stop forever all his movements. Still laughing and joking, these gentlemen and officers would ride away. Why not? The corpse was only an Irish peasant, and probably a sympathiser with these rebels, and anyway what did it matter? One more or less made no difference, and it was part of their duty to strike terror into the hearts of all the Irish.

The Auxiliary force had been allowed to bluster through the country for four or five months, killing, beating, terrorising, and burning factories and homes. Strange as it may appear, not a single shot had been fired at them up to this by the IRA in any part of Ireland, to halt their terror campaign. This fact had a very serious effect on the morale of the whole people, as well as on the IRA. Stories were current that the 'Auxies' were super-fighters and all but invincible. There could be no further delay in challenging them.

On 21 November a column of thirty-six riflemen were mobilised at Farrell's of Clogher, north-west of Dunmanway, for a week's training, preparatory to opening the attack on this super-force. On that Sunday a brigade meeting was held at Curraghdrinagh, and although many battalion O/Cs reported the assaults of Auxiliaries in their districts, no mention was made that it was proposed to attack them on the following Sunday.

After the meeting, I turned north to meet the new flying column. This unit was composed of new men, only one of whom had fought previously at Toureen, and only three had been through camp training. They were mostly quite untrained, but many appeared to be splendid natural fighters. They looked a fine body of the best type of Volunteers, and with some exceptions, lived up to this estimate afterwards. The column was divided into three sections, section commanders were appointed, and training started early on Monday morning. Training was interrupted three times by enemy military raiding parties who came so close that twice a fight was nearly forced on the IRA. The column had a definite objective for the following Sunday and was not to be diverted, so it was moved on and evasive action was taken. Starting on Monday at Togher it was thirteen miles south-east of its first billets on the following Saturday, when training was completed. On the Friday, accompanied by Michael McCarthy, vice-commandant of the Dunmanway Battalion, I rode on horseback to select the ambush position.

We returned to the flying column. That night Paddy O'Brien came to speak to me as I was pondering on the problem of how best to ensure that the Auxiliaries would slow down before the attack opened. Paddy was wearing a fine IRA officer's tunic. Suddenly the thought came that the Auxiliaries could never have seen a man wearing one of these. If on coming into the ambush position, they were to see a man wearing such a uniform, with an officer's field equipment such as I wore, they would be certain to slow down to investigate. Paddy O'Brien was told to change his tunic for my civilian coat for a couple of days.

At 2 a.m. on Sunday, the flying column of thirty-six riflemen fell in at O'Sullivan's, Ahilina. Each man was armed with a rifle and thirty-five rounds. A few had revolvers, and the commander had also two Mills bombs, which had been captured at Toureen. At 3 a.m. the men were told for the first time they were moving in to attack the Auxiliaries between Macroom and Dunmanway. Father O'Connell, PP, Ballineen, had ridden out to hear the men's confessions, and was waiting by the side of a ditch, some distance from the road. Silently, one by one, their rifles slung, the IRA went to him, and then returned to the ranks. Soon the priest came onto the road. In a low voice he spoke: 'Are the boys going to attack the Sassanach, Tom?'

'Yes, Father, we hope so.' He asked no further question, but said in a loud voice, 'Good luck, boys. I know you will win. God keep ye all. Now I will give you my blessing.' He rode away into the darkness of the night.

The column started its march against lashing rain. Everyone was drenched, but the march continued by road, by-roads and cross-country. Noiseless, silent and only smoking in the cover of a ditch during the short rest halts, no one knew of its passing as it went towards Kilmichael. During a rest halt, when the column was three miles from its destination, Flyer Nyhan came up from the rear section to report that young Pat Deasy had followed the column all the way and was now fifty yards behind the last section. Pat, a lad of sixteen, was already battalion lieutenant of signalling in the Bandon Battalion. Quiet and serious beyond his years, he was still a merry boy and a favourite with all the column. His enthusiasm for Volunteer work and training was exceptional, and, when all others were tired out, he could be seen practising arms drill outside his billet. He had been ill for two days previously and before we left I had told him he would have to miss this fight. He was instructed to hand over his rifle and equipment to a local man selected to take his place in the column. He was also told to return to the Bandon Battalion area until he would be recalled in a week or two. Now here he was again after trailing the column to within three miles of the ambush position.

Flyer Nyhan was ordered to bring him forward and Pat was asked most formally: 'Lieutenant Deasy, you have disobeyed orders. Why?'

'No, Commandant, honestly. I have not. I can go back to the Bandon area this way, but I thought if you saw I was able to march with the column you would let me wait for the fight. I am not sick. I could march twice as far again without a stop.' It was difficult to resist the plea in Pat's voice. It sounded as if his boyish pride was terribly hurt, so he was given back his rifle and his deputy sent home.

The column reached the ambush position at 8.15 as the late winter dawn crossed the sky. The ambush was in the centre of a bleak and barren countryside, a bogland interspersed with heather and rocks. It was bad terrain for an ambushing unit because of the lack of roadside ditches and cover, but the column had to attack in some part of this road between Kilmichael Cross and Gleann Cross of three roads, a few miles to the south. The column could not engage the Auxiliaries on the Macroom side of Kilmichael, as enemy reinforcements could quickly arrive from their base. It could not select a position south of Gleann, because on the previous four Sundays, the terrorists had diverged from Gleann Cross to four different districts. There was no certainty of meeting them, except on the road between Kilmichael and Gleann which they never once failed to travel.

The point of this road chosen for the attack was one and a half miles south of Kilmichael. Here the north-south road surprisingly turns west-east for 150 yards and then resumes its north-south direction. There were no ditches on either side of the road, but a number of scattered rocky eminences of varying sizes. No house was visible except one, 150 yards south of the road at the western entrance to the position. It was on this stretch of road it was hoped to attack the Auxiliaries.

Before being posted, the whole column was paraded and informed of the plan of attack. They were also told that the positions they were about to occupy allowed for no retreat, the fight could only end in the smashing of the Auxiliaries or the destruction of the flying column. There was no plan for a retirement until the column marched away victorious. This would be a fight to the end and would be vital not only for west Cork, but for the whole nation. If the Auxiliaries were not broken that day in their first fight with the Irish army, then the sufferings and degradations of the Irish race would surely continue until another generation arose. The Auxiliaries were killers without mercy. If they won, no prisoners would be brought back to Macroom. The alternative now was kill or be killed; see to it that it is those terrorists die and are broken.

All the positions were pointed out to the whole column, so that each man knew where his comrades were and what was expected of each group. The dispositions and details of the plan were:

1. The command post was situated at the extreme eastern end of the ambuscade and faced the oncoming lorries. It was a small narrow wall of bare stones, so loosely built that there were many transparent spaces. It jutted out onto the northern side of the road, a good enfilading position but affording little cover. Behind this little stone wall were also three picked fighters, John (Flyer) Nyhan, Clonakilty; Jim (Spud) Murphy, also of Clonakilty; and Mick O'Herlihy of Union Hall. The attack was to be opened from here and under no circumstances whatever was any man to allow himself to be seen until the commander had started the attack.

2. No. 1 section of ten riflemen was placed on the back slope of a large heather-covered rock, ten feet high, about ten yards from the command post. This rock was a few yards from the northern edge of the road. By

moving up on the crest of the rock as soon as the action commenced, the section would have a good field of fire.

3. No. 2 section of ten riflemen occupied a rocky eminence at the western entrance to the ambush position on the northern side of the road, and about 150 yards from No. 1 section. Because of its actual position at the entrance, provision had to be made so that some men of this section could fire on the second lorry, if it had not come round the bend when the first shots were fired at the leading lorry. Seven men were placed so that they could fire if the lorry had come round the bend and three if it had not yet reached it. Michael McCarthy was placed in charge of this section.

4. No. 3 section was divided. Stephen O'Neill, the section commander, and six riflemen occupied a chain of rocks about fifty yards south of the road. Their primary task was to prevent the Auxiliaries from obtaining fighting positions south of the road. If the Auxiliaries succeeded in doing this, it would be extremely difficult to dislodge them, but O'Neill and his men would prevent such a possibility. This section was warned of the great danger of their crossfire hitting their comrades north of the road and ordered to take the utmost care.

5. The remaining six riflemen of No. 3 section had to be used as an insurance group. There was no guarantee the enemy would not include three, four or more lorries. Some riflemen, no matter how few, had to be ready to attack any lorries other than the first two. These men were placed sixty yards north of the ambush position, about twenty yards from the roadside. From here they could fire on a stretch of 250 yards of the approach road.

6. Two unarmed scouts were posted 150 and 200 yards north of No. 2 section, from where they were in a position to signal the enemy approach when nearly a mile away. A third unarmed scout was a few hundred yards south of the command post to prevent surprise from the Dunmanway direction.

All the positions were occupied at 9 a.m. when up the road came John Lordan with his rifle at the trail. He had heard that the column was looking for action and had followed it. Now he asked if he could take part and was posted to No. 2 section. John was the vice-O/C of the Bandon Battalion, a fine type of Volunteer officer and a splendid fighter. He was a welcome addition to the flying column.

The column had no food. There was only one house nearby and although these decent people sent down all their own food and a large bucket of tea, there was not enough for all. The men's clothes had been drenched by the previous night's rain and now it was intensely cold as they lay on the sodden heather. Except for a few visits in the sections there was nothing to do but wait, think and shiver in the biting cold. The hours passed slowly. Towards evening the gloom deepened over the bleak Kilmichael countryside. Then at last at 4.05 p.m. the distant scout signalled the enemy's approach.

As soon as the signal was received the order – 'Lie flat and keep your heads down until firing commences' – was given twice. Then around the entrance bend, unconscious of the enemy behind them, riding on a sidecar pulled by a grey horse, came five fully armed IRA. These men should have reached the flying column on the previous Sunday, but failed to receive the mobilisation order in time. Now, as well as endangering their own lives, they very nearly upset the operation and endangered the whole column, for nobody could foresee the consequences if the Auxiliaries had come on them at the entrance to the ambuscade. Luckily there was a ditchless lane, leading to the house and immediately the order was given, 'Gallop up the lane, the Auxies are here. Gallop, gallop.' The grey horse galloped, and in thirty seconds the small party disappeared from sight and were not to reappear until the fight was over.

Fifteen seconds later, the first lorry came round the bend into the ambush position at a fairly fast speed. For fifty yards it maintained its speed and then the driver, apparently observing the uniformed figure, gradually slowed it down until at fifty yards from the command post, it looked as if it were about to stop. But it still came on slowly and, as it reached thirty-five yards from the small stone wall, the Mills bomb was thrown, an automatic barked and the whistle blew.

The bomb sailed through the air to land in the driver's seat of the uncovered lorry. As it exploded the rifle shots rang out. The lorry lurched drunkenly, but still came on impelled by its own weight, the foot brake no longer pressed as the driver was dead. On it came, the Auxiliaries firing their revolvers at the IRA who were pouring lead into them, and then the lorry stopped a few yards from the small stone wall. Some of the Auxiliaries were now fighting from the road and the fight became a hand-to-hand one. Revolvers were used at point blank range, and at times, rifle butts replaced rifle shots. So close were the combatants that in one instance the pumping blood from an Auxiliary's severed artery struck one attacker full in the mouth before the Auxiliary hit the ground. The Auxiliaries were cursing and yelling as they fought but the IRA were tight-lipped, as, ruthlessly and coldly, they outfought them.

It was not possible to see the efforts of the IRA except those near me. There Jim (Spud) Murphy, John (Flyer) Nyhan and Mick O'Herlihy were fighting splendidly. Once I got a side glimpse of Flyer's bayonet being driven through an Auxiliary, whom I had thought dead as I passed him, but who had risen to fire and miss me at four yards' range. There was no surrender called by these Auxiliaries and in less than five minutes they had been exterminated. All nine Auxiliaries were dead or dying, sprawled around the road near the little stone wall, except the driver and another, who with the life smashed out of them were huddled in the front of the lorry.

At the opening of the attack I had seen the second lorry come around the entrance bend, but did not know of the progress of the action at that part of the road. Now that we had finished with the first lot, we could see the second lorry stopped thirty yards at our side of No. 2 section. The Auxiliaries were lying in small groups on the road firing back at No. 2 section, at about twenty-five yards' range. Some men of No. 2 were engaging them. Waiting only to reload revolvers and pick up an Auxiliary's rifle and some clips of ammunition, the three riflemen from the command post, Murphy, Nyhan and O'Herlihy, were called on to attack the second party from the rear. In single file, we ran crouched up the side of the road. We had gone about fifty yards when we heard the Auxiliaries shout 'We surrender'. We kept running along the grass edge of the road as they repeated the surrender cry, and actually saw some Auxiliaries throw away their rifles. Firing stopped, but we continued, still unobserved, to jog towards them. Then we saw three of our comrades on No. 2 section stand up, one crouched and two upright. Suddenly the Auxiliaries were firing again with revolvers. One of our three men spun around before he fell, and Pat Deasy staggered before he too went down.

When this occurred, we had reached a point about twenty-five yards behind the enemy party and we dropped down as I gave the order: 'Rapid fire and do not stop until I tell you.' The four rifles opened a rapid fire and several of the enemy were hit before they realised they were being attacked from the rear. Two got to their feet and commenced to run back past No. 2 section, but both were knocked down. Some of the survivors of our No. 2 section had again joined in and the enemy, sandwiched between the two fires, were again shouting: 'We surrender.'

Having seen more than enough of their surrender tactics, I shouted the order: 'Keep firing on them. Keep firing, No. 2 section. Everybody keep firing on them until the ceasefire.' The small IRA group on the road was now standing up, firing as they advanced to within ten yards of the Auxiliaries. Then the 'ceasefire' was given and there was an uncanny silence as the sound of the last shot died away.

I ran the short distance to where I had seen our men fall and scrambled up the rocky height. Michael McCarthy, Dunmanway, and Jim O'Sullivan, Knockawaddra, Rossmore, lay dead, and a few yards away, Pat Deasy was dying. As we bandaged him his face grew pale, but he was quite conscious as I spoke. 'They are all dead, Pat. We will move you safely to a house in a few minutes and will get a doctor. Are you in pain?'

'No, Commandant, but give me water.' I knew enough first aid to understand that any liquid might quickly kill him, so he was told he would get a cup of tea when he reached the house. I turned away and ordered all the survivors, except the two who were to remain with Pat, to get down to the road. The whistle blew, and the order 'Fall in at the double' was given. Down the road with rifles at the trail came the insurance party of six riflemen; out from behind their rocks doubled Stephen O'Neill and his men; and from behind their high position slithered No. 1 section hastening to join the others. After numbering off they reloaded. Four men were sent hurrying for a door to bear Pat Deasy away: six were ordered to protection positions; eighteen detailed to remove the armament and papers from the dead Auxiliaries; the remainder to make the lorries ready for burning. The first unarmed scout to reach the scene of the fight hurried for a priest and doctor, the other two collected the personal effects of Michael McCarthy and Jim O'Sullivan, and made preparations for the removal of the bodies of those gallant comrades.

Within seven or eight minutes Pat Deasy was borne away, and the flying column 'fell in' with its task completed. Eighteen men carried the captured equipment over their own, the enemy rifle slung across their backs. One man had a sandbag full of the Auxiliaries' paper and notebooks. Jack Hennessy of Ballineen, whose head wound had to be dressed, reported his fitness to march. He was told to remain sitting on the roadside until the column moved.

The flying column came to attention, sloped arms, and was inspected. Some showed the strain of the ordeal through which they had passed, and a few appeared on the point of collapse because of shock. It was of supreme importance that these men should be jerked back to their former efficiency, particularly as another engagement with the British might well occur during the retirement. They were harshly reprimanded, and then the column commenced to drill and march. The lorries were now ablaze. Like two huge torches, they lit up the countryside and the corpse-strewn, blood-stained road, as the flying column marched up and down, halted, drilled and marched again between them. For five minutes the eerie drill continued until the column halted in front of the rock where Michael McCarthy and Jim O'Sullivan lay. There it executed the 'Present Arms' as its farewell tribute to those fine Irish soldiers.

The column formed sections, and the order of march was given. A half-an-hour after the opening of the fight, it moved away to the south, aiming to cross the Bandon river before the British-held Manch Bridge. Soon it commenced to rain again and the men were drenched. The rain continued as the IRA marched through Shanacashel, Coolnagow, Balteenbrack, and arrived in the vicinity of dangerous Manch Bridge. With full precautions, the Bandon river was crossed, and Granure, eleven miles south of Kilmichael, was reached at 11 p.m.

On the road I had decided that the column could not be risked in numerous billets that night as was usual. Hourly the threat to it would develop as the British sought it out and endeavoured to surround it. The column would have to remain together in a single house, ready for instant action. Paddy O'Brien and Dan Hourihan had reported an empty labourer's cottage at Granure, and it was in front of this the column halted. The local Ballinacarriga Company had been mobilised before our arrival and the members were eagerly waiting to help. They posted an outer ring of scouts, provided candles, bread, butter, buckets of tea and placed bundles of straw on the floor. They dumped the surplus rifles and equipment. All ammunition, bombs and revolvers were distributed to the flying column.

It was now 1 a.m. and the scouts and sentries were inspected. When I returned half an hour later the men were all sleeping in their wet clothes on the straw-covered floors. I looked at them and a thrill of pride ran through me as I thought that no army in the world could ever have more uncomplaining men. They had been practically thirty hours without food, marched twenty-six miles, and were soaked through, nearly frozen on exposed rocks and had undergone a terrifying baptism of fire. Their discipline was of the finest. Compulsion or punishments were not required for this Volunteer army; they risked their lives and uncomplainingly suffered.

I poked out a corner near the door and lay on the straw. I could not sleep as my mind worked rapidly. Lying on my back, staring up at the ceiling of the dimly lit kitchen, thoughts crowded in on me. The Auxiliaries had had it. They were looking for it for a long time. But they were now smashed, and their reign of terror against west Cork men and women was ended. The IRA had outfought them, and not more than fifteen or sixteen of our riflemen had had the opportunity to fire at them because of their dispositions. The 'super' force! Who was this Colonel Crake who had commanded them and who now lay dead on the road? Close quarter fighting did not suit them. It does not suit the Essex or the Tans. Keep close to them should be our motto, for generally they must be better shots than we, because of their opportunities for practice and their war experience. There are no good or bad shots at ten yards' range. Our dead! Two of them might be alive now had I warned them of the bogus surrender trick which is as old as war itself. Why did I not warn them? I could not think of everything. Liam will be cut up but he will understand. Pat *would* come. What will Mick and Jim's people say? War means death to some and can't happen without deaths. The Auxies paid, though. Could we have managed three lorries of them? A good enough haul, eighteen rifles, 1,800 rounds, thirty revolvers and ammunition. And the Mills bombs. They were badly wanted. We are well armed now. I must sleep. If they find us before day and come on us from the north we will have to —— I must sleep. I must sleep as I want to be fresh when they come. Some day they will surround us. Sleep, sleep!

I awoke with a start as someone gently pressed my shoulder. It was Commandant Charlie Hurley, the Brigade O/C. I looked at my wristwatch and saw that I had not slept for more than half an hour. We tip-toed to an outhouse so that the sleepers would not be disturbed. There, as we smoked, I told him of the fight. Charlie had been in the Clonakilty area, and on his way to us had heard some extraordinary rumours of what had happened. The best news he had got was that two Auxiliaries and six of the column were killed; the worst, that the whole column had been wiped out with no British losses.

We talked for an hour, and I went back to sleep more easily as Charlie had taken over charge of the sentries and scouts. Until morning he would prowl round, tireless and watchful. Again I thought of what an extraordinary army we were. Where in all the world would a brigadier walk alone and armed for fifteen miles to find a fighting unit and mount guard himself while it slept in safety? But then, there was only one Charlie Hurley, and there never was his equal in all the units that fought for freedom in 1920 and 1921.

On the following day the column was confined to the cottage while reports of intense enemy activity came in steadily. Large bodies of the British were gathering in Dunmanway, Ballineen, Bandon, Crookstown and Macroom before converging on Kilmichael. One unit of 250 steel-helmeted soldiers moving on to Dunmanway about noon, passed 200 yards from the cottage, while the column stood at the alert.

Other enemy units were moving at the same time a few miles away on to Manch Bridge. No risks were taken by them as it was nearly 4 p.m. when all their force reached Kilmichael. The British were aware at 6 p.m. Sunday evening that the Auxiliaries had been ambushed, yet it was late evening on the following day before they ventured to the scene of the fight. It was clear enough to me that they thought a large IRA force was engaged and waiting for a stand-up fight with the British reinforcements. That morning Charlie moved east at my request to attend to several urgent matters, including the burial of our three dead comrades. When night came, while the British were concentrating north of the Bandon river, the column drove further south to Lyre. For three days it zig-zagged, avoiding at times, by only a few hundred yards, clashes with other fresh British troops which had been sent to west Cork. It was possible to engage one of these units, although there was a great probability that if the IRA had attacked again, the other enemy units a few miles away would have got at the rear or flanks of the column before a decision was reached.

During those days other British forces converging on Kilmichael, carried out large-scale reprisals around the ambush area. Shops and homes, hay barns, outhouses, were destroyed at Kilmichael, Johnstown and Inchigeela. Proclamations were posted up and printed in the daily press.

NEW POLICE ORDER IN MACROOM

December 1st, 1920.

Whereas foul murders of servants of the crown have been carried out by disaffected persons, and whereas such persons immediately before the murders appeared to be peaceful and loyal people, but have produced pistols from their pockets, therefore it is ordered that all male inhabitants of Macroom and all males passing through Macroom shall not appear in public with their hands in their pockets. Any male infringing this order is liable to be shot at sight.

By Order,

AUXILIARY DIVISION, RIC

Macroom Castle

December 1st, 1920.

NOTICE

December 2nd, 1920.

> The General Officer commanding 17th Infantry Brigade, Cork, requests that all business premises and shops be closed between the hours of 11 a.m. and 2 p.m. Thursday, December 2nd, 1920, as a mark of respect for the Officers, Cadets and Constables of the Auxiliary Division, RIC killed in ambush near Kilmichael, 28th November, 1920, and whose Funeral Procession will be passing through the city on December 2nd.
>
> F.R. EASTWOOD, Major,
>
> Brigade Major, 17th Inf. Bde

This 'request' was enforced on the unwilling citizens by large forces of military, Black and Tans, and Auxiliaries, who lined the funeral route through the city.

Later came the Martial Law Proclamation on 10 December 1920, from Field Marshal Lord French, Lord Lieutenant of Ireland:

> Because of the attacks on crown forces, culminating in an ambush, massacre, mutilation with axes of sixteen cadets, by a large body of men wearing trench helmets and disguised in the uniform of British soldiers, and who are still at large, now I do declare Martial Law proclaimed in the county of Cork, East and West Riding, the city of Cork, Tipperary, North and South Riding, the city and county of Limerick.

Impartial students of guerrilla warfare may agree that the Kilmichael ambush justified Field Marshal Lord French in proclaiming martial law in the south of Ireland. I anticipated such a step as a logical sequence. It was even welcomed, as it connoted our recognition by the enemy as an army in the field, instead of their previous pretence that our status was that of a gang of rebel murderers.

However, this proclamation was based on lies. Firstly, Lord French referred to sixteen casualties only, whereas the British government had officially announced their losses at Kilmichael as sixteen dead, one missing and one in a dying condition. Secondly, Lord French used the word 'cadets' to describe those hard-bitten terrorists, all veterans of the

First World War who were ranked in the British official communique announcing their deaths as majors, captains, etc., etc. The calculated use of this misnomer 'cadet' was intended to arouse sympathy from the outside world. Thirdly, Lord French stated the attackers used British uniforms as a disguise. No officer or member of the IRA attacking force wore uniform of any kind, except the column commander, who had an official IRA tunic. Fourthly, the proclamation alleged that the IRA mutilated the bodies of the Auxiliaries with axes. The foulest of all British weapons has ever been 'atrocity' propaganda. No axe was in possession of the IRA and no corpse was interfered with. This mutilation allegation was a vicious and calumnious lie. Well may one ask from where Lord French got his information. Of the eighteen Auxiliaries, sixteen were dead, one reported missing (after he had been shot, he crawled to the boghole near the side of the road, where he died and his body sank out of sight), and one died of wounds. The last-mentioned never regained consciousness before he died. There were no spectators to the fight.

To clinch this exposure of lying British propaganda, it is as well to state here that after the Truce with the British in July 1921, Sir Alfred Cope, then assistant British under-secretary for Ireland, called on me in Cork for a written statement that the IRA had killed the Auxiliaries at Kilmichael, since this was essential before the British government could pay compensation to the dependants. He informed me that the British government had no evidence of how these men had met their deaths as there were no survivors to testify in court and the dying Auxiliary had never recovered consciousness. Incidentally, he was refused any statement.

THE SACKING OF CORK CITY BY THE BRITISH

11 DECEMBER 1920

by Major Florence O'Donoghue

(formerly Adjutant, Cork No. 1 Brigade, IRA)

THE BURNING OF Cork city by the British army of occupation on the night of 11 December 1920, was the most extensive single act of vandalism committed in the whole period of the national struggle from 1916 to 1921. But it would be a mistake to regard it as an isolated incident, or to accept in explanation of it the conventional excuse that the armed forces of England, drink-sodden and nerve-racked from a contest in which they were being worsted, had run amok and destroyed the city in a fit of frenzy. Indeed, to that ignominious excuse the spokesmen of the British government were ultimately driven; having passed through the successive stages of denying 'that there was any evidence that the fires were started by crown forces', of charging the burning of their own city first upon the IRA, and then upon the citizens themselves, and finally, in ignorant and reckless desperation, assuring the world that the fires in the City Hall and Carnegie Library had spread from Patrick Street across the river and several intervening blocks of unburned buildings. It was an excuse, nevertheless, and one that was very far from the truth.

The burning and looting of Cork was not an isolated incident, but rather the large-scale application of a policy initiated and approved, implicitly, or explicitly, by the government from which all authority of the British forces in Ireland was alleged to derive. That was a policy of subjugation by terror, murder and rapine; of government by force of arms; of the deliberate destruction of those industries and resources whose absence would inflict the greatest hardship and loss upon the nation; of ruthless hunting down and extermination of those who stood for national freedom. The policy was, of course, presented to the world in a coat of smooth lies. 'Great Britain had no quarrel with Irishmen; her sole quarrel is with crime, outrage and disorder' – thus General Macready; the 'crime, outrage and disorder' being the acts of war of an Irish army, constitutionally acting under the authority of a national government elected by the vast majority of the Irish people, and engaged in a righteous war to expel the armed forces of an alien government. And that master of the art of mystification, Mr Lloyd George, with his eye on the influence of our people in the United States, had this to add: 'fundamentally, the issue is the same as that in the war of North and South in the United States; it is an issue of secession and union', forgetting, or hoping that the public would forget, that this was a nation older than England, that had in every generation asserted its claim to independence, that had six times in the past 300 years asserted it in arms and that there was no analogy between our relations with England and the relations of North and South in the American Civil War.

A brief glance at the record of the British forces in Ireland in the six months before the burning of Cork will be sufficient to indicate how this policy was being put into effect and how well these forces were carrying out their mission of 'preserving law and order'. The records of that time bear witness to the cold-blooded murder of men identified with the republican movement; to the arrest and imprisonment, in jails and internment camps, of thousands of Irishmen; to the deliberate drowning of unarmed men; to the shooting of unarmed prisoners on the pretence that they were attempting to escape; to the killing of untried and unarmed prisoners; to beatings, threats, insults, and the whole litany of savage brutality by the forces of a powerful empire striving to extinguish in blood the nationhood of this people. In one month these 'forces of law and order' had burned and partially destroyed twenty-four towns; in one week they had shot up and sacked

Balbriggan, Ennistymon, Mallow, Miltown-Malbay, Lahinch and Trim. These armed forces comprised three main groups – the army, the Royal Irish Constabulary and the Auxiliaries. The Royal Irish Constabulary included the remnant of the original force which had not retired or resigned, and a reinforcement of British jail-birds and down-and-outs, who had been hastily recruited into the force in England when candidates had ceased to offer themselves in Ireland. These instruments of despicable policy were the origin of the expression 'Black and Tans'. Owing to a shortage of uniforms in the early days of their appearance in Ireland they wore the khaki trousers of the regular army and the dark green, almost black, tunic of the Royal Irish Constabulary. As fighting material they were of the poorest type, untrained, undisciplined and vicious; as policemen it would have been difficult in any country to assemble a more incongruous set of ruffians for police work; but they were not intended for police work; the Royal Irish Constabulary had ceased to be police force except in name.

The Auxiliary force was of a different type. About 1,500 strong, they were organised as a separate command, and consisted exclusively of ex-officers of the British army and navy, most of whom had seen service in the Great War. The establishment of this force was the last desperate effort of the British government to forge a weapon to defeat the IRA. They had fifteen companies scattered throughout the country; the men were very highly paid and were a reckless, courageous, desperate force, hard-drinking and unprincipled. They were fitting instruments for the work they were intended to do, and the doubtful honour of leadership in the work of burning, shooting and destruction fell to them. Ultimate responsibility for the acts of all these forces rested on the British Cabinet. The Auxiliaries were not uncontrolled soldiers of fortune, acting without authority, which they were sometimes conveniently represented to be; nor were their crimes the unpremeditated reaction of men exposed to the hazards of guerrilla warfare. Their action had the sanction of a higher authority, although it was the policy first to give an indignant denial to any charge made against these forces, to stigmatise such a suggestion as a base calumny on heroes who fought in the Great War; and later, perhaps, under stress of undeniable proof, to admit grudgingly that a few Auxiliaries did get a trifle excited here and there. Neither were the Auxiliaries an irregular force, as was sometimes suggested. Lloyd George, in his letter to the Bishop of Chelmsford on 19 April 1921, states specifically: 'There are no "irregular forces of the crown". The Auxiliary division of the Royal Irish Constabulary is a regular force.' Logically, then, when it is proved that these forces burned Cork, there can be no ambiguity as to where responsibility rests. Notwithstanding that there was a confusion of control and divergence of policy in the British command in Ireland, and possibly in the British Cabinet on Irish policy, the burden of responsibility for what happened here is inescapable.

To understand the lack of cohesion that existed between the British forces in Ireland, it must be realised that there were two authorities representing Great Britain in this country, the civil and military. Normally, the civil authority, represented by Dublin Castle, controlled the police force and when the Auxiliary division was established it was nominally under the control of that department. But the work which this or any other section of the police forces was doing was not police work; they were all armed military forces engaged in savage repression. The control of the regular military forces was in the hands of a military officer. In the martial law area (and Cork was in this area on the night of the burning) the police force, Black and Tans, and the Auxiliaries were under the control of the military governor; in Dublin the Auxiliaries were subject to the military authorities, but the Royal Irish Constabulary were not. In the remainder of the country, outside the martial law area, the Auxiliaries were alleged to be under the control of the senior Royal Irish Constabulary officers, divisional commissioners and county inspectors. In this confusion of control it is not surprising to find each section acting without the knowledge or co-operation of the other sections, and not infrequently one section solemnly going through the farce of investigating offences committed by members of another section. The one shining example of their unanimity, in desire and action, was their co-operation in the burning of Cork.

A company of the Auxiliaries (K Company) had been stationed at Cork military barracks since October 1920, and had indulged in raids on houses, holding up and searching civilians in the streets, robbery and insulting behaviour. In November and December their drunken aggressiveness became so pronounced that no person was safe from their molestations. Age or sex was no protection. Poor women were robbed of their few shillings in the streets by these 'gentlemen' in broad daylight. After their raids on houses, articles of value were frequently missing. Whips were taken from shops with which to flog unoffending pedestrians. Drink was demanded at the point of the revolver.

The IRA determined to put an end to this intolerable situation. Ambushes were laid at various points in the city over a period of several weeks, and that at Dillon's Cross on the night of 11 December was the first to come off. The difficulties faced by the IRA in operating in the city in this period were immense. Enemy forces had barracks in all parts of the city; they were equipped with fast cars, lorries and armoured cars, in which they could swoop on any part of the city at short notice. They were, of course, vastly superior in numbers and armament to the IRA. One thing they lacked which the IRA had in generous measure – the co-operation of the people – and without it they were blind and impotent. That a group of armed men could frequent a particular locality for long periods day after day without their presence being remarked upon was inconceivable. Yet IRA men frequently did duty of this kind, and no word was ever passed to the enemy by the hundreds who must have seen them daily.

The ambush at Dillon's Cross took place within a couple of hundred yards of the military barracks. Lorries of Auxiliaries were bombed and raked with revolver fire. At least one Auxiliary was killed and twelve were wounded. The IRA party of six men got away without injury to a single man. An ambush had been laid in the same position two weeks earlier, but did not come off. Indiscriminate shooting in the main streets of the city commenced shortly after eight o'clock; and it was remarked that it was Black and Tans and not the Auxiliaries who were so engaged. Curfew was at ten o'clock, but long before that hour the streets were almost deserted. An air of impending disaster was evident everywhere; many had been warned to get to their homes, as trouble was expected that night. This was before the ambush took place. It is difficult to say with certainty whether or not Cork would have been burned on that night if there had not been an ambush. What appears more probable is that the ambush provided the excuse for an act which was long premeditated and for which all arrangements had been made. The rapidity with which supplies of petrol and Verey lights were brought from Cork barracks to the centre of the city, and the deliberate manner in which the work of firing the various premises was divided amongst groups, under the control of officers, gives evidence of organisation and pre-arrangement. Moreover, the selection of certain premises for destruction and the attempt made by an Auxiliary officer to prevent the looting of one shop by Black and Tans: 'You are in the wrong shop; that man is a loyalist,' and the reply: 'We don't give a damn: this is the shop that was pointed out to us,' is additional proof that the matter had been carefully planned beforehand.

About ten o'clock two houses at Dillon's Cross were set on fire by Auxiliaries and Black and Tans. Auxiliaries patrolled the roads in the neighbourhood to prevent any attempt being made to extinguish the fires. One man who attempted to save his furniture from a house next door to one of those on fire was immediately fired upon and assaulted. He was dragged through a neighbour's back yard, put up against a wall and threatened to be shot. Only the intervention of some women saved his life. When these fires were started a call was sent to the fire brigade, and a section of the brigade from Grattan Street started out to go to Dillon's Cross. On arrival in Patrick Street, through which they had to pass on their way, the firemen saw that Grant's drapery warehouse was on fire. They decided, on seeing the immensity of this conflagration, to go to the fire brigade headquarters at Sullivan's Quay for assistance. From there the military authorities at Cork barracks were asked on the phone to send their fire-fighting appliances to the fires at Dillon's Cross. No notice was taken of the request and the fires at Dillon's Cross blazed on until the houses were charred ruins. Before the curfew hour at ten o'clock motley groups of armed ruffians appeared upon the streets; the emptying city rang to the crack of indiscriminate rifle and revolver fire. Some in these groups wore uniforms, some were in civilian attire: here and there a police greatcoat was observed over civilian clothes, or ordinary overcoats over police or military uniforms. Auxiliaries, Black and Tans, soldiers, some half drunk, many shouting and jeering, all wild, furious, savage, exultant in the urge to destruction. A tram car going up Summerhill, full of passengers and on its last journey for the night, was set upon by Auxiliaries and Black and Tans; the passengers were dragged or pushed out upon the road, searched, threatened, abused, beaten with rifle butts and fired upon. A priest who was a passenger in the tram was singled out for special attention. He was put up against a wall, his overcoat, jacket and vest, and collar were torn off; he was knocked sprawling upon the ground and told to say: 'To hell with the Pope.' He refused and was told he would be shot. Another group intervened; he was kicked again and told to run. He was unable to do so after the treatment he had received, and was pushed up the hill with the muzzle of a rifle in his back. His clothes were kicked before him some distance up the hill, and he was fired at while attempting to pick them up. As curfew hour approached the few pedestrians upon the streets became the targets for the shots of the incendiaries. Some were fired at without warning, the moment they appeared round a bend or a street corner. Others were held up, beaten, asked to sing 'God Save the King', ordered to run and then fired at. A tram was set on fire near Patrick's Bridge. By ten o'clock the centre of the city was deserted except for its despoilers.

From their great barracks on the hill above the city, fresh hordes of armed men now issued forth, lorries laden with petrol tins swept through the empty streets and over the river bridges into the main thoroughfares. From the city police barracks other groups emerged, and soon the central streets of the city were overrun by swarming masses of violent men intent upon loot and destruction. All discipline was not quite lost at first; the group that fired Grant's, the first premises in the city to be given to flames, marched up the street in military formation, though most of them were in civilian attire. They were under the command of Auxiliary officers. Later the group setting fire to Cash's were directed by the sharp commands of a military officer. But soon all discipline relaxed and the uncontrolled orgy of burning and looting began. One after another all the principal business houses in Patrick Street were set on fire. At the Munster Arcade, where a number of persons were residing, shots were fired through the doors, the windows were smashed and bombs were thrown into the building. The men and women who were on the premises were ordered out at the point of the revolver, and kept on the street under the guard of two RIC men for several hours. These men and women saw a military officer and an RIC man take tins of petrol and go upstairs into the Munster Arcade; they saw some of the police put masks over their faces; they heard the predominant English accents above the smashing of glass, the crash of bombs and the crack of rifle shots.

Looting was going on all the time. Some of the looted shops were burned; other were not. From many shops groups emerged laden with suitcases; silks and articles of clothing protruding from some of those cases, where the looters, in their greed and haste, had failed to pack them properly. The lurid flames rose ever higher into the night sky, and in their ruddy glare the passing lorries of curfew patrols cheered the furious incendiaries. The raging fires were spreading with every passing minute, and soon it seemed as if the whole city must be involved. The fire brigade was doing its heroic best to cope with a situation far beyond the capabilities of its resources. The firemen did marvellous work in confining the fires at some points; but their efforts were hampered, not alone by the inadequacy of the hose lines to deal with an unprecedented conflagration, but by the more serious factor that they were continuously under fire from the incendiaries, and literally took their lives in their hands throughout that awful night. A new line of hose at the General Post Office was got out to assist in quelling the fires in that locality. It was deliberately cut with bayonets and rendered useless. Firemen were frequently fired at, one at least was hit, and the ambulance taking him to the North Infirmary was again fired on. As the night wore on the effects of drink became more and more evident. Hotels and public houses were raided; stocks of spirits were consumed or taken away. The smashing of bottles was added to the all-pervading sounds of destruction. Attempts were made to fire other premises. They failed only because of the drunken exhaustion of the sated incendiaries. There was no sleep for the residents in the centre of the city that night. Those who had been driven from their homes and had seen them given to the flames, sought shelter with friends or in hotels. Residents in houses threatened by spreading fires tried to save their household goods and furniture by removing them to the streets or to houses in a safer position. The awesome roar of raging flames rose like the sound of a great wind above the clamour that marked the flowing tide of destruction. Great pillars of fire produced marvellous combinations of brilliant colour and wreathing form; the crashing of roofs and walls sent up effervescent showers of glowing sparks; over the whole city there hung a dense, dull pall of heavy smoke.

Attempts were made to start fires in shops on the Grand Parade and Washington Street. A fire was actually started in a shop next door to Saint Augustine's church and priory in Washington Street. If this blaze had not been extinguished by some civilians before it had got a firm hold on the premises, it is probable that not alone the shop, but the church and priory as well, would have been destroyed. The shutters were torn down from a jeweller's shop on the Grand Parade, the windows were smashed and armed bands of looters invaded the shop. Later they were seen emerging with kit bags filled with the contents of the looted shop and making off with their booty in the direction of the Union Quay barracks of the Royal Irish Constabulary. An armed party, led by a military officer, went through Marlboro Street smashing windows on both sides of the street until not a ground floor window was left intact. Boots and shoes were looted from Tyler's shop in Winthrop Street and carried away by the incendiaries.

The City Hall and the Carnegie Library close by it were destined to suffer the same fate as Patrick Street. The City Hall had withstood several previous attempts at burning it; windows that had been broken in an earlier attempt to effect an entrance were now protected by corrugated iron shutters. A few firemen were on duty there every night as a precautionary measure. But this building, which had so many historic associations with the national and civil life of Cork was, because of these associations, an object specially marked out for destruction by the British forces. In this hall Tomás MacCurtain had been elected first republican Lord Mayor of Cork – he who was soon afterwards to make the supreme sacrifice for his faith in that kindly, Gaelic way of life which he himself had personified. Here his body had lain in state, his face serene in death, while his nation mourned for one so well beloved, and the endless crowds, patient in the bleak March wind, waited silently to pass before that guarded bier. And here his successor, Terence MacSwiney, a soldier with calm foreknowledge stepping into the breach of death, had spoken deathless words that called forth a supreme courage in the whole people at a time when it was sought to break their spirit by terror: 'It is not to those who can inflict most but to those who can suffer most that the victory is assured.' This place was forever hallowed by their memory; all their enemies could do was to destroy it. Here the Volunteers had been started; in the shadow of its walls the heartening sound of marching men of an Irish army – the first to be heard in Cork city for a generation – had carried a measure of hope and encouragement to those who, in patience and obscurity, had laboured through long years for this day. Under its roof those associated with the national movement had passed many a happy night in concert and ceilidhe; into it flowed, and there coalesced, in the years 1917 to 1919, all those elements that went to make a great national resurgence, that helped to build up an organisation that withstood the terrific strain of the following years.

This place was now marked down for destruction. About two o'clock on Sunday morning heavy firing from incendiaries gathered round it, drove the firemen on duty in the hall into the comparative safety of the Bandon railway station behind it. The raiders effected an entrance by getting over the library wall, and with axe and sledge breaking a door into the back corridor of the hall. For over two hours they were in possession of the building, while their comrades brought tins of petrol from the Union Quay barracks close by. Deliberate and thorough preparations were made for the total and effective destruction of the building. Explosives were placed in position, and the whole contents soaked in petrol. Shortly after four o'clock the 'all clear' was sounded, the raiders emerged and a terrific explosion was heard. This was followed by about ten lesser explosions in the next half-hour and the fire spread with great rapidity to all parts of the building. Equally thorough and effective preparations were then made for the destruction of the Carnegie Library adjoining the City Hall, and soon this fine building, with its hundreds of thousands of volumes, was a mass of flames. The firemen got a line of hose playing on the Carnegie Library, but a party of police who were on duty close to the hydrant turned the water off as soon as the firemen had turned it on. This party of policemen was under the control of a head constable and three sergeants, and they deliberately turned off the water at the hydrant every time the firemen turned it on. The firemen protested to the head constable; he said he had no control over these men. After nine or ten attempts to keep the water turned on, the firemen were forced to desist and take their line of hose into Patrick Street. There was then no hope for the City Hall or the library. The clock on the City Hall tower still rang the quarters above that raging inferno; it struck six for the last time on that tragic Sunday morning, and then clock and tower crashed into the ruins below.

The following extract from the official report of the then Superintendent of the Cork Fire Brigade, Mr Alfred J. Huston, requires no comment:

> I have no hesitation in stating that I believe all the fires were incendiary fires, and that a considerable amount of petrol or some such inflammable spirit was used in one and all of them. In some cases explosives were also used, and persons were seen to go into and come out of the structures and breaking an entrance into same, and in some cases that I have attended the people have been brought out of their houses and detained in by-lanes until the fire had gained great headway. I have some of the petrol tins left behind in my possession.

The most ghastly deed in all that night of horror was the cold-blooded murder of two Volunteers, Con and Jeremiah Delaney, at their home at Dublin Hill, just outside the city. These two brothers had been active Volunteers and their house and farm had been used for safe storage of arms and ammunition. About two o'clock on the morning of 12 December loud knocking at their doors awakened members of the family. A party of armed raiders who had arrived in a lorry were outside and demanded immediate admission – demanded it loudly and threateningly. Daniel Delaney, father of Con and Jeremiah, admitted them, and was asked his name and if he was a Sinn Féiner. He answered that he was an old man and not interested in politics. He was next asked who was in the house and he replied that there was no one but his family, who were in bed. Eight men had entered the house and they demanded to be shown to his sons' room. They entered the room occupied by Con and Jeremiah Delaney, and their uncle, William Dunlea. At the point of the revolver, the raiders ordered them out of bed and asked if their name was Delaney. Immediately they said 'Yes' they were fired at and mortally wounded. William Dunlea was fired at and wounded in two places. Jeremiah, who was fired at first, died almost immediately, his sister holding a crucifix to his lips. Con survived almost a week, until Saturday 18 December. Their dreadful work accomplished, the murderers went downstairs, but they did not leave the house. The sisters of the wounded boys, terrified and distracted though they were by the stark horror of that awful calamity, were doing what they could for their brothers. One of them on her way downstairs to go for a priest was met by one of the raiders rushing upstairs again, a revolver in one hand, a flashlamp in the other, demanding: 'Is anyone belonging to me up there?' The grief-stricken father answered him: 'Nobody but dead men.' Miss Delaney attempted to get out through the kitchen door to go for a priest and medical assistance. She was prevented from doing so by one of the raiders, who remarked: 'If the house is all right what is the need for a priest?'

The murderers remained for about a quarter of an hour before they left in a motor lorry. The members of the family were all in agreement that the raiders wore military uniform, spoke with foreign accents, and that some had handkerchiefs over their faces. A message was sent to the city for the ambulance, but it was too fully engaged to come out. A priest came from the North Presbytery about 4 a.m., and at eight o'clock the ambulance came and removed Con to the Mercy Hospital.

When the cold dawn broke on that December Sunday morning, revealing the results of the night's madness, what a scene of ruin and desolation the city presented! Many familiar landmarks were gone forever, many a remembered contour and skyline had given place to gaping cavities where whole buildings had collapsed, here and there a solitary wall, windowless and heat-blistered, leaned at some crazy angle from its foundation. The streets ran sooty water, the footpaths were strewn with debris and broken glass, ruins smoked and smouldered, and over everything there was the all-pervading smell of burning. Three million pounds' worth of goods and property had been destroyed.

There was an immediate universal demand for an impartial public inquiry into the burnings. The Cork Corporation, Chamber of Commerce, Harbour Board and other public bodies joined with the Sinn Féin leaders and local unionists in asking for such an inquiry. The Parliamentary Labour Party offered to prove at such an inquiry 'that the fires were the work of crown forces'. Every party was anxious for the fullest possible investigation, except the British government. The British Labour Commission, which was in Ireland at the time investigating the outrages by British forces, intimated their conviction, after investigation on the spot, that the fires were caused by crown forces, and offered to produce reliable evidence to prove it. Press and public demanded an inquiry. The British government resolutely refused. 'The best inquiry, and the most impartial,' said Hamar Greenwood, 'will be made by the general officer commanding on the spot.' 'In the present condition of Ireland,' declared Bonar Law, 'we are much more likely to get an impartial inquiry in a military court than in any other.' And so the 'impartial investigation' was made by the criminals themselves. And the findings of even that 'inquiry' were never published.

Cork Corporation sent the following reply to a telegram received by the city engineer from the commanding officer, Cork barracks, asking him to appear before the 'inquiry':

> We have instructed the city engineer and other corporate officials to take no part in the English military inquiry into the burning of this city, with which we charge the English military and police forces before the whole world. We adhere to the offer made by the City Members and the Lord Mayor to submit evidence already in our possession before an impartial international tribunal, or before a court of fair-minded Englishmen.

The curfew report for the night of 11–12 December concocted by the military officer in charge of the curfew patrols, in consultation with the officer in charge of the Auxiliaries, is worth quoting as showing what little reliance can be placed on any official document issued by the army of occupation at that time:

> 1. Three arrests were made.
>
> 2. At 22.00 hours Grant & Co. in Patrick Street, was found to be on fire. Warning was at once sent to all fire brigades.
>
> 3. At about 00.30 hours Cash & Co. and the Munster Arcade were reported on fire.
>
> 4. At 05.30 hours the majority of the troops were withdrawn, and the remainder at 08.00 hours.
>
> 5. Explosions were heard at 00.15 hours, but were not located. No shots were fired by the troops.
>
> F.R. Eastwood, Major,
>
> Brigade Major, 17th Inf. Brigade,
>
> Cork, 12/12/20

To these depths of evasion and lying the campaign in Ireland had reduced the great British army.

There was an implication in the British government's insistence that the inquiry should be held by General Strickland that whatever had happened in Cork that night, the military, as distinct from the Auxiliaries and police forces, had no responsibility for it. The curfew report itself is an indication of how far from the truth this contention is. In fact, of the armed forces in occupation of the city, the prime responsibility rested on the military. The area was under martial law. All responsibility for the preservation of public order had been forcibly taken out of the hands of the citizens. A military governor was in control. Curfew commenced at 10 p.m. and no person had authority to be on the streets between that hour and 3 a.m. without a permit from this military governor. Yet it was precisely at the time when the military were in absolute possession and control of the city that the destruction took place. General Strickland and his officers failed utterly to take any steps to prevent the fires, to limit their extent or to stop looting in the area under their command. They had sufficient force to do these things, but the will to do them was absent.

One of the minor mysteries of the night is what became of much of the looted property. General Crozier, who was in charge of the Auxiliary forces in Ireland, put it on record that one member of this force opened up a depot in the north of England for the sale of property looted in Ireland. Whether the Cork loot found its way to this depot or not is still unknown; what is certain is that the military authorities did prevent the sending away of some looted property which had been committed to the post by Auxiliaries. What became of this property ultimately, since it was never returned to the owners?

When it became clear that no impartial inquiry into the burnings would be permitted by the British government, the Sinn Féin organisation took the matter in hand and proceeded to collect evidence in connection with the events of the night of 11 December. Sworn statements were taken from nearly 100 witnesses, including American citizens and Englishmen, as well as many local persons who were not in sympathy with the national movement. This evidence was detailed and specific, and was so overwhelmingly conclusive that no doubt could remain in the mind of any reasonable person but that the city of Cork had been deliberately burned by the British army of occupation on that night.

QUICK CHANGE OF PLAN WAS NECESSARY TO COUNTER THE ENEMY AT MONREAL

MID-CLARE BRIGADE, 18 DECEMBER 1920

by Joe Barrett

(formerly QM Mid-Clare Brigade IRA and O/C Mid-Clare Brigade flying column)

THE ACTIVE SERVICE UNIT of the Mid-Clare Brigade was astir early on the morning of 18 December 1920. Long before the dawn of that winter day had broken over the hills there had been a clatter of arms and equipment and an urgency of movement under the roofs of Tullagha in the Kilfenora district where, in the homes of the O'Donoghues, the O'Loughlins and the McCormacks, the column had been billeted on the previous night. O'Donoghue's was its headquarters whilst in Tullagha, for Andy O'Donoghue was the O/C of the 5th Battalion of the brigade, and it was by his house that fifty-six fighting men stood to arms that morning, under the column commander, with Peadar O'Loughlin and Ignatius O'Neill, prior to setting out on a four-mile march across country, to an ambush site that had been selected at Monreal, on the road between Ennistymon and Ennis.

Some twenty-five column men carried service rifles, valuable trophies from the disarming of seven British soldiers in Ennis, an attack on an RIC patrol at Rineen and a big haul from Ruan RIC barracks. The remainder of the men had shotguns, which weapon the Mid-Clare Brigade had adapted for military purposes in a way that was peculiarly its own. The idea belonged to an old fowler whose reputation for shooting wild duck was a by-word in a large part of the county, and its implementation had made the shotgun a deadly weapon at many times its normal effective range. To achieve this with an ordinary twelve-bore sporting gun his method was simple and inexpensive, and it was readily adopted in the Mid-Clare Brigade, in the absence of a sufficiency of service rifles. It simply entailed melting candle grease into a cartridge charged with buckshot, and the ammunition thus made was proved capable of penetrating quarter-inch timber at 250 yards' range. The destructive effect achieved by it at 100 yards or thereabouts can readily be visualised.

Over paths that led across rock and bog and heather the column moved in a south-westerly direction, in the darkness of that winter morning. In addition to their rifles and shotguns some of the men carried hand grenades that had been captured at Ruan. Their objective at Monreal was the destruction of two lorries of military and police which had been observed to make daily routine journeys between Ennis and Ennistymon, and the capture of their arms and ammunition. It had been noted that each lorry carried a complement of between twenty-five and thirty officers and men, and that the patrol usually left Ennistymon between nine and ten o'clock in the morning. The value of the potential booty could be reckoned between fifty and sixty rifles with a plentiful supply of ammunition, a machine gun or, maybe, two, with adequate pans of ammunition, and some revolvers.

Ennis lies about sixteen miles in a more or less southerly direction from Ennistymon which, in turn, is about three miles from the position selected for the ambush. There the road from Ennistymon faces rising ground before turning sharply to the south-east. Around Monreal the landscape conforms to a pattern found a great deal west of the Shannon. Heather, moss and outcrops of rocky ground predominate all around whilst the road is fenced on both sides by the loosely piled stone walls that are well-known to all travellers in the west. The walls and small folds in the ground provided the only cover available to the attackers. For that reason it was considered necessary to engage the enemy at quarters closer than what might be deemed advisable in places where the face of the countryside had been cast in a different mould. Withdrawal under fire from positions such as those taken up at Monreal presented obvious difficulties. On the other hand, there was the decided advantage of having the enemy exposed to a wide, uninterrupted field of fire from the section lying in wait for him, and that factor, in conjunction with the closeness of the range, invariably resulted in heavy losses being inflicted on him at the beginning of such an encounter. Monreal provided an outstanding example of an ambush fought under such conditions.

From the point where the road from Ennistymon turns sharply round the high ground towards the south-east, a stone wall straddles the hill and stretches east. Part of the wall forms the northern side of a rectangular cattle or sheep shelter which comprises four stone walls, built to a height of seven feet or thereabouts, open overhead and with a little gap at its south-eastern corner, that can be quickly opened or closed. Men of the No. 2 section were posted inside the rectangle and they manned the wall facing north, with signallers higher up to the east and armed flankers on protective duty on the rising ground south of the shelter and above it towards the east. The little gap in the shelter had been cleared of obstacles to permit the men inside to withdraw that way should an evacuation of their position become necessary. It was in this manner that the column commander had disposed his forces on the east of the road, where Commandant Ignatius O'Neill was in command.

On the opposite side of the road the main body of the No. 1 section had cover behind a stone wall, about thirty yards away from the road and more or less parallel with it. They were appreciably south of the No. 2 section, an arrangement which permitted fire to be brought to bear on the enemy from both sides of the road without the possibility of either section being endangered by the crossfire of the other. In a little fold of ground south of the stone wall the column commander took up his position and he had with him there John Joe Neylon, Martin Slattery and John Minihan. Each section had about twelve riflemen and a fair number of grenades, and had two men detailed to guard the flanks. Men with

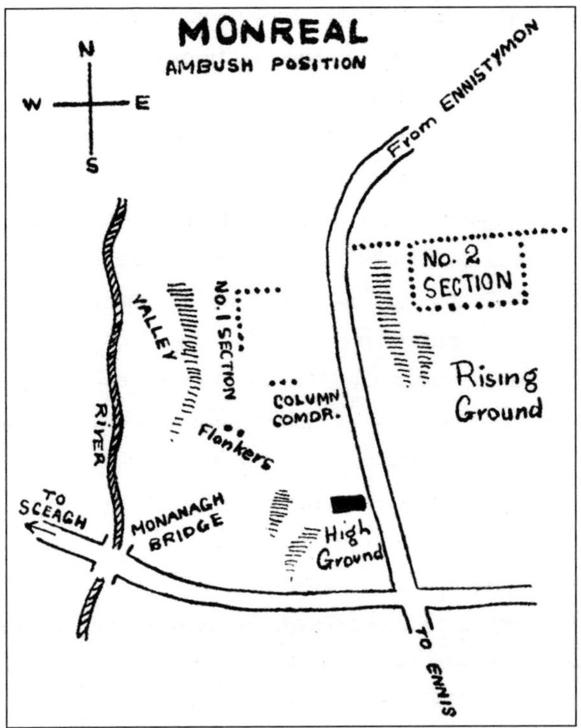

grenades occupied selected positions behind the roadside fences. There was an outer ring of shotgun men on protective duties around the entire position.

It was a morning of heavy frost and the coming of daylight revealed ice crusts on the many little bogholes west of the road. The men felt the cold intensely as they quietly awaited the enemy, in their positions behind the stone walls or in the ground folds amongst the heather. To the west, below the rear of No. 1 section, the ground sloped sharply towards a long valley through which the River Inagh flows. The river is bridged at Monanagh where the by-road to Sceagh leads westwards over a hill that rises up from the far bank.

The approach of the enemy was not signalled until 9.15 a.m., when the IRA officers found to their concern that three lorries would have to be dealt with instead of the two for which they had prepared. They were travelling about 400 yards apart which meant that the third lorry would still be outside the ambush position when the leading one was engaged, and that the enemy elements aboard it would be free to engage the IRA section from outside the ambush position. That situation was bound to present the column with a serious problem, for the dispositions of the two sections had been made with only two lorries in mind, and the men in ambush would be fully occupied with the first and second lorries. There was the added factor that the enemy had an additional twenty-five or thirty fighters available, which gave him a substantial numerical advantage over the column. Even with two lorries his firepower would have been vastly greater than that of the attackers. Thus it happened that, from the outset, the dice was heavily loaded to the disadvantage of the waiting column; but it was a risk that attended most actions by the IRA and had always to be accepted as a possibility.

As the lorries approached a single shot rang out clearly in the frosty air. One of the men facing the oncoming enemy had accidentally discharged his weapon when endeavouring to improve his firing position behind the stone wall on the rising ground east of the road. The incident was unfortunate, for, whilst it did not cause the enemy to pull up, it undoubtedly alerted him. Immediately that the leading lorry had rounded the bend of the road it came under a deadly fire from the men of the No. 1 section who raked it at a range of about thirty yards. A stream of lead was poured into its mixed complement of military and police, and dead and wounded fell from it onto the road. One apparently unwounded soldier made a flying leap out of it, but his feet had scarcely touched the ground when he fell riddled to death. The driver who had miraculously escaped being hit, took the lorry through at top speed and it disappeared in the direction of Ennis. It subsequently transpired that all in the first lorry had been killed or wounded, and that most of the British losses, which amounted to sixteen killed and fourteen wounded, were numbered amongst its occupants.

The second lorry, which also carried a mixed force of military and police, drew up as it reached the ambush position and its occupants jumped down on the road, though not before their numbers had been reduced by the fire put down on them by the No. 2 section in the high ground above the road. The police amongst them in particular lost no time about getting to work on the men inside the animal shelter, and largely by the use of grenades, they had soon made the place untenable. O'Neill realised that his whole section was in danger of being outflanked, so he withdrew it across the hill in accordance with a prearranged plan; its capture was averted by a stern and skilful rearguard action fought over a couple of miles of country.

In the meantime, the No. 1 section, which had wrought such havoc on the leading lorry, was engaged by enemy elements from the second lorry, who had remained on the road and who had not taken part in pressing home the attack against O'Neill's men. Whilst this was taking place the occupants of the third lorry deployed, and, from outside the ambush position, they also laid down a heavy and accurate fire on the No. 1 section which had been placed west of the road. There was also imminent danger of that section being outflanked, so that the column commander had no choice but to withdraw his men from their hazardous positions. It was arranged that the commander, with Martin Slattery and John Minihan, would cover the withdrawal of the section as it fell back towards the little river that flowed through the valley at their rear. The section would later keep the enemy to ground with well-directed fire whilst the trio was pulling out. To men firing from the road, the valley was dead ground, so it was thought that the men of the No. 1 section would have an interval of security as they went through it. Before they had succeeded in doing so, however, the British had established command of the high ground east of the road, and having mounted a Lewis light machine gun there, they were able to play it on the men in the valley. Another party of the enemy had worked its way along the road in the Ennis direction under cover of a stone fence that screened and gave it protection from the fire of the commander, Minihan and Slattery. This enemy party, which had another Lewis gun, entered an old cabin that commanded the valley from high ground on which it had been built. From where they lay in the relative security of the fold of ground, the three column men watched two soldiers make a breach in the cabin wall that faced towards the valley. They were, of course, working from the inside. When the breach was sufficiently large and otherwise to their liking, they pushed the nose of a Lewis gun through it. So placed it would have a clear field of fire on the men who were wading across the river that flowed through the valley, and who were already under the fire of the Lewis gun mounted on the high ground east of the road. Inside the cabin two gunners sighted their weapon and made ready to send its contents ripping into the men below. They never got started. Calmly the three IRA rearguard men in the fold of ground waited until the breach had been completed. The larger the British gunners would make it, the lesser would be their chance of ever again handling the round magazine of a Lewis. One of them had the butt of the weapon at his shoulder, ready to open fire, when a rifle cracked and there was one gunner less in His Majesty's army of occupation in Ireland. Having pulled the dead body of his comrade out of the way, the second gunner grasped the butt with his left hand, rammed the gun to the shoulder and in doing so exposed himself to the satisfaction of an IRA marksman who squinted his sights and squeezed his trigger to send the gunner following his comrade into eternity. The column rearguard had made its presence felt and, covered by some of the men down by the river, the trio which comprised it then withdrew. The British had by that time succeeded in getting the machine gun out of the cabin, and having mounted it on a piece of high ground to the rear of the structure, they attempted to bring it to bear upon the river. In order to achieve an effective field of fire it was necessary to operate the gun from an exposed position. This they tried to do repeatedly, but they gave up the attempt when five of their number had fallen to the accurate fire of the section's covering party.

Fire from the first Lewis gun ripped the river as the men of the main body of the section waded across it towards the opposite bank. There were flecks of red here and there on the ice-cold water, for

Paddy O'Loughlin, Bill MacNamara and Bill Carroll had been hit and were being helped along by the others. Fortunately none of them had been wounded seriously and all three, with the rest of the section, reached the safety of the far side of the hill that rises up from the western edge of the river. There a halt was made and a check showed that there were two men missing, Jack Hassett and Jim Kierse, who had been covering the right flank, and who had not succeeded in getting away. Immediately that their absence had been discovered, the commander asked for six volunteers to return with him to the scene of the ambush and try to rescue their missing comrades. It was a nasty proposition for men who had just withdrawn with difficulty from a severe engagement under heavy fire from machine guns. To accomplish the task that lay ahead the volunteers would probably be called upon to face the same thing again, with the likelihood that some of them would not come back next time. Yet, when the call for six volunteers was made, not a man hung back; it was answered by every one of them. With pride in his eyes, John Joe Neylon turned to his commander and said simply: 'By heavens, Joe, but there are great men in Ireland still.'

Reconnaissance revealed that Kierse and Hassett were standing up to their waists in water under Monanagh bridge, and that the British were on the bridge directly over their heads, having advanced up the by-road that leads west off the main Ennis-Ennistymon road in the direction of Sceagh. It transpired that one of the column flankers had been hit when attempting to get away towards the south, which was not the withdrawal route followed by the main body. Both were then unable to continue across the river, so they went under the bridge. Apparently, the British had observed them do so, for when the column had withdrawn behind the hill, police and soldiers advanced on the bridge with the object of killing or capturing the two men. They would undoubtedly have succeeded in accomplishing either one or the other, had the section's return to the scene been delayed a moment longer. Hassett in particular was in bad shape, with two wounds in each leg and the lead having remained embedded in them. Each had a trying ordeal that December day, standing wounded and waist high in the icy water with a pitiless enemy closing in.

Having sized up the situation, the section commander manoeuvred six men into a position from which they put down on the bridge a heavy fire that drove the enemy back to the crossroads. The British returned the IRA fire from the roadside, but, whilst these exchanges were taking place, the column O/C succeeded in getting the wounded Volunteers from under the bridge and, having availed of the cover provided by surrounding fences, he had them conveyed safely to the security of the far side of the hill. There the full section answered the roll-call. The British made no attempt to follow the section beyond the bridge, and, untroubled by further enemy interference, it withdrew towards Sceagh. Whilst on the way the men had adequate evidence of the enthusiasm of the people for the cause for which the war was being waged. Buttered cake, raw eggs and chunks of cooked bacon awaited them, together with cans of tea and milk. Horses were provided to carry the wounded and various other forms of assistance were forthcoming to get them quickly to relatively safe billets in which medical men who attended the wounded were Dr Hillary of Miltown-Malbay, Dr Peterson of Lisdoonvarna and Dr Hayes of Kilmaley. Bill Carroll, who had been wounded whilst crossing the river during the withdrawal, had been an RIC man stationed in Ruan barracks at the time of its capture by the IRA. Taken as a hostage by the attackers, he had volunteered to fight with them for Ireland and subsequently took part in many a stern encounter.

THE AMBUSH AT GLENWOOD

EAST CLARE BRIGADE, 20 JANUARY 1921

by Donal O'Kelly and George Mulvey

The authors are indebted to officers of the brigade staff, who were members of the ASU and who took part in the action described, for the verification of the military details contained in this article, including the nominal roll of participants and the list of houses destroyed during reprisals by crown forces.

THE CLOSING MONTHS of 1920 found the East Clare Brigade, commanded by Austin Brennan, engaged in a series of sharp encounters with British forces. On 20 October the police patrol at Feakle had been attacked and in the following months similar actions took place at Broadford and O'Briensbridge. Casualties had been inflicted on the enemy in each case and at O'Briensbridge, Michael Brennan, brother of Austin and brigade director of operations and O/C of the active service unit, had been wounded and put out of action for some weeks. During the lull that ensued the country was shocked by news of the murder in cold blood by the Auxiliaries at Killaloe of four unarmed prisoners taken in raids in the Whitegate and Mountshannon area after the action at O'Briensbridge. Martial law was proclaimed in County Clare on 1 January 1921, and accordingly, when Michael Brennan rejoined his command in the first days of the new year, immediate offensive action was decided on both to express IRA reaction to the imposition of martial law and to relieve the enemy pressure in neighbouring brigade areas.

The intelligence staff, thanks mainly to the good work of Jack Egan of Pullough, had already noted a suitable objective, a police patrol car, which travelled frequently between Sixmilebridge and Broadford, enemy posts about twelve miles apart by the most direct route. Broadford is situated in a valley between the Slieve Bernagh mountains and Knockaphunta and for the better part of the way the direct road between the two posts skirts the lower slopes of the latter hill. The country was suitable for ambush and quick dispersal, and the principal difficulty in waylaying this patrol lay in the fact that the crown forces in east Clare were becoming gun-shy and wary. An intricate network of roads offered them a choice of routes coming and going, and it had been noted that whatever route they took on the outward journey, they always returned by a different one. From Sixmilebridge the direct road to Broadford led through Castlelake and Belvoir Cross, the alternatives most often favoured being the road through Kilmurry and Enagh or through Kilmurry and Kilkishen. It had been hoped that it would have been possible to stage an ambush at Castlelake, which covered two of the three routes most likely to be taken by the enemy, but close inspection proved that the terrain was unsuitable. Michael Brennan, in consultation with the IO, Jack Egan, finally decided to set the trap at the entrance gate of Glenwood House, trusting to his IO's belief, based on long observation, that the enemy would come that way.

The ambush position was a good one. At Glenwood the road skirts the slope of Knockaphunta. The curved wall to the north of the entrance gate commanded the road approaching it, and on either side of the gate the ground to the east of the road was eight or nine feet above the carriage way and topped by a wall which afforded cover from view and from fire. West of the road the ground was level and open as far as Belvoir woods, about half a mile to the north.

The action was originally planned for the first week in January, and the ASU had received orders to assemble at Glenwood, on 6 January. A postponement was decided, however, and the next activity of the column took place on 11 January, when it assembled at Oatfield, taking up quarters at Kelly's, O'Grady's and other local houses. On 13 January it moved to Cratloe with the intention of attacking the enemy transport moving north-west along the Red Gate-Cratloe road. A brief action ensued, followed, as was usual in Clare, by house burnings

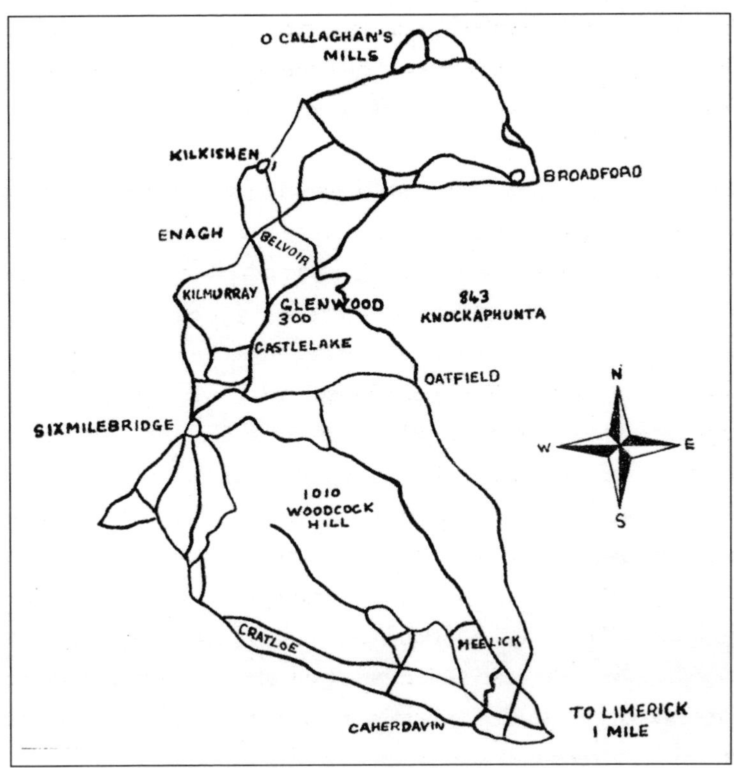

and outrages against the civilian population. It is worth noting here that while murder and arson were familiar weapons of the crown forces throughout Ireland in 1920–21, they were employed by them more consistently and systematically in County Clare than anywhere else. One of the houses to go up in flames after the Cratloe action was the family home of Thomas McGrath, vice-commander of the brigade.

Following the action at Cratloe, the column moved to Woodcock Hill and from vantage points on the high ground watched an impressive sweep of the countryside by the military, who approached the area along the Meelick-Sixmilebridge road. As, however, the soldiers did not leave the road, or even dismount from their lorries, the display of military power was more spectacular than effective. A member of the column, an ex-soldier named Martin MacNamara of Kilkishen, told the officers in advance that the military would act in this manner, because junior officers had strict order not to commit their troops to action unless they were aware of the strength of the opposition they were likely to meet. In practice, of course, they never were, and such British officers as possessed initiative and an inclination for aggressive tactics, were restrained by the realisation that the probable reward of zeal would be a court martial.

On 14 January the column dispersed and the men returned to their battalion areas, with order to re-assemble half an hour before daylight on the morning of 20 January at Belvoir Cross. The brigade staff had decided to mount the previously postponed attack at Glenwood on that date. On the night of 19 January the men of the 2nd and 3rd Battalions assembled at Kelly's House in Oatfield, where they were sheltered and fed. The contingent from the 5th Battalion mobilised at Donnellan's of Clonloun near O'Callaghan's Mills, while the 6th Battalion and 4th Battalion men met at the houses of Jimmy Slattery and Martin Gleeson of Bodyke.

Members of the 1st Battalion and those of the Kilkishen Company proceeded direct to Belvoir Cross. The scene of the ambush was in the 5th Battalion area, almost on the line dividing it from the 2nd Battalion.

At the appointed hour thirty-seven men reported for duty at Belvoir Cross. They included the Brigade O/C, Austin Brennan, and Tom McGrath, Vice-Commandant. Command of the action was, however, in the hands of Michael Brennan, the O/C of the ASU, and for the occasion the brigade staff officers acted as section leaders under his orders. The remaining personnel was as follows: 1st Battalion: Jack Grady, Danny O'Brien and Jack Curley, all of Quin; 2nd Battalion: Mick Hehir, Jack MacCormick of Clonlara, Martin Naughton of Oatfield and Seamus Hogan of Galway, who was temporarily attached to the East Clare Brigade at the time; 3rd Battalion: Jackie Ryan; 4th Battalion: Michael Clery and Tom MacInerney, both of Mountshannon, and Dinny Minogue of Scariff; 5th Battalion: Joe Clancy, Martin MacNamara, Mick Neville and Jimmy MacInerney of Kilkishen, Jack Egan (intelligence officer) of Pullough, Pat (Tadhg)

McGrath, Dan Lenehan, Peter St Ledger, Michael Shaughnessy, Mick Moloney of O'Callaghan's Mills, Michael O'Dea, Paddy Quinn, Paddy Hanrahan, and Paddy MacCarthy of Tulla, Joe MacNamara and Paddy Cox of Bodyke; 6th Battalion: Matty McGrath, Joe Tuohy, Joe Rocheford, Joe Nugent, Mick O'Brien, Matty Moloney and Mick Tuohy, all of Feakle.

Something less than half the column was armed with rifles; the remainder, except for the scouts who were unarmed, were equipped with revolvers and shotguns. Dan Lenehan carried a Mills grenade.

Michael Brennan inspected the men, checked their arms and ammunition, and issued his orders. He divided the column into three sections, commanded respectively by himself, Austin Brennan and Tom McGrath. He posted his own section, armed with rifles, along the curved wall on the north side of the entrance gate to Glenwood House, where they could command the enemy's route of approach from good cover, a stone wall over which the riflemen could fire. Austin Brennan's section, armed with rifles and shotguns, took up position some fifty yards to the north, also under a covering wall, and Tom McGrath's men, armed with short-range weapons and the grenade, were placed about 100 yards south of the gate to Glenwood. All sections were on the eastern or right-hand side of the road coming from the Sixmilebridge direction, on ground some eight or nine feet above the carriageway. The orders were that the O/C's section would open fire first, after which the other section leaders would take independent action. All was ready and the men in their combat positions in good time. It had been noted by Jack Egan that the lorry usually made its outward journey to Broadford about eleven o'clock, but of course no one knew if it would take the Glenwood route on that particular day. There was no sign of it up to about 11.30, and accordingly, Michael Brennan sent a scout into Kilkishen to find out if it had passed through there. Incidentally, it was Fair Day in the village, a fact that had contributed to the selection of 20 January as the day for the attack. Many a likely ambush had been made abortive by the presence of civilian traffic on the road at the critical moment, and the staff felt that the danger of such a mishap would be minimised on Fair Day when it could be assumed that most of the local traffic would be concentrated in the village during mid-morning.

In due course the scouts reported that the enemy patrol had not passed through Kilkishen up to noon, so the column settled down to a further tedious wait. It was 3.30 in the afternoon when at last scouts signalled that the enemy were approaching. The roar of a Crossley engine at high speed was heard and, as the lorry came in view, Michael Brennan's section opened rapid fire. Austin Brennan joined in and so did Tom McGrath. Thanks to perfect timing by the O/C, the lorry was almost directly under McGrath's section when the action started. The short-range weapons took their toll and Dan Lenehan lobbed his grenade fairly into the lorry, a fine effort, as it is not easy to make such a score on a vehicle travelling at forty miles an hour. It was ineffective, however, as the grenade failed to explode. Then occurred one of those freak episodes that sometimes happen in war. As always on such occasions, fire was directed specially against the driver of the vehicle, but the lorry with its load of dead and dying, instead of crashing, drew up normally, right at the entrance to Glenwood House and a man, who must have been the driver, jumped out, apparently unhurt, and under the rifles of the amazed attackers, made his way off the road on the left-hand side and got clear away to the shelter of Belvoir woods. Driver or not, it was certainly his lucky day. Another unwounded policeman also made his escape, but the rest of the police party was dead or mortally wounded. The dead were District Inspector Clarke, Sergeant M. Molloy and Constables P. Doogue, M. Moran, W.J. Smith and F.E. Morris, Sergeant J. Egan and Constable Selve were wounded. Eight rifles, six revolvers and a considerable quantity of ammunition were captured, and the enemy lorry was destroyed by fire. The column suffered no casualties, which is not surprising as the accuracy of its fire had destroyed the enemy before he could retaliate.

When the firing ceased, the wounded, who were beyond aid, were made as comfortable as possible, and were cared for until the end by Fathers Daly and O'Dea of Sixmilebridge, who were summoned quickly to the scene, together with local helpers. The booty was collected and the lorry set on fire, after which the column retired to Oatfield. As they climbed the mountainside a sharp explosion on the scene of the ambush told Dan Lenehan that at last his well-aimed grenade had come to life in the heat of the burning Crossley.

The men of the 1st, 4th and 6th Battalions, and those of the Tulla Company of the 5th Battalion, dispersed in the vicinity of Glenwood, while the remaining members of the column moved on to Kelly's of Oatfield, and later to Vaughan's of Sallybank, where they spent the night. Next day they moved on to MacNamara's of Kilmore; the following day to Kilbane where they stayed at the three houses of the Gunning family and the night after to Ryan's of Cloneconry, whose house had been looted, wrecked and set on fire by Auxiliaries from Killaloe the night before. The Ryans, had, however, got the fire under control after the departure of the Auxiliaries and the shell of the house was still habitable. Here they stayed until the following Monday, when Paddy Donnellan, now clerk of the District Courts in the area, guided them across country to Callaghan's and Skehan's of Clonloun, in the O'Callaghan's Mills district, from which point the men finally returned to their respective battalion areas.

Following the ambush there ensued a night and day of terror, not likely to be forgotten by those who experienced it. Darkness had set in when lorries filled with RIC Auxiliaries and Black and Tans converged upon the Kilkishen area, from Killaloe, Broadford and Sixmilebridge. Their courage stimulated by liquor, these upholders of law and order fired their weapons indiscriminately as they bore down upon Kilkishen, feeling reasonably certain that by that time the IRA would have withdrawn from the area. Homes along the roadside were fired into by the passing lorries and their occupants terrorised. The usual reprisals, which meant the destruction by fire of the houses and other property of unarmed civilians, were carried out in a wide area, the principal incendiaries being the Auxiliaries from Killaloe. Joe Clancy, a prominent member of the East Clare flying column, who had served as a captain in the British army during the 1914–1918 war, had his home near the village of Kilkishen. He had rarely seen the inside of it for more than a year previously, and neither had his brother, Paddy, as both of them were 'on the run'. At the time of the Glenwood ambush it was occupied by their aged father, John Clancy, and by their sister, Winifred, then a member of Cumann na mBan, and now Mrs Murphy of Ennis. Knowing that the enemy would soon return to the locality to wreak his vengeance upon the defenceless people, and that he would very likely burn the house and shoot her father, Winifred quickly took him to a place of relative safety, near Newmarket-on-Fergus. As she had more or less anticipated, their house was the first entered by the enraged enemy. The entire contents of the place were smashed to smithereens by the wreckers who, for some reason, did not give it to the flames. The Auxiliaries from Killaloe were less squeamish, and that night a chain of flaming homesteads marked their progress from Killaloe to Kilkishen via O'Briensbridge and Broadford. The Hayes and Ryan houses at Cloneconry were the first to blaze; and they were quickly followed by Savage's of Lissane, Broughton's of Ballykelly, Duggan's of Aclare, Fitzgerald's of Belvoir, Mack's of Knockatureen and Casey's of Sixmilebridge. Even this list does not complete the tale of destruction.

A curious feature of the enemy behaviour that night was that, except for the burning of hay and out-offices belonging to Mr Dwyer, no damage was caused to the village of Kilkishen itself, though its some 400 inhabitants were terrorised by the reckless shooting and brutal behaviour of the drunken constabulary. The police were so drunk and firing so wildly that many of them had to be disarmed by their own officers, so great was the risk that they would inflict casualties upon each other. At many points around Kilkishen that night could be seen the red glow sent up by flames from the burning homes of the people.

Police returned to the district early next day, and, this time accompanied by military detachments, they proceeded to the scene of the ambush. Houses were entered by them, people questioned, threatened and beaten up, and the contents of farmyards destroyed by fire. The reprisals were extended to embrace a wide area of east Clare and about twenty homes went up in flames in the orgy of destruction that followed. The extent of the damage was reckoned at many thousands of pounds. Twenty-two arrests were made, though all but two of the arrested persons were released following a short period of detention. But though the British might destroy the countryside for many miles around Glenwood, they could not kill the unconquerable spirit of the people of east Clare. A couple of nights later a Black and Tan dispatch rider was killed at the same bend on the road at Glenwood where the ambush had taken place. This time no reprisals followed. Speaking of the morale of the East Clare flying column to the writer, Joe Clancy declared: 'You can take it from me, that in my four years in France during the war, I never came across a braver or a better disciplined lot of lads. They were ever ready for a scrap, and always cheerful and good humoured.'

A beautiful Calvary has been erected in the village green in Tuamgraney, as a memorial tribute to the men and women of east Clare who took part in the fight for independence. About half the cost of the memorial was subscribed by east Clare exiles in America. It was blessed and unveiled by the Very Rev. D. Flannery, PP, Bodyke, in the presence of Most Rev. Dr Rodgers, the Co-adjutor Bishop of Killaloe.

Within a few days of the reprisals carried out by the British in east Clare, following the ambush at Glenwood, startling disclosures concerning the violence and burnings caused throughout Clare by crown forces, were made in a report published by Judge Mathew Bodkin, County Court Judge for Clare. Judge Bodkin stated that in the period covered in his report, it had been proved before him that criminal injuries had been done by British crown forces in 139 cases and that compensation to the amount of £187,046 had been awarded. That amount he described as an impossible burden on the ratepayers of the county, and he expressed the opinion that it should be paid by the British Treasury. He stated that in none of the cases was there any evidence that the victims had been guilty of an offence, and that in a large number of cases women and children had been treated with great violence.

Publication of the full text of the judge's report was made in *The Manchester Guardian*, and *The Westminster Gazette* made the following comment on it, early in February 1921:

> What the judge reports in Clare has been going on, more or less, in nearly all Irish counties, and is still going on. Germans in Belgium were able to guarantee a reasonably quiet life to their victims after a few weeks of terror. The government in Ireland has been able to offer no such guarantee to the victims of its reprisals ... There is only one way to recover what is lost and that is for the government definitely to recognise that the method of terror has failed, and to withdraw all forces which have been instruments in the proceedings that Judge Bodkin describes, to proclaim a truce and re-open the door to negotiations.

'It is humiliating,' declared *The Star*, London, 'that England should first send a great force to coerce Ireland and should then be condemned to pay compensation for crimes outside and beyond either the laws of nations or humanity.'

An example of the crimes referred to by *The Star* had taken place at Canada Cross, Miltown-Malbay, when RIC and soldiers opened fire without warning on a harmless gathering of youths and girls. For many years 'illuminations' provided by a display of lighted candles in the windows of the homes of the people, and by lighted tar barrels in the streets and near rural assembly places, had been symbols of rejoicing through the provinces. Consequently, the lighted tar barrel always attracted a happy crowd of people, men, women and children, and such gatherings were never disorderly. The night of 14 April 1920, was an occasion for special rejoicing, as men who had seemed doomed to die on hunger strike, many of them Claremen, had been saved by their release from prison that day. The gathering by the tar barrel at Canada Cross was typical of the hundreds of similar expressions of the people's joy and relief, made in most parts of the country. Young people attracted by the candle-lit windows and the 'bonfire', laughed, sang, and generally enjoyed themselves in the ways of young people when there is cause for merriment. But their joy was short-lived. Out of the encircling darkness, a murderous blow was struck at them by police and British military, who poured volleys of rifle fire into the assembled people. These uniformed assassins had ranged themselves in firing positions over a stretch of approximately 200 yards, from the corner of Matt Lynch's premises to those of Mrs Honan. An order to disperse was shouted to the people near the tar barrel, and volleys of rifle fire rang out immediately afterwards. Scenes of panic followed as people scattered in terror, seeking to escape the lethal weapons that had been turned upon them. Three youths were killed and about fifteen persons were wounded. The dead were Patrick Hennessy, John O'Loughlin and Thomas O'Leary.

Public feeling all over Ireland, and to some degree in England too, had been shocked by this murderous action by crown forces. Mr Denis Henry, the Attorney General, had an official explanation. The police and military had been provoked, he told the House of Commons, by about 150 men, who had marched defiantly in procession, carrying flags. Missiles had been thrown and shots had even been fired by the marchers, stated Mr Henry.

But British terrorism could not force the Clare people to suppress the truth. 'A monstrous mis-statement of facts; an absolutely untrue allegation,' was how Very Rev. Canon Hannon, parish priest of Miltown-Malbay, described the version of the occurrence given in the House of Commons. 'There were,' said Canon Hannon, 'no procession, no marching, no flags; instead of 150 there were not thirty men in the crowd fired on; and they were shot at without being given one minute to disperse.' Who will deny that Canon Hannon of Miltown-Malbay was not in a better position to obtain the true facts about the shootings than the King's Attorney in London, whose version of the report had been provided by the uniformed murderers themselves? The statements of the parish priest were supported by the facts revealed at the inquest, at which the next-of-kin of the dead were represented by Mr Paddy Lynch, KC. Evidence brought forward by Mr Lynch showed that RIC Sergeant Hampson, who commanded a combined RIC and Highland

Light Infantry force that night, was the man who planned and ordered the savage action. Hampson had been drinking heavily for months prior to it. Two ex-British soldiers testified that no shots had been fired or missiles thrown by the crowd, and that nothing had been said or done to justify the shooting by the police and soldiers. Traders of the town swore that Hampson 'was under the influence of drink' on the night of the shooting, and that when leading the enemy force out of the RIC barracks he had told them 'to be getting ready'. One of the RIC constables with him had been overheard to use a foul expression and say that it was right to kill them (the victims of the shooting). There was a significant omission from the records of the night as given in the RIC diary in the Miltown-Malbay barracks. It had entries in respect of the going out and return of Sergeant Hampson, six RIC constables and the military; details of the routine examination of three revolvers and three bombs by Hampson. But it included no reference to the fact that three people had been killed and many wounded. The medical evidence given at the inquest showed that two of the dead had been shot in the back.

In the House of Commons, persistent questioning by Commander Kenworthy (afterwards Lord Strabolgi) embarrassed the attorney general. The commander wanted to know why the crowd had been interfered with on the night in question. Mr Joe Devlin, the Nationalist MP for Belfast, described Mr Henry's previous answers as 'a series of falsehoods'. Henry's reply was weak. He said: 'The inquest which is being held on those who have been unfortunately killed is not yet concluded. The whole matter will be considered by the Irish government.'

When the inquest was concluded, Hampson and a number of his RIC and military collaborators had been found 'guilty of wilful murder without any provocation'. In addition of Hampson, those whom the jury found guilty of murder were Constables Thomas O'Connor and Thomas Keenan of the RIC; Lance-Corporal Kenneth McLeod and Privates William Kilgour, James McEwan, Peter McLoughlin, Robert Bunting and Richard Adams, all of the Highland Light Infantry. On the application of Mr Lynch, KC, the coroner issued warrants for arrest on charges of murder against the three RIC men and six Highlanders named. The warrants were served on the district inspector of the RIC, a man named Mooney; but they were never executed. The British government allowed the murderers to go free as the air, despite the findings of a coroner's court functioning under the much-vaunted code of British justice. Later, the British were to forbid the holding of coroners' inquests in Ireland.

Viscount Simon, the noted advocate, then Sir John Simon, was scathing in his criticism of the conditions brought about in Ireland by the terrorist policy of Lloyd George's coalition government. Speaking at Stedham in February 1921, he declared:

> When we talked of preserving the rights of small nations they meant it not only of the Belgium and Poland, but of Ireland. When they talked of a League of Nations they meant it not as a peroration for a speech, but of flesh and blood. As long as they remained under the domination of the coalition how could anybody really believe anything? The recent condition of Ireland was poisoning the relations of England with America; it was holding up the name of England to contempt among critics throughout the world, and it made their protestation that they would go to all lengths to protect a small country like Belgium seem futile. History would write them down as nothing less than a set of humbugs. There was no justification for treating the present Irish race as though they were a lot of cut-throats and assassins. The government's policy was replying to outrage by visiting people who could not answer and were never shown to have had anything to do with it at all. It is quite possible to suppose that these attacks, made night after night upon towns and villages by crown forces, are not carried on with the connivance of their superiors. They were not justified by the government, for the government said: 'We have no information.'

But the campaign of terrorism continued unabated and remained one of the principal weapons used by the British enemy against the people of Ireland and the Irish Republican Army. Exclusive of casualties in armed conflicts, 203 were killed in Ireland in 1920, according to *The Irish Bulletin.* Of the victims, 172 were young men; twelve were children under seventeen years of age; six were women; ten were aged sixty or over, and three were boys of eighteen. The casualties included two Catholic priests. The heaviest casualties were in November, when sixty-four persons were shot dead. In December, the number killed was fifty. Executions of prisoners of war, murders of defenceless civilians, burnings of property, and lootings, were events of almost daily occurrence. In that terrible period the people of Clare were comforted by their beloved and patriotic Bishop, Most Rev. Dr Fogarty. In the course of his Lenten Pastoral, in that momentous year, 1921, he had the following to say:

> Peace will yet come, and come, I believe, sooner than most people imagine. Meanwhile, what Ireland needs in her deep distress are the two divine virtues of fortitude and wisdom – fortitude to endure, and wisdom to choose the right way. It has been truly said that, in the conflict with evil, final victory lies not with those who can inflict most, but those who can endure most.
>
> The calamitous days we live in have made Ireland a veritable purgatory for all of us. Anyone who knows the psychology of the Irish people is well aware that brute force will never appease them nor intimidate them into a surrender of their natural rights. Ireland will never consent to be led around the world for all time like a dog at the end of a chain, by Sir Edward Carson and his friends.

QUICK ON THE UPTAKE: IRA INTELLIGENCE PAVED WAY TO SUCCESS AT TUREENGARRIFFE

CORK NO. 2 (NORTH) BRIGADE AND KERRY VOLUNTEERS, 28 JANUARY 1921

As told by participants to Patrick Lynch

THE CORK-BOUND TRAVELLER coming out of Kerry by Castleisland of the Moonlighters, journeys over winding roads that give ascent to windy uplands and then gradually dip eastwards. All around the high country and in the valleys among the hills are to be seen white banners of *ceannabhán* that wave against the dark backcloth of windswept bogland; here and there is the diamond-bright gleam of moonadawn [*sic*] nestling amongst the fern. It is a rugged way by sweep and bend through rocky, heather-coated glens, where blue-black whortleberries cluster beneath the shapely bells that dangle rich red from the graceful stems of foxglove. It is a landscape typical of the entire stretch of country which extends along the eastern edge of Kerry, from Abbeyfeale over the Limerick border to Millstreet in County Cork.

Through it lies the route followed on a January day in 1921 by Major-General Philip Armstrong Holmes, divisional commissioner of police for the counties of Cork and Kerry, when returning to his Cork headquarters with his escort, following an inspection in Kerry. The escort consisted of a sergeant and five constables. They were ambushed by the Newmarket Battalion column and some East Kerry Volunteers under Commandant Seán Moylan, at a place about two miles west of Ballydesmond, where the Castleisland road dips into the glen of Tureengarriffe.

During the early weeks of 1921, the Newmarket Battalion column was quartered in Kiskeam, a more or less remote County Cork village some three or four miles east of the Kerry border, and about equidistant from Mallow and Tralee. The column, which was commanded by Commandant Seán Moylan, was made up of some twenty or so fighting men drawn from the different companies which comprised the battalion. Its armament consisted of about five rifles, a Hotchkiss light machine gun, and a number of revolvers and shotguns.

During the last week in January, two large touring cars of the enemy were observed to pass through Kiskeam and take the Ballydesmond road into Kerry. High-ranking British officers were in the habit of using such transport, so word of the enemy movement was immediately conveyed to Commandant Moylan. He decided to mobilise the column and to prepare an ambush without delay at the most suitable place to be found nearby, on the chance that the British would return by the same route. The chosen spot was in Tureengarriffe Glen in County Kerry, about two miles west of the Cork border. As the cars in which the British party was travelling were driven by high-powered engines, it was thought that the best road block would be a trench cut across the highway. This was dug, and about thirty yards north-east of it were posted the riflemen and shotgun men in positions along a fence facing west. North-west of the trench Mount Falvey commanded a considerable stretch of the road to Scartaglen and Castleisland.

On that vantage point the column's signal section was posted. South of the trench and more or less parallel with the fence lined by the riflemen and shotgun men, the ground rose steeply to a rocky eminence on which the Hotchkiss gun was placed. There also Commandant Moylan made his command post. He had selected his position and disposed of his force with competence. Hardy, tenacious, a product of the rural areas, Moylan, then in his early thirties, had been a Volunteer organiser and was known as a man of study and wide reading. The men who waited with him on the glenside were hard in sinew and shrewd of mind. Farmer's sons and labourers, sons of small town traders, artisans and workers of many kinds, they knew what had to done and the best that was in them went into the doing! The men for whom they lay in ambush were to prove themselves worthy foes.

It was 27 January when the column moved into positions, and that day passed without sign of the enemy. About noon on the following day the approach of the touring cars was signalled from Mount Falvey. They were returning along the same route after all, and the waiting IRA men made ready for them. The element of surprise was a distinct advantage to the attackers, provided that they utilised it properly; so was the choice of ground. Also, they were more numerous than the approaching enemy. Such favourable circumstances were necessary to counterbalance the superior training of the battle-tried British, especially as the IRA ammunition was scarce, and because the Hotchkiss was an unreliable weapon with a tendency to jam. It was trained on the trench as the column awaited the approaching cars, all eyes on the stretch of winding road along which the enemy would travel. Behind the Hotchkiss, which dominated the scene from the rocky eminence, lay Bill Moylan of Newmarket, with Seán Healy of Kilcorney and Denis Galvin of Clonbanin. With the Volunteers who lined the fence north of the trench were Captain Dan Vaughan of Ballydesmond and Captain Danny Guiney of Knocknanaugh, outside Kiskeam. Every man was ready; in a matter of seconds they would be in action.

Into the glen came the cars, and when the driver of the first one saw the trench he increased his speed with the intention of jumping it. Engine flat out, he was racing up to it when Moylan ordered a burst of rapid fire by the Hotchkiss. The trench had proved its effectiveness as a road block when Moylan called upon the British to surrender. Theirs was the swift reaction of brave men and experienced fighters; for in a flash they were out of the cars and blazing at Moylan's position, from places of cover by the roadside. The bark of the Hotchkiss cut through the sound of rifle and revolver fire. Shotguns went off as the men of the column marked down their targets. Bullets spattered and whined, and the sides of the touring cars were perforated. Little swirls of smoke floated upwards, and there was the rank smell of cordite in the noon-day air.

Down on the roadway, Holmes directed the police fire, and not an inch was yielded though he and his party were trapped in a rugged glen, with little hope of escape. Again the ceasefire order was given by Commandant Moylan, and again his call for surrender was answered by a defiant negative backed up by an intensification of fire. The IRA responded with heavy fire and the fight continued to rage.

Through the glen ran a ravine. Moylan directed a Volunteer to cross it, with the purpose of taking the enemy in the rear. To the utter astonishment of his commander, the Volunteer looked at him blankly, and said, 'Commandant, don't you know that I can't take part in this fighting.' Scarcely crediting what he had heard, Moylan asked him why the hell he couldn't. 'Surely you remember, Commandant,' he replied, a broad grin on his face, 'that I was bound to the peace by the republican court at Ballydesmond, a few weeks ago'. What Moylan said then is not recorded, but it packed enough punch to wipe the grin off the humorist's face and set him to his allotted task without further delay. Some few weeks before the ambush, the Volunteer, as a civilian, had participated in a faction fight at Ballydesmond and, having been charged with a breach of the peace, before the republican court for the area, he was found guilty, and bound to the peace. Moylan had been well aware of that lapse of his at Ballydesmond, but was not in the mood to appreciate his humour at Tureengarriffe.

Lead had been exchanged for about half-an-hour when the British were given another opportunity to surrender; but as before, they scorned it and fought on, stubbornly disputing the issue with the IRA, whose fire was taking a terrible toll of them. At last their position had become so desperate that they had no alternative to surrender. They held their hands up and called out that they were ready to give in. When the IRA came down on the road, it was found that one of the British had been killed outright and that all the remaining members of the ambushed party had been wounded, Divisional Commissioner Holmes very seriously. The dead policeman, Constable T. Myles, fell to the first IRA volley. Amongst other injuries suffered, Holmes had a bullet wound in the head and a fractured arm and leg. Of the other members of his escort, Sergeant A. Charman had an arm fractured by a bullet; Constable J.H. Andrews was wounded in the face, right arm and leg. Constables J. Hoare and F.D. Calder were slightly wounded. Holmes would not authorise a surrender until the ammunition of his party had given out. Weakly he asked for the IRA commandant to be brought to him, and when Moylan came up he made the badly wounded major-general as comfortable as possible on the roadside. A folded overcoat was placed beneath his head and a lighted cigarette between his lips.

All the while, the other British wounded were being given first aid, and many of them expressed their appreciation of the chivalrous treatment accorded them. A car owned by an inspector of schools was stopped coming out of the west, and sent back to Tralee with the divisional commissioner and the more seriously wounded British, who were immediately taken to the County Infirmary. A party of British military proceeding from Killeagh to Tralee picked up the other members of the ambushed escort and the body of Constable Myles. Early next morning a special train brought two prominent Cork city surgeons to Tralee to attend to Holmes. They had him removed to Cork that evening and he died in the military hospital there on the following morning. Holmes, who was about forty-five years of age, was a native of Cork city. He joined the RIC as a cadet in 1898, and during his career received five police awards for good service. During the war he served with the Royal Irish Regiment, and was wounded and gassed at the front. Holmes' predecessor in office, the notorious Colonel G.V.B. Smyth, had been shot dead by IRA men in the County Club in Cork city on 17 July 1920. Smyth had just returned from an inspection tour in Kerry, where he had ordered the RIC to 'shoot on sight and ask questions afterwards'. Summary justice dictated just that end for himself. His orders to the RIC in Listowel barracks in June 1920 almost led to mutiny by the men stationed there. 'You must go out six nights a week,' said Divisional Commissioner Smyth to the men, 'and get out of the barracks by the skylight or back door, so that you won't be seen. The more you shoot the better I will like you. We want your assistance in carrying out this scheme of wiping out Sinn Féin.'

'You forget, Mr Bloody Smyth,' retorted one of the RIC men, 'that you are taking to Irishmen. Your own brains may be plastered on that ceiling first. To hell with you.'

Smyth ordered him to be placed under arrest, but the other RIC men in the barracks became so menacing in support of their comrade, that the divisional commissioner and his party had to hasten away. A few weeks later two armed Volunteers walked into the lounge of the Cork County Club and shot him dead. His brother, Major G.O.R. Smyth, who was serving with the British forces in Palestine at the time, vowed that he would take vengeance for his brother's death. With that purpose in view, an immediate assignment in Ireland was obtained for himself and some of his friends in the force. In Dublin the major was attached to military intelligence, and was soon reputed to be the best IO in the city. He was killed with four other officers on 12 October 1920, when leading a large force of military in a vain attempt to trap the Tipperary men, Seán Treacy and Dan Breen, in the house of Professor Carolan, at Drumcondra, Dublin.

Vengeance was also in the minds of the RIC and Tans who swooped upon the villages of Knocknagree and Ballydesmond, on the days following the ambushing of Holmes and his party at Tureengarriffe. Children playing ball in a field near Knocknagree were brutally machine-gunned. A boy named Kelliher, aged fourteen years, was killed and two others, aged nine and eleven, were wounded. Amongst the survivors was a lad named O'Herlihy, who is now Monsignor O'Herlihy, Rector of the Irish College in Rome. In Ballydesmond police bombed and burned the houses of Timothy Vaughan and William McAuliffe, and the homes and business premises of T. O'Sullivan and M.J. Cronin.

One of the cars used by the divisional commissioner's party at Tureengarriffe was so badly damaged that it was of no further use, and the IRA burned it. The second was driven away to Glantanefinane and was later hidden in the vicinity of Caherbearna, between Millstreet and Rathmore.

The ambush at Tureengarriffe is an example of the rapid evaluation of military intelligence by the IRA, and of the constant state of preparedness of the fighting columns. Indicative of the quality of leadership was the selection of terrain and the competent planning and direction of the fight. The booty taken by the IRA comprised three service rifles, one Winchester shotgun and seven revolvers.

DROMKEEN AMBUSH RESTORED THE MORALE OF THE LOCAL IRA AND PEOPLE

EAST AND MID-LIMERICK BRIGADES, 3 FEBRUARY 1921

by Lieut-Colonel J.M. MacCarthy

(formerly adjutant, East Limerick Brigade IRA)

Flaunting defiance from the highest point of a large, detached building in the village of Pallas,* County Limerick, a conspicuous flag in the sombre colours of black and tan strikingly, if unconventionally, identified the local police barracks throughout the winter of 1920–21. Pallas was the headquarters of a police district in charge of an officer ranking as a district inspector, RIC, but whose special category, and that of the greater part of the large garrison, was plainly indicated by the unofficial emblem so prominently displayed. The hoisting of this banner reflected the tension prevailing in the area at that period and was expressive of the challenging sentiments of the garrison towards the countryside at large, but particularly towards the East and Mid-Limerick Brigade IRA. These two units were equally involved through the fact that, though Pallas itself was in the East Limerick domain, the inter-brigade boundary ran close by, while the police district – and, needless to say, the police activities – extended into both areas.

For long the operations, and more especially the methods, of this garrison had made its personnel exceptionally feared by the general public, and had proved a very sharp thorn for the two brigades to which it offered a challenge that had to be met. The police were definitely in the ascendant when, early in 1921, they scored what, in the circumstances of the time, was a big success, and for the local IRA a correspondingly serious reverse, by locating and capturing the arms dump of the Mid-Limerick Brigade. The police raiding party took good care to celebrate their feat by visiting the house of Dick O'Connell of Caherconlish, the 'on-the-run' O/C of the brigade's active service column, and staging a *feu-de-joie* with the captured weapons in the presence of the occupants paraded to witness, so they were assured, this proof of defeat and final end of the column's activities.

These events brought matters to a head. Consultations, already in progress between the two brigade staffs with a view to common action, were hastened to a conclusion. Plans considered for an attack on the barracks disclosed serious difficulties to be surmounted in view of the pitiably poor armament of the IRA. The nature of the building, its position and defences, made for difficulty of approach and ensured a protracted fight before the defenders could be overcome. Despite the fairly extensive experience of the East Limerick column in conducting prolonged and successful barrack attacks, such as that at Kilmallock in the previous May, when the attack was sustained for over six hours, the time factor in this case was a definite obstacle to success. The proximity of Pallas to large military and police centres (Limerick city, ten miles; Tipperary, twelve miles) made it probable that the garrison would be relieved long before the barracks could be destroyed or captured, notwithstanding all that might be done to impede the arrival of reinforcements. With a mere sniping, or demonstration, attack being of no value since the situation required that the IRA should register a clear-cut success, an awkward problem seemed to defy solution when John Purcell, the IO of the Mid-Limerick column, came to the rescue. He was able to report that a considerable portion of the Pallas police garrison regularly travelled with a lorry convoy to Fedamore, eleven miles distant, making the return journey on the same day. Further, he was able to indicate the route normally followed, and even to fix the usual date of the movement as the first Thursday of each month.

With this information the decision to attack and destroy the convoy was taken, the first Thursday of February being fixed for the effort as a joint operation by East and Mid-Limerick columns, the OC of the former, D. O'Hannigan, taking charge of the combined units for the occasion. An examination of the route led to the further conclusion that a carefully laid ambush along a particular stretch of road (see sketch) at Dromkeen, some three miles from Pallas, offered the best method of attack. There a straight section of the route extended for 300 yards, slightly downhill from a bend at its western (Fedamore) end to a road junction at its eastern (Pallas) limit. A house at the bend afforded observation both over the whole ambush position, and westward for a considerable distance towards Fedamore. The road junction presented almost full right-angled turns to vehicles travelling in any direction, and was an obvious site for barricades which would be out of sight until the turn was about to be taken. From this point, too, observation over the entire position and extending as far as the western bend and Dromkeen House, was feasible from a ruined house at the road fork.

These facilities, and the lay-out of the road section, were definite advantages in light of a number of factors. As the intention was to destroy the convoy completely, a fairly lengthy stretch of the route had to be held to ensure that all the vehicles were within the position before the action opened. The position had also to be capable of being sealed off at both ends when the convoy had entered it. The length, at first sight over-long, was therefore not excessively so in the circumstances, especially when there was no certainty as to the number of lorries likely to be encountered, nor as to the distance between the lorries.

To reduce this uncertain element to the minimum, and for other reasons, it was decided to intercept the convoy on its return rather than on its outward journey. In this way its strength would be known on its departure from Pallas and might be counted on to be approximately the same when it set out on its return trip from Fedamore, though it had varied somewhat on occasions. With this knowledge any necessary last-minute adjustment in dispositions could be made. Also, there was the point that some local residents had seen IRA officers in the vicinity a few weeks previously. Although not connected with the planned

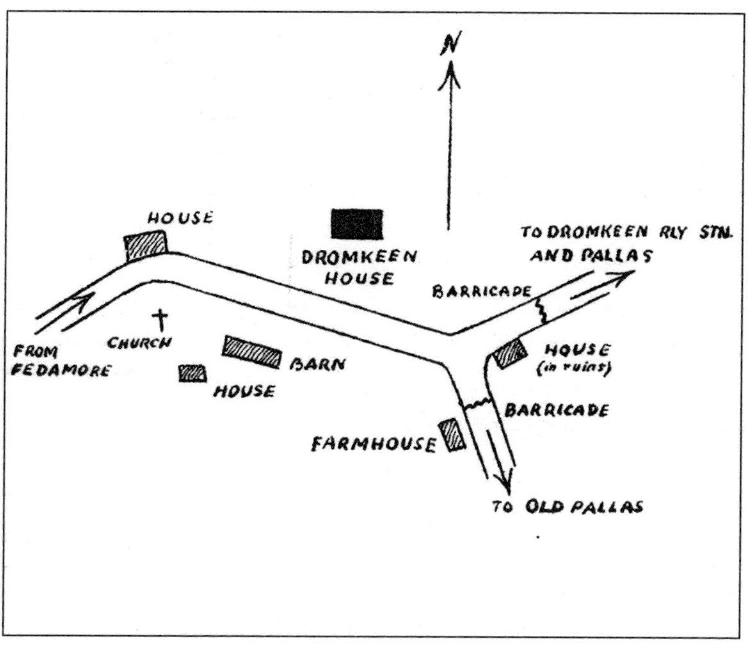

attack, this circumstance had given rise to not a little gossip locally that the area was being marked out as the scene of an action. There was always the possibility that this gossip had reached further afield and enabled the hostile garrisons in the neighbourhood to have planned a counter-move to any IRA attack. Allowing the convoy to pass unmolested on its outward trip would permit observation of hostile movements in the area during that period and reveal any preparations for such a counter-move. Furthermore, the later in the day the action opened the better from the standpoint of the column's withdrawal, which it was desired to effect under cover of darkness as far as possible because of the elaborate military and police reactions anticipated. The other grounds for interception on the return journey were that it made actual occupation of the position unnecessary until confirmation of the movement of the convoy was received, and by that very fact, lessened the possibility of a long and perhaps fruitless wait in the position itself. Also, by ensuring that occupation would not be effected at all if the convoy did not move out, possible disclosure of intentions was avoided and the same site could be used another day. This consideration was important in view of the suitability of the location, and the distinct chance that the intelligence officer's estimate as to the date of the movement might not be borne out by events.

Keeping this valuable consideration in mind, as well as the special caution needed in this particular area, the arrival of the two columns, and their junction with another, was so timed that neither would be in the immediate vicinity of Pallas longer than was absolutely necessary. The more distant of the two, the East Limerick unit was mainly concerned in this 'approach march'. By the day preceding that fixed for the attack, it had reached a billeting area, nine miles away, near Emly on the Limerick-Tipperary border. At nightfall it moved forward some four miles to the neighbourhood of Kilteely, where it remained for a few hours before continuing, while darkness still prevailed, to a previously agreed-on 'assembly area', and rendezvous with the Mid-Limerick column. This rendezvous was at Bennet's farm at Cloverfield, Kilteely, a secluded locality away from dwellings and a little over a mile short of the selected Dromkeen position.

There contact was made between the two columns just before dawn. The combined force, some forty riflemen strong, then lay up to await developments. A dilapidated shed afforded the shelter required, both because of the need for secrecy and because of the fact that the weather during the moves on the preceding nights had been very bad and had continued so. Communication was soon established with the local scouts who, from early morning, were keeping movements in Pallas, and on the adjoining roads, under observation. It was not, however, until close to noon that calculations were in great part fulfilled by the news that two lorries, carrying about twenty policemen, with the district inspector in charge, had started out along the road towards Fedamore.

A move was at once made to the site for the intended interception through which, as further information soon indicated, the lorries had passed, travelling fast and close together. The weather had then cleared, and luckily, as matters developed, little time was required for taking up positions, these having been assigned beforehand. Excepting the farmhouse at the turn of the road to Old Pallas, and Dromkeen House, all the houses and the barn provided fire positions, and were occupied in varying strength according to accommodation and the field of fire available. The farmhouse, left unoccupied, was used to detain passers-by, some half-dozen being thus 'interned'. The house on the road bend at the western end held a party detailed to observe the route towards Fedamore, signal movements from that direction and prevent a withdrawal by the lorries or their occupants by that route. Among the members of the column who comprised that party were Captain D. Guerin (Kilteely Company); Captain Seán Stapleton (Oola Company) and Volunteer M. Meade (Elton Company), all of the East Limerick Brigade. The last-mentioned had the distinction of having served with Roger Casement's Irish Brigade in Germany and was a very experienced soldier, who acted as weapon and drill instructor in the column.

The command post was located in the ruined house at the road junction, its occupants being the East Limerick Column Commander D. O'Hannigan; the writer, as column adjutant, and a few Volunteers, including David Clancy of the Cush Company. This position was the nerve-centre of the operation, being, as already indicated, well placed for observation, fire and control. Any vehicle entering the ambush would face it head-on, and the only doubt about the suitability of its location was whether one or more of the fast-driving police lorries might not crash into it before being stopped by fire and so demolish not only the already tumbled-down structure, but its garrison as well. However, that risk had to be taken. Small detachments also took positions at intervals on both sides of the straight stretch of road along its low boundary walls, in the yard of the farmhouse used as a place of detention, and at the fences covering both the road fork and two barricades erected there. The main body of the Mid-Limerick column was placed on the northern side of the straight stretch of road and included the O/C of that column, Dick O'Connell; Seán Carroll of Castleconnell; James Horan, Johnny Vaughan, Joe Ryan and Ned Punch. A few of the

Mid-Limerick men – Jimmy Humphreys, the noted county hurler among them – were also detailed to garrison the barn on the opposite side, a position that allowed plunging fire to be brought to bear from the top of its contents, onto the road. The other fire positions on this (southern) side and on the barricades were manned by East Limerick Volunteers, with Liam Hayes, Dan Allis, Ned Tobin, Owen O'Keeffe and Danny Moloney in charge of sections of the column so located. Other prominent members of the East Limerick column with these sections included Jim Greene, Tom Howard, who was killed in action a few months later and – such is the ubiquity of men of Cork – two natives of that county, Bill Bourke of Ballindangan, Mitchelstown, and David Barry of Glanworth. The latter subsequently served in his native county as brigade adjutant of one of the hard-fighting Cork brigades.

The barricades were made with farm-carts in preference to other forms of obstruction so that no outward signs need remain should there be a postponement. For the same reason no artificial fire positions were constructed, except at the northern boundary wall of the road where loose stones, readily replaceable, permitted a limited number of loop-holes. Elsewhere fire was to be brought to bear from the tops of the walls and the fences, the hay in the barn, and the windows of the houses. A passing ass and cart conveying a bag of flour was commandeered to form one of the barricades, and the woman owner 'interned' in the crossroads farmhouse, loudly bewailing the fate of her flour. As events turned out, this barricade was so violently struck by the leading police as to burst open the bag and scatter its contents. This incident, however, had a happy ending for the owner, as she persisted in a claim for compensation which was fully met years later by the state.

The dispositions of the combined columns were then complete except for two measures intended to secure the authors of the projected surprise against being themselves surprised. One was the occupation by a party of armed local Volunteers of a position near Dromkeen across the intended line of retreat, to keep open that route and cover the withdrawal of the column. This step was considered essential in view of the heavy military traffic in the vicinity. The other security measure was the use of a screen of scouts provided over a wide area by the local Volunteer companies to signal hostile approaches from an unexpected direction. The frequency of enemy patrols in the locality generally, and on the main Limerick-Tipperary road, only three-quarters of a mile distant, made such a happening not improbable. Whether or not it was appreciated at the time, the fact is that these scouts had no effective means of delaying, or rapidly communicating the progress of any hostile formation should the latter, as was likely, have been motorised. Consequently, had an occasion for action by the scouts arisen, this protective measure would in all probability have broken down badly.

It was a little after 12.30 p.m., with all in readiness. After an uncomfortable night and morning, and a long cross-country march to their next billeting area in prospect, the Volunteers hoped for an early end to their vigil. In this they were not disappointed, for nearing one o'clock the approach of the lorries was signalled. Hardly had the signal been amplified to indicate the number of vehicles as two, when the first appeared around the road bend, quickly followed by the second at about fifty yards' distance. Orders had provided for the opening of fire when the first of whatever number of lorries might comprise the convoy took the turn at the road junction. In the event, fire was opened a few seconds before this occurred, due probably to the riflemen in the western half of the position having difficulty in judging the exact moment of the leading lorry's arrival at the road fork. As matters went, the plans of the attackers were not harmed by the premature firing, though it might have been otherwise had there been a larger convoy or a wide interval between the lorries. The happening did serve to emphasise the necessity for a check on details, lest danger should result from a small oversight on a future occasion.

After the opening volley, the first lorry continued along the short distance which separated it from the road junction. To the occupants of the command post it gave a feeling akin to what must be the reaction of riflemen in a trench when confronted by a tank charging directly upon them. The lorry towered to huge size in the eyes of the command post garrison as it thundered down the sloping road almost onto the muzzles of their rifles. Would it maintain its course and crush them in a sickening crash into the ramshackle cottage? Would its driver survive long enough to avoid the crash and take either the left or right turn? Amazingly, he did survive despite the point-blank volleys which struck his lorry from the front and from both sides. Confronted with the barricade as he was taking the left-hand turn on the usual route to Dromkeen Station, he swerved violently to the right in an effort to take the other turn. Faced there with the second barricade, the lorry struck both it and the fence adjoining the ruined house. Thrown, or having jumped clear, the driver, who happened to be the district inspector, and another policeman, reached the adjoining field unharmed. Aided by the fact that they alone among the police were wearing their civilian clothes, they succeeded in making good their escape and eventually proved to be the only survivors of a total police party of thirteen. A stronger police escort had been expected, but a reduction in the original number had probably been made at Fedamore. Of the five occupants of the first lorry three remained, one of whom was mortally, and two slightly, wounded at the outset. The latter two took cover at the roadside, but shortly after were again hit, this time fatally.

The second lorry contained eight policemen. It had arrived a little beyond mid-way in the ambush when the first shots were fired. Halting at once, in occupants began to dismount. Some were hit while doing so; others as they took up positions at the roadside; of these five were killed outright, and one suffered severe wounds that proved fatal some days later. Two managed to get into positions beneath the lorry, from which they fired from behind the wheels. Refusing to surrender, they maintained a steady exchange of shots, and might have prolonged the situation indefinitely as they were practically secure against being hit by fire from the initial positions of the attackers. A move to get on their own level by firing on them from the actual road-bed was undertaken by Volunteer Johnny Vaughan, a Limerick city member of the Mid-Limerick column. Assisted by the fire of his comrades, he engaged in a close-range duel by taking up a new position on the roadside, from which he quickly put an end to this last-ditch stand of the police remnant. The two policemen responsible for this determined fight against hopeless odds were two of only three members of the regular RIC in the police party.

In the course of the attack on the second lorry the combined columns suffered their single casualty when Liam Hayes, in his position on the wall near the church, had his hand shattered by a bullet.

Nightfall saw the Volunteers safely installed in billets some twelve miles from Dromkeen.

In the particular circumstances outlined at the outset, the action at Dromkeen had a not inconsiderable effect on the morale of not only the IRA in County Limerick, but of the civil population as well. Perhaps its achievement in this respect is best illustrated by the remark of a local 'character' who, having accosted the Mid-Limerick commander following the operation, registered his disbelief in rumours then current of an impending political compromise, by enquiring, facetiously: 'Would you take Dominion Home Rule now, Dick?'

* Author's Note – This is the form of the name by which the village is normally known except when necessary to distinguish it from Old Pallas, 1½ miles to the south-west. According to local usage, it then becomes New Pallas. The Ordnance Survey map versions are respectively, Pallas Grean (New) and Pallas Grean, but in some map editions Old Pallas is given as an alternative to the latter name.

DRISHANEBEG TRAIN AMBUSH YIELDED FOURTEEN RIFLES TO MILLSTREET COLUMN

CORK NO. 2 (NORTH) BRIGADE, 11 FEBRUARY 1921

As told by participants to Patrick Lynch

THERE IS AN old saying that 'the watched pot never boils'. It is aptly used when a period of waiting or watching for something to happen drags interminably, as for instance, on the night of 11 February 1921, when a score or so of armed men lay in ambush on the southern lip of a railway cutting about two miles east of the town of Millstreet. Eight of them had rifles and the remainder handled shotguns of various makes and calibres. They were members of the Millstreet Battalion column of the IRA, and it was the tenth successive night of vigil they had kept at a place called Drishanebeg. Their purpose was to attack any party of armed British military on its way in or out of Kerry, whether on the quarter past six train from Mallow to Tralee or the six o'clock train from Tralee to Mallow. Night after night they had assembled and had moved into positions on the damp grass above the railway cutting which yawned beneath them in the darkness. They had watched the night trains pass through and waited vainly for the pre-arranged signal which would indicate that the period of waiting was at an end and the time for action at hand. Nine times it had happened thus, with nerves on edge in the anticipation of battle, and with nothing happening save the anti-climax of a silent withdrawal in the winter darkness that had come down on the rugged hills of Muskerry and Duhallow. It was a period of strain for the indifferently armed men, who cannot have been unmindful of the analogy of their situation and the 'watched pot'.

The object of the attack on the British was the capture of arms and ammunition, of which there was an acute shortage – particularly of rifles and rifle ammunition – in the Millstreet Battalion. In this respect the battalion was no different from any other unit of the IRA, for all of them were hopelessly deficient in warlike materials. The Dooneen and Coole Cross Company officers had seen a way to add to their meagre store by ambushing one of the parties of armed military then in the habit of travelling on the night trains. Millstreet railway station is at Dooneen, a little over a mile from the town itself, so that it naturally followed that amongst the tasks of the Dooneen Company was that of keeping close watch on the use the enemy made of the trains. Having observed the fairly regular use of the night trains made by parties of armed military, the Dooneen and Coole Cross men concluded that one of them could be ambushed successfully, and that rifles and ammunition could be captured from the troops. The place chosen for the attack was Drishanebeg, about a mile and a quarter from Dooneen and some two miles from Millstreet town. There the line runs through a cutting, and it was believed that an attack would succeed if the train could be halted in the cutting. Though they did not possess a single rifle, the companies which had conceived the idea of the operation were anxious to carry it into effect themselves, and set about making plans to do so. At the time there were eight rifles in the possession of the battalion column, but there was understandable reluctance on the part of the commanding officer to loan them for the job. That was the position when Commandant C.J. Meaney, who had charge of the Millstreet Battalion, issued an order stopping the preparations of the Dooneen and Coole Cross Companies, on the grounds that it was impracticable for them to proceed without rifles. To permit them to go ahead with the project on their own, with no weapons other than shotguns and a handful of cartridges a man, would be to risk failure and the certainty that the opportunity for such a valuable capture would not occur again. There was too much at stake to permit that chance to be taken; the enterprise offered too much in the way of a haul of arms and ammunition to allow it to be embarked upon without the employment of every available element that would be conducive to its success. For that reason, it was taken out of the hands of the Dooneen and Coole Cross men and made an objective of the battalion column.

Before Drishanebeg had been chosen as the site for the ambush, the railway station at Dooneen was considered, and the first idea was that the train should be rushed whilst it was stationary by the platform, and the troops disarmed. There were too many weak points in this plan, so it was discarded and the decision was then taken to go ahead with the operation at Drishanebeg. The battalion column went into camp at Kilcorney, and for a number of weeks the men were put through a course of intensive training. When it ended, morale was high and so were the standards of fitness and efficiency. Preparations for the ambush had been completed. In command of the column during the training period was the Battalion Adjutant Jeremiah Crowley, with Captain Con Meaney, officer commanding the Mushera Company, as second-in-command. Mobilised for flanking and other duties each evening whilst the column lay in ambush were the Dooneen, Coole Cross, Rathcoole and Derrinagree Companies.

The column left the training camp at Kilcorney on 2 February, and crossed the Blackwater at Keale, which is across the river from Drishanebeg. There it went into quarters. Each evening the men stood to arms and, joined by members of the Derrinagree and Coole Cross Companies, they crossed the river under cover of darkness, and took up ambush positions which commanded the railway line, at the Drishanebeg cutting. No train was to be attacked until the approaching engine had signalled by a long blast that there were armed troops aboard. Once the warning blast had been given the ambushers were to place a lighted bicycle lamp in the centre of the track to indicate the exact point at which the engine was to stop.

Between Mallow and the terminus in Kerry the permanent way is but a single line, which means that trains cannot pass one another along the route, except at railway stations, at each of which there are a number of lines. The down-train from Mallow to Tralee, and the up-train from Tralee to Mallow have always passed each other at one of the intervening stations. They did so at Dooneen, the station for Millstreet town, at the time of the Drishanebeg ambush. They always remained there long enough to let down and take on passengers and freight. The up-train's stop at Millstreet, which was about a mile west of the ambush position, had its part in the carefully laid plan of the IRA. Each night the train was inspected there by men of the Dooneen Company to ascertain whether it carried armed troops. If it did, they were to board the engine with drawn revolvers and take control. The driver was to be ordered to give the long signal blast as they approached the Drishanebeg cutting, and to stop the train at the spot indicated by the bicycle lamp. Similar arrangements had been made for the inspection of the trains approaching the ambush position from the eastern, or Mallow side, and for the warning signal to be given when armed troops were carried. Every evening a member of the Rathcoole Company travelled to Banteer, which is about four miles east of Rathcoole. There he inspected the train from Mallow on route for Tralee, whilst it was stopped at Banteer station. If he found armed military aboard, he was to return on the train with a ticket for Rathcoole, a small station mid-way between Banteer and Dooneen, at which the train never stopped unless there was a passenger to get off there. At Rathcoole he would be awaited by another IRA man, and together they would board the engine and take over control for remainder of the journey to the ambush position.

For nine successive nights, which began with the night of 2 February, this routine had been carried out, but no armed military had been found on the train, though several unarmed parties had passed up and down. On the night of 10 February, the observer at the Banteer end noticed six British soldiers on the train, but they carried no arms. When the train had passed the ambush position and pulled up at Millstreet station, the man on duty there saw that the six soldiers had rifles. There could be only one explanation. The soldiers were hiding their weapons

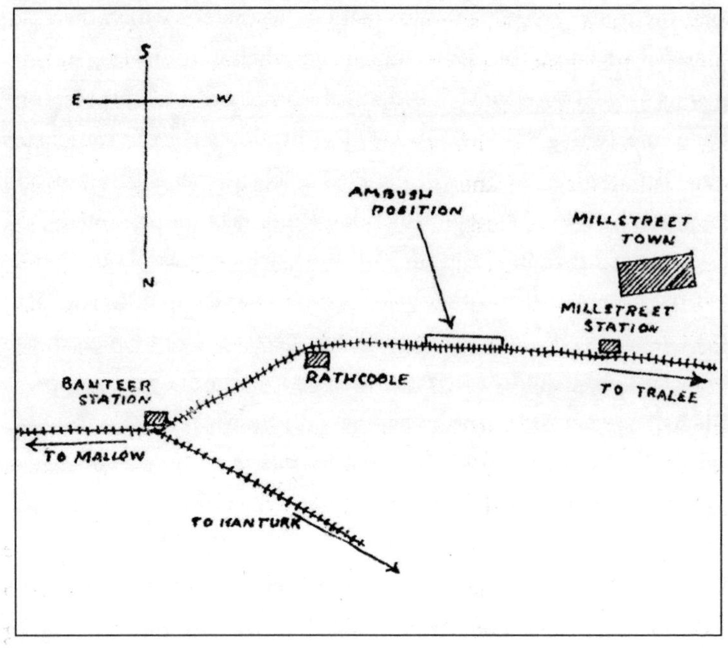

under the seats of the carriages during a portion of their journeys, at least. Something seemed to be going wrong. Nevertheless, the IRA leaders decided that they would maintain the ambush for one more night, with a slight change in the inspection routine at the Banteer side. The watcher at that end that night had orders to join the train if it carried military so that on the journey from Banteer to Rathcoole he could make certain whether they had arms. So it happened on the night of 11 February that the Rathcoole man boarded the train from Mallow, having found that it carried fourteen or fifteen soldiers. Calmly he entered one of the compartments occupied by the military with whom he joined in conversation and exchanged cigarettes. He saw that they were all armed. As he had a ticket for Rathcoole, he got down there and was hurriedly joined by a comrade whom he had beckoned. Together they walked to the engine and boarded it quickly, revolvers in hand. They told the driver and fireman of the orders that would have to be carried out. Secreted around the station house and platform was a shotgun section of the Rathcoole Company, available on call in the event of a mishap. But everything went well. The train pulled out in a perfectly normal manner, and there was nothing to suggest to soldiers or civilians on board that anything unusual was afoot. Through the darkness it chugged its way westwards, and about a mile from the ambush position the long whistle blast gave the awaited signal. Immediately the men at Drishanebeg placed a lighted bicycle lamp in the centre of the tracks. The lamp had been lighted long before train time every night since 2 February and, concealed by a sack, it had lain by the side of the rails until the train had passed. This was a precaution to avoid such risk as the failure of the none-too-reliable carbide bicycle lamps then in use, to light when required, at the last moment, and to ensure that it was placed in position with the minimum of delay. Alerted by the engine signal, the men of the column lay tensed for action in their positions on the southern lip of the cutting. Their excitement mounted apace with the increasing rumble of the approaching train and produced a last-minute concern for the condition of weapons which had already been attended to over and over again. Into view came the lighted carriages, and in a matter of seconds the engine was pulling up with a loud hiss of escaping steam. It had over-run by a few yards the stationary marking light on the tracks. Down from the cab jumped the two IRA men, Volunteers Dan Coakley and Jack Keeffe. Out of the darkness above the cutting Commandant C.J. Meaney called upon the military to surrender to the Irish Republic.

The engine driver and fireman dived for cover amidst the coal in the tender, and terrified civilian passengers stretched flat on the floors of the carriages. A rifle shot answered the summons to surrender, and immediately rapid fire was poured into the compartments occupied by the military. These were brilliantly lit up by blazing torches of timber and paraffin-soaked sacking which the attackers had tossed down the embankment. For ten to twelve minutes the line resounded to the crack of rifles and the loud report of shotguns, until cries of 'We surrender', 'We surrender', were heard from the sorely pressed military.

The IRA ceased fire. A compartment door opened and an officer who crouched inside blazed upwards at the top of the cutting. His action was a complete surprise, but fortunately his shots struck none of the attackers. Instantly Captain Con Meaney had his rifle trained on him and confidently squeezed the trigger. To Meaney's amazement, nothing happened; no sharp crack had rung out, for the striker of the weapon had broken. The British officer jumped off the train just as a shotgun was discharged at him by Volunteer John Joe O'Driscoll. He had been hit, apparently, for he lay still below the train, and Captain Meaney ordered O'Driscoll not to give him the second barrel. The 'Tommies' in the train also resumed firing but accomplished nothing other than drawing upon themselves a well-directed load of lead from the men on the embankment. All was over in another couple of minutes. Despite the trick they had just used, the British offer of surrender was again accepted, and firing stopped for the second time. It was a bizarre situation in the cutting, with the stationary train still steaming, and the groans of the wounded soldiers emanating from dimly lit carriages. Into the open came the unwounded soldiers, their hands above their head, and up the bank they struggled in compliance with an order of the IRA officer in charge. Civilian passengers, recovering some of their composure, were beginning to take an interest in what was happening about them, as the train was boarded by men of the column and some from the local companies who had been on protection duty in the area surrounding the ambush site. The British wounded were made as comfortable as possible and given first aid. Seven of the military had been hit, some severely. One was dying and another, Sergeant Boxall, was already dead. When the IRA sought the body of the officer on the line, he was not to be found. He had shammed injury in the first instance and had made good his escape into the night. All the enemy party belonged to the 1st Royal Fusiliers.

Fourteen rifles and 600 rounds of ammunition were taken from the British. As the attackers were about to push off, an unarmed British soldier emerged from the civilian section of train, and bounded up the slope, shouting: 'I'm all right, lads, don't fire. I'm a Munster

Fusilier.' He was a soldier out of Kerry, going home on leave. And he wanted a rifle to fight for Ireland. When told that his request could not be entertained, he was greatly crestfallen, but volunteered to tend wounded soldiers during the journey into Kerry. As the train moved out of the cutting, the Millstreet men withdrew with their booty. On arrival in Killarney station the body of the dead soldier was removed, and the wounded were borne away on stretchers by military and police. Two ladies and the Munster Fusilier, who was a native of Ballybunion, were taken off the train at Killarney and charged with having shouted 'Up the rebels' after the ambush. The soldier's papers were taken by an officer, but all three prisoners were released soon after the train had left for Tralee. Police under Sergeant P. Mulcahy, and military who were soon at the scene of the ambush, searched the country round about and interrogated a great many persons. None of the attackers were captured. The IRA in Kerry was to get a new recruit. Soon after his arrival home the 'Munster' repeated his offer to serve in the army of his country and was accepted.

ESCAPE OF THREE LEADERS FROM KILMAINHAM WAS AIDED BY BRITISH SOLDIER

DUBLIN BRIGADE, 14 FEBRUARY 1921

by Simon Donnelly

(formerly Vice-Commandant 3rd Battalion Dublin Brigade)

On Thursday 10 February 1921, I was arrested in Dame Street, Dublin, and brought to Dublin Castle to be questioned by British intelligence officers. Following the preliminary interrogation, I was taken to the guardroom of the Castle, and detained there until Friday 11 February, when I was summoned before the notorious Captain Hardy.

The captain was infamous throughout Ireland at that time as a bully and for his brutal methods of attempting to extract information from prisoners. He tried his usual system on me, warning me that I was accused of being implicated in the shooting of British intelligence officers on 'Bloody Sunday,' and giving me a pretty fair idea of what I and any other prisoners were to expect if evidence could be found connecting us with that operation.

From the Castle I was sent under heavy escort to Kilmainham jail, and there I soon recognised a number of my old comrades, who were awaiting trial on various charges. The identity of one of the prisoners puzzled me. I was sure that I knew him, and yet I could not place him at first. He was known as 'Mr Stewart', and I could not recollect having previously met anybody of that name in the Dublin Brigade. I quickly learned, however, that he was none other than Ernie O'Malley, without doubt one of the bravest soldiers who had fought for Irish independence. He had grown a heavy moustache and had generally altered his appearance.

Our men had to be careful of fellow prisoners of whose identity they were not certain, because it was usual for the British to 'plant' spies amongst us, who were supposed to be prisoners, in the hope that we would unwittingly betray ourselves to them. Once my comrades were sure that I was the man I represented myself to be, they took me into their confidence and told me that they were working on plans for an almost immediate escape. Among the prisoners who were in Kilmainham at that time were Captain Paddy Moran, NCO Frank Flood, Volunteers Thomas Bryan, Pat Doyle, Thomas Whelan and Bernard Ryan, all of whom were afterwards executed on 14 March 1921; Frank Teeling, who had been wounded and captured on 'Bloody Sunday'; and Ernie O'Malley. There were so many of us there charged with murder – for England did not recognise us as prisoners of war, although a state of war had been in existence – that we used to talk about our part of the prison as 'Murderers' Gallery'.

'Murderers' Gallery' was, incidentally, in the old and disused part of the prison, and it had been reopened to cope with the increasing number of prisoners which the British had been incarcerating there since the commencement of the War of Independence. Fortunately for us, as it transpired later, this old wing had never been fitted with modern lock and key systems, and the old bolt and padlock method was still in vogue there. As well, the older peep-hole, four inches square, was also retained there while the modernised portion of the prison had been fitted with the new sized peep-hole, inch-and-a-half square. These two factors were to prove invaluable to us when the time came to attempt our break-out from the prison.

The Irish Republican Army was never known to shirk coming to the rescue of comrades in danger, so we were full of confidence that our people outside were doing everything in their power to rescue us from the clutches of the enemy. For some time prisoners had been kept in touch with plans that were under consideration to effect a rescue, for, with the aid of two friendly soldiers, communication had already been established with the IRA outside. Immediately that my identity had been satisfactory established I was brought up-to-date with these plans, which were that, with luck, the escape would be attempted on the following night, Sunday night, 13 February.

Grave difficulties and dangers had to be overcome by our deliverers, for with curfew in force it meant almost certain death for anyone found loitering near the prison after nightfall, and, of course, the rescue could not be effected in day-time. In addition to that, Kilmainham was no easy place to penetrate, with its high surrounding walls, barbed wire entanglements, machine guns mounted at every strategic position, and its heavy guard of soldiers. At first the IRA had almost despaired of rescuing prisoners from Kilmainham, but the news from inside the prison that two friendly soldiers had been found who were willing to help brought a ray of hope. The first plan, quickly abandoned as impracticable, had been that a drug should be smuggled in and administered to the guards in their tea.

Eventually, it was a ship-yard worker who had suggested the plan and furnished the implement which was successfully used to set us free. This man used a bolt-cutter in the course of his work, and assured the O/C of the Dublin Brigade that it would be just as simple to cut a prison bolt as any mere 'civilian' bolt. A bolt-cutter is an implement as long as a pair of garden shears, and there were difficulties to be surmounted before one could be smuggled into Kilmainham. First, this tool had to be procured, and this could only be done by breaking into Dublin dockyards, not an easy thing to do with curfew in full swing and with the military and Tans combing the streets of Dublin for 'rebels'. One was duly obtained, however, and the next problem was to get the big, unwieldy instrument into the prison. One of our soldier friends undertook to try, and as he had himself to run the gauntlet of the sentries, it was necessary to reduce the size of the cutters by sawing away the handles, so that he could bring it in concealed in his clothing without being detected. Minus handles the cutter would not have the necessary leverage to cut bolts, so detachable handles of tubular steel had to be provided to replace the original wooden ones. There was a right and a wrong way to fit the new handles, and if they were fitted the wrong way the instrument was not workable. Accordingly, the soldier had to be given demonstrations of the correct way to adjust the handles. When he felt that he understood the correct procedure, he assured the O/C that he was ready to carry out his part of the job as planned. He succeeded in smuggling into the prison, not only the cutters and handles, but a number of revolvers as well.

An alternative plan for the rescue, made in case the bolt-cutters should fail, provided that a rescue party with a rope ladder and a rope tied to it, should take up positions close to the prison wall near a certain rarely used gate. Following an agreed signal they would throw the rope over the prison wall so that we could haul the ladder over to our side. We were not sure whether the bolt-cutters would work, and we were not counting upon more than one or two prisoners making their escape if the rope-ladder alternative had to be employed. Our principal concern was to save the life of Frank Teeling, who had already been sentenced to death. Ernie O'Malley's escape was also essential, for had his real identity been established he could expect from the British the same brand of treatment which they had given to Dick McKee, Peader Clancy and Conor Clune. The fate of the rest of us had not been decided at that time. No general jail-break was intended, therefore, so that the chances of Teeling and O'Malley might be all the greater, for the bigger the number who tried to break through, the greater the risk of detection by the prison guards. For my own part, I merely tagged along with Teeling and O'Malley, intending to take my chance of getting away only when I felt sure that they were safe.

Member's of 'F' Company of the 4th Battalion of the Dublin Brigade, who had been detailed for the rescue operation, had to leave their homes every night during the period in which the agreed signal might be received from us. They had first to get outside the city boundary in order to avoid enemy patrols along the city approaches to Kilmainham, and then make their way stealthily back by the railway lines, so as to be near the jail gate when needed. Meanwhile the revolvers had been concealed amongst a lot of old lumber and boxes in an unoccupied cell convenient to our own. We had decided that, when making the break, we would get through a disused gate that led on to a side road.

Two circumstances aided us considerably at the actual moment at which the escape was to be attempted. Our cell doors were, as we have seen, fitted with the old-type bolts, padlocks and peep-holes. The warders rarely troubled to use the padlocks, and merely pushed home the bolts. A man could slip his hand out through the peep-hole and ease back the bolt from its socket. This we were able to do on the night of the attempted escape. Also, evidently confident that the thirty foot wall which surrounded the prison could not be scaled, the prison authorities seldom locked the door leading from the prison building out to the yard, and so it was possible for us get from our cells to the gate on the outer wall through which we hoped to escape.

Our plans having been perfected, we sent word to our friends waiting outside the walls that we were on our way. These rescuers, as they approached the gate, had come upon some soldiers with their girlfriends loitering around the side road outside the wall, and for the purpose of ensuring that no alarm could be passed to the prison guards, the soldiers and the girls had to be taken into custody and removed to a place of safety, a fact which interfered with the plans which our friends had originally mapped out for themselves.

Meanwhile, armed with revolvers and the bolt-cutter, we reached the gate and were actually in sight of the rescue party when to our dismay we found that the cutter would not work, for, as it later transpired, the make-shift handles had been wrongly fitted and so they did not afford sufficient leverage for cutting through the stout iron bolt. We whispered urgently to our friends outside to throw over the rope that was attached to the rope-ladder. Over it came; but another disappointment awaited us. When we commenced to haul over the rope we could make no headway. The harder we pulled the more securely did the rope seem to fasten on top of the wall. It transpired that it had sunk into a joint in the masonry, and the more we pulled, the tighter it got locked. With one terrific heave we got the rope loose, only to find that it had broken. So, baffled and dispirited, we had to say a sad good-bye to our friends outside, not knowing whether we would ever see them again, and return to our cells in 'Murderers' Gallery'. In our disappointment over the failure we were tempted to think that the soldier who had provided us with the cutter was not playing straight with us, and we doubted whether the instrument could be of any use to us for jail-breaking. The soldier, however, was sincere in his sympathy with us, and in his wish to help us: but he had either misunderstood or forgotten his instruction, and had gone the wrong way about refitting the handles of the bolt-cutter. He was so ashamed of the muddle he had made that he went to the O/C again without delay and told him that he was sure that none of us trusted him any longer, and that the O/C himself must think that he was double-crossing. The O/C took him very kindly and patiently demonstrated again how the handles should be fitted in order to get the correct leverage. The soldier then said that if we would make another attempt he himself would cut the bolt for us to prove his sincerity.

Prior to the formulation of the escape plans prisoners had been grumbling about the dirty condition of the prison. The complaints had ceased, however, since the urgent problem of making an escape had been seriously considered. To our great consternation we learned on Monday morning, 14 February, that the prison authorities had decided to clean out the place immediately, including the disused cell in which our weapons and the cutter were hidden. Discovery of these would remove our last hope of escape. Something had to be done quickly to save the situation, so we established an uncommon precedent for IRA prisoners in enemy hands by volunteering to do fatigue duty and to clear up the cell ourselves. The soldiers fell for the ruse and so we were able to prevent the discovery of our weapons. We had reason to believe that our jailers suspected that some escape plan had been made and had failed, for the newspapers that morning hinted at 'rumours' of escape. Having weighed up the situation we decided that we would make another attempt to get away about 6.30 p.m. that same night, and sent word to that effect to our collaborators outside. The position of Teeling was desperate – he was to be executed a few days later. Should 'Mr Stewart' be recognised as Ernie O'Malley his fate would be little better. I was facing a murder charge, but even then my position was not so urgent as that of Teeling and O'Malley.

When the hour had come for the break to be made O'Malley and Teeling began to make their way down to the gate, a trying ordeal, for all the while they wondered whether they would run into a sentry and be bayoneted or shot. I remained behind for a few minutes talking to a soldier named Roper who was on duty that night. He told me he was due for his discharge from the army the following week, and was happy to be going home. I encouraged him to talk and did all I could to hold his attention while my comrades were slipping away towards the gate. When I considered that they must have reached it, I, too, managed to slip quietly away. On my way I passed the cell of Paddy Moran. It was open, and I tried to persuade him to accompany us. He was also to be tried in connection with the shooting on 'Bloody Sunday', but, having a clear alibi, he was so sure of his acquittal that he absolutely refused to leave, and said that any attempt by him to get away would be interpreted by the British as an admission of his guilt. Paddy Moran was to pay with his life for his reliance on British justice.

When I found that I could not bring Paddy with me, I began the hazardous journey across the yard in the wake of my two companions. It was a nerve-racking ordeal to cross that yard, for it was covered with a substance called breeze, and each time I set my foot on a bit of this breeze it crunched under my boot with a sound that seemed to me as explosive as a clap of thunder. So, every second I expected to feel a bayonet plunged into me by the sentries. When at length I reached the gate I found that this time the bolt-cutter had done its work. But even then the danger for us was not past, for it was a tedious and critical task to work back the rusted bolt from its socket. We greased it with some butter which we had saved from our prison rations, and after some minutes of hard work and extreme anxiety we finally eased back the bolt. By slow degrees we opened the gate, always keeping a sharp eye out for any soldiers who might be hanging about in the side road outside; but there were none and so our way to freedom was open before us. We had our revolvers at the ready all the time we had been working on the gate, for had we been discovered then we intended to fight our way to freedom; but thanks to our comrades outside we met with no opposition, for, as on the occasion of our first attempt, our friends had made sure that there would be no alarm given from outside by arresting any soldiers they found in the vicinity of that gate.

So we three ex-prisoners walked casually out of Kilmainham. Down a back road we went and hid our revolvers in the garden of a private house. We passed close to another enemy stronghold, Richmond barracks, and along the banks of the canal. There we got something of a fright, for as we were about to cross a bridge an enemy armoured car drove up. We flung ourselves flat in the grass, and only just in time, for the armoured car flashed out a searchlight. It missed us, however, luckily for us, for as we were now unarmed, we would have been entirely at the mercy of the enemy had we been discovered.

After a few minutes the armoured car passed on its way. We picked ourselves up out of the grass and boarded a tram for the city. At different points along the route we got off the tram, and each in his own way set to rejoin his respective unit, free to assume once again his part in the fight for freedom.

BRITISH GENERAL KILLED IN ACTION AGAINST CORK AND KERRY IRA AT CLONBANIN

CORK NO. 2 (NORTH) BRIGADE AND KERRY NO. 2 BRIGADE, 5 MARCH 1921

As told by participants to Patrick Lynch

ONE OF THE peculiarities of war is the rapidity with which the names of remote localities spring into prominence overnight. Long after the lights had gone up in the rooms and corridors of the British War Office, on the night of 5 March 1921, the name of an obscure Irish townland was being flashed across the telegraph wires. On a huge map in the intelligence department it was picked out and appropriately marked and shaded on the demarcation line between the counties of Cork and Kerry. In diaries and 'situation journals' it was painstakingly recorded. A file was opened on it, and reports were asked for and prepared. It was given an index number and identification letter. In a matter of hours adjutants and assistant adjutants, clerks and orderlies, had become familiar with yet another spot in Ireland where British arms had suffered a severe reverse. In the buildings that housed the great daily newspapers of London, sub-editors and re-write men were scanning 'copy' that told of an engagement in southern Ireland that afternoon in which a British brigadier-general had fallen among the bodies of many members of his escort. International press agencies telegraphing their accounts of the fight were sending the same strange placename to the far corners of the globe. Clonbanin was in the news.

Ten hours earlier the average traveller on the main road from Mallow to Killarney might recognise Clonbanin as the spot where the signpost pointed north-west along the direct route to Tralee. Few who glanced at the passing landscape saw in it more than the snug farmsteads and rolling pasture lands that there mark the beginning of the long, wooded valley of the Blackwater, which extends the full breadth of County Cork, from west to east. Certain it is that none could have thought that before night had come down on the encircling hills, the name of Clonbanin would have been written in fire across the pages of the story of Ireland's fight for independence.

How did a relatively unknown place come to be selected as the scene for one of the largest actions of the guerrilla war in the south? What was the object of this ably planned engagement so courageously fought in that most unlikely spot for an ambush? Why did the leaders of the republican army in north Cork and east Kerry decide to give battle at Clonbanin, but a few miles from the heavily garrisoned town of Kanturk and the strongly manned enemy posts at Millstreet and Newmarket?

Thereby hangs a tale which turns back the calendar to the closing months of the previous year. It traces the course of events from the bounds of Kerry to the eastern gateway to Cork; to the deep woodlands and smiling valleys that surround the town of Fermoy, and to the heather-covered hills that sweep upward and southward from the banks of the Bride and the Blackwater – an area barely across the border from Waterford, but nonetheless closely related to the drama of the smoking rifles that was played to a conclusion at Clonbanin on the opposite side of the county.

During the weeks which led up to Christmas 1920 and in the early months of the new year, few stretches of the country were subjected to a closer scrutiny and to a more continuous and systematic search by enemy raiding parties than that tract then known to the IRA as the Fermoy Battalion area. Convenient to the great military centres of Fermoy and Moorepark, it was a place where members of the republican army were constantly in danger of arrest or death; a locality in which enemy agents were busy. It was due largely to British intelligence in the Fermoy area that the opening months of 1921 found the local IRA battalion without a commandant, a vice-commandant, a quartermaster or an adjutant. In short, the entire battalion staff had been arrested and, consequently, the nerve centre of the resurgent movement in the districts concerned had been dealt a staggering blow. But those responsible for the betrayal and imprisonment of the unit officers were greatly mistaken if they thought that their activities had paralysed the nation's army along the Cork and Waterford border. They reckoned without the capability and high personal courage of General Liam Lynch and the officers who were concerned with him in the over-all administration of the 2nd Cork Brigade, as well as those responsible for affairs in the Fermoy Battalion area.

Into the Fermoy area, in January 1921, came General Lynch and one of his best staff officers, Commandant Paddy O'Brien of Liscarroll. The purpose of their visit was to carry out a tour of inspection and reorganisation, and to appoint battalion officers to replace those who had been arrested. The general idea was to ensure that the battalion would continue to operate as part of the widespread fighting force then striking with increasing intensity and with telling effect in almost every parish of Cork.

From farmhouse to cottage and from cottage to farmhouse the brigadier and his staff officer moved rapidly in the course of their tour. They were meeting the men of the hidden army; discussing, investigating, organising, instructing, planning. Despite the speed of their movements and the security measures that surrounded and preceded and followed them, spies were on their trail everywhere they went. The districts through which they passed were combed soon afterwards by impatient search parties of British military; the houses in which they snatched a few hours' sleep were quickly raided. 'The Defenders of the Realm', as Pearse would have known these enemies of the Republic, were working well, both secretly and in the open.

It was this pertinacious probing by the enemy throughout the Fermoy area that provided one of the principal reasons for the action at the opposite side of the county. From it grew the decision which resulted in the large-scale and successful fight at Clonbanin, where the

British were engaged by a number of North Cork Battalion columns and a Kerry Brigade column.

To obtain a proper picture of the situation that then existed throughout the north Cork area, and to facilitate a more complete appreciation of the events that led up to Clonbanin, it must be realised that the pattern of the fight had undergone a change over the Christmas period. Prior to Christmas, a brigade column had been operating against the British in the area. Organised in September 1920, the column was drawn from the different battalions in the brigade, and during the closing months of the year it was continuously harassing the enemy. As Christmas approached, the brigade commander decided that the men of the column would return to their own localities to form the nuclei of battalion columns, with a view to a more active and extensive campaign by all units after the holidays. To ensure further that every district would be able to participate, it was also decided to run a brigade training camp at Nadd, to which men from all the battalions would be called.

And so it was that for a period of fourteen days, at the beginning of 1921, there were billeted in closely guarded valleys high in the Boggeraghs a number of men from the IRA battalions centred in Millstreet, Kanturk, Newmarket, Charleville, Castletownroche and Fermoy. For the fortnight, their training went on intensively under the direction of the brigade staff, and when the work had been completed the men returned to their respective districts to impart to their comrades the knowledge gained at Nadd. Immediately following the termination of the camp, General Lynch and Commandant O'Brien entered the dangerous and more-or-less leaderless Fermoy Battalion area. As a result of what they had heard and seen, and experienced during their tour, it was agreed that every other battalion in north Cork should make a special effort to relieve the pressure on the particular corner of the brigade area occupied by the Fermoy unit. As a preliminary there was a widespread campaign of road trenching and this succeeded in considerably disrupting the enemy's transport. It prevented him from freely using his lorries for the continuous raids he was then conducting in every corner of the area.

The intelligence service of the IRA was widely organised throughout the 2nd Cork Brigade area at that stage of the war, and was working with dispatch and accuracy. Due to the courage, nerve and shrewd intellect of the Irish intelligence agents, enemy movements, and intended movements, were quickly made known to the leaders of the republican army. As a result appropriate orders and directions went out rapidly to the battalion columns to enable them to lie in wait for convoys of military and police.

All through that month of February 1921, the British in north Cork ran the gauntlet of well-informed, better-trained and more highly organised harassing elements than they had hitherto encountered. Towards the end of the month information reached the IRA that the British officer commanding Buttevant barracks, Brigadier-General Cummins, intended to travel into Kerry in the course of a tour of inspection of his command.

Thus did it happen that in or around 1 March, the leaders of the IRA in east Kerry sought the aid of a North Cork column for an ambush they were planning for a locality in the Kerry No. 2 Brigade area. The request was received by Commandant Seán Moylan, who was then in charge of the Newmarket Battalion. He immediately forwarded a dispatch to the O/C of the Charleville Battalion, Commandant Paddy O'Brien, asking that the men of the Charleville unit should join the Newmarket Battalion column on the evening of 2 March, in the vicinity of the schoolhouse at Drominarigle, a remote rural townland lying south-west of Newmarket.

The receipt of that dispatch by the O/C of the Charleville Battalion column on the evening of 1 March marked the commencement for him and the men of his unit of a period of activity that was to call forth from each man the utmost in mental fortitude and physical endurance. It was to set in motion a train of events that left them little opportunity for rest, whilst imposing on them the necessity for strategy and daring; it was to see them, in common with the other units from North Cork and Kerry, going into battle following long, gruelling marches, with little food and inadequate equipment.

Before the arrival of the dispatch from Newmarket, the column had made arrangements to engage a patrol of police in the town of Charleville on the morning of 2 March. When the dispatch arrived it was decided to go ahead with the commitment in Charleville, as arranged, prior to setting out with all speed on the long trek to Drominarigle. Into the town, then, at nine o'clock on the morning of 2 March, the men of the battalion column moved to take up a position in the vicinity of Lyons' Corner. It was intended to wait there for a cycling patrol of police which was known to travel each morning from its barracks on the Kilmallock road to collect mail at the Charleville post office.

The IRA plan was to permit the enemy patrol to collect its mail and to attack it on the return journey. When returning, however, the police divided and took two separate routes, half of the patrol going back by Lyons' Corner and the other travelling by Broad Street. This left a smaller force to be dealt with, initially, by the men in position at Lyons' Corner. But its destruction was not to be, for as the police came within the field of fire of the ambushers, a group of children passing along to school also entered the danger zone. Although the children were quickly rushed into the protection of the schoolhouse lane, the incident delayed the action sufficiently to enable the police to escape without a casualty, even though they were attacked.

From Charleville, on the Limerick border, the column had to retreat without more ado and begin the long journey to Drominarigle. Horses and traps were waiting on the outskirts of the town and in these the men of the column travelled at a galloping pace along the Newtownshandrum road, while trees were felled in their rear to eliminate the possibility of enemy lorries quickly following them up. Beyond the village of Newtown they were met by other members of the column and all then proceeded to Dromina on foot. Having rested for a few hours at Dromina, they marched as far as Freemount, where some horses and traps were procured to take them to Allen's Bridge, about midway between Kanturk and Newmarket. The remaining few miles to the meeting place were completed on foot, and on arrival there they found Seán Moylan awaiting them.

Commandant Moylan explained that they would have to travel overnight to reach the Kerry area at the pre-arranged time. When they had had a meal, the combined force of between thirty and forty men set out on the night march into Kerry. Travelling by Knocknagree and Gneeveguilla, they reached 'The Bower', between Rathmore and Barraduff, at daybreak. All the North Corkmen were armed with rifles. They also carried a Hotchkiss light machine gun, taken in the successful raid on the Mallow military barracks during the previous September. Commandant Humphrey Murphy and the men of the Kerry No. 1 and 2 Brigade column were waiting to receive them on their dawn arrival at 'The Bower'. The projected action was discussed, and it was decided that Seán Moylan would command the combined Cork and Kerry IRA columns. When the Kerry O/C had pointed out the site he had already selected for the ambush, Commandant Moylan and Commandant O'Brien immediately went over the ground.

There then occurred one of those humorous incidents which interlace themselves through the warp and woof of war. Wearing a soiled and well-worn trenchcoat, unshaven and unwashed after his long night march from Drominarigle, and generally bearing marks of the rigours of continuous campaigning, Seán Moylan presented anything but the appearance of a well-groomed Sandhurst product on that bleak March morning. Paddy O'Brien was in similar shape. There remained in both, however, sufficient of the leaven of humour to absorb the caustic comment of a Kerry column man whom they overheard to remark: 'God help us, lads! Are they the officers we're going to have?' Apparently their appearance suggested decrepitude to the man from Kerry and he consequently considered them far beyond the age of active service!

When the different sections had been placed in position and the situation generally organised, a number of mines brought along by the North Cork column were laid on the roadway over which the enemy transport was expected to pass. It was then early morning, and all through the day the columns remained in position. But there was no sign of the British, and at four o'clock in the afternoon the entire force was withdrawn to a number of pre-arranged billets provided under the direction of the Kerry officers. The billeting occasioned no small hardship to the residents of the locality, when close on forty men from North Cork, and fifty or sixty from Kerry, had to be fed and housed for the night by people who, for security reasons, had no chance to provide for such a contingency in advance. Furthermore, the district was a mountainous one in which great difficulty would present itself any time a force of 100 men sought food and shelter in it. Yet, food and shelter the men of the columns received, and on the following morning they again occupied the ambush position.

The greater portion of the second day passed uneventfully until about three in the afternoon, when a dispatch arrived from Killarney containing information that the enemy was aware of the IRA position. Following a hurried council of the leaders, it was decided to withdraw immediately and occupy a position on the Cork side of the county boundary next day.

Simultaneously with the decision to withdraw, and while transport was awaited, men of the Kerry column were delegated to provide food for the entire force. The extent of the provisioning problem already referred to becomes clear when it is noted that the men sent out for supplies failed to find any food other than two four-gallon buckets of eggs. The afternoon was waning and as the men had eaten nothing since morning, those who felt able for such repast quickly disposed of the eggs without any preliminaries like boiling or frying!

Horses, traps and side-cars comprised the transport made available to take the North Cork columns to Knocknagree, where they were to be billeted for the night. As there were not enough vehicles to take all, it was arranged that a number of the men would march until the transport could return to pick them up, when the first detachment had been conveyed to Knocknagree. The Kerry column was to find billets in Kerry and to move on to rejoin the Corkmen at Cullen on the following morning.

Through one of those hitches that can beset the best of arrangements and impede the most carefully organised movements, the men who went on foot towards Knocknagree were to suffer added hardship. It transpired that the transport which was to shorten their march never materialised and, furthermore, as they tramped into Knocknagree in the early hours of the morning, cars were already waiting there to take them to Cullen where a new position was to be occupied. Weary from their long march through the night, their second night without sleep and their second night of marching in a matter of a few days, they immediately moved towards Cullen to prepare to fight. Be it remembered that on the night of 2 March, these men completed a long night march from Drominarigle to 'The Bower' where they immediately went into battle positions. On the following night they rested in billets in Kerry. Then, on 4 March, they remained in position all day, appeased their hunger with raw eggs in the evening, after which they marched all night to Knocknagree. On arrival there they were immediately ordered on to Cullen, without a break for sleep or rest. In these events there is surely an example of the discipline, determination, and splendid spirit of service that characterised the Irish Republican Army during the grim fight in which it was engaged. They provide an instance of the hardship and privation that were the daily lot of the men who voluntarily served the nation in arms.

At an assembly point in the vicinity of Cullen schoolhouse, some of the local men suggested that there was a good ambush position at a spot about half-a-mile to the east, on the main road to Mallow. The place was inspected but, as the enemy would undoubtedly employ armoured cars, the ground was considered too exposed, and so the columns moved further east into Cork until they came to the forge west of Clonbanin crossroads. On the previous night word had been sent from Knocknagree, summoning the Millstreet Battalion column which, under Commandant C.J. Meaney, was billeted at Lackadota and which had been mobilised to move against the Black and Tan garrison in Millstreet town. On the evening of 4 March, the Millstreet men, having received Seán Moylan's dispatch, moved by cars to Drishanebeg. From there they travelled along the southern bank of the Blackwater to Keale Bridge where they crossed the river. Then, proceeding across country, they came to Clonbanin in the morning, by way of Derrinagree. Meanwhile, the combined North Cork and Kerry columns, which had moved east from the position rejected at Cullen, were resting at the forge west of Clonbanin Cross, whilst their leaders inspected the site of a suggested ambush position.

From the point of view of security, it was by no means an attractive proposition that faced the IRA officers charged with the plan of battle. From Clonbanin Cross, roads branched off to Boherbue, Kanturk and Mallow, and a little to the south-east was the road junction for Mallow, Kanturk, Banteer and Millstreet. The road through the ambush position was the main highway from Mallow to Killarney. North of the position, and to its rear, ran the road to Boherbue, which was also the main road to Tralee. To the south, and only a few fields away, was the road from Mallow to Millstreet, and running into the back of the position was the direct road from Kanturk to Clonbanin. On that same road, a little over four miles distant, was a full battalion of British infantry, the Gloucesters, who, with a number of detachments, then occupied the Kanturk workhouse on the Clonbanin side of the town. In front of the ambush position a by-road ran from the north and the south to connect with the Killarney road.

A more unlikely spot for an ambush could hardly be found. Examined on the map, or viewed on the ground, it would seem that such a place had little to commend it to the IRA leaders' purpose, but its very improbability made it valuable and ensured to the IRA the vital advantage of surprise. The position had other advantages. Rising ground to the north and south-east enabled the ambushers to overlook the roadway. Fences provided cover from fire, particularly fire from the heavy Vickers machine gun of an armoured car. Hedgerows gave cover from view. Also, there were several lines of withdrawal and these were eventually used with skill and effect.

Taken by and large, the position was the best available for the ambush, though only daring men would elect to fight virtually on the enemy's doorstep. British reinforcements were less than half-an-hour away. But the attacker must strike where his blow is least expected.

And every blow must tell. He must crouch like a boxer seeking an opportunity to deliver a telling punch. Such maxims apply particularly to men who are inadequately armed and equipped. They must not only seize their opportunities; invariably they must make them also.

The situation having been considered, and the position decided on, battle stations were allotted. Some of the sections were already moving into position when the Millstreet Battalion column arrived. When these men had been given breakfast, they took over part of the ground to the south of the road where the Kerry column was also in position. Some men of the Millstreet column were detailed to cover the approach roads to the position, to deal with possible enemy reinforcements. In the haggard of Shaughnessy's farmhouse, on the left of the road, the Hotchkiss gun was put in position and manned by Bill Moylan, Denis Galvin and Seán Healy. North of the road were the Newmarket and Charleville Battalion columns, while on the flanks were the signallers under P.J. Dennehy. Two mines were placed at what were judged to be the eastern and western extremities of the ambush position.

Shortly before 10 a.m., and just as the mine was being laid at the eastern end, a signal was received that lorries were approaching from the east. Most of the sections were already in position and the section leaders were with Seán Moylan near the eastern mine. A hurried consultation resulted in the decision to attack this approaching convoy, despite the fact that the party for which the ambush had been laid was expected from the west. Section leaders hastily rejoined their sections with orders to hold their fire until the western mine had exploded, while the operator in charge of the eastern mine was instructed to allow all the lorries to pass through with the exception of the last which he was to 'blow'.

Seán Moylan and Paddy O'Brien took up position by the switch of the western mine, and Moylan said to O'Brien: 'You fire the first shot. When I am switching the mine I will tell you to fire.'

Into view from the Mallow direction came three lorries of troops. As arranged, the first two passed over the eastern mine and when the

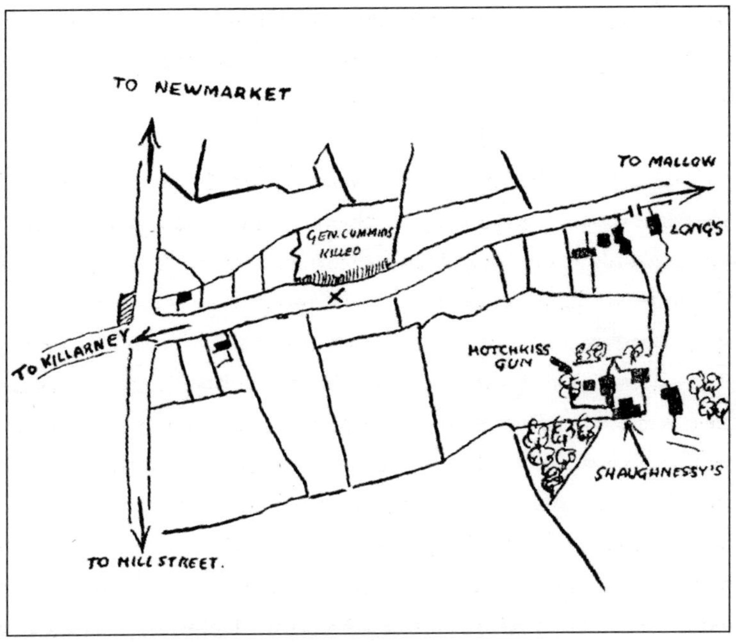

leading lorry reached the western mine Seán Moylan threw the switch and shouted 'Fire' to Paddy O'Brien.

Then occurred an amazing coincidence. Anticipating the order, O'Brien had his rifle trained on the leading lorry, and as Moylan threw the mine switch, his comrade pressed the trigger. Nothing happened. The rifle did not fire and the mine did not explode. In obedience to orders, the waiting sections held their fire, puzzled no doubt by the absence of the explosion that was to be the signal for the attack to commence. Unmolested and unaware that death had stalked so near, the troops passed into Kerry aboard their lorries. Commandant O'Brien lowered his rifle. It was at half-cock, an occurrence which is remarkably rare and which, it need hardly be said, prevents the striker of the rifle from functioning. But what of the mine? A prompt examination proved it to be a dud, because high tension detonators were being used with low tension batteries. The eastern mine was found to be in the same useless state. As mines and their use were in their infancy in north Cork at that time, what happened at Clonbanin is understandable. Though the knowledge that their mines were useless left the leaders of the ambushing party more than a little perturbed, it was decided that any enemy force coming their way would be engaged with the rifles and the Hotchkiss. Incidentally, the four sections on outpost duty covering the approach roads around the position were armed mainly with shotguns. And so, having made their decision to fight without the valuable aid of the mines, the leaders and the men of the different sections awaited the foe.

A seemingly interminable wait it must have been, even allowing for the fact that at intervals the men were relieved systematically to obtain food at neighbouring farmhouses. What were the thoughts of those men of the hillsides who waited patiently at their posts? Along what channels did their minds work as they lay there in the cold, damp ditches of Clonbanin while noon came and passed, and the early afternoon set in? Before and below them the road stretched westwards towards Kerry, long and empty, before it turned out of sight. Down that road would come the enemy on his powerful, rumbling lorries, one, two, maybe a dozen vehicles; nobody could say how many. Perhaps the high-ranking officer they were expecting would bring a large escort from the garrisons at Killarney and Tralee. He might not come that day or the next. These were amongst the possibilities, and must have been in the thoughts of the waiting men; these, and the secret musings that none may guess. If the fight did come, how many would survive? Ahead, by intent and surmise, lay battle with the crash of rifle fire, the staccato rattle of machine guns, the tangy smell of cordite, the filmy scarves of smoke drifting upwards from levelled muzzles and the rude disturbance of a peaceful place where men would go suddenly to meet their God. Behind were homes, parents and sisters; warm meals, firesides and comfortable beds. Inevitably, there were wistful memories of sweethearts and moonlit laneways, of the whirl of the dance and of cosy pubs at the end of a long fair day. For events and associations of the past will cross the screen of the soldier's mind when he has thrust upon him the lot to watch and wait. And to watch and wait demands no less nerve and courage than to fight.

They were waiting and watching at ten minutes to two when the signallers on the left flank indicated that five motor vehicles were approaching from the west. The first of these came into view almost immediately. Commandant Moylan had ordered that the first lorry was not to be engaged until it reached the more easterly positioned sections. His object was to ensure, as far as possible, that all the vehicles would be in the ambush before firing started. The instruction was implicitly obeyed, and in the words of one of the officers in charge of the ambush: 'It worked out more than satisfactorily.' Right into the position came the entire convoy of five vehicles: the leading lorry, another lorry, a touring car, an armoured car and a Crossley tender bringing up the rear. Thus it happened that the leading lorry was engaged and halted by the sections at the eastern end, just before the other vehicles were taken on by the section disposed at both sides of the road. The Crossley tender came under the fire of the men at the western end. Actually, the first shots came from the Hotchkiss gun concealed in Shaughnessy's haggard, and were directed against the leading lorry as it passed on to be engaged by the eastern sections positioned north of the road. Its occupants having exchanged a few shots, the lorry lurched to a stop on the grass margin by the roadside.

For nearly two minutes there was not a sound other than the noise of the vehicles as they moved down the road through the ambush position, which extended about a quarter of a mile in length. Firing resumed with two rifle shots in quick succession, and the touring car, swerving across the road, ran into the ditch. The Hotchkiss gun sprayed the second lorry with a leaden hail. That, too, was quickly brought to a standstill, and a heavy toll taken of its occupants.

Having also come under the fire of the Hotchkiss, the armoured car collided with the back of the tourer and bogged down on the soft ground beside the road. It was afterwards ascertained that the driver had been wounded by a bullet from one of the Hotchkiss bursts which entered his cabin.

The moans of wounded military were clearly audible above the din of battle. Soldiers taking cover by the roadside answered the shots directed at them from north and south. A tall officer leapt from the touring car as it careered into the fence. In answer to an IRA call to surrender, he defiantly replied: 'Surrender to hell! Give them the lead', as he dived for cover at the other side of the road. Those were the last words of Brigadier-General H.B. Cummins, DSO, for they had scarcely been uttered when he fell, shot through the brain by a bullet from an ambusher's rifle. He was the first British general in Ireland to take civilian hostages on his lorries and his escort that day at Clonbanin carried a hostage who escaped during the fighting.

From both sides of the road rifles cracked, and troops on the highway crawled to positions from which they could return the fire. For an hour or an hour and a half the battle raged. The IRA Hotchkiss gun jammed and could not be got to function again; but the Vickers heavy machine gun in the stationary armoured car swept the hedgerows. From positions on the road itself the British brought Lewis light machine guns into action; but the IRA rifles and marksmen proved more than a match for these, so that gradually all enemy weapons were silenced save the Vickers in the armoured car. Though bogged down and jammed in a standstill position, the armoured vehicle and its gun more or less dominated the ambush scene, and prevented the rounding up and disarming of the military left alive.

At the start of the fighting some troops from the last vehicle sought refuge in a cottage south of the road and west of the ambush position. When the battle had continued about an hour and a half, a group of IRA men on the high ground to the north saw a parson come down the road from the western direction, accompanied by a British officer and some troops. Presumably his purpose was to give the last rites of his Church to those of the enemy who might need them. When the party reached the last lorry, one of the IRA column commanders, Paddy O'Brien of Liscarroll, ordered two officers to cover the men on the road, and further instructed that if they had to fire, to do their utmost to avoid hitting the clergyman. The two officers, Tom McNamara of

Newmarket and Pat J. O'Brien of Effin, levelled their rifles at the men below. The column commander then mounted the fence and called on the British to surrender. The enemy officer backed slowly towards the lorry near which a soldier was standing. Suddenly he snatched the soldier's rifle and fired at the column commander on the fence. As he did so, the clergyman dived for shelter in the nearest ditch. Both the watching IRA officers immediately fired at the British officer, but failed to hit him. Paddy O'Brien vanished off the fence, but not before he had been struck on the face by a lump of earth thrown up from the fence top by the bullet fired at him. The enemy party immediately jumped under cover, and by that stage no soldier on the road was in a position to engage the IRA. All the while the stationary armoured car was acting as a pill box and with its Vickers blazing away, it dominated the road. Captain Con Meaney of the Millstreet Battalion column, had his rifle trained on it from the moment that it had entered his field of vision at the commencement of the ambush. With him was Captain Michael O'Riordan of Millstreet. They took careful aim with their rifles and fired at the bonnet from the position they occupied on the fence of Shaughnessy's haggard, a little to the south-west of the Hotchkiss gun section. They wondered whether it was a bullet from one of their rifles that had put the car out of control. Seán Moylan, taking with him some of the Newmarket column, made a detour and crossed to the ground south of the main road, with the purpose of crawling up to the armoured car to capture or destroy the heavy Vickers gun. The task proved to be impossible, however, and the columns south of the road were then withdrawn in good order. No feasible objective remained to be dealt with by them.

North of the road the IRA remained longer in position. There some of the Newmarket and Charleville Battalion columns had a narrow escape. Some twenty minutes or half an hour after the Millstreet and Kerry columns had withdrawn, Commandant P. O'Brien was near the western extremity of the position with Captain Dan Vaughan of the Newmarket Battalion column, and Tom McNamara, when he noticed that a section of British had worked its way up from the road and was closing in on the right flank of the IRA position to the north. Speed and courage were essential if the Charleville column was to be safely withdrawn, so Tom McNamara was sent with all haste to convey the Charleville men along the withdrawal route. Meanwhile, the advancing enemy was engaged by Commandant O'Brien and Captain Dan Vaughan. Both officers fought a valiant and completely successful rearguard action while the Charleville column to which the only remaining IRA men in the position belonged, was being extricated by Tom McNamara. Only when the men reassembled some distance away and were rejoined by the column leader and Captain Vaughan, was it fully realised how fortunate they had been to get out, and how much they owed to Captain Vaughan and his brother officer. For it was then found that many of the men were down to their last round of ammunition, and that no man had more than five rounds. Had they been surrounded by the British their fate would have been sealed.

As matters went, all IRA sections withdrew from Clonbanin without suffering a casualty, whilst under the barking Vickers they left thirteen enemy dead and fifteen wounded. By well-known paths the Kerrymen withdrew to Rathmore, the Millstreet column towards the steep sides of Clara, and the men of Newmarket and Charleville towards Kiskeam, where they were billeted that night. It is of interest to note that, when he came out of Kerry on the morning of the fight, Brigadier-General Cummins brought a heavy escort with him as far as Rathmore, at which point he dismissed it, judging the remainder of the route to be safe. It is clear that he seriously under-estimated the ability, intelligence and daring of those who led the flying columns of the IRA. The general had commanded the Kerry Brigade, and his escort at Clonbanin was composed of men of the East Lancashire Regiment. About a month previously, the rank of brigadier-general had been abolished in the British army, and that of colonel-commandant substituted for it.

ENCIRCLING BRITISH FORCES TAKEN ON IN TURN AND SMASHED AT CROSSBARRY

CORK NO. 3 (WEST) BRIGADE, 19 MARCH 1921

As told by participants to Flor Crowley

THE ROLL AND rattle of guns was stilled at last; the wicked whine of bullets had ceased. A shattering blow had been struck, a decisive victory won. Weary but exultant, scarred and begrimed as men always are who fight to the death, yet rejoicing in soul and exalted in spirit for work well and ably done, for a battle truly and nobly fought and won, the victors withdrew slowly towards the north-west, to seek that rest of body, that relaxation of mind and muscle, which they had so dearly earned.

Far towards the south and west and towards the north-east too, other men withdrew, the vanquished! Withdrew in the abject confusion of a hopeless retreat; withdrew, broken and beaten, towards the safety of their strongholds in Bandon and Kinsale and Ballincollig and Cork!

That was a great day for our land, a glorious day for Ireland and Irishmen, that day of 19 March 1921.

In generations of the future when historians have finally written up the fruitful period of the war of 1920 and 1921, it is doubtful whether any other engagement of those dire years, not even Kilmichael itself, will be accorded a place equal to that of Crossbarry. Up to that day our tactics had of necessity to be hit-and-retreat tactics. But at Crossbarry it was different. Here, more than in any other fight of the time, our forces embarked upon a calculated campaign, one in which our superior generalship and superior fighting ability overcame superior numbers and greater firepower.

Here were two opposing forces at full strength; the one side little more than 100 strong, the other 1,000 or more. It was a numerical advantage which, by all the tenets of warfare, should have brought victory to the stronger force. But that advantage in numbers which the British enjoyed at Crossbarry was off-set by the greater fighting capacity, the greater determination, the greater daring and courage of the 100 who opposed them.

Were things otherwise, Crossbarry could have had but one result – the complete destruction of Tom Barry and his column. There at Crossbarry waited 100 men with limited arms and limited supplies of ammunition, with, however, unlimited courage, unlimited confidence in a leader who had never failed them, unlimited faith in themselves. Opposed to that 100 were more than 1,000 men, a great encircling force of men and guns and armour, steadily gravitating upon Crossbarry from the west and south and east, and from the north-east. With every passing minute the circle closed more surely upon the little waiting unit at Crossbarry. Only one line of retreat remained, should retreat be necessary, that towards the north-west, and even that might at any moment be sealed off, too, so deliberately thorough were the movements of the British columns. But retreat did not enter into the mind of the leader of Crossbarry, or into the minds of his men. To fight, not to retreat, was their duty that day, to fight and show the world that the spirit which won Benburb and Clontibret and Oulart Hill was not yet dead in the hearts of Irishmen.

The early spring of 1921 marked an introduction of new methods on the part of the British forces in Ireland. By that time they had come to realise that in one way only could they achieve victory over the Irish; that was to annihilate completely the flying columns, and firstly to annihilate the one column which was the inspiration of all others, that of the 3rd West Cork Brigade. But before anything can be destroyed it must be cornered – and to corner Barry's column became the object of all the occupation forces in the extensive area between Cork city in the east; Macroom and Ballincollig in the north and north-east; Kinsale in the south; Bandon, Dunmanway and Skibbereen in the west.

On 16 March 1921, came the first suggestion of the great and concentrated encircling movement by the British which was to have its climax at Crossbarry three days later. Lying in ambush at Shippool on the Innishannon-Kinsale road, the column learned that the Kinsale garrison knew of its whereabouts. In a few hours all the other garrisons in the area knew as well, and there began that movement of men, that movement and counter-movement, which raised Crossbarry to the plane of a campaign rather than a chance engagement. Each side appeared to know all there was to be known about the other, and each planned accordingly. A force as ponderous as that on the British side could not move in secret, so Barry knew through his scouts every move his enemies were making on all sides, and so exactly did the several British contingents converge upon Crossbarry on the morning of the actual engagement that it is a moral certainty that they too knew a great deal about Barry's movements.

In slow and secret movements, the column withdrew from Shippool, to Skough, east of Innishannon, and onwards towards Ballyhandle. An advance party scouted well to the front of the main body of the column, with scouts advancing inside both road fences to detect possible attack – for Barry planned to attack rather than to be attacked. By midnight he had made his headquarters and settled in for the night – but by three o'clock in the morning word had come through that Percival's men were moving from Bandon towards Kilpatrick and Upton and Crossbarry. Soon the flares of their headlights and the sound of the engines could be detected in the clear, still night. It was a moment of tension for the men of the column and for their leader, for neither entertained any false ideas regarding their own position, and each of them knew that for them the big engagement of the entire war was imminent. That the British were planning a large-scale movement was obvious to them from every report received from their scouts, and by daybreak they knew that 400 troops had left General Strickland's headquarters in Cork, travelling towards the west; that 200 had left

Ballincollig; 300 had left Kinsale; and more than 300 had left Bandon, all gravitating upon the one point – Crossbarry!

Having reached what were apparently pre-arranged points, west, north-east and south-east of Crossbarry, the British troops formed into raiding units and proceeded to make a slow and systematic search of the countryside, but all the while gradually closing in upon the focal point at Crossbarry. The lorries followed behind the raiding columns, and as the troops drew slowly nearer, the sound of their engines became more and more clearly audible to the men waiting at Crossbarry.

By 3 a.m. the column stood to arms and the decision was made to engage the enemy no matter what his strength, for, almost surrounded as it was, the column could scarcely hope to evade contact with some one of the encircling British contingents, with the result that they would be compelled to fight on the retreat. A series of skirmishes might easily develop from which the column could not hope to escape lightly. Then, ammunition supplies were small, so that a short, sharp attack was preferred to a prolonged, perhaps, day-long action.

As well as this, it became apparent to Barry and his officers that organisation on the part of the British troops was by no means good, for every report seemed to confirm the belief that Percival's men from Bandon were moving faster than the others, and would be at Crossbarry some time before the other British forces. This position, allowing that the various British columns could be taken in individual engagements, was exactly what Barry hoped for, and he had no doubt of his ability to cope with each British attack as it came.

With the entire column standing to arms, Barry spoke to his men, as he had spoken to them at daybreak before Kilmichael. He reviewed the position, explained the seriousness of the engagement before them, and exhorted each section and each man of each section to give of his best that day. There was to be no withdrawal, no matter how heavy the pressure, until a general fall-back order was issued. Each section was given a special task and was made responsible for its own individual part of the expected fight.

Mines were to be laid, one at each end of the ambush position, and no shot was to be fired at the leading units of the enemy as they passed through the ambush lines until they had reached the mine at the eastern end. This was then to be blown up, the explosion to be taken as the signal for a general open-fire on the nearest enemy.

At 4.30 a.m. ambush positions were taken up just west of Crossbarry village on the road to Bandon. The men of the column occupied the 200 yards of high ground immediately north of the road between Moore's Lane on the west and the Creamery road leading towards the north-east from Crossbarry.

Seven sections in all, with fourteen men and an officer comprising each section, lined up for action. No. 1 section under Seán Hales, occupied the extreme western position of the ambush, and commanded the entrance to Moore's Lane and the road approach to the ambush from the west. Its task was to hold Moore's Lane clear of the enemy, so that no flanking movements could be attempted after fire had been opened at the advance units further east. As well, Hales and his men held a strong attacking position from which they could open fire upon fresh troops arriving at the scene of the ambush after the start of the engagement.

Along the two farmyards skirting the road just east of Moore's Lane – Harold's and Beasley's farmyards – three sections were posted under, respectively, John Lordan, Mick Crowley and Pete Kearney. These were to comprise the chief striking force of the column once the enemy had come within their field of fire. They were well covered in outhouses and sheds, with a strong hedge of whitethorn as a screen in front to cover them until the moment for action arrived.

A further section under Denis Lordan was placed on the high ground at the eastern end of the ambush, eighty yards from Crossbarry village. This was to engage any troops approaching from the east or south-east, from which directions the Cork and Kinsale columns might at any moment appear.

Tom Kelleher's section held a rear line in the Castle field, 400 yards behind the main column position. The task of the section was to hold up any British troops approaching from Ballincollig after the attack began.

Further to the west on the high ground overlooking Sein na nEan Cross, Christy O'Connell was entrenched with his section, a quarter-mile on the western flank of the ambush. From this commanding position O'Connell's men could guard the column flank from unexpected attack and, at the same time, engage any further enemy forces that might arrive from Bandon and the west.

Three armed scouts were detailed to patrol to the rear of the column positions, so that no sudden attack could come from that direction, and so the scene was set for Crossbarry, set as well as a capable leader with a small but virile force could set it. A stone fence was erected across the road just behind Finn's corner, so that none of the enemy lorries could speed through the ambush and escape. The mines were set. Barry was ready! The time was just 5.30 a.m. on 21 March.

Suddenly, just as the morning sun rose over the hills to the east, a volley of shots broke the dullness of the dawn somewhere between north and west. What they signified the men of Crossbarry could not guess. They knew only that they must be enemy shots – and perhaps it was well for them that they could not know the exact meaning of that volley, for it was the volley which took from them one of their best-beloved leaders and comrades, which deprived them and Ireland of one of the greatest men of his day! Severely wounded in the Upton ambush of 15 February, Brigadier Charlie Hurley had been recuperating at the house of Humphrey Murphy of Ballymurphy. In the general round-up of that morning, Charlie awoke to find the house already surrounded by the British. There could be no escape for him, no hope of hiding. One thing remained for this unconquerable man, and he accepted that thing willingly; it was to go down fighting. Rushing down the stairs towards the door of the farmhouse, he opened fire upon the British outside. In confusion they retreated before his blazing guns. One leap and he was out into the yard. But a blast of gunfire from a dozen rifles and as many revolvers caught him then, and he fell with a British bullet in his brain. It was the death which Charlie Hurley would have chosen for himself, that fair-haired, mildly spoken country boy whom patriotic fervour and hatred of British rule and oppression turned into a soldier who was fearless and irrepressible, a leader who feared for his men but never for himself.

The knowledge that Charlie Hurley was dead was denied to the men of the column waiting at Crossbarry for the British who had killed him. It was, perhaps, well that it was so, for if there was one thing on earth which would have stirred to fury and to recklessness the souls of those waiting men, it was the thought that Charlie Hurley was dead. Reckless men do reckless deeds for which they sometimes pay with their lives. It is possible that many more would have died at Crossbarry if the men who fought there had known of, and tried to avenge, the death of Charlie Hurley. That his death was amply avenged is very true, but no vengeance can repay a nation for the loss of a man of his stature.

So the wait at Crossbarry dragged on through the hours of the early morning, until in the strengthening light of 8 a.m. the first of a long line of Essex Regiment lorries nosed its way beyond Sein na nEan towards Moore's Lane and Crossbarry. In five minutes a dozen lorries of British were within the ambush position. The leading tender was just abreast of the column command post at Beasley's Grove, when suddenly it jerked to a halt – a Volunteer had shown himself for a second at Harold's barn window and had been seen. Sensing danger, the British leaped from their lorries for the shelter of the hedges, but the 'open fire' was called, and volley after volley was poured into them from the three sections in the main ambush position. With the range at less than ten yards, the execution was shattering, and in five minutes the British had broken in disorder and fled over the fences and fields towards the railway on the south, leaving their dead and wounded, many of their guns and ammunition, and all their lorries behind them on the roadside. Out on the roadway leaped three sections of Barry's men, firing after the fleeing British, who did not stop or try to re-organise until they reached Bandon many hours later.

The first part of that great day's work was done. The first engagement of Crossbarry had been a crushing defeat for Percival and a resounding victory for Barry. But Barry knew even then that the day had further work in store for himself and his men; that this was no more than the preliminary to other and sterner fights to come. He could then have ordered a general withdrawal, could have marched away to the south, to the west, or north-west in perfect safety, and considered his day well spent with one column of the enemy broken and in complete rout. But that was not Barry's way. He chose to await the further attacks from the east and north-east which he knew would soon develop.

Ordering the men of Crowley's, Kearney's and Lordan's sections to collect the captured arms and ammunition – among which was a new British Lewis gun – Barry set about burning the captured lorries. Just as they caught fire, Denis Lordan's riflemen went into action at the eastern approaches to Crossbarry village. A long and steady blast of fire told the column commander that a further British contingent, probably Strickland's Hampshires from Cork, had arrived at Crossbarry through Killeady and Ballinhassig on the east, a new threat to be met and dealt with.

The three sections on the roadway, by then well supplied with captured arms and badly needed ammunition, rapidly regained their original attack positions along the farmyards and grove. The firing on their left flank increased in volume as Denis Lordan's men strove to repulse the advance of the British units, 200 strong, which had then reached Crossbarry bridge, and were returning a strong, concentrated fire. To meet this fresh attack, the column commander ordered Pete Kearney and his section to move up to the assistance of Denis Lordan's men. The increased volume of fire which the combined sections kept up steadily for five minutes was more than the British attackers seemed to relish, and, breaking off into a desultory exchange of shots, this contingent soon retreated at the double back through Crossbarry village and Killeady, leaving, as the Essex had done a half-hour earlier, their dead and dying on the road. They, like the Essex, never stopped to re-group and offered no further threat to Barry's men that day.

So in the space of thirty minutes the powerful pincers movement so carefully planned by Strickland at his Cork headquarters – the movement which was to put an end to Barry's column for all time – had been curbed and crushed. The circle of British arms and armour had been burst wide open on two sides and Barry was free to withdraw his men to the south or south-east as well as to the north-west had he chosen to do so. More than 500 British soldiers had come within the range of his fire and had been defeated ingloriously. His column had captured dozens of rifles, a Lewis gun, thousands of rounds of ammunition, had burned and destroyed most of the lorries abandoned by the Essex and, generally, had given the British a lesson which they were not likely to forget. Surely with all this already achieved he will now retreat towards safety!

But if the events of that momentous morning had taught the British a lesson, it had taught Barry a lesson too – the lesson that he and his men could meet and break the enemy in a stand-to fight. Only four sections of his column had so far gone into action, fewer than sixty men in all, and they had shattered a British force of 500! It was a heartening realisation for the man himself and for the men he led! Yes, he might have then withdrawn and avoided further engagement with the enemy. But it was not his plan to withdraw or to evade further action. Already he knew he had broken the morale of the British force, and he knew also that, with their fighting spirit now aflame, his men were capable of routing the other British units which were still advancing towards Crossbarry from the west and north-east. The day would only be complete when those units were broken as their compatriots had already been broken!

From the west came the rifle fire of the third engagement of the morning. A reinforcing British unit, endeavouring to outflank the column on the high ground over Sein na nEan, had come within range of Christy O'Connell's section. Taken completely by surprise, this British platoon fell back immediately the firing opened and offered no further resistance to the column. So the third engagement was won.

Meanwhile, Tom Kelleher's section had been deployed on the

column's left rear to meet the advance they knew the British had been making from Ballincollig. During the initial engagements by the column proper, this section had been entirely inactive, but they were well aware that their turn was coming. It came fifteen minutes after the last shots of O'Connell's men had turned the third British attack at Sein na nEan.

Two hundred British, in extended formations, advanced on Kelleher's position through Ballyhandle in the north-east. In the fight which followed, this British unit showed far greater combat ability than their comrades had done earlier that day, and it was only after a desperate engagement that they were finally beaten into flight. They were met with heavy fire from Kelleher's men as they advanced upon the Castle field, but they continued to advance. From covered positions inside the old castle ruins, two Volunteer snipers, Dan Mehigan of Bandon and Con Lehane of Timoleague, poured telling fire upon them, and though the British were virtually closing on the castle, these two stood courageously to their posts and held the position under heavy fire.

On the column front no further units of the enemy were in sight, and the column commander dispatched a reinforcing party of eleven men under Jim ('Spud') Murphy to the aid of Kelleher's section. Under the intensified fire the British were forced to retreat, followed closely by Kelleher and Murphy and their combined groups, forming a force of twenty-six men, including Mehigan and Lehane who had then rejoined their section after the enemy had been driven from the Castle field. With a few selected Volunteers to assist him, Tom Kelleher detoured in an endeavour to carry out an outflanking attack upon the retreating British. This was a profitable strategy on Kelleher's part, for he soon discovered that the British had themselves planned a similar attack upon the advancing column. The enemy flankers did not observe Kelleher and his Volunteers until they were close up to them. Then at point blank range the IRA opened fire, killing the British officer and many of his men with the first volley. The others turned and ran for their lives, once more leaving their dead behind them.

The fight on the column front was over, and, leaving O'Connell's section to hold their vantage point to the west in case a fresh attack might develop from that direction, Barry ordered his remaining sections to fall back towards Kelleher's position, where firing was still going on. He had reached the position just as Kelleher's flankers returned from their successful foray against the retreating enemy. It was then observed that the British were making an attempt to reform, several hundred yards away – the sole British unit which showed sufficient spirit to do so that day. Falling his men in, Barry positioned them along a fence and gave the 'open fire!' After three volleys the re-grouping British broke completely and fled – and Crossbarry was over and won! Barry's men had stood against the might of Strickland and Percival, and crushed them in a fair fight! Then at last they could retire with glory!

But let us be just, even to our enemies, though 1,000 of them had broken ignominiously before a tenth of their number. Neither we in Ireland, nor any other race which has faced them in battle, have found the soldiers of England the abject cowards they appeared to be at Crossbarry. How then did they fail so utterly before Barry's column in the one big battle of the Anglo-Irish War? The answer is that they were already broken in nerve and in spirit before ever a shot of Crossbarry was fired. Consider their mode of life for months before. Close confinement to barracks, never-ending vigilance, ever-present fear of sudden attack, no normal life or relaxation or amusement, always with the cold shudder of dread sheering through their beings – that was the state of mind and soul through which these men of the British occupation forces had lived for months.

Then the frequently recurring periods of guard duty, the long nerve-fraying hours of sentry and guard-room duty – the severest strain a soldier can undergo even in peacetime – that, too, added to the misery of the British soldier in those uncertain days when one shot or one Mills bomb at midnight meant an entire garrison standing-to until dawn. There could be no relief from duty for them. In trench warfare of the orthodox type, the soldier stood out a measured period and was relieved. In Ireland the British were in the line of fire from the moment they set foot on Irish soil until the last shot of the war was fired. And to every man of the British forces that last shot might not be fired for years, for there was no knowing how long the war might drag on – for each of them it might be fired at any second from any window they passed, from any fence they approached, by any man they might meet during any hour of the twenty-four. Their lives were an endless misery in west Cork, made so by the unrelenting menace of Barry and his men, those almost spectre-like figures which hovered eternally around them to harass and to haunt them.

So, many of those British soldiers were literally wrecks before a shot was fired at them in Crossbarry. Barry and his men had beaten them before they ever met them; they had beaten them by the insistence of their attack, by never allowing them to forget that death hung close to them every moment of their lives, for in that war of nerves the names of Barry and his fighters bore as deadly a menace as their guns bore in the actual struggle.

But victory is rarely achieved without its price, and victory in battle claims its price in human blood. An engagement of the extent and intensity of Crossbarry could not be won without cost, and the cost of victory there was the lives of three young Volunteers – and the miracle was that in the hurly-burly of that terrible day the cost was not much greater. Peter Monahan, one of Denis Lordan's section, was killed in repulsing the second British attack, that which advanced through Crossbarry from the east. Two rounds he had fired when a British bullet caught him. Another caught Dan Corcoran of Newcestown on the hip, crippling him, but a comrade, Dick Spencer of Castletownbere, bore him to safety over his shoulder under the heavy fire of the enemy, an act which would have won him a high military decoration in any other army in the world.

Of Tom Kelleher's section, two Volunteers were killed in action soon after his men engaged the enemy. They were Jerry O'Leary of Coronagh, Leap, and Con Daly of Ballinascarthy. Two others were slightly wounded. The traveller who passes through Crossbarry today will see on that historic roadside a small and unimposing iron cross on which are inscribed the names of the three dead Volunteers – a slight and very humble token of our respect for the memory of the men who died at Crossbarry.

The British admitted thirty-nine killed, including five officers, and forty-seven wounded. The column had good reason to believe that the British losses were much greater. The *Cork Examiner* of 21 March 1921, reporting, as it claims, from 'reliable sources', stated that eight of the British forces were killed in the initial attack. Later it appeared to contradict this statement when it printed this: 'Reinforcements of the Hampshire Regiment arrived from General Strickland's Headquarters at Cork to find "All the first party killed or wounded".' It further remarked that, following the departure of the IRA, the Beasley and Harold families ventured out to find 'the road strewn with dead and wounded'. It may, therefore, be safely assumed that the British suffered heavily at Crossbarry. In all four phases of the fight they lost men, but particularly at Beasley's Grove, where the first engagement took place. Denis Lordan's men accounted for several others, and so did O'Connell's at the west, while Kelleher and his section were responsible for many others. So, in mourning the loss of our three dead, we may console ourselves with the thought that they were amply avenged that day.

The stillness of midday had followed the roar and rumble of the morning as the victorious little column marched away from Crossbarry. Behind them they left the shambles of a defeated enemy who had been twenty-four hours before resplendent in all the pomp and array of a conqueror. Before them lay all west Cork, with every man and every woman and every child to make them welcome.

TOO EARLY ARRIVAL OF TRAIN ROBBED IRA OF FRUITS OF VICTORY AT HEADFORD

KERRY NO. 2 BRIGADE, 21 MARCH 1921

As told by participants to Edward Gallagher

'THE BEST LAID schemes of mice and men gang aft a-gley.' In no sphere of action more than in war have the words of Robert Burns been proved true. A commander plans his action down to the last foreseeable detail, but it is often the unforeseeable factor upon which the tide of battle turns.

So it was at Headford railway junction, in County Kerry, where, on a bleak March day in 1921, the Kerry No. 2 Brigade column planned to ambush and disarm a military ration party coming in by train from Kenmare. The column commanders relied upon the railway timetable when planning their coup, but the train came in some fifteen minutes before it was officially due. The fight that ensued was a bloody one, and one that struck a heavy blow at British morale in the county, but the unforeseeable factors – in this instance the train that came in before time and a delayed dispatch – cheated the column of the fruits of victory – the arms and ammunition that were so badly needed.

The fight at Headford took place on Monday 21 March. The previous week the column, which numbered thirty men of all ranks at full strength, had finished a fortnight's training at the Gap of Dunloe, headquarters of the brigade. The men were fit and eager for a fight but they lacked battle experience. Only twelve of them, in fact, had ever been under fire and their leaders were anxious to put the fortnight's training to the test.

Five days before Headford, on Thursday 17 March, they had planned an ambush at Dysert, Castleisland. The column had taken up positions while the local Farranfore and Firies Companies had staged a sham attack on the police barracks at Farranfore. It was hoped that the sham attack would have drawn military and police reinforcements from Castleisland into the ambush position. But the operation had failed. No enemy forces had appeared and after a seven-hour wait in the icy cold the column had withdrawn.

Cheated of an engagement, the column made a series of marches across country to Kilquane, Barraduff, a village near Headford. They reached there on Saturday night and their leaders decided to billet there for twenty-four hours. The local company and its captain, Jim Daly, thought it better that the column should strike for Gortdarrig, closer to the shelter of the massive mountains and away from the main Killarney-Mallow road.

But there was to be a wedding party at a neighbour's house on Sunday night. The men of the column, nerves taut in the presence of ever-constant danger, wanted relaxation. They went to the celebrations. There was dancing, music, song and laughter. Then came the order to move on. Too many young men at a wedding might arouse suspicion, it was thought, and the main road was near.

Another factor that influenced the column leaders in their decision to move on was the fact that a man called Sandy, an itinerant, who was over-fond of the company of the enemy forces, had suddenly left the locality.

The local company had been keeping their eyes on Sandy's movements, for he was known to be friendly with a Captain O'Sullivan, a British intelligence officer stationed in Killarney. And on that day one of the company had reported that Sandy had disappeared and was possibly headed for Killarney.

A number of men from the company set off on bikes in pursuit of Sandy and overtook him on the road to Killarney. He was all innocence, but his interrogators were not satisfied. He was arrested and turned over to the column who already held two British army deserters. When the column set out for Headford it could not afford to set guards over the captives, so they were all securely tied up in a cowshed and picked up after the ambush.

Before following the column on the road that led to Headford, we might here dispose conveniently of Sandy's subsequent brief but eventful story. After the ambush he was court-martialled. Star witness was an IRA man who, while a prisoner in Killarney barracks, had heard someone give information about IRA activities to Captain O'Sullivan. The witness had been unable to see the informer nor had he recognised his voice until he had sung for the intelligence officer. The song was 'Take me back to my dear old mother and there let me live and die'. That was well known in the district as Sandy's song and the way in which it was sung gave away the identity of the singer to the listening IRA man. That evidence helped to seal Sandy's fate and he was duly executed as a spy.

When the column moved off from Kilquane to Gortdarrig, which it reached in the early hours of Monday morning, the leaders had no particular action in mind, but when, about midday, they read a dispatch brought in by Con Moynihan, the information it contained suggested to them that here was just the opportunity for which they had been looking.

Once a week – but not on any set day – a military ration party went from the barracks in Killarney to the military post in Kenmare and back by train. The information brought in by Moynihan was that the ration party was probably returning by the afternoon train. The train was due into Headford at 3.15 p.m. and the decision was taken to ambush the military while they were changing trains at the junction.

Briefly the column commanders, Dan Allman and Thomas McEllistrim, told the men of the column what had to be done. They were familiar with the procedure that would be followed by the military party on arriving at Headford. They would disembark from the train on the Headford platform, move over the line to the other platform to which the Killarney train, coming from the Mallow direction, would come in soon after, form up in two ranks with protective flanking squads of five men each, and hold that position until their train came in.

The commanders planned to post the column on the embankment on either side of the station and, when the military party had taken up position on the Killarney platform, to blast them with rifle fire. They reckoned they should be able to finish the job with two volleys; those of the military who might not have fallen victim to the fire of the column would be in no condition to prevent the latter from seizing all the rifles and ammunition and – most important – a Vickers machine gun which the ration party always carried in a wagon next to the engine. With its booty the column would then retire to the shelter of the Pap mountains.

The leaders estimated that they had about one and a half hours in which to get to Headford and take up positions before the train came in. Equipment was checked and then the column fell in and set off on a forced march across country from the shadows of the snow-capped mountains to the boggy valley where the station stands in a cutting.

When it had arrived within about 300 yards of the station, the column was halted and ordered to fall out. The column commanders now reckoned that they had from fifteen to twenty minutes in which to carry out a reconnaissance of the position and to post their force. So, while the rest of the column rested, Allman, McEllistrim, Dan Healy, Jack Cronin and Moss Carmody entered the station to make their dispositions. In order not to arouse suspicion they left their rifles in charge of Johnny O'Connor.

Headford Junction has two platforms, one at the centre and one at the side. One side of the central platform, that next to the stationmaster's house, is the starting and stopping place of the Kenmare branch-line train; on the other side of the central platform comes in the main line train from Tralee and Killarney to Mallow. To the side platform comes in the main line train from Cork and Mallow to Killarney and Tralee. We are concerned here with the side of the central platform on which the Kenmare train arrives, which we shall call for the sake of convenience the Kenmare platform,

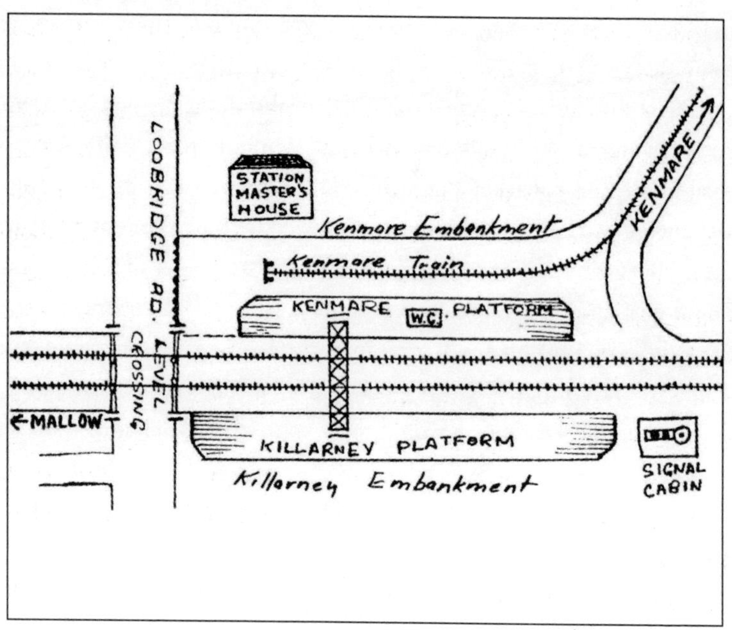

and the side platform on which the Killarney train draws up, which we shall call the Killarney platform. The embankment facing the Kenmare platform will be called the Kenmare embankment. Behind it are Crohane and the Pap mountains. Overlooking the Killarney platform is a steep embankment, which will be called the Killarney embankment. Tucked in underneath this embankment at the Kerry end of the station is the signal cabin. Into that end, on the dead-end branch line, would come the Kenmare train. At the other – or Cork end – of the station is a level crossing with gates. Into that end would come the Mallow-Killarney train.

First due was the Kenmare train. The time was just past three o'clock as McEllistrim and Carmody climbed the steps to the signal cabin. Carmody's job was to mount guard in the cabin to provide against the danger of the signals being set against the incoming Kenmare train.

It was at this point that the unforeseeable factor – the time factor – upset the column calculations. The commanders reckoned that they had a reasonable margin of time in which to complete their dispositions

– and so they had according to the train's scheduled time of arrival. They were not to know that the train from Kenmare, which was a mixed passenger and goods train, had started from Kenmare with a full load and that consequently she had not to utilise the time allowed her for taking on goods at the intermediate stops. At the military inquiry held in Killarney after the ambush, the engine driver, Con O'Mahony of Tralee, was closely questioned on this point of his train coming in before her time. The enemy were concerned to know whether he had deliberately brought her in before her normal time to enable the 'rebels' to deal with the British forces before the arrival of the Cork train. His perfectly legitimate explanation, however, had to be accepted.

McEllistrim learned of the train's too early approach – without, of course, knowing the reason why – when, on asking the signal man how she was running, he was informed to his consternation that she was due within a few minutes. Leaving Carmody in charge of the signal cabin he dashed for the central platform to inform the others.

The work of shifting wagons out of the field of fire, which had been going forward, had to be suspended and the column got into position at top speed. Time was now the essence of the contract.

Johnny O'Connor flung their rifles to the five men on the platform and then clambered up the Killarney embankment to join his section there.

McEllistrim ran across to the stationmaster's house which is at the Cork end of the station and, as has been stated, faces the Kenmare platform. This was to be operations headquarters. There with him were John Flynn, an ex-British army man who had trained the column, and young Paddy Lynch. When the Kenmare train drew up, the engine would more or less come in line with the house.

Peter Browne joined his section on the Kenmare embankment. And here again the time factor crops up. Had the column commanders had the time – which they reckoned they had – to reconnoitre the position carefully, they would never have posted men on that section of the Kenmare embankment to which a portion of the column was directed in the race to nullify the new time element. The position was excellent in so far as it gave a commanding view of the station, but it lacked cover. Men lying there would be fully visible to anyone on the train. Hastily they ran back and took up position behind a fence about sixty yards from the station. The snag was that, from the front of the embankment which overlooks the station, to the fence behind which the men of the column took up position, the ground slopes downwards. The result was that the fire of the section here was rendered ineffective as it no longer commanded a view of the station. The consequences of that ineffectiveness will be described later.

A section of six crouched or knelt behind the Cork end of the Kenmare platform which at that time ended in a sharp drop but which now ends in a sloping ramp. Jack Brosnan of Castleisland and Tom 'Scarteen' O'Connor of Kenmare were among those who occupied this position designed to smash the British with enfilading fire.

Despite the too early arrival of the train, which had forced the men of the column to occupy hastily improvised positions, the operation at Headford might still have gone according to the designs of the leaders and have gone down in the history of the Anglo-Irish War not merely as a very gallant action – which it was – but also as a highly successful one.

But the fates had still to deal the column a further blow. Allman, Healy and Jim Coffey, an ex-British soldier and fine fighter, had taken refuge in the lavatory which stands about half-way down the platform. The idea was that they might remain there undetected until the military party should have moved over to the Killarney platform when they would have been able to engage them from a strategic position. But, as we have said, the malignant fates had not yet finished with the column.

Inside the lavatory Healy, who had brought along Allman's rifle as well as his own, was told by Allman to load the latter's gun. Healy began to do so while they waited tensed for the train to come to a stop.

Into the station eased the train carrying the ration party comprising of Lieutenant Adams, two sergeants, a corporal and twenty-six other ranks of the 1st Royal Fusiliers. As the train came to a stop, doors were flung open and soldiers and civilians began to pile out onto the platform. There was that momentary pause, which happens when people get off a train and bags are looked at, parcels adjusted and coats straightened. Then a young Fusilier began to walk across to the lavatory. The fates had now done their worst.

When the Fusilier entered the lavatory the first person he saw was Coffey standing with rifle in hand. In his amazement he blurted out the incongruous exclamation, 'Hello, Paddy!' Coffey made a grab for his rifle and the Fusilier backed out hastily. Allman presumably recognised that the game was up. The soldier was going to give the alarm and possibly enable the enemy to dictate the course of the action as they wished to fight it. The issue was joined in any event and Allman, we must suppose, decided to get his blow in first and give the column the advantage of what measure of surprise remained with them. As the Fusilier backed out of the lavatory, Allman's revolver spat fire and the man slumped to the platform and rolled over.

There was a split second of stunned silence and inactivity while the reverberations of the shot rolled across the cutting to the distant mountains. The Fusiliers faced towards the sound of the explosion and their officer paused in the carriage doorway in the very act of getting off the train. It was possibly his last conscious action.

The men of the column knew that the balloon had gone up. There was no waiting for fire orders. A rifle volley shattered the stillness of the March afternoon and its echoes sang away among the mountain fastnesses.

At this distance of thirty-one years it is not easy to conjure up the scene of pandemonium that the Kenmare platform must have presented when the column opened fire on it. The whole thing happened so suddenly – so unpreparedly, if one likes – that even the recollections of those who took part in it are blurred. It happened not the way the column commanders had planned to fight the action. They had reckoned that they would be dealing solely with a military party on the Killarney platform. They never visualised having to deal with them on the Kenmare platform – and having to deal with them when the action was complicated by the presence of civilians.

Let us try to recapture as best we can what happened when the column opened fire. A Fusilier, moving for the lavatory in the wake of his comrade-in-arms who was shot by Allman, was dropped in his tracks by a marksman on the Killarney embankment. Lieutenant Adams, halted in his carriage doorway by the crack of Allman's revolver, was riddled by bullets from the column riflemen. Others of the military party who were the first to jump out were sent reeling to the platform, dead or wounded. Fusiliers who had not been caught in the first volley, or who had been behind their comrades leaving the train, jerked up their rifles and let fly, but their fire was wild and indiscriminate as they had not got their bearings. Their shooting was, in fact, more dangerous to the civilians than it was to the men of the column.

The civilians were mostly cattle dealers returning from Kenmare fair. They and the other civilians dashed wildly for shelter or safety. A woman dragging two children by the hand ran screaming along the platform towards the Kerry end. She leaped over the bodies of the first two Fusiliers who had been claimed by the column and dashed out of sight. Two little girls in white ran sobbing and shrieking towards the other end of the platform and also reached safety. But other civilians were not so fortunate. Two cattle dealers named Paddy Donoghue and Seán Breen were wounded and Breen subsequently died on the way to hospital. A Loo Bridge publican named McCarthy and his little daughter were injured by flying bullets. A Cork cattle dealer named Tangney was shot by the indiscriminate fire of the military as he dashed down the platform.

The ration party, though torn and shaken by the fire of the column riflemen, was not demoralised. Many of them were seasoned Great War veterans and battle discipline now stood them in good stead. Though their officer was dead and numbers of their comrades were lying around dead, dying or grievously wounded, they rallied behind a sergeant who led a dash down the platform towards the Cork end.

His dash was short-lived, for a column bullet sent him sprawling to the ground. This stopped the rush and the Tommies paused, uncertain what to do next. That pause was a fatal one. Bunched together in momentary bewilderment they presented a sitting target to the column, who poured volley after volley into their ranks. It was at this stage that the greatest execution was done among the enemy forces. From the opening shot to the end of this phase of the action it is estimated that their casualties totalled twenty-five in dead or seriously wounded. The column had suffered one fatal casualty. Jim Baily, lying behind his rifle on the Killarney embankment, had been shot through the head and killed instantly.

Among the remnant of the enemy who had survived the merciless blasting by the column riflemen, the instinct of self-preservation or battle experience asserted itself and the survivors, led by the second sergeant, jumped down off the platform, some crawling under the train and others trying to get round the engine. But fire from the stationmaster's house picked these latter off, though one soldier did manage to dash across the line and find concealment in a fold of the field in front of the column position on the Kenmare embankment. He emerged only ten feet from the position, crawling frantically, either because he was wounded or for concealment. A shot rang out and he slumped down into the grass.

The position now was that the four or five survivors of the military party were sheltering under the train with the platform protecting them from the fire of the column men on the Killarney embankment. Owing to the fact that, as we have stated previously, the section on the Kenmare embankment had had to retire sixty yards back to a position below the level of the bank overlooking the station, the fire of this section could not be brought to bear against these Tommies on the Kenmare, or unprotected, side. The Vickers machine gun, which might have played havoc with the column, had been immobilised practically from the start of the fight. After a few bursts of fire from the wagon in which it was carried, it had lapsed into silence as the gunners were blasted into oblivion.

There ensued a lull punctuated by sniping fire on both sides. When the survivors of the military party went to earth under the train, the column men on the Killarney embankment could not bring fire against them effectively because of the intervening platform, nor could the men on the Kenmare embankment because they did not command an effective fire view of the platform on their side. Driver Con O'Mahony who, with his fireman, was lying flat on the footplate sheltering from the bullets, related that a soldier in shirt sleeves, and with a fresh bullet scar on his neck, swung into the cabin and ordered him to reverse the train along the Kenmare line. Whether he came from under the train or from the wagon next to it, in which the Vickers gun was kept, he does not know. O'Mahony stalled him and got rid of him by pointing out that if he moved the train the Tommies sheltering under it would be cut to ribbons. At the end of the fight, when the column had withdrawn, the same soldier mounted the machine gun on the platform and blazed away at the stationmaster's house.

One of the reasons for the lull in the fighting was that liaison had not been so far established between the two wings – so to speak – of the column. When the enemy sought refuge under the train the column men on the Killarney side could no longer hit them up because of the intervening Kenmare platform. Their role was reduced to one of sniping. And they had no knowledge of what the column men on the Kenmare side were doing. On the Kenmare side McEllistrim, who had been hotly engaging the enemy under the train from his stationmaster's house position, had repeatedly called on them to surrender, to be met every time with the defiant shout 'Never!'

The lull was to be short-lived. When the balloon had gone up Allman, with Healy and Coffey, had come out of the lavatory and, lying down on the platform to the side of it, had fired on the military. Subsequently the three had retired to the end of the platform and with a sloping ramp giving them some cover, had continued to engage the enemy from that position. Carmody, who had been unable to leave by the door of the signal cabin on account of the fierce firing, was now released by Johnny O'Connor who, crouching on the bank, rammed his rifle through the glass panes at the rear of the cabin, making an opening for his trapped comrade to climb through.

Allman was determined to get the rifles and ammunition now for the taking, if only the battle-seasoned Fusiliers under the train could be silenced or dislodged. The problem was how to do that. A Mills bomb, pegged like a stone, which had exploded with shattering effect under the train, had failed to do the trick. Allman's idea was that the only way in which it could be done was to get onto the line and shoot it out with them. Alternatively he thought that if they got out behind the guard's van, which was stopped just below the start of the ramp, they might be able to fire underneath the train and force the enemy out into the open where they could be dealt with.

The repercussions of the old bad luck time factor which had dogged the column were still being felt. Liaison had not yet been established between the forces on both sides of the station. Men who, as a result of having had to occupy hastily improvised positions, had never had a chance of getting effectively into the fight, and others whose fire had been rendered ineffective as a result of the enemy survivors getting under the train, had withdrawn. It is believed that at this stage of the fight fewer than a dozen of the column remained in the ambush position.

Coffey, who had edged out from behind the shelter of the ramp and essayed a shot up along the train, had had the experience of having his arm seared by a bullet the moment he exposed himself. He warned Allman that all around that position seemed to be covered off by a deadly marksman. But Allman was determined to try to break the stalemate. He came out from behind the shelter of the ramp, knelt down on the line and lifted his rifle. Next moment the hidden sniper had sent a bullet through his lung.

Healy and Coffey pulled him back into cover. It was obvious that he had been fatally hit, for blood gushed from his mouth, ears and nostrils and a green-and-gold rosette worn on the lapel of his coat was in a trice dyed a vivid red. They heard him gasp 'water', and he tapped his breast. Coffey knew that the dying man was referring to the little bottle of holy water which he carried in a vest pocket. He took out the bottle and sprinkled him with the water.

The position of Healy and Coffey was a difficult one. They wanted to take the dead or dying Allman with them, but burdened with his body they would have presented too good a target for the British snipers. These latter, flushed with success, were sending bullets screaming off the rails all around. Reluctantly then they left Allman's body lying behind the van.

With Allman's death McEllistrim would now assume sole command and Coffey made his way across the line to acquaint him of the new position that had arisen. On the Kenmare embankment he was directed by Browne to the stationmaster's house which, as has been previously stated, was operations headquarters.

The position of the remaining men of the column was now critical. The Mallow-Killarney train had been held up on the line some 300 yards from the station by the signals being set against her. Unknown to the column there were military on the train. Their presence was first realised by the enfilading section at the end of the Kenmare platform. An officer was observed standing on the footplate of the engine. Presumably he had come along to the driver to enquire the reason for the stop. Immediately the section proceeded to open fire against the train. McEllistrim, made aware by their action of the presence of enemy reinforcements, ordered a retreat on the Kenmare side and crossed the line to the Killarney side to order the men there to withdraw.

When he gained the Killarney embankment O'Connor pointed out to him where the bodies of Allman and Baily were lying. In the meantime the military on the signal-halted Mallow-Killarney train, who were also drawn from the 1st Royal Fusiliers, advancing on foot along the line, had arrived on the scene. For the four men of the column remaining – McEllistrim, O'Connor, Browne and Jack Brosnan – it was time to retreat, and to retreat as fast they could.

At the back of the Killarney embankment the four column men found a bohereen which wound a quarter of a mile between stone-bound ditches before spilling into a little coarse field surrounded by black ditches of bog mould. They split into two parties. McEllistrim and O'Connor had made the centre of the coarse field without mishap when bullets clipped the grass around their feet. Their plight was perilous in the extreme. The field was devoid of cover, but even had there been any they were in no position to engage the enemy as their ammunition was practically exhausted. Fifty yards away beckoned the safety of a black bog ditch four feet high.

McEllistrim dropped to the ground while O'Connor raced for the ditch and cleared it in a single bound. McEllistrim, unhurt and getting to his feet between the volleys, followed him and cleared the ditch in a flurry of black earth and bullets.

Fortunately for the men of the column the British did not keep up the pursuit but contented themselves with scouring the countryside from the railway line and the roads.

When they had crossed the Flesk River on their trek to the friendly shelter of the hills, the column men were comparatively safe, but they had to keep moving. Through gullies, over mountain paths, across rivers and ravines, they made their way to Shrone, in the district of Rathmore, on the Kerry-Cork border, where the column mustered that night under the guidance of members of the local company.

Thus ends the story of the Headford ambush. Two gallant soldiers of Ireland had lost their lives and the column had been cheated of the spoils of victory. But at least the enemy had been dealt a heavy blow and the men of the Kerry No. 2 Brigade column had written an imperishable chapter in the history of their country's fight for freedom. If they had not achieved complete success they had deserved it.

SCRAMOGUE AMBUSH DID NOT MAKE FOR HAPPY RELATIONS BETWEEN LANCERS AND TANS

NORTH AND SOUTH ROSCOMMON BRIGADES, 23 MARCH 1921

by Seán Leavy

(formerly O/C 3rd Battalion, North Roscommon Brigade, IRA)

In the spring of 1921 all the energies of the North and South Roscommon Brigade staffs were directed towards intensification of activity against the enemy. Morale was high in the county, thanks mainly to the organising ability of Seán Connolly of the Longford Brigade, who had been sent to Roscommon by GHQ. Connolly was, undoubtedly, one of the great guerrilla leaders that the IRA had so far produced, and his sojourn in Roscommon had borne good fruit. The battalions had been reorganised, the men had full confidence in their officers and, at last, sufficient arms for some offensive activity had been assembled. After organising Roscommon, Connolly was transferred by GHQ to organise Leitrim county. He had asked me to apply to GHQ to have him sent back to Roscommon for a further period but, when parting, he mentioned to me that he had a strong presentiment that we would never meet again. Soon after going to Leitrim he was dead, as well as five of his gallant comrades, for, sad to relate, the whereabouts of the column had been betrayed to the enemy by two of his own compatriots. One of the traitors was promptly executed near to his own home; the other made good his escape to England, where, however, he did not live long to enjoy the fruits of his treachery. He was crushed to death on his own doorstep by a runaway lorry.

The Roscommon men, for whom Connolly had done so much, were naturally anxious to balance the account, but there was also a sound military reason for immediate action in the county – the urgent necessity of diverting enemy pressure in the Longford and Leitrim areas. The enemy had taken a heavy hammering from Seán MacEoin and had reacted sharply. It was imperative that some of their forces be diverted, and so Michael Dockery, O/C of the North Roscommon Brigade, called a conference to discuss ways and means. At the conference he offered £50 for the purchase of arms to the battalion that first submitted a feasible plan for attack on the enemy and then carried it out. He also promised to stage another ambush immediately after the first, so as to draw off enemy pressure. It may be mentioned that both promises were faithfully carried out; but more of this later.

Following the brigade conference, as O/C of the 3rd Battalion, North Roscommon Brigade, I called together the officers of the battalion and laid before them plans which had been formulated already for an ambush at Scramogue, some two miles south-east of Strokestown, on the Strokestown-Longford road. The ground was well-known to me, as indeed it should be, for the ambush position chosen was within eighty yards of my own hall door. In fact, the extreme unlikelihood of the hall door and the house to which it was attached surviving the ambush for more than a couple of hours was pointed out to me at the brigade conference. The ambush proposal was approved by the officers, as was also a suggestion that the 3rd Battalion of the South Roscommon Brigade be invited to participate in the action. Martin Fallon, O/C of the North Roscommon flying column, and myself, therefore, arranged a conference with Pat Madden and Luke Duffy of South Roscommon, which took place at my house. It was at this conference that the proposal received final approval and that final plans were made for a joint attack by the men of the 3rd Battalions of both the Roscommon Brigades. It should be mentioned here that Scramogue lies almost on the line of demarcation between the two brigade areas and was as easy of access to the men from South Roscommon as it was to those from the northern half of the county. It should also be mentioned that the area of south Roscommon was hopelessly unsuited for guerrilla warfare, consisting as it does of wide rolling plains devoid of cover, large fields separated only by low stone walls and banks that afforded no cover from view or from fire. The first essentials of a successful guerrilla action are the ability to break off action at will and a covered line of retreat. One has only to study the terrain around Roscommon town, with its open vistas and all round field of fire, to realise its hopelessness; but it must be added that these disadvantages did not prevent the men of South Roscommon from carrying out a highly successful ambush at Fourmilehouse.

One problem that did not worry us was the question of finding a target. The road through Scramogue was one of the main highways for military traffic from the garrison town of Longford to north and west Mayo, crossing the Shannon at Tarmonbarry, five miles south of the ambush position. Military lorries passed at almost hourly intervals, but, owing to the nature of the terrain, only south-bound traffic could be attacked with any hope of success.

The attacking position was, in itself, a strong one, and the great danger to the attackers lay in the proximity of enemy reinforcements. Barely a mile away, at Strokestown house, there was a squadron of the 9th Lancers and a half company of the East Yorks, while there were some sixty-five RIC and Tans in Strokestown police barracks. There were also police and Tans in Elphin, and military garrisons in Roscommon, Tarmonbarry, Rooskey and Longford, while Athlone had a huge military establishment of all arms. The Lancers offered the greatest potential menace, as well-officered cavalry could play havoc with the withdrawal of the IRA column, particularly as most of the men, as will be seen, were armed with short range weapons. The Lancers were commanded by Captain Sir Alfred Peek, Bart, DSO, a capable and vigorous soldier who had shown violent hatred of the IRA. Captain Peek was of an arrogant and bullying disposition and had declared that if one of his men was injured he would not leave a house standing within five miles. This threat was made at Scramogue post office following the seizure of military mails by the IRA. One of Captain Peek's letters, intercepted by the IRA, contained his will and another the statement that 'all the local IRA leaders are safely under lock and key except Fallon and Leavy and we do not consider these two dangerous'. Captain Peek showed wisdom in the making of his will.

It was decided to mount the attack in the early hours of Spy Wednesday, 23 March 1921. The column from the South Roscommon Brigade was picked and armed by Luke Duffy, Frank Simons and Pat Madden, and came in small numbers to the assembly area between 2 a.m. and 6.30 a.m. The men of the North Roscommon column, picked by Martin Fallon and myself, assembled about the same time, and food was provided by my parents and by James Early and his sister. The total strength of all ranks, contributed fairly evenly by the two battalions, was thirty-nine. The armament consisted of seventeen rifles, two or three revolvers and twenty shotguns with slugged cartridges. All the companies had been alerted and during the early hours all roads leading to the ambush position were blocked, except those leading through Strokestown to Sligo via Elphin and to Ballina via Tulsk.

The approach to Scramogue from Strokestown is along a straight, low-lying road with level marshy fields on either side. At Scramogue the road ascends the eastern flank of Slieve Bawn in a double bend. The place was a known danger point, but captured documents revealed that the enemy considered the most likely ambush position to be the wooded area at Scramogue post office some 500 yards further on. The ambush site chosen is indicated by the centre of the circle on the map. To the east of it the land rises rapidly and, as will be seen by the map, the road takes a sharp turning to the left, so that an approaching motor vehicle would have to reduce speed considerably. The house marked 'A' on the map was on much higher ground than the road over which it held a commanding position. At the point 'B' the road fence, which was also considerably higher than the carriageway, consisted of an earthen bank. Inside this bank there was a trench which provided

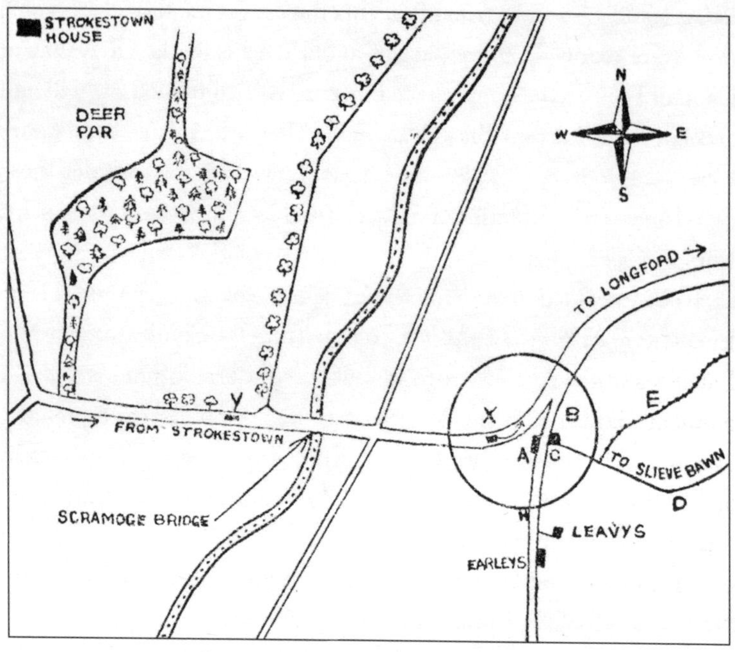

excellent cover. From it a doorway opened into the house marked 'C', and another door in the opposite wall of that house gave access to the lane, 'C-D'. This laneway was fenced on either side by high banks topped by hedges, and the entrance to it was completely hidden from view from the main road, by the houses, 'A' and 'C'. The lane leads to high ground containing excellent cover and eventually to the lower slopes of Slieve Bawn. In the house marked 'A', which was suitably loop-holed, there were posted ten shotguns and five rifles, and there were ten shotguns and six rifles at point 'B' in the trench. To cover the flanks there were four rifles at point 'C' and two rifles at point 'D'. At Early's house two men guarded civilians evacuated from houses nearer to the scene of the action.

With the coming of daylight everything was ready. The men had been fed, final orders issued and combat positions occupied. The civilians in the adjoining houses had been removed from the scene of the action. No one knew what target would appear, but the orders were clear and the men knew precisely the circumstances under which they were to open or hold fire. Meanwhile, in Strokestown house, Captain Peek was early astir and in not too good a temper. He had ordered the Black and Tans, between whom and the military relations were not good, to provide a lorry and escort at 7 a.m. to bring two Tans, under arrest for smashing the windows of Elphin Church, to Longford. The Tans had phoned to say they could not start their lorry, and so Captain Peek decided to provide his own escort and transport. In a few minutes they were ready, a sergeant and four men of the Lancers and the two prisoners, the latter in civilian dress. At the last moment Captain Peek, who intended to go to a coursing meeting in Longford that afternoon, decided to accompany the lorry and to take with him his second-in-command, Lieutenant Tennant. As they were on the point of departure the lorry-load of Tans turned up and Captain Peek decided to take them too. It was about 7.10 a.m. when the two lorries left Strokestown house, the Tans lorry leading, but, strangely enough, pulling very badly, and Peek's lorry took the lead soon after, leaving the second lorry stopped and apparently having engine trouble about 600 yards behind. When the first lorry had reached the point 'X' on the map, fire was opened by all arms. The lorry proceeded the short distance indicated on the map by the line along the road, and then crashed into the wall at the point shown by the arrowhead. A Hotchkiss machine gunner got off a few ineffective bursts of fire, before he was put out of action. In a few minutes it was all over. Lieutenant Tennant received a fearful abdominal wound from which he died the same day. Captain Peek succeeded in staggering some hundreds of yards before he collapsed and died on the road. The only survivors were the prisoners, who by some miracle, were untouched. Meanwhile, IRA riflemen higher up the hill engaged the broken-down Tan lorry, which was at the point marked 'Y' on the map. In a short time the engine of this lorry miraculously sprang to life and conveyed a badly shaken body of Tans at all speed back to the safety of their barracks in Strokestown, whence hasty calls for aid went out to Roscommon, Longford and Athlone.

The brief action had been a complete success, with no IRA casualties. The enemy had been wiped out and valuable booty obtained included five rifles, two revolvers and, greatest trophy of all, a Hotchkiss gun, with ammunition. Unfortunately, none of the Volunteers, not even the British ex-service men among us, was able to operate the gun. The lorry was set on fire, the arms collected and the withdrawal began. The Tans in Strokestown showed no inclination to re-enter the fray and the Lancers did not appear, probably because Captain Peek, when he took his second-in-command with him, had deprived them of the only officer capable of taking decisive action in his absence. Whatever the reason, troops and police from Roscommon, travelling via Tulsk and via Kilteeran, Ballagh and Curraghroe, were on the scene as soon as the local troops, and we had thus gained an invaluable half-hour's grace. British troops from Longford were unable to pass the road blocks.

The dispersal proceeded according to plan. Most of the North Roscommon men dispersed to their homes, while the South Roscommon men moved off by the sunken lane, in the direction of the Shannon. It was only then that it was discovered that the two unwounded men in civilian dress, who had been captured from the lorry were, in fact, Black and Tans under arrest. Unfortunately for them, these men had seen the faces and learned the names of many of the men in the column so that, should they escape or be released, the lives of every man in the column would be in their hands. The British hanged or shot every soldier of the Republic found in arms against them, and it was this refusal of the British to observe the rules of war that was to cost the two unfortunate Tans their lives. No responsible commander could expose his men to such terrible risks and, accordingly, the two prisoners were shot. It was a hard decision for the commander, but he had no possible alternative. Both men met their deaths bravely.

When the troops from Roscommon arrived on the scene, the usual intensive comb-out of the district took place. Two members of the North Roscommon column had, contrary to orders, delayed in the vicinity of Curraghroe and were captured emerging from a shop. Isolated groups of IRA men, trying to make good their own escape, heard the shots but were powerless to intervene. The two men were captured and conveyed to Strokestown military barracks and subsequently to Athlone. In both places they were severely beaten up, but they remained staunch and gave away no information, but captured documents revealed the fact that the brother of one of them was an IRA officer. The brother was shot and killed in his own house the next day by RIC and Tans from Roscommon, and was the only IRA casualty resulting from the action. On the day of the ambush the Coffeys, Murphys, Treacys and Earleys, with my parents and other members of my family, were arrested and taken to Strokestown military barracks, where they were interrogated and kept overnight in an open shed. Next day they were conveyed to Athlone barracks where they were again interrogated. Needless to say, they all proved faithful to the IRA.

The ambush at Scramogue had far-reaching consequences. First of all, the very peculiar behaviour of the Tan lorry on the morning of the ambush had convinced the military that, in some way, the Tans had suspected an ambush and had let Captain Peek go to his death. No one will ever know the truth of this and, on the face of it, it seems unlikely; but the military were strained to breaking point, to the great advantage of the IRA, who fostered this dissention by every means in their power. Scramogue was followed up with another blow which well and truly shook the already low morale of the crown forces. A death sentence had been passed on a local British Secret Service man and the order confirming his execution had been received from GHQ some days before the Scramogue affair. The execution was deliberately postponed until after the ambush had taken place and then it was carried out almost in the same place. The lesson was taken to heart by the enemy and no officer was found to order the usual reprisals. Even my own house remained immune.

As stated earlier, Brigadier Dockery was true to his word. Fifty pounds were paid to the 3rd Battalion, who invested the money in four Lee Enfield rifles and a case of Mills grenades. Three days after Scramogue, the second promised ambush took place near Keadue, relieving pressure on the 3rd Battalion and striking yet another blow at enemy morale. Soon after this the brigadier was himself captured and taken to Boyle military barracks, which was then garrisoned by three companies of the Bedfordshire Regiment, and was a stronghold far beyond our power of attack. This time the brigade and 3rd Battalion used guile instead of force, and the story of Brigadier Dockery's escape makes a fitting postscript to this brief account of the action at Scramogue.

About the end of April 1921, Brigadier M. Dockery and Brigade Adjutant John Clancy of the North Roscommon Brigade, IRA, cycled from Drumlion to Cootehall, to make arrangements for the building of a dugout in the Cootehall area. They arrived in Cootehall village about midnight and contacted Joe O'Hara, who, with his brother William, both IRA men, kept a licensed premises. When they had been in O'Hara's house about half-an-hour, it was surrounded by RIC and Auxiliaries from Boyle, and the encirclement had been so thorough that no avenue of escape remained open. Dockery and Clancy were armed with service rifles which had been captured from the RIC in the ambush at Keadue a few weeks previously; but they had no chance to make a fight against the overwhelming numbers of the enemy who had surprised them in Cootehall. With the two O'Hara brothers, they were taken outside and handed over to a guard, while the house and premises were being searched. Before the searchers had finished their task Dockery made a determined bid to escape and had all but succeeded when he was brought down by a chance shot that hit him in the foot. The four prisoners were then brutally beaten up by their captors, and subsequently they were taken to Boyle military barracks.

About the same time Captain James Molloy of the South Sligo Brigade was wounded and captured during an attack on a police patrol in Ballymote town. He, too, was taken to Boyle military barracks. Dockery and Clancy were put in separate cells, with Commandant Jim Hunt of the South Sligo Brigade occupying a third cell. There were only three cells in the barracks so Molloy and about forty other prisoners from Roscommon, Sligo and Leitrim, were imprisoned in the rifle range.

Plans were made to rescue Dockery and Molloy. George McGlackin, a corporal in the Bedfordshire Regiment, was on friendly terms with Miss Maggie Judge, who kept a shop in the main street, Boyle, convenient to the barracks. Miss Judge, who was a member of Cumann na mBan, took McGlackin into her confidence and told him of the plans to rescue the two IRA leaders. He promised to assist. Miss Judge next contacted Pat Delahunty of Bridge Street, Boyle, who was brigade intelligence officer, and outlined to him the progress that had been made with the planning of the rescue. Delahunty was to arrange that outside assistance would be organised. Amongst the prisoners in the barracks rifle range were three IRA officers from Boyle town, James Feely, Martin Killalea and Phil Murray, all three of whom had a good knowledge of the internal lay-out of the barracks and of its surroundings. They would make the inside arrangements for the escape. It was decided that Molloy should escape first.

About six o'clock every morning the prisoners in the rifle range were marched to the wash house, under a guard of ten soldiers. The wash house overlooks the Boyle river, and there was a window in the river side of it that measured about 2½ feet by 2 feet. A door and three windows were to the front of the building. All the windows were guarded by light bars. There was not sufficient room in the wash house to permit all the prisoners to perform their ablutions together, so the guard of soldiers remained outside with those of the prisoners who were awaiting their turn to wash.

Word from Pat Delahunty had reached the prisoners to the effect that, so far as the outside arrangements were concerned, everything was in readiness for Molloy's escape bid. By a certain morning all plans were watertight. Molloy was amongst the first batch of prisoners to enter the wash house that morning. Within a matter of minutes the bars that guarded the escape window had been bent by his comrades, who then lowered Molloy into the river, which he succeeded in crossing without having attracted the attention of his gaolers. Concealed in a grove on the far side of the river and within twenty yards of the barracks, were a number of armed IRA men from the Boyle Company, in case their assistance should be needed to cover Molloy's escape bid. These men were Pat Brennan, Luke Dempsey, Tom Lohan, Batty Reid, Tom Daly and the brigade intelligence officer, Pat Delahunty. They got Molloy away to safety. He went straight to the house of Mrs Roche, near Ballinameen, and subsequently to a dugout near the house in which he remained for a few days before returning to his own brigade area.

Plans were then made for Dockery's escape. Because of the position of his cell it was found to be impossible to get him out of it without assistance from one of the soldiers. With the help of the three Boyle men, Feely, Killalea and Murray, Corporal McGlackin agreed to open Dockery's cell, so that he could gain access to a part of the building from which it would be possible for him to escape. McGlackin got a late pass one night and, having returned to the barracks about 2 a.m., he stole the key to Dockery's cell from the guardroom. He went immediately to the cell, opened it and escorted Dockery to a wall overlooking the river. Dockery got across the wall and jumped into the river which he crossed also. On the other side he too met Brennan, Dempsey, Lohan, Daly, Reid and Delahunty, who had been waiting to give such assistance as might be needed and who conveyed him to Roche's of Ballinameen.

When Dockery had got away, Corporal McGlackin returned to the guardroom and put the cell key back in the same place from which he had taken it. The military authorities suspected that he had some part in the escape, so he was placed under arrest and heavily guarded, and was taken to England, where he was court-martialled. Though they failed to prove a case against him, he was kept in prison for about six months and then discharged from the army. McGlackin returned to Ireland in the spring of 1922, married a girl from Boyle and still lives near Boyle.

HEAVILY GUARDED, WOUNDED PRISONER RESCUED FROM MONAGHAN COUNTY HOSPITAL

MONAGHAN BRIGADE, 30 MARCH 1921

As told to Donal O'Kelly

The author wishes to express his indebtedness to Dr F.C. Ward of Monaghan, now the last Monaghan survivor of the staff of the 5th Northern Division, for the information concerning the planning and carrying out of the activity described and the reasons which impelled the IRA authorities on the spot to undertake it. The author also acknowledges his debt to Mr J. McConnon, Waterworks, Threemilehouse, and to Mr John McKenna, Newbliss, both former IRA officers, for the information given about the actual carrying out of the rescue.

It will be very evident to even casual students of the Anglo-Irish struggle in 1920–21 that the overall strategic objective that governed the pattern of IRA action was the infliction of casualties and damage on the enemy. Circumstances, however, sometimes call for different methods, and, in the story of the rescue of Commandant Matt Fitzpatrick from Monaghan County Hospital we have a classic example of a brilliantly conceived and executed plan, carried out under the nose of a strong enemy garrison, wherein the participants had strict orders to avoid the infliction of casualties and to keep shooting to a minimum.

In the early part of 1921, north Monaghan was a centre of IRA activity along the newly created border. In districts such as this the IRA had to face many problems of a kind that were unknown to their fellow fighters in other parts of the country. Our story is only concerned with one of these, the fact that if the IRA wanted arms, as of course it did, it had in the main to fight for them at loyalist houses, in many cases occupied by armed 'B' Specials of the Royal Ulster Constabulary. Thus, in the province of Ulster, raids for arms, which were almost a routine activity in the south and west, became in many cases assaults upon enemy strongpoints.

It was in one such raid that Commandant Matt Fitzpatrick, a young officer of exceptional popularity and of great character and soldierly ability, was severely wounded. He received a charge of shot in the left side and right forearm – his side being severely torn and his right wrist shattered. His comrades conveyed him by pony and trap to Joe Duffy's house on a mountainside near Newbliss and from there, following the usual safety measures adopted in such cases, he was moved from time to time to other friendly houses in the vicinity. One day Matt was visited by a member of his own Wattlebridge Company and it is believed that, all unknowingly of course, it was this incident which led to the discovery of his whereabouts by the enemy. Matt's visitor had come by cycle and on the way back to Clones he met a party of RIC and Black and Tans. Cleverly enough, the police did not molest him, although he was suspected of IRA activities. Instead, they followed the tracks of his bicycle back along the muddy roads and by this method, after raiding several houses along the way, they eventually found their severely wounded quarry. Matt was arrested and taken to the County Hospital in Monaghan, where he was placed under armed guard. This guard, consisting of two NCOs and six men, placed one sentry in the prisoner's ward and one in the ground floor corridor near the improvised guardroom. An armed RIC sergeant was placed as a 'patient' in the next bed.

Word of the arrest reached the IRA nearly as soon as it was made; Captain Jim MacConnon of Threemilehouse learned of it from the conversation of two British Secret Service men, which he overheard in a barber's shop in Monaghan while he was being shaved. Jim hastened with the information to Dr Ward, Monaghan, who then was a divisional staff officer. There was no certainty as to how soon the prisoner would be brought to Belfast gaol and, in the light of his record in the IRA, it was believed that once there, nothing would save him from the hangman's rope. The only hope, therefore, lay in immediate rescue. Dan Hogan, O/C, and other available members of the divisional staff were immediately informed of the facts and a conference was held at Mr H. Farmer's house at Cornasoo. At this conference the possibility of rescue was discussed and it was decided that detailed rescue plans should be worked out. It soon became evident that the difficulties were enormous and that only the most meticulous planning and split-second timing could bring off the job successfully. The presence of an armed guard and the armed policeman in the bed beside Fitzpatrick was bad enough, but in addition to this there was a garrison consisting of a company of military and some sixty RIC and Black and Tans in the town. There were many civilian patients in the hospital, some of them seriously ill, who must be disturbed as little as possible. If the job was to be done at all, it must be done swiftly and in silence; the guard must be taken completely by surprise and the prisoner rescued before people knew what was happening. Detailed plans of the approaches, the lay-out, position of guard and times of changing guard were submitted by Dr Ward to Dan Hogan, who decided to take command himself, choosing as his associates Jim MacConnon, Pat Kierans, Phil Marrin, John MacCarville, James Flynn, Seamus O'Donoghue, Joe MacCarville, Frank Tummin, Pat Mulligan, Joe Shannon, Paddy McCarron, Jimmy Winters and Pat Monaghan. At a further conference between Hogan, Dr Ward and members of the flying column, arrangements were made for the requisitioning and placing of transport and for the alerting of the different companies for road blocking. Paddy McCarthy, town surveyor, Monaghan, furnished to Dr Ward a plan of the hospital and its approaches, together with a report setting out the day and the hour when the guard was due to be changed. It had been ascertained that the guard did a forty-eight hour tour of duty and it was decided that 2 a.m. on the second night of duty would be the hour most likely to find the guard at the lowest pitch of vigilance. Paddy McCarthy had also arranged with a friendly member of the staff to leave a door unlocked but, lest there be any hitch here, duplicate keys were prepared. A stretcher was provided for the removal of the wounded man, and on Jimmy Winters was placed the all-important task of disconnecting the telephone immediately the rescue party entered the grounds. The attempt was finally fixed for 2 a.m. on the morning of 30 March.

On the evening of 29 March the rescue party assembled at Cornasoo, with three commandeered cars driven by John McKenna, Newbliss, Jas Nolan and a garage worker named Stephen who was a native of Donegal. Dan Hogan once again repeated his orders, the Rosary was recited and the party moved out. The curfew hour for cars was then 8 p.m. Two of the cars, with their drivers in charge, were stationed some distance from the hospital and left facing in the direction of Tyholland and Clonribret crossroads. The men took off their boots and, as silently as possible, manoeuvred the third car into a position of readiness outside the hospital, with Johnny McKenna at the wheel. On a perimeter outside the town of Monaghan parties stood ready to block the roads at selected points after the rescue party had passed through. The laying of road blocks earlier was prohibited lest their presence might alert the enemy.

The stealthy approach of the party through the hospital grounds passed unnoticed and the hospital door was unlocked as had been arranged. In the corridor the sentry drowsed, his rifle beside him. One of the party grabbed the rifle and Dan Hogan overpowered the sentry but not before the latter had been able to utter a shout of warning. In the guardroom some of the men off duty were asleep, but one who was sitting on his bed at the time, had been alerted by the sentry's warning cry, and, seconds later, when Paddy McCarron appeared in the doorway he was halted by a rifle bullet which wounded him in the arm. Pat Monaghan then fired both barrels of his shotgun high over the heads of the guard, blinding them with mortar and plaster which fell from the ceiling. The guardroom was rushed in the confusion which followed and the guard surrendered.

The report of rifle and shotgun fire in the dead of night destroyed all further hope of surprise and the wonder is that the British forces outside the hospital were not alerted. The RIC man in the bed beside Matt Fitzpatrick jumped up, drew his gun and covered the prostrate prisoner; while the sentry in the ward, evidently a resolute man, opened fire through the door. Fitzpatrick said to the RIC sergeant: 'Are you going to shoot a wounded prisoner?' and in reply the sergeant, from what motive we do not know, threw his revolver onto an adjoining bed and went back to his own. Whatever his motive may have been, by not shooting Fitzpatrick there and then, he undoubtedly saved his own life by throwing down his gun. Had he killed Commandant Fitzpatrick the men on the rescue job would have given him short shrift. The problem of the remaining sentry had still to be solved and very quickly at that. Dan Hogan tied the hands of the disarmed prisoners in the guardroom behind their back and forced them to proceed him into the ward, shouting as they went: 'Don't shoot.' Confronted with this situation, the sentry, a brave man, could only follow his comrades' example and surrender, which he did.

MacConnon and Kierans with all haste, then placed the prisoner on a stretcher and started off for the car whither the wounded McCarron, having had first aid applied, had already gone. Before he was carried out Matt Fitzpatrick told Dan Hogan of the RIC sergeant's action and where he had thrown the gun. Hogan collected the gun, at the same time telling the sergeant he would not be injured. Other members of the party collected the arms and equipment of the military guard – eight rifles, ammunition, a .45 revolver and some bandoliers. They then reassured the civilian patients and the staff of the hospital and quietly took their departure. They retired along their pre-arranged route, leaving MacConnon, Kierans, Mulligan and Shannon to make their way to Threemilehouse along the railway line.

So ended an entirely successful action, carried out against heavy odds but so well planned that even a serious hitch could not mar it. The whole operation took less than fifteen minutes, there were no casualties on either side, except for McCarron's flesh wound in the arm, the rescued prisoner got clean away and a valuable addition was made to the brigade's slender store of offensive weapons. So effective were the security measures taken that the first news the enemy garrison received of the affair was when the sad, dispirited and unarmed members of the guard made their way to the barracks, to tell their story as best they could to their infuriated superiors.

Besides attaining its immediate object, the rescue had a remarkable moral effect in Monaghan, in particular on the large loyalist minority in the town. British propaganda had consistently pictured the IRA as a gang of irresponsible 'murderers' and 'corner-boys'. To very many people, whose minds were not completely closed by prejudice, there was little of the murderer in men who risked their lives to save the life of a comrade and who spared their enemies when they had them at their mercy. It must be admitted that the brilliant staff work and execution of the rescue showed a genius, daring and chivalry that commanded the respect of the most bitter opponents of the IRA.

ACTION BY WEST CONNEMARA COLUMN AT MOUNTEROWEN

WEST CONNEMARA BRIGADE, 23 APRIL 1921

by Peter J. McDonnell

(*formerly O/C West Connemara Brigade IRA and Commander, West Connemara Brigade flying column*)

GALWAY AND MAYO did not come actively into the fight for freedom until the spring of 1921. That they had not been in it earlier was by no means due to reluctance on the part of the men to fight, but mainly because GHQ had delayed the formation of independent brigades in these areas until late in 1920. Prior to that battalion officers were not permitted to carry out operations which did not have the approval of their brigade authorities. As a result, opportunities for action were lost whilst detailed plans were being examined at brigade level, and the enemy was able to concentrate his strength against IRA forces who were active in other areas.

Richard Mulcahy, Chief of Staff of the IRA, came to Connemara, under an assumed name, in September 1920, to convalesce following an illness. While in the west he was the guest of Thomas O'Malley, Kilmilkin, Maam, who was a brother of surgeon Michael O'Malley, Galway. Mulcahy told me that GHQ had considered the army organisation in Galway too unwieldly to be effective, and that it had been decided to break it down into independent brigades, each responsible to GHQ only. Connemara was to constitute one such brigade. A meeting of the principal Volunteer officers of the area was immediately called and the new developments were explained and discussed. In order to be in readiness for the change-over, four battalions were formed and their officers appointed. The commanding officers were: No. 1 Battalion (Leenane), Thomas O'Malley; No. 2 Battalion (Rosmuck), Colm O'Gaora; No. 3 Battalion (Roundstone), Jim King; No. 4 Battalion (Clifden), Gerald Bartley. The battalion commanders were instructed to proceed at once with the organisation of their areas and to collect money for the purchase of arms. By the end of October I had received the sum of £120 from the battalion officers, which was a very good return, considering the poverty of the area and the fact that neither the members of the IRA nor its supporters were amongst the wealthy.

About the first week of November 1920, I received a dispatch from GHQ confirming my appointment as commanding officer of the newly formed West Connemara Brigade, and instructing me to report to GHQ on 12 November. (Michael O'Droighnean, Furbo, was appointed O/C East Connemara Brigade). When I attended there, the members of the staff wanted to know when we could go out on active service, and I replied that we were ready and would go when we had sufficient arms. I handed over the £120, which I had brought with me, and was given an assurance that the necessary arms would be sent to us with the least possible delay. Following several visits to Dublin by Brigade Quartermaster J. Feehan, we had acquired eleven rifles by the end of February 1921. Five of these rifles were magazine type, five Martini single-shot carbines and one Howth rifle. In addition we had about a dozen revolvers and automatic pistols, and a similar number of shotguns. We had approximately sixty rounds of ammunition for each rifle and about a dozen for each revolver and shotgun. The brigade council had decided that an active service unit should be mobilised at once, and on 10 March the men assembled for that purpose at a previously arranged rendezvous in the Twelve Pins, within easy reach of the Clifden-Galway road, and about seven miles from Clifden, across country. For the four days following we manned an ambush position on the Clifden-Galway road as a result of information we had received that a lorry or a couple of lorries of RIC used that road almost daily. We had no luck, or, considering our armament, we might, in fact, have had all the luck that was going. At all events, the enemy did not appear there, so we decided to go into Clifden to make contact with him. On the night of 16 March the column entered the town, six of the men carrying sidearms, to engage a party of four RIC and Black and Tans, who comprised the usual nightly patrol of Clifden, while the remainder of the IRA force occupied positions to keep the barracks covered and prevent reinforcements going to the assistance of the patrol. Only two of the enemy went out on patrol that night, and they were duly eliminated. When their arms and ammunition had been collected, the six IRA men linked up with the main body again and the column then moved out. On 6 April we collected a Lee Enfield rifle and two Webley revolvers with ammunition, after a partly successful ambush at Screebe, Rosmuck.

In our headquarters in Padraic O'Maille's house at Mounterowen, we received information from a source that we considered to be reliable, to the effect that the enemy had planned to carry out an extensive round-up of the Maam Valley, from Cornamona to Leenane, with both regular military and RIC employed for the purpose. We decided to await their coming to Mounterowen and to give a good account of ourselves against them. Mounterowen House was set on the side of a hill, and faced north, about 250 yards from the Maam-Leenane road. Between it and the main road flowed the Maam river, about fifty yards in from, and almost parallel to, the road. The river is about twenty yards in breadth at that point and was crossed there by stepping-stones, with a shallow ford for horse-drawn traffic. The stepping-stones have since been done away with, and the river is now spanned by a bridge about 100 yards west of where they had been. Immediately behind the house the land rises steeply to a height of about 300 feet, beyond which the broad Leagh Valley stretches south to the Maamturk mountains. To the west Mount Roighne rises to about 1,400 feet.

In preparation for the expected raid, every rifleman had been allotted a fixed position on the face of the hill to the rear of Mounterowen House, to both sides of the house itself. Every man knew the position he was to occupy when the enemy arrived. We assumed the enemy would set out from Cornamona at daybreak and arrive at our positions about noon. Constant watch was maintained for him, but day followed day without his forces being sighted, and we had begun to think that it might have been the RIC who had started the rumour, with the intention of scaring us out of the area. There was no fear that the column would withdraw to avoid contact with the enemy, for we were anxious for a good fight to justify our existence as a fighting unit. As our headquarters was less than three miles from Maam RIC barracks, sentries were posted on the look-out during daylight, and at night a regular guard was mounted with an officer in charge, who changed the sentries every two hours. This was done to prevent our being taken by surprise during the night.

On the night of 22 April the guard was mounted as usual, and the sentries had instructions that anything suspicious should be reported immediately to the officer of the guard. Before daylight I was awakened by someone shaking my shoulder. I opened my eyes and saw the officer of the guard standing by my bed. In response to an urgent question by me, he replied that there were dark objects approaching over the road from Maam but that, because of the darkness, he had been unable to determine whether they were men or cattle. I jumped out of bed immediately and told him to rouse the rest of the men and get them outside, while I was going down to have a look. I just pulled on my breeches, jacket and boots which remained unlaced, grabbed my rifle, bandolier and haversack, rushed downstairs and out to the front of the house. It was then about three o'clock and starting to get bright, so that I had no difficulty about identifying the objects as police. They were clustered in a group, about 100 yards from the point where the path turned off the road and led to the river and the stepping-stones, and it looked as though they were then being given last-minute instructions for a raid on Mounterowen House.

The men of the column were all ready when I rejoined them. I then gave them instructions to man the fences that extended from both sides of the house and not to fire a shot until the RIC at the end of the stepping-stones would be in a cluster on the bank. We were then to fire as fast as we could before the enemy broke for cover. The range was 200 yards. My men quickly spread out to occupy their positions, and while they were doing so the police began to mount their bicycles and to cycle towards the stepping-stones. Three of them had already entered the by-path when a revolver shot was accidentally discharged by a policeman amongst the group still on the main road. Almost immediately an answering rifle shot rang out, fired by one of my own men from the right of the position, despite orders that fire should be withheld until the police had come to the river. The element of surprise, on which we had counted, was thus destroyed, for the police immediately scattered without attempting to advance against the house. Some of them dashed to the north side of the road and took cover in a depression made there by a mountain stream that flows beneath the road and into the Maam river. Others got down behind low banks near the road. They were already down by the river when the rifle shot was fired. I had one of them in my sights from my position beside the pillar of a wicket gate to the left front of the house. He was standing at the far end of the stepping-stones, apparently making up his mind whether to cross the river or not. I squeezed the trigger. There was a faint click. The cartridge had misfired. I quickly ejected the dud cartridge and shoved up another, but found that I could not get the bolt quite home. Apparently the bullet from the faulty cartridge had remained in the breach, so I took a stone off the top of the wall and used it to hammer the bolt home. The extra seconds required to do this had probably saved the policeman's life as, before I was ready to fire, he had taken cover behind a big block of bog oak which had been left on the river bank following a flood. When I fired my double-bullet shot I was extraordinarily lucky to get away with nothing worse than a severe 'kick' on the shoulder, in return for the doubtful satisfaction of lifting a sod in front of the policeman's position.

Early in the engagement some of our men were inclined to waste ammunition in their excitement, but the officers quickly got them under control, reserving their fire for visible targets. As the enemy kept well under cover, our fire was eventually reduced to what was sufficient to keep him engaged. Most of his fire seemed to be controlled and in volleys that were to a great extent concentrated on the house, which was then empty of men. All through that day Mrs Eamonn O'Maille, with her two young children and her sister-in-law, remained in the kitchen at the rear of the house and managed to send out to us some welcome hot tea with bread and butter. Although we were only 250 yards from the police positions, it was impossible to see a target to fire at, and we concentrated on keeping them pinned down.

When the fight had been in progress for some time, it occurred to me that the force of police, which I estimated to number no more than twenty-five, could hardly expect to capture us unaided and that its purpose must be to hold us there while another enemy party was crossing the mountain and coming through Leagh Valley, to take us in our rear. Accordingly, I decided to send a man to the shoulder of the hill from which he would have a view of the valley, and be able to give us timely warning of an enemy advance from that direction. The man I picked for the task was John Dundass, Adjutant of the Roundstone Battalion, whom I knew to be a fearless soldier. I told him what I wanted done. It was a dangerous mission, as it entailed running up the face of the hill, carrying his shotgun and haversack, with twenty or twenty-five RIC firing at him from 250 yards' range. I told him to wait until the police had fired one of their volleys and then to run for it. Behind the fence he was on his toes like a sprinter waiting for the starter's gun, and as soon as the next volley had crashed out he was away up the hill. The police fire lifted immediately as they tried to get him, and I held my breath as their bullets kicked up sods at his heels and all about him. To my intense relief, he arrived safely at the crest of the hill and then, instead of diving to safety, he deliberately turned round to thumb his nose at the police and give them the 'international phrase' which was, however, drowned in rifle fire.

Around noon the fine weather which had prevailed gave way to heavy showers and these, at times, reduced visibility to about thirty yards. I decided to avail of the cover thus created to withdraw my entire force to the shoulder of the hill, where we would have greater freedom of movement should enemy reinforcements arrive. To get there we had to work our way along towards the right, under cover of the fence we had manned, until we reached a sheep path which leads into the valley. About thirty yards of the steepest part of the path had been in plain view of the police, with no cover, but the shortening of visibility enabled us to negotiate that exposed stretch in relative safety. Once behind the shoulder of the hill we were able to take stock of the situation and to see whether anything could be done to dislodge the police from the positions they were holding. As there was no cover between them and the house that would enable us to close on them, it was decided to send G. Bartley and R. Joyce to the right, and J. Feehan and J. King to the left, to work behind the police in order to encircle them. Because of the nature of the ground, these four men had to make wide detours to get round unobserved by the police. When they had succeeded in doing so, they found that, though within 150 yards of the police and directly above and behind them on the mountain, such was the conformation of the ground that they could get no sight of them. They saw only one of the enemy lying near a bank and fired a few shots at him before they realised that he was already dead.

Three men, armed with shotguns only, were sent towards Leenane to demolish or barricade a bridge about a half-mile distant on the Leenane road in order to hold up lorries of reinforcements that might come from Clifden. While they were procuring some tools in a house near the bridge, Thomas F. Joyce of Leenane drove by in a Ford car, and had passed before they had time to get back to stop him. There was a workman in the car with him, and they had some stakes and wire to repair fences on grazing land of Joyce's at Kilmilkin. Apparently there was a lull in the firing at the time and Joyce, unsuspectingly, had driven into the middle of the ambush when an RIC man suddenly appeared, leaped on the running board of the car and ordered him to drive through, at revolver's point. Gerald Bartley and Dick Joyce fired on the policeman immediately that they saw him on the car, but they had to be sparing of ammunition, as they had less than fifty rounds apiece when the engagement began. The RIC man was hit on the arm but managed to hold on until the car had reached Maam. There he got a police driver to take a lorry to Maamcross and phone for reinforcements. Soon afterwards a beggarman sauntered along the road from Maam, going towards Leenane, and apparently the police must have given him a message to take with him, for about an hour and a half later a Ford car arrived from Leenane. A tall man dressed in black got out of it. About that time we were spread out along the shoulder of the mountain, roughly about 700 yards from the police position and through the haze caused by the showers, the newcomer looked very like one of the RIC. Some of the boys loosed off a few shots at him, and a number must have passed too close to be comfortable, for he made a dive for cover. Not until that night did we learn that he was not a policeman, but the Rev. Father Cunningham, PP, who had got word through the tramp to go out to the scene of the ambush to attend some wounded policemen. He was annoyed by what had happened when he arrived there, as he thought we should have recognised him and not interfered while he was ministering to the wounded. When he got out of his car he threw his travelling rug over one of the doors. Due to the distance and bad visibility, the rug looked, to Christy Breen, one of the boys, like an RIC man taking things easy and, as Christy so far had the opportunity to fire but a few shots, this seemed a heaven-sent target. When he had fired four shots at it without apparent effect Christy decided that he was either a rotten shot or that he had been mistaken in his surmise that the object was one of the enemy. It was learned next day that three of his bullets had struck the rug and car panel, which was remarkable shooting, considering the visibility and range.

At that time we were firing very few shots, just one now and again to show that we were still about. Ammunition was running low, and we had nothing to show for it. From our elevated position it was then possible for us to look down on the enemy positions. Following the most careful search with my glasses, the only movement discernible was that made by a few policemen under cover of the bank on our side of the river. They had apparently gone to ground there in the first flurry of excitement and they were not finding it comfortable. The other members of the raiding force were packed down under cover at the end of the culvert on the far side of the road, with the river between them and our positions. With the aid of the glasses I could make out their rifle barrels sticking up over the edge of the bank, but there was no sign of any heads behind them. I got the idea that if two more men could work their way down and get close enough to the river without being seen, then with the assistance of the four men already behind the enemy, it might be possible to rush his positions. I decided to try to go down myself, and took with me Volunteer Tommy Coyne, a member of my old company and a man in whom I had plenty of confidence. We set out on our trek downwards, carrying only side arms, as rifles would be a hindrance, having in mind the nature of the ground. We alternated between crawling on our stomachs and rushing from cover to cover. We did not get by unobserved. Our progress was spotted by a lone rifleman who tried out his marksmanship on us. Sometimes a bullet of his would smack off a stone and there would be a sound as though an angry hornet was buzzing past. We kept on and, following what had appeared to be an age, we reached the shelter of a good mound, where we sat up and stretched ourselves. When we had rested, we looked about to size up the possibilities of the situation and were disappointed to find that these offered no hope for the successful carrying out of our idea of rushing the enemy. We were still more than 150 yards from the river, between us and which there was not a scrap of cover. I decided that it would be foolhardy to try further. We could make a detour towards Maam and cross the river, but we would still be too far from the culvert in which most of the enemy force lay. There was also the fact that some hours had elapsed since the RIC man had got away in Joyce's car, so that enemy reinforcements might be expected at any time. If they caught us in the positions we then occupied, we would be dead men. Nothing remained but to withdraw up the mountain, and we got safely back without the unknown marksman having succeeded in registering a hit. That we had returned unscathed could not be attributed to his concern for our personal safety, as several of his shots had come very close to us.

Immediately that we had regained cover behind the shoulder of the mountain, I searched the Maam road with the glasses, for movements that would indicate the approach of enemy reinforcements. Sure enough, I spotted a line of lorries coming down from Maamcross to the Maam bridge. We had barely returned to our mountain position in time. I decided to move the column further up the mountain, for in the position we held behind the shoulder of the hill, we would be in plain sight of anybody coming along the road from Maam. It was then 4.30 in the afternoon, and we had been engaged for thirteen hours.

From the cover of a boundary fence, higher up on the mountain, we watched with interest the arrival and disposal of the reinforcements. An armoured car was first on the scene, and it was followed by thirteen lorries loaded with military and police. Some of the lorries had halted half-a-mile away from the place where the police had been held to the ground, and the soldiers who had come out in them were then spread in extended order and were advancing over river and bog towards Mounterowen House. The place was black with men running and firing their rifles and Lewis guns. Had we ammunition to spare we would have inflicted casualties, even though the range was about 800 yards. I had only five rounds left myself, and practically all the others were similarly circumstanced.

Apparently the enemy had a healthy respect for those he considered to be inside the house. To our amusement, his forces spent three-quarters of an hour getting to grenade-throwing distance of it, advancing in rushes that were covered by rifle and machine-gun fire. When they had worked in close they bombed it by throwing grenades through the windows. Finally, they captured the place, empty except for Mrs Eamonn O'Maille, her two young children, and Miss Jane O'Maille, who were found at the back, in an out-office in which they had taken shelter before the arrival of the reinforcements. When the house was found to be empty the police moved in and started to remove clothes, bedclothes and anything that took their fancy. They then set fire to the house and out-offices. The women and children were made prisoners and taken as far as Leenane, where they were released. There Michael B. King took them in for a time.

We then pushed on to Cuilleaghbeg, a village of a few houses, on the Leenane side of the scene of the fight, and about a mile away from it. We sent messages to Leenane for food, and I can tell you that we were well and truly hungry by that time. We did justice to the food when it arrived and, having posted sentries, we rested a few hours. While in Cuilleaghbeg we learned that the police had one man killed and two wounded, and that when the reinforcements had turned up, the police who had been engaged in the fight were immediately sent in two lorries to Maam barracks. Nearly all of them had to be lifted into the lorries, they were so badly cramped through having been pinned down all day in positions that had permitted of no movement. Some of the police had to kneel in the stream without moving from the time that they were driven into the culvert. It was the good fortune of the police that they had been able to get one of their number away to summon reinforcements. They had been on the point of surrender prior to that, as after the first half-hour they saw no hope of extricating themselves from the position in which they were pinned. Most of them had come from Oughterard in two lorries in which they also brought bicycles. At Maam RIC barracks they picked up the sergeant and some more men, all with bicycles, and then the entire force pushed on, in their two lorries. The Maam sergeant, it seems, had reported that the police would have no difficulty about capturing the IRA men in Mounterowen House. It was his belief that, once the police had fired a few shots, we would bolt up the face of the mountain, and they could then pick us off whilst we were running. They had left their lorries and two drivers about a mile short of Mounterowen House, and had cycled the remaining distance in order to take us unawares, by the silence of their approach. When the firing had broken out and continued without any sign of the police returning, the drivers moved up to investigate. We permitted them to approach as far as the culvert, and then forced them to take cover in it with those of their comrades already sheltering there. None of the men sheltering in this difficult position were able to move out of it until the arrival of the reinforcements, the RIC elements amongst which were under the personal command of Chief Commissioner Cruise.

The driver of the car which had brought Father Cunningham out to the two wounded RIC men, was the vice-O/C of the brigade, J.J. Connolly, who was employed as a driver mechanic at Leenane Hotel which is situated on the south shore of Killary Bay. Though most anxious to come out on active service with us, he was ordered to remain in his employment at the hotel, for the contacts he made there provided us with useful information. He had spent some time with the British army transport during the 1914–1918 war and, as he had never been openly identified with us, he was able to mix around with the police and military who patronised the hotel. When he had brought Father Cunningham to the ambush site, he found that it was not healthy to remain in the car, so he went down to the stream where the police were under cover and heard their conversation.

When we had rested a few hours at Cuilleaghbeg we retraced our steps and passed the scene of the recent fighting. The enemy had then withdrawn from the place. We turned north across the mountains to the village of Touwnaleen, where we remained for two days. At the end of that period we crossed the mountains to Killary Harbour, which we crossed by boat to the north shore and went to the house of Michael Wallace, father of two members of the column. Whilst in Wallace's we had refreshments drawn from supplies that had been sent there for us by Mrs Cuffe of Leenane. We also found there a small marquee which J.J. Connolly had obtained for us from Mr McKeown. Having packed our supplies and the marquee, we continued across the shoulder of Ben Gorm mountain and entered the deep, bowl-like valley of Luggacorry, where we had cover on every side. We pitched our camp and decided to remain in the valley for some days, or until we had obtained more arms and ammunition from GHQ. Our attempts to collect armaments from the enemy had been attended by little luck.

Our headquarters had been set up in the valley for some days when J.J. Connolly arrived one night with a case that contained four Lee Enfield rifles, two .45 calibre revolvers, 105 rounds of .303 ammunition,

120 rounds of .45 ammunition and ten hand grenades. He had crossed from the south shore by boat, for there was difficulty about having a motor car on the road after dark, and besides, it was easier to bring us the case of arms by boat. Connolly laughed heartily and gave us reason to laugh too, when he told us that soon after he had taken delivery of the case from Mr Kelly, the stationmaster at Maamcross railway station, the car he was driving was held up by a sergeant and two constables from Maam RIC barracks, who wanted a lift to Maam. 'Yes, of course,' he replied, but added that the two constables would have to sit on a crate of china he had in the back of the car for Leenane Hotel. One of them talked all the way to Maam about the fight at Mounterowen, and wondered where we had got the up-to-date rifles with which we had pinned them to ground. He would have been greatly surprised to know that he was sitting on a box of the best weapons that had come our way so far.

Because of our limited armament and the terrain over which we had to operate, it was impossible for us to engage the enemy patrols that were sent out after we had fired the first shots of the campaign in the west, in Clifden, on the night of 16 March. After that it was seldom that patrols comprised as few as two lorries, and never fewer than two. More often than not they were composed of four lorries, well spaced out. The bleak Connemara countryside, bare as the Twelve Pins, offered no approach cover to roads which, themselves, were not even bordered by fences. Bearing these factors in mind, and the meagre armament at our disposal, it will be realised that in such circumstances we would have no chance to survive against strong enemy forces. Kylemore Pass, the one place in the entire area where we could engage them with reasonable hope of success, they avoided like a plague. British convoys from Leenane to Clifden went round by Recess in order to avoid passing through Kylemore.

During the fortnight which comprised the last week of June and the first week of July, a huge round-up was carried out, over the country from Ballina to Killary, through Castlebar, Newport, Westport and Louisburg. We were on the Mayo side of Killary on 29 June, and about midnight information reached us that troops were being landed from destroyers to join in this great enemy operation. The men of the column were immediately roused and we marched to Bundorragha, where we obtained two boats and crossed to the Galway side just before daylight. We had barely disembarked and moved up the mountain when we saw two enemy observation planes circling the islands off the mouth of Killary and along the Mayo coast. Soon afterwards two destroyers arrived off the coast and hundreds of men were put ashore from them on the Mayo coast to the north of Killary. One of the destroyers came into the bay and landed about 100 men on the north shore, at the foot of Mweelrea mountain. All boats and curraghs were collected by the enemy and taken in tow to where the destroyer had anchored near Leenane. The operation continued until 10 July, on which day there were nine lorries of Auxiliaries drawn up at Leenane when an IRA courier arrived from Dublin and contacted J.J. Connolly who brought him to me. The courier was the bearer of the Truce notice. Michael Kilroy of the West Mayo column, and three of his officers were with me at the time. They had almost been encircled in the huge round-up, but had managed to keep outside the enemy ring. As happened in the case of the round-up which followed the Mounterowen fight, not a single IRA man was captured.

One good result of our entry into the fight, late though it was in coming about, was the upset to enemy plans and calculations caused by the extension of the general campaign to our area, which he had hitherto considered to be quiet and safe. Our activities drew upon west Connemara military and police, who had previously formed part of forces that had been pressing the IRA columns in other places west of the Shannon, and the diversion thus created accorded more breathing space to the columns concerned. Soon after the Mounterowen fight the British launched a great round-up in our area and employed more than 1,000 troops and police on the operation, with planes to guide them. All males between the ages of sixteen and sixty were brought to Maam RIC barracks to be identified. Not a single IRA man was caught in the net, though we had barely crossed over to the north of

Killary before all the mountains to the south were combed by the enemy.

Here is the list of names of the men who participated in the fight at Mounterowen, without ranks except in the cases of the brigade and battalion officers: P.J. McDonnell, brigade O/C: J. Feehan, brigade QM; Martin Coneely, brigade adjutant; Colm O'Gaora, O/C No. 2 Battalion (Rosmuck); Jim King, O/C No. 3 Battalion (Roundstone); Gerald Bartley, O/C No. 4 Battalion (Clifden); Thomas Coyne, John C. King, Richard Joyce, Peter Wallace, Patrick Wallace, William King, Padraic O'Maille and E. O'Maille, all of No. 1 Battalion. John Dundass, Michael Conroy, John Coneely, Denis Keane, Stephen Mannion, all of No. 3 Battalion. Thomas Madden, Paul Bartley, Christy Breen, William Coneely, Laurence O'Toole, all of No. 4 Battalion. The men are now scattered. Many have found a livelihood in foreign lands, and some are already in their graves. The cause for which they fought and were willing to give their lives, lives on, and it may be that those of us who still remain will yet witness its fulfilment and share in the complete freedom of all our country from foreign rule. If that privilege is not to be ours, we can but hand down the traditional love of freedom that ever animated our race, to those who come after us, and pass on to join our departed comrades, thanking God to have lived in a generation that succeeded, at least, in driving the British invader out of twenty-six of our thirty-two counties.

THIRTY IRA MEN DEFIED 600 BRITISH TROOPS AT TOURMAKEADY

SOUTH MAYO BRIGADE, 3 MAY 1921

by Edward Gallagher

Based on the account of the engagement written by Tom Maguire, O/C South Mayo Brigade, and published in the issue of An t-Óglach *of 21 August 1921; and on information gathered at the scene of the action.*

IN ITS ISSUE of 21 August 1921, *An t-Óglach*, the official organ of the Irish Volunteers, carried an account of an action which, for modesty and understatement can rank with anything that Caesar ever wrote in his commentary upon his wars in Gaul. The account was written by Tom Maguire, the officer commanding the South Mayo Brigade, and narrates his brigade column's action against enemy forces at Tourmakeady.

The secret of successful guerrilla fighting is to strike hard, to disengage quickly, and never to take on a force stronger than one's own. In practice, of course, these ideal regulations do not always work out. Time and again during the War of Independence, republican forces set themselves limited objectives, which their numbers and armament gave them reasonable hope of achieving, and, for one reason or another, found themselves opposed to superior forces and committed to fighting a defensive action. Such was the action at Tourmakeady.

May 1921 was a grand month for guerrilla fighters – dry and warm for men who had to lie out on the hills, but it had the disadvantage that the days were lengthening – darkness came too late for those who, in the presence of superior numbers, had to rely on the cloak of dusk and local knowledge for a safe retreat.

Tom Maguire's column had a limited objective which they should have been quite capable of achieving. The column – mostly Ballinrobe men – numbered about twenty-five men, but when it mobilised in the Shrah area on the morning of 3 May, with the assistance of local companies, it was strengthened to about sixty strong. It was weak in firepower. As far as one can ascertain the column possessed six to eight rifles, the balance of firepower being supplied by shotguns. Under the pressure of buck-shot, many of the older shotguns went out of action and, at a crucial period, the column's effective armament was not what it appeared on paper.

In south Mayo, IRA action and public opinion had been taking their toll. On the main road to Westport and Ballinrobe the RIC barracks at Partry had been evacuated; so had the barracks at Ballyglass. At Derrypark – or more correctly, Cappaghnacreich – the enemy still maintained a garrison of about twelve constables. The republican intelligence service had noted that a convoy bearing pay and provisions went out from Ballinrobe to Derrypark on the 3rd of each month. The convoy normally consisted of two Crossley tenders and a car. Tom Maguire decided to ambush the convoy at that point between Ballinrobe and Derrypark called Tourmakeady. One might mention here that although the action has gone down in history as taking place at Tourmakeady, this is a misnomer. Actually the fight stretched along the road in the townlands of Gortfree, Gorteenmore and into Cappaghduff. Tourmakeady is only a field at the back of Tourmakeady Lodge near the village of Derryveeney. Tourmakeady Lodge is also in Gortfree.

Early on the morning of 3 May, the column, with local support, mobilised at Tourmakeady. The brigadier expected three vehicles, a short action and a quick retreat. No provision was made for blocking roads leading into the ambush area, a lack of precaution which was to cost the column dearly later in the day. Scouts were posted and the remaining force divided roughly into sections. North of the village Michael O'Brien, the brigade adjutant, was put in charge of a section at the Fair Green; Maguire himself took command of the central section at the post office; Paddy May of Ballinrobe was in charge of the section posted at Drimbawn gate. Each position was about 200 yards from the other, and the plan of operation was to allow the first vehicle to proceed as far as Drimbawn gateway where it was to be engaged; the other sections would then take on the second or third vehicle, as the case might be, which would be by then well inside the ambush position.

About one o'clock the first vehicle was sighted and allowed to proceed up to Paddy May's section at Drimbawn where it was engaged. On the first discharge the driver of the vehicle – a Ford car – was killed instantly, and the car crashed into the entrance wall. The three remaining members of the RIC in the car were quickly disposed of, and three rifles, three revolvers and holsters, and rifle and revolver ammunition captured.

In the meantime the position further down the ambush position was not so satisfactory. The second vehicle, a Crossley tender, containing ten to twelve police in the charge of a head constable, had pulled up between the two positions on hearing the first shots at Drimbawn. The enemy spilled out and, despite the efforts of the two sections, fought their way into a hotel – now a shop owned by James O'Toole – from where they hotly returned the fire of the column men. The fight was unequal. Behind cover and with a plentiful supply of rifle grenades, the enemy easily defied the column's efforts to close with them. After half an hour's fusillading on both sides, Maguire, realising that there was no chance of dislodging the police, and fearing that enemy reinforcements might arrive, ordered a withdrawal.

The situation was more critical than the brigadier realised. At Derrypark barracks there was a wireless transmitter, and enemy garrisons in surrounding posts had already been alerted and were converging on the area.

Dismissing the local men, except for a few Shrah Volunteers to act as guides, Maguire led the balance of his force, about thirty strong, up the Partry mountains, intending to retreat northwards in the direction of Westport. Above Shrah he ordered a rest. After about an hour, scouts reported to him that they had observed enemy activity in the direction of Ballinrobe and on surveying the position through his field glasses, he saw that the information was only too true. Twenty-four lorries, bearing troops from Galway, Claremorris and Ballinrobe, were converging on the position. Some of the lorries roared up the roads on the south-east and south-west of the position, others halted on the southern side and opened up machine-gun fire on the men on the hillside.

Maguire's column was in a nasty spot. The hills here, bleak, tree-less and comparatively level, offer little in the way of cover. With enemy machine-gun fire licking their heels, the men of the column retreated in a northerly direction, only to find troops from Castlebar and Westport barring that line of retreat. There was nothing for it but to select a position and hold it – if they could – until darkness gave them a chance of slipping through the enemy lines. Above the village or townland of Tournawoade, Maguire found such a position – a fold in the ground with a rise behind it. It was not ideal, but it was the best that could be found. He ordered his men to lie down and to put their diminishing stock of ammunition to the best possible use.

The enemy fire was intense. Rifle and machine-gun bullets plastered the column position, but the men remained calm and steady, each man reserving his fire until an attacker exposed himself. Any attempt by the enemy to get close to the column position was blasted by steady and accurate fire, and enemy casualties were high.

The column, however, had suffered a grievous blow. A bullet from a Lewis gun had hit the brigadier in the forearm, passed through at the elbow point and, issuing on the inside of the arm near the armpit, fractured the bone. It was now about 4 p.m.

Michael O'Brien, the brigade adjutant, crawled over to the wounded leader and proceeded to give first aid. He had slit open Maguire's sleeve and was in the act of attempting to staunch the flow of blood, when there was a shout behind him of 'Hands Up!' Swinging round, he beheld an enemy officer, a Lieutenant Emmerson of the Border Regiment, divested of cap, coat and puttees, and carrying a rifle. Some distance behind the officer were eight soldiers. Making use of every bit of cover, and unobserved by the column men, who were pinned down by the intense enemy fire, the party had practically reached the column position.

Quick as thought O'Brien picked up his rifle, but in the very act of bringing it up to his shoulder the officer fired and killed him instantly, the bullet subsequently passing through Maguire's back under the right shoulder blade, and inflicting a flesh wound. A column shotgun man fired, knocked the officer's rifle out of his hand with the discharge from the first barrel and sent ten grains of buckshot into his stomach from the second barrel. The officer turned and ran, falling after going twenty yards. That seemed to knock the heart out of his party. Seeing their leader fall, they also made a run for it, but they were caught between their own fire and the fire from the column. Six of them fell.

It is related that Emmerson crawled on hands and knees to a house in one of the villages above Shrah. The sole occupant of the house was an old woman who was nearly blind. He crawled in and sat himself on a chair. The old lady, because of his hair, mistook him for a certain Volunteer who also had red hair. Shortly afterwards an old man with a jaunting car came to the house. Emmerson produced his revolver and forced the old man to take him to the main road at Shrah where he was picked up by troops on their way from Tourmakeady that evening. Emmerson recovered from his wound and was promoted for his action.

Hungry and thirsty, their leader badly wounded, their second-in-command dead, the men of the South Mayo column clung tenaciously to their position. The enemy continued to hit the position with grenade, rifle and machine-gun fire. Ammunition had to be conserved and every shot had to tell – and every shot did tell! As they watched, fired and reloaded, they prayed for darkness, but darkness came slowly, on leaden feet it seemed to the gallant men fighting for their lives on the hillside. But finally it came. At 10.30 p.m. the enemy withdrew in force, leaving a skeleton party behind who kept sending up Verey lights throughout the night. The column men, under the cloak of darkness, successfully made their way through this party.

The difficult part of the retreat was getting the wounded brigadier – and he was hit six times in all during the fight – down from the hillside. But the feat was managed. He was brought that night to the house of a Mrs Lally, in Tournawoade, and received first aid treatment from Tom Costelloe, an ex-soldier and Volunteer. Later he was treated by a Dr Murphy. For two days Maguire was kept in the village, being moved from house to hillside when raiding parties of the enemy came too close to the locality. Finally, he was removed by horse and cart to a place of safety.

It is estimated that the column fought its position on the hillside against 600 troops. In the circumstances, its losses – Michael J. O'Brien, the adjutant, killed, the brigadier seriously wounded, one Volunteer slightly wounded, and shotguns captured by the enemy – were not so heavy as they might have been. The enemy, on the other hand, lost heavily. As usual, of course, no exact figures can be given as they were not disclosed. However, Maguire reports that, in front of his own position, two policemen and two soldiers were killed, an officer wounded, and six soldiers knocked out, whether dead or wounded he was not in a position to say. Four policemen were killed in the ambush, a policeman was killed outside Kinnury village, on his way to the fight, and one was killed on the Tourmakeady side of the hill.

On the evening of the fight, Michael Kilroy and the men of the West Mayo column got word that the South Mayo men were being hard pressed by enemy forces. Very gallantly they volunteered to go to their assistance, but when, after a forced march, they arrived in the area that night, they found the fight over and that the column had got safely away.

The action at Tourmakeady had very concrete results. As a result of it the RIC garrisons at Derrypark, Kinnury and Cuilmore were immediately withdrawn.

CAPTURED ARMOURED CAR DRIVEN INTO MOUNTJOY IN ATTEMPT TO RESCUE MACEOIN

DUBLIN BRIGADE, 14 MAY 1921

by Professor Michael Hayes, Colonel Joe Leonard, formerly of 'The Squad', and General MacEoin

PHYSICAL FIGHTING AGAINST the British was of a rather different character in the country to what it was in Dublin. In the country, attacks on RIC barracks were first undertaken by men who assembled at night and who, after an attack on a barracks, resumed their ordinary civilian life. Later, small bodies of men in flying columns remained on full-time active service in the country, getting food and shelter from the country people, using assistance from local Volunteers and civilians in their activities, and operating on the hit-and-run method. Leadership of these columns required certain qualities. The column leader had to be fearless, and as well as that he had to be resourceful, alert and responsible. In many cases, he had first to disarm members of the RIC or British military to provide his men with arms and ammunition. He had to keep in touch with units in adjoining counties and with GHQ in Dublin.

A point was reached when the RIC was unable to hold all its positions throughout the country and many of its barracks were evacuated. These barracks were promptly burned by local Volunteers acting on orders from Volunteer headquarters in Dublin. A new problem then presented itself to the local IRA leader, because, as well as fighting, he had to take his share, sometimes a very important share, in the administration of justice in the area from which the constabulary had been withdrawn.

Seán MacEoin, a young blacksmith from Ballinalee, County Longford, was leader of the Longford flying column, and was also vice brigadier and director of operations for Longford and a portion of Leitrim and Cavan. He had shown not only great courage, but also ingenuity, military knowledge and a capacity for taking responsibility. By 1921 he had many big exploits to his credit and had become a well-known figure. The British had warned him that they would shoot him on sight.

On 9 January he observed RIC and Black and Tans closing in on his headquarters in Miss Martin's cottage near Ballinalee. In order to avoid a fight in the cottage, MacEoin rushed out to meet the enemy, his blazing guns clearing a way though them. District Inspector McGrath of the RIC fell fatally wounded and MacEoin escaped. On 2 February MacEoin's column ambushed a British punitive party moving in lorries near Ballinalee. Two Auxiliaries and a district inspector of the RIC were killed in the fight, which had continued for almost an hour when the British surrendered. There were fifteen survivors, of whom eight were wounded. MacEoin released the unwounded prisoners and let them have one of the captured lorries to take their wounded comrades to hospital.

About a month later the British captured Commandant MacEoin. Though handcuffed he attempted to escape, but was shot at, wounded and recaptured. His captors beat him up with their rifle butts before taking him away.

While awaiting trial in prison he was elected a member of Dáil Éireann for Longford and Westmeath. On 14 June he was charged before a field general court martial in Dublin with having murdered District Inspector McGrath. Several Auxiliaries gave evidence that after the fighting in Ballinalee he had, in fact, sent a doctor to attend them. The relatives of the dead DI made a plea that 'the man who spared and protected his prisoners shall be spared and protected himself when a prisoner'. But he was sentenced to be hanged and was lodged in Mountjoy jail, Dublin, with a special guard of Auxiliaries to watch over day him day and night.

The jail was an old building with a strong outer gate reached by a long passage from the main road and two inner gates, which, under prison rules, had always to be kept closed. The ordinary staff of the jail, all Irishmen, was augmented by Auxiliary police, and regular British military furnished the outer guards.

It will readily be understood that the loss of MacEoin was considered a very grievous one, and there was passionate anxiety that he should not suffer the supreme penalty; but the problem of effecting his rescue seemed impossible to solve.

Like the flying columns in the country, there had been formed in Dublin in September 1919 a full-time active service unit called 'The Squad'. The men who belonged to it gave their whole time to active service. They operated in Dublin city and got co-operation not only from members of the Volunteer organisation, but also from many civilians, from some police, prison warders, civil servants and others. Conditions under which they operated were different from those in the country, with crowded streets instead of lonely places. Intimate knowledge of the city by-ways and the help of friendly civilians often brought men to safety when they had carried out a 'job'.

Michael Collins called 'The Squad' into play to attempt a rescue of Seán MacEoin. The attempt is described in the narrative that follows, by Colonel Joseph Leonard, a member of 'The Squad'.

Michael Hayes

LEONARD'S STORY – OUTSIDE MOUNTJOY

IN MAY 1921, Collins conceived a plan to rescue Seán MacEoin from Mountjoy jail. The plan was in three parts: (1) to capture and man a British armoured car for the purpose of gaining entrance to the jail; (2) having gained entrance to get possession of MacEoin's body; (3) to make sure that it would be possible to come out of the jail again.

British military lorries drew meat rations for various barracks from the Dublin Abattoir two or three times a day. The lorries were accompanied by an armoured car, a Rolls single-turret Whippet. Having in mind the use of an armoured car for the Mountjoy job, Collins instructed Charlie Dalton to take up quarters in the abattoir superintendent's house and to watch through the window the movements of the car. Charlie noticed that some days, on their first visit, which was at 6 a.m., the car crew would become restless, so that eventually the last soldier would get out to stretch his legs and, having locked the car, would ramble about the place. This led to the conclusion that it might be possible to capture the car. Collins took immediate action and, in Jim Kirwan's public house, he had a consultation with Emmet Dalton, myself and a warder of Mountjoy jail, who gave full information about warders, the positions of military guards, meal times and relief times for police and Auxiliaries. Meantime, through another source, MacEoin was instructed to make some complaint or pretext every day to ensure that at 10 a.m. he would be with the governor in his office. The governor's office is outside three obstructing gates, and the governor was usually alone in his office at ten o'clock in the morning, to interview prisoners. If we could get in at that time and find MacEoin in the office the rest would be easy.

The organisation of the parties was done by Paddy O'Daly. It was made the task of one group to capture the car, of another to man and drive it, and of a third party to force an entrance through the main gate of Mountjoy after the car had been driven in. The last party was to reopen the gate and keep it open until the armoured car had come out again. I shall take these three parties in order.

One morning Charlie Dalton noticed that, on their early visit at 6 a.m., the soldiers were in a jaunty mood, and he guessed that the last soldier would probably leave the car on their next visit. He made his report, returned to his watch-out post and the job was on.

The car with the same crew returned on its second journey and the crew behaved as Charlie Dalton had guessed it would. The last Tommy got out and went for a stroll. Volunteers, wearing corporation uniform caps, who had been waiting about the abattoir, closed in at a prearranged signal, and held up the Tommies, shooting some of them who resisted. They secured the keys of the car, and a Rolls single-turret Whippet armoured car, became for the first time the property of the IRA.

Pat McCrea, a quiet and most reliable man, had never seen the inside of a car like this in his life. But he got in calmly and stepped on the gas. He was accompanied by Tom Keogh, Bill Stapleton and Paddy McCaffrey as machine gunners, and went off down the North Circular Road. Emmet Dalton and myself were waiting for them, dressed and armed like British officers. Emmet was wearing his own British uniform and having worn it for a long time when in the British army, he had all the appearance and manner of a British officer. He knew how to adopt the right tone when serving a prisoner's removal order on the jail authorities. I had served for six months in Mountjoy and knew the prison well. Besides, Emmet's second uniform fitted me to perfection.

When he had picked us up, McCrea drove to Mountjoy jail. Emmet Dalton, who was sitting outside as the officer usually did, waved an official-looking paper at the look-out warder. The gates opened wide and shut-to with a clang behind us. Two more iron gates were opened for us. McCrea used his head, driving the car in one long sweep around by the main entrance and back through the two iron gates we had just entered, carelessly jamming both open, and so leaving the main gate only to be negotiated in the get-away. Dalton and myself jumped smartly out of the car. We posted Tom Keogh, dressed in British dungarees and a Tommy's uniform cap, outside the main entrance door to cover our rear or give the alarm as necessary. Dalton and I entered the main door at 10.30 a.m., as the warders were coming from their quarters on duty. One of them, Warder Kelly, had known me as a prisoner and was so surprised at seeing me in a British uniform that he said, 'Oh cripes, look at Leonard', and then, clapping his hand over his mouth, he dashed back upstairs, knocking down all the warders who were descending. We were refused entrance to MacEoin's wing by the warder in charge, and as it was not possible for us to break down two massive iron gates and MacEoin's cell door as well, we continued on to the governor's office. The situation in the office at ten o'clock should have been that there was only one warder on duty, but when we went in we received a shock. Instead of finding Governor Munroe alone, there were seven of his staff present and as we went in the door slammed shut behind us. The governor received us nicely and all went well until he mentioned that he must ring up the Castle for confirmation of the order to remove MacEoin. I sprang for the telephone and smashed it while Dalton, drawing his gun, held the staff at bay. We then began tying the staff up, in the hope that we might secure the master keys, when a fusillade met our ears. It was now or never, if we were to get out of the building. We forced the door open, goodbyes were said quickly, and we left with all haste.

MacEoin was not in the governor's office. We had arrived half-an-hour late for that appointment through no fault of our own.

The plan for holding the main gate open was that Miss Aine Malone would approach with a parcel and have the wicket opened and that Volunteers in several groups would then rush the gate. Miss Malone, with her parcel, arrived in good time, the wicket gate was opened and the main gate rushed. But a sentry on the roof, having seen the civilians rushing the gate, fired a shot which wounded one of our men and raised the general alarm. Tom Keogh, ever on the alert, shot this sentry dead from the courtyard with a Peter the Painter, and the sentry's rifle fell down to the pavement. As Dalton and myself were rushing to the door, I spotted the rifle. Auxiliaries were on the roof with their rifles at the ready. A guard of regular soldiers turned out on the ground near the gate, but were naturally confused at the sight of British uniforms. Acting the part of a British officer, I ordered them to retire, and, on their refusal to obey, I took up the rifle, knelt down and threatened to fire. The soldiers, seeing an officer kneeling in the firing position, retired to their quarters. But the Auxiliary police were advancing from the other side, so it was time to jump on the back of the Whippet and go, taking our rifles with us. We shouted to Pat to let her rip, and Pat McCrea drove down that drive and onto the North Circular Road at a speed that was very satisfactory, seeing we were exposed to rather heavy fire from the jail. Pat McCrea had instructions to drive the Whippet to the Finglas Brigade area, but as the engine overheated badly on the way, he decided to abandon the car at Marino and having stripped it of its guns and ammunition, he set it on fire and went back to his brother's shop to continue his daily work.

Dalton and I had no plan of action agreed upon and we transferred into a waiting taxi at end of the street. We arrived in Howth and dismissed our taxi. It then dawned on me that my sister had good friends among the Sisters of Charity, so we decided to go and see them. We were very nicely received by a sympathetic sister, who listened to our tale of woe, and who, having produced a lovely cup of tea and set out the best china, went to see the Reverend Mother. A messenger was dispatched to Cassidy's public house on the Summit, and returned with two suits borrowed for the occasion. Our uniforms were packed away for dispatch and we emerged less showy, perhaps, but feeling more comfortable and more pleased with ourselves. We returned to town by tram.

On arrival in Dublin we learned that the English military had confined all armoured cars to barracks, having got a scare at loss of their baby Whippet.

Joseph Leonard

MacEOIN'S STORY – INSIDE MOUNTJOY

In May 1921, I received a dispatch from Michael Collins informing me that a new attempt would be made to rescue me from Mountjoy jail. The dispatch instructed me to contact Warder Breslin. Later that evening I received information and instructions from Collins, also in dispatch. These were to the effect that an armoured car, manned by Volunteers would enter Mountjoy jail at any time between ten and twelve o'clock on the following morning, and that I must take such steps as were necessary to be in the governor's office and remain there for that time. When I came in from exercise that same evening I made contact with Breslin who informed me that everything was ready for action the next morning. On return to my cell I immediately sent for the deputy governor, Mr Meehan, and made a violent attack upon the conduct of (a) the warders, (b) the Auxiliaries, and (c) the Black and Tans who were in charge of C (1) Wing and were our jailers. In accordance with the rules, I demanded an immediate interview with the governor and succeeded in arranging the interview for the following morning. Everything was working according to plan and I arrived in the governor's office escorted by an Auxiliary officer and a warder. I succeeded in remaining in the office with thc governor, Charlie Munroe, until about 11.30, when I informed Munroe that I had future complaints on behalf of many of the prisoners and that I would return to my cell and prepare notes for use next morning. This was simply a makeshift as I did not know what had happened.

When on my way out to exercise after lunch, Breslin contacted me again and informed me that the car had not been taken that day but the attempt would be made on the following day, and that the same plan must work. I then sent out a dispatch to Collins informing him that I could be in the governor's office on the following morning, and that I would be accompanied by an Auxiliary officer with a revolver, but that when our men would arrive, I thought that I could handle him. As arranged on Thursday morning I was once more in the governor's office, and remained there for about the same time, with the same result, and, on going out to exercise, I received a repetition of the same message from Breslin. On the third morning the interview was again arranged with the governor for 10 a.m., but, in the meantime, something had occurred which we had not foreseen.

The members of the Auxiliary and Black and Tan guard, who were in charge of the wing, were being relieved and a new body of Auxiliaries and Tans were taking over the duty. The officer commanding the new party insisted that every prisoner in C (1) wing should be locked in his cell. This was done; then the new party accompanied by the officer commanding the old party came and saw every prisoner. This was for the purpose of identification. Each prisoner was carefully scrutinised and notes taken of him by each member of the guard, so that each one would know and recognise each one of the prisoners who was being handed over for the first time into their custody. It was then believed by the authorities that the warders could not be trusted and that prisoners might be enabled to exchange cells so that they would have wrong names and wrong cells.

While this was going on I protested and claimed my interview with the governor, which I had arranged. Mr Meehan, the deputy governor, was present and explained to the commander that I had an interview arranged with the governor. The Auxiliary officer replied that my interview with the governor would be in time enough, that his orders took precedence. While this inspection was taking place the armoured car arrived into Mountjoy and the first indication I had of its presence was the firing of shots. The Auxiliaries manned the inner gates of C (1) wing and a short time afterwards they returned and opened my cell; they were very excited and proceeded to search every corner of the cell and my person. While this was proceeding Breslin came into the cell and said to the Auxiliaries 'we are all safe', at the same time giving me the 'glad-eye'. From that wink I realised that the car had come in and gone out and that those with it were all safe. I bluffed the Auxiliaries a bit by saying, 'when you meet the armoured car down town you will have a very hot time if I get much more abuse'. They then informed me that they were aware of my line of communication and that they would be able to end it. I wished them luck in their efforts, feeling satisfied that they could not have secured any information upon the line of communication, which was a very simple and very old method. That is another story. When the excitement had died down I was blandly informed that the governor was now ready to receive me, not in his usual office, but in a cell at the end of C (1) Wing, and all interviews with the governor thereafter, while I was a prisoner in Mountjoy, were in this cell.

The capture of the armoured car and the attempt at rescue were a first-class effort, and, had they succeeded in capturing it on either of the first two days on which it was planned, I would have been in the governor's room and would have had no trouble in being able to accompany the two Volunteer officers who were dressed up in the uniform of the enemy forces.

Seán MacEoin

CONCLUSION

To GIVE A really satisfactory account of this episode one would require a corroborative narrative from a prison official or from some member of the British military or police force on duty in the jail. An account from the governor, Munroe, or the deputy, Meehan, would have been easy to get, but I do not know whether any steps were ever taken to obtain it.

The reason for the failure is clear. The armoured car could only be captured, when, contrary to regulations, the soldiers had left it. Separated from the car they could be mastered; inside it they were impregnable. Unfortunately, on the morning when an opportunity arose to capture the car, a new guard had come on duty in the jail. As General MacEoin points out, a more stringent and intelligent step had been taken about prisoners. It is clear that the exploit involved risk of death for the crew of the armoured car, and indeed, for MacEoin himself, but these things, as Colonel Leonard observes, were all part of the day's work at that time.

Although the prisoner was not rescued, the attempt was not without very valuable results from the point of view of the Volunteers. It was a great shock to public opinion in England to find that an armoured car could be captured from the regular British army, could be driven straight into a prison, and that the raiders could escape unscathed in broad daylight in Dublin.

Leonard's story is told with great modesty, but the nature of the exploit itself emerges clearly. There was great daring, resourcefulness and a fierce determination not to be stopped by any kind of danger. Above all, the incident showed well-directed organisation, good planning and afforded added evidence to the British that members of their administration in Ireland, apart altogether from the civilian population, were collaborating with the Volunteers. In fact, British administration in Ireland at that moment, showed symptoms of a complete break down. General MacEoin's narrative indicates assistance on the part of members of the prison staff.

Answers by the chief secretary for Ireland in the House of Commons constantly repeated that 'outrages' in Ireland were the work of a small band of 'murderers'. Here in the attempted rescue of MacEoin from Mountjoy was proof positive of the existence of an armed force, widespread in its membership, well led, disciplined and daring.

The exploit, therefore, made its own substantial contribution to bring about the Truce, and the subsequent negotiations which resulted in the establishment of a sovereign Irish State.

Michael Hayes

THE BURNING OF THE CUSTOM HOUSE IN DUBLIN CRIPPLED BRITISH CIVIL ADMINISTRATION

DUBLIN BRIGADE, 25 MAY 1921

by Oscar Traynor, Minister for Defence

(formerly O/C Dublin Brigade IRA)

The story of the destruction of the Custom House is one of brave endeavour as well as one of outstanding success. To it has been ascribed, rightly or wrongly, the ending of the war with the forces of occupation. What is certain is that it will always be linked with the ending of that gallant struggle for the restoration of Irish independence, because in a matter of about one month Mr Lloyd George invited Mr de Valera to a conference. This invitation was followed by arrangement for a truce which eventually took place on 11 July 1921, at noon. Thus was brought to an end one of the most successful fights in our long history for the restoration of our independence.

Early in the new year of 1921, I received a note informing me that there would be a meeting of the army council in the home of the O'Rahilly in 40 Herbert Park. These meetings were seldom held twice in the one place, and this was the first time I had been summoned to Herbert Park. I was later informed, verbally, that the meeting would be a rather important one and I should come prepared to discuss the activities of the Dublin Brigade and matters pertaining to it. I was also told that the President (Éamon de Valera), who had just arrived back from America, would be present. I arrived at Herbert Park at the appointed hour and found most of my colleagues already there.

Those present, as far as my memory goes, were Cathal Brugha, Austin Stack, Richard Mulcahy, Diarmuid O'Hegarty, Michael Collins, Gearóid O'Sullivan, Liam Mellows, Seán Russell, J.J. O'Connell, Seán McMahon, Piaras Béaslaí and, I think, Eoin O'Duffy.

There may have been one or two others, but I cannot remember them at the moment. However, we were assembled there for some little time when word was brought to us that the British forces had drawn a cordon across the entrance to the road. It was immediately assumed that this activity was in some way connected with our meeting. The position we were in was being discussed, ways and means to meet it were being planned, when to our surprise the president was ushered into our presence. Everyone naturally wanted to know how he managed to get through the cordon. His reply was simple. He said: 'I was held up, questioned and finally passed through.' Later the word came through that the cordon had been withdrawn. As it was then a very ordinary procedure on the part of the occupying forces to throw out these cordons, little further notice was taken.

The meeting proceeded in a very normal way for some time and then the president spoke and he made it clear that something in the nature of a big action in Dublin was necessary in order to bring public opinion abroad to bear on the question of Ireland's case. He felt that such an action in the capital city, which was as well known abroad as London or Paris, would be certain to succeed. He suggested that the capture of the headquarters of the Auxiliaries, which was situated in Beggar's Bush barracks, would capture the imagination of those he had in mind, apart from the serious blow it would constitute to the enemy. As an alternative to this he suggested the destruction of the Custom House, which was the administrative heart of the British civil service machine in the country. It was finally decided that I, as the officer commanding the Dublin Brigade, should examine these propositions and report back to the army council in due course.

I immediately set to work and was given the help of GHQ intelligence. Two weeks were spent on the investigation and examination of the possibilities of capturing Beggar's Bush. The experience of the men engaged on this work was such that they reported against such an operation. My activities were then turned to the alternative suggestion – the Custom House. I made a personal examination of this building. Armed with a large envelope, inscribed with OHMS on its front, I made my way all over the building. I was greatly impressed by its solidity, its granite walls, and what appeared to me its complete lack of structural material which would burn. However, each office into which I penetrated was surrounded by wooden presses and shelves, which held substantial bundles of papers and office files. It could also be presumed that the presses contained papers and other inflammable material. Immediately after my examination I took Commandant Tom Ennis of the 2nd Battalion into my confidence and asked him to make a similar examination and let me have his views. He carried out his task by methods similar to my own and his report more or less confirmed my views. My next step was to secure plans of the building. These were secured for me by Liam O'Doherty, O/C 5th Battalion. A perusal of these indicated the magnitude of the task. There were three floors to be dealt with as well as the basement floor, numerous corridors and hundreds of offices. The staff probably numbered upwards of 400 with the control of large numbers of telephones. In the course of our investigations it was also discovered that there was a direct line to the Castle for emergency use. There was also the problem of the general public, who were continually entering and leaving the building. There were no military guards on the building, they having been withdrawn some short time before. There was, however, a number of police patrolling both the front and rear of the building. All these and many other points had to be given careful consideration. I spent nearly three months on the preparation of the plans. They were in my mind day and night. They were altered dozens of times as weaknesses or better points occurred to me. Finally they were submitted to a sub-committee of the army council for their imprimatur or otherwise. This body met at six o'clock one Sunday morning in May, in 6 Gardiner's Row, which was the headquarters of the Dublin Brigade. Those present were Richard Mulcahy, chief of staff, Michael Collins, director of intelligence, J.J. (Ginger) O'Connell, ASC, and a man named Dowling. I got the impression that he was a specialist in engineering. The plans in general were accepted. But one portion which arranged for the throwing up of barricades in the vicinity of the various city barracks was objected to. This operation was designed to operate only if any attempt was made by enemy forces to leave during the twenty-five minutes from 12.55 p.m. to 1.20 p.m. when it was hoped to have destruction of the building and its evacuation completed. It was designed solely as a delaying action and to give the men operating within the Custom House an opportunity of returning in safety when their task was completed. The barricades were to have been covered by riflemen operating from a distance of 200 or 300 yards.

The DI's objection to this part of the scheme was very strong. He regarded the throwing up of barricades all over the city as being suggestive of a general uprising and finally stated, in reply to my arguments, that if it could not be carried out without this precaution it should not be carried out at all. Having withdrawn my arguments in favour of that part of the plan, the date of 25 May was agreed upon for the carrying out of the operation.

My next step was to inform the senior officers of the brigade of the proposed action together with an outline of the plan. They on their part were to start on the selection of their officers for the varying tasks which they would be called upon to fill. In the course of a number of meetings the whole plan gradually unfolded. As the target was in the 2nd Battalion area it was decided that the actual destruction of the building would be entrusted to that unit. Commandant Tom Ennis was appointed to take sole control of the party within the building. The 2nd Battalion was reinforced by the addition of 'The Squad', a party of about twelve men who were attached to the DI's department, and some men of the ASU.

To the 1st Battalion was allotted the task of protecting the outside of the building. In the event of a surprise attack by enemy forces, the battalion was to engage them with grenade, rifle and machine-gun fire. This was a later addition to the plans which I had submitted to the Army Council's sub-committee. I had hoped to be able to tell the men who had to enter the building that they would be completely protected against surprise by reason of the ring of barricades to which I have already referred, but, following the elimination of that part of the plan, I decided to adopt these measures which would give at least partial protection. In addition to this task the 1st Battalion was also to deal with any fire stations in its area. In other words, the men were to put all fire-fighting appliances out of action by the removal of vital parts of their machines. The 3rd and 4th Battalions dealt in a similar way with the stations in their areas.

To the 5th Battalion was given the very important task of cutting off the Custom House from all communication, telephonic or otherwise, with the outside world. This was a highly technical job and the most skilled men of the engineers were called on to carry out the work. Communications could not be cut until the last minute as otherwise suspicions would most likely be aroused. As quite a number of manholes and high telephone poles were involved, the difficulty of their task can well be imagined.

The preparation for the main task of destruction brought about the necessity for a number of lesser actions. For instance, I decided right from the beginning that in no circumstances was petrol to be used. This necessitated the commandeering of a large quantity of paraffin oil and the transferring of the oil from steel casks and tanks to petrol tins. It also necessitated the holding-up of an oil concern and their staff for a number of hours and the commandeering of a motor lorry to bring the tinned paraffin to the Custom House precisely on time. When this lorry arrived at the back entrance to the building, which is opposite Lower Gardiner Street, the men detailed for the inside operation entered, at the same time taking with them from off the lorry a tin of paraffin. The building was also entered from the Quays and Beresford Place entrance, opposite Liberty Hall. In this way the number going in by one door was not excessive and did not arouse suspicion. Their immediate job on entry was to control all telephonic communications as an added safety device, even though these had been cut by our engineers, precisely on the entrance of our men to the building.

Within the building each captain had been allotted a landing or floor and all the offices and men on that landing to deal with. His job was to see that every person employed on that floor was sent down to the main hall where they were kept under the vigilant eyes of the men of 'The Squad' and the ASU. With this part of his task completed he was then to see that every office on his landing was thoroughly saturated with paraffin oil. This could not have been done if petrol was used as the gas manufactured by the contact of the petrol with air would have made a very dangerous explosive mixture. When the job of saturation had been completed the officer was to report to the O/C, Commandant Ennis, on the ground floor, and the actual firing was to take place on an order given by him by a single blast of his whistle. Two blasts were to signify the completion of the job and the withdrawal of all men to the ground floor. Everything went perfectly according to plan except that just before all floors had given Commandant Ennis the 'all ready' signal someone blew two blasts on a whistle and all retired to the main hall. One officer reported, however, that he had not completed his saturation task. He and his men were sent back at once to finish the job. The few minutes lost here, not quite five, was the difference between the successful retirement of all the participants and the arrival of large numbers of enemy forces in lorries and armoured cars. These forces swept into Beresford Place at exactly 1.25 p.m., just five minutes after the time allotted in the plan for the completion of the operation. They were engaged on entry to Beresford Place by the 1st Battalion units with volleys of revolver shots and the throwing of a number of hand grenades. For some unknown reason the machine gun which our men were to have mounted inside the Custom House docks at the far end of Beresford Place did not come into action. Just before the entry of the enemy forces I was talking to Captain Paddy Daly, just outside the main back entrance. We were discussing the delay in the men leaving, as 1.20 had just passed. The sudden entrance of the enemy put an end to our discussion as at this point they were firing wildly from the different lorries as they came through. Captain Daly made away towards Abbey Street. I made towards the supports of the Loop Line Bridge opposite Brooks Thomas' building stores. As I reached the road here I came under fire from a lorry of Black and Tans, but due to the speed and movement of the lorry the firing was erratic. As I reached the pathway, however, the lorry had come to a sudden halt. I was still being fired on and at the same time there were shouts of 'Hands Up'. At this point I saw a young Volunteer jump out from the cover of the bridge supports and throw a bomb into the middle of the Black and Tans' lorry, with disastrous effects to the occupants. I was later told that he was Volunteer Dan Head and that he was killed either then or sometime later during the action. By this time 'The Squad' in the Custom House had gone into action with their Parabellum and Mauser automatics with still further disastrous effects to the Black and Tans who were attempting to storm the main back entrance. Before I managed to get away I saw several enemy bodies lying motionless around the entrance and, as far as one could see and judge, dead. Those who were blown out of the lorry with which I was concerned were unconscious on the ground, if not dead. I eventually got out through Gardiner Street and Talbot Street and back to Abbey Street where I made contact with Captain Daly again, just outside the Abbey Theatre. Here we were informed that Tom Ennis, who had shot his way out, was taken away in a lorry seriously wounded. At this time enemy reinforcements were coming up in lorries together with additional armoured cars. We then knew that the only hope for the men inside was to escape by the Custom House docks, a slender enough chance considering the strength of the forces now on the scene. Actually, a goodly number did escape by various ways and ruses. Some were killed in their attempt. Altogether we lost five killed and about eighty captured. Some short time later I received a message to the effect that Tom Ennis had reached his home in Croydon Park House, Fairview, and that he was in a very serious condition. Captain Daly and myself immediately went to the brigade first aid post in Gardiner's Row, where we collected some first aid equipment and cycled to Tom's home. His wife, who was nursing a young infant, brought us to Tom's bedside where we found him in a semi-conscious condition. He had an awful-looking bullet wound in his groin. The bullet entered from the buttock and made its exit through the groin. In its passage it was apparently deflected and tumbled on its way through, as the exit wound was a large gaping hole with portions of bone protruding. This looked so bad that I at once ordered Daly to get into immediate touch with Michael Collins's motor driver, Batt Hyland, and ask him to come over at once. While awaiting his arrival I gave first aid treatment to the wounds, having earlier in my Volunteer career done a course in that service.

When the car arrived Daly and I had considerable difficulty in getting Tom down the stairs from his flat, every movement causing him excruciating pain. The car then made its way very slowly to the O'Donnell's Nursing Home in Eccles Street where all our Volunteers were treated. On our way there we twice had to pass through police cordons – once on Ballybough Bridge and later on, on the bridge on Jones's Road. On both occasions the police, after peering into the car, gave us the 'all clear' and passed us through. I think they sized up the situation and decided on a non-interference policy. On arrival at the home we had to carry Tom to the very top of the building. He was then only barely conscious. He was attended almost immediately and operated on, I think, that night. He spent a considerable period of time in that home. In the course of one of my visits he told me that the doctor assured him that the first aid attention which he had been given helped considerably in saving his life. I merely mention this to show that the special services in the brigade were of considerable and genuine value, especially when it was not always safe to call in outside help without some knowledge of the individuals called on, or the time to make inquiries as to their friendliness or otherwise.

The operation, apart from these losses, was entirely successful. Everything within the four walls of the building was reduced to ashes. The fire was still burning ten days after the attack. The fire brigades were unable to go into action for a considerable time. This delay, as well as the use of the paraffin oil, played a decisive part in the total destruction of the inside of the building.

That evening the Dublin Brigade again went into action in a number of places in the city, mainly as a gesture of defiance, as well as to show that our heavy losses that day did not impair our ability to carry on the fight.

The nuns of the Mater Hospital later told me the story of the death of Seán Doyle. As he lay on his death bed, they said his one worry was 'Are the boys beaten?' and that night as the sound of nearby explosions shook the air, Seán's face was wreathed in smiles as he turned to the nun who was attending him and feebly whispered: 'Thank God, Sister, the fight goes on.' That simple statement of a man who had given his all for the cause of Ireland symbolised the determination of the Irish people down through the centuries.

UNLIKELY AMBUSH POSITION WAS DELIBERATELY CHOSEN NEAR CASTLEMAINE

KERRY NO. 1 BRIGADE, 1 JUNE 1921

As told by participants to Edward Gallagher

THE FIRST DAY of June dawned bright and clear and with the promise of making another of those hot, cloudless days that had characterised the month of May. As the morning broke and the residents of the Kerry villages of Castlemaine and Milltown drew up their blinds or took down their shutters, they saw before them another listless, enervating day of scorching heat. They were not to know that the day would be neither listless nor enervating. They were not to know that before the sun should set many men were to die on the three-mile stretch of road between them.

Summertime, with its long bright days, is not the ideal campaigning season for the guerrilla fighter. The screen of friendly darkness is missing. So a stay had necessarily been put upon the activities of the republican forces in the area. Nevertheless when, about eleven o'clock, Michael Gallivan brought word to Dan Mulvihill, adjutant of the local or 6th Battalion, that a cycling party of nine Tans, led by a district inspector, had passed through on their way to Tralee, it was decided to ambush them on their way back.

The villages of Castlemaine and Milltown lie on the main Tralee to Killorglin road, about three miles apart. The cycling party of Tans were members of a detachment stationed in Killorglin. Their object in going into Tralee was to collect pay for their detachment. It might be asked why an ambush had not been set for these Tans before this. The answer is simple. These crown forces had been most circumspect in their behaviour. Their movements had been designedly irregular. They had not, in fact, essayed a trip into Tralee for two months before this day.

Orders were sent out to members of the battalion in the area, and eighteen to twenty men were mobilised near Castlemaine. Their armament consisted of one long Lee-Enfield rifle, one police carbine, and shotguns loaded with buck-shot.

The problem was to select the most effective ambush position. The main road in this area is of an unusually winding character, with the bends very close together. The enemy had been reported cycling in extended order. At what point could the whole party be brought simultaneously within an effective field of fire? Just outside Milltown an ambush position with excellent cover offered itself at Kilderry Wood, but the IRA men decided to ignore it. They decided to ignore it because they reckoned it was the obvious spot at which the enemy, on guard against an ambush, would expect to be hit up. Boldly they decided to take up a position which gave them little cover and, on that account, one that the enemy would not expect them to occupy.

Just around the bend from Castlemaine railway bridge on the Milltown road, there is a straight road in the district. Today the banks or ditches on each side of the road are heavily wooded; thirty-one years ago they were bare. Here it was decided to ambush the enemy. Today as then, there is a cottage at the beginning of the straight stretch of road – or opening of the ambush position – and another cottage at the end of the straight stretch or end of the ambush position. It was decided to place the shotgun men behind the left-hand ditch at intervals of roughly ten yards from cottage to cottage. The men with carbine and Lee-Enfield were to be stationed at the cottage at the end of the ambush position. When the head of the enemy cycling party came abreast of the cottage the riflemen were to open fire. This was to be the signal for the shotgun men to go into action against the remainder of the party.

The Castlemaine Company was contacted and its help enlisted. Between Castlemaine and Tralee lies a winding mountain road, and

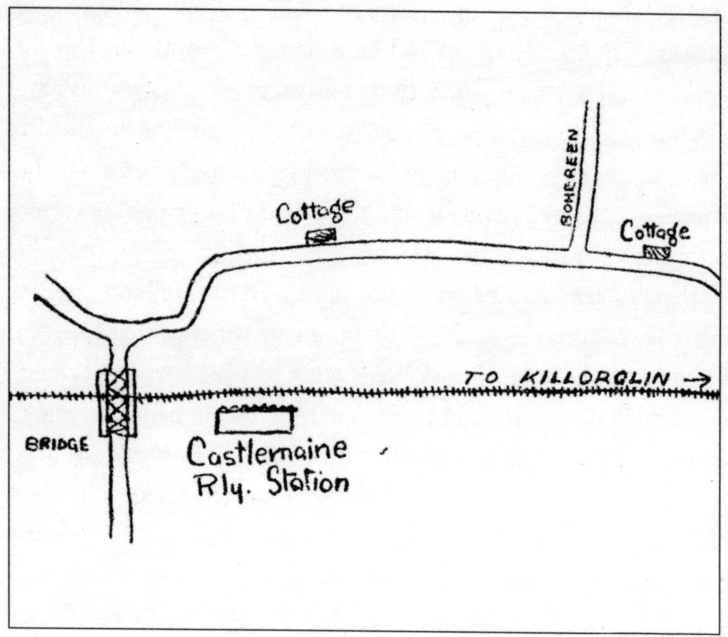

scouts were posted from the top of the mountain back to Castlemaine to signal the approach of the enemy. In addition, to guard against surprise, scouts were posted on both flanks.

The ambush position selected and security measures provided for, the IRA men were prepared to try conclusions with the enemy. Tactically, however, they suffered under a big handicap. They required more riflemen. With but two rifles at the end of the ambush position to bear the brunt of the rapid and accurate firing, it was but too probable that the shotgun men would be unable to prevent many of the mobile enemy force slipping out of the ambush position.

Mulvihill sent a messenger across to Keel, about eight miles away, where his Battalion O/C, Tom O'Connor, was 'on his keeping', to inform him of what he had done, and asking him to join him with what assistance he could get from the Keel Company. He also requested him to contact Paddy Cahill at 'The Hut', acquaint him with what they proposed to do and solicit the support of some riflemen to help them out in the intended action.

A word of explanation must here be said about 'The Hut' and its occupants. These men, members of the Kerry No. 1 Brigade column, were mostly from Tralee and, apart from other considerations, could not return to their homes as they were all on the 'wanted' list. Earlier in the year the brigades in Kerry, Cork, Waterford and west Limerick had been welded together into the 1st Southern Division with Liam Lynch as officer commanding. Following the formation of the division a certain amount of reorganisation had taken place. Andy Cooney, a GHQ staff captain, had been appointed acting O/C Kerry No. 1 Brigade in place of Paddy Cahill. Other changes on the brigade staff were also made. These changes caused some understandable confusion and a great deal of resentment. The upshot of the matter was – as far as our story is concerned – that the column men at 'The Hut', as their quarters in Keel were called, pending clarification of the position, still looked upon Cahill as their O/C.

Tom O'Connor did as requested. He informed Cahill what it was proposed to do, asked for assistance, but made it clear that the action would go forward in any event. He then set out himself for Castlemaine with members of the Keel Company.

Going into battle men's nerves are keyed up. They think quickly but remember slowly. The men who planned the action reckon that their party got into position between 2 and 2.30 p.m. Their position and dispositions were inspected and approved by Tom O'Connor, Jack Flynn, vice-O/C and now deputy for South Kerry, and Dan Mulvihill.

Then came the testing time for all fighting men – the waiting time, the waiting for the suspense to cease and the action to start. The minutes crawled past on leaden feet. Fifteen minutes passed, then thirty, and still no word from beyond that tantalising bend of the road of the arrival of the enemy in Castlemaine. Approximately an hour of doubt and misgiving passed before the IRA men got certain tidings of the approach of the enemy. Then William Keane, of the Castlemaine Company, whose scouting mission it was to keep ahead of the Tan party, arrived into the ambush position with the information that the latter were halted on Castlemaine railway bridge holding, presumably, a council of war.

The reason for this consultation on Castlemaine railway bridge was as follows: when the Tans arrived in the village there was a common desire for liquid refreshment. Apart from this fighting force's weakness for the cup that more than cheers, it was not out of the way that men who had cycled over a mountain road on a hot day should have a thirst to slake. They proceeded to slake it, and in the course of slaking the district inspector was informed that suspicious activity had been observed on the road between Castlemaine and Milltown. It might be that the 'boys' were planning to ambush his party. He might be well advised to take an alternative route.

To this advice the inspector turned a deaf ear. He would not turn off his road for any 'Shinner'. He would shoot it out with any of them and be damned to 'em. Nevertheless, when the party arrived on the railway bridge the order to dismount was given and the possibility of being ambushed debated. The inspector would not hear of turning off the main road but, by way of precaution, ordered his party to ride in closer formation. The party remounted and, headed by the district inspector and a sergeant, rode off in a line that covered roughly about 250 yards of road.

In the meantime the pendulum had swung in favour of the waiting IRA men. Under the command of Tadhg Brosnan of Castlegregory, Paddy Cahill had sent over a section of riflemen from 'The Hut'. Their firepower was not merely welcome, but might prove all important. A number of them under Brosnan went down towards the opening of the ambush position, and a number were stationed at the cottage closing it.

The orders still stood. When the leaders of the enemy party came abreast of the end cottage the men stationed there were to open fire. Now, however, instead of but one rifle and a carbine to carry out this opening phase of the fight, there was the additional firepower of five rifles carried by Paddy Paul Fitzgerald, Mick O'Leary, Jerry O'Connor, Eugene Hogan and Jerry Myles, all from 'The Hut'.

The district inspector and his sergeant, closely followed by two Tans, appeared around the bend at the beginning of the straight stretch of road. They passed the first cottage and entered the ambush position. Cycling steadily, eyes wary for any untoward movement, they moved up the road. The last of the Tans passed the first cottage, and the whole party were within the ambush position.

The district inspector comes abreast of the cottage. Zero hour! There is the thunderous crash of the rifle volley and the inspector and the two leading Tans, hit by a hail of bullets, are tumbled lifeless from their bicycles. Miraculously the sergeant is unhurt and passes the cottage. His escape, however, is short-lived. Jerry O'Connor, armed with a grenade, lobs it accurately on the road, and the sergeant goes down riddled with shrapnel fragments.

Down the road the remainder of the IRA party have gone into action, and there is fire and counter-fire, but for the Tans it is but a matter of time. Caught between two fires, their fate is sealed. In the heat of the action two of them, flinging away their rifles and ammunition, manage to scramble over the bank on the other side of the road. This bank, of course, could not be occupied by the IRA men because of the danger of some of their own party being hit by crossfire. The two Tans, divesting themselves of their tunics, made their way across the fields down towards the railway line. They were the only ones who did escape.

The one IRA casualty happened when the action was to all intents and purposes over. Running along the ditch behind which the attackers were lying was a deep gully. A Tan rolled into this when fire was opened and lay there undetected until the firing ceased. He stood up then, presumably to take stock of the position and looking over the ditch the first person he saw was Jerry Myles, who was also standing up. Instantly the Tan swung up his rifle and fired. Myles ducked instinctively and the bullet entered at the back of his neck and travelled down his back inflicting an ugly and serious wound. The Tan ran crouching along by the ditch towards a bohereen on the right of the road. When he came out at the bohereen he made the target the IRA men were waiting for, and was brought down lifeless.

Myles was now conveyed by his comrades up the bohereen to a cottage. On the way the party were met by Dr Sheahan, the Battalion MO, who did what he could for the wounded man who was taken into the cottage and laid on an improvised stretcher consisting of two mattresses placed on a kitchen door. Gently the stretcher was raised by ready hands and a little party set out, with flanking scouts, to convey the wounded man to a place of security where he might receive medical and nursing attention. Fording the Flesk river, the party made Beaufort and stayed in a house there for the night. The next day a carefully planned movement to a safe retreat in the Glencar area was carried out, and there for three months the wounded man was devotedly nursed back to health by Mary O'Brien, the battalion nurse.

Judged by the casualties inflicted on the enemy and the amount of equipment captured, Castlemaine must be accounted a most successful ambush. When the IRA men had sorted out the weapons and equipment which littered the road, they found themselves in possession of eight or nine rifles, six Webley revolvers, 800 rounds of .303 ammunition, 100 rounds of .45 ammunition and in addition, the bicycles of the whole party – and all of them brand new!

LANDMINES USED AGAINST LORRY-BORNE AUXILIARIES AT RATHCOOLE

CORK NO. 2 BRIGADE, 16 JUNE 1921

As told by participants to Patrick Lynch

GOOD SUMMERS, WITH months of almost continuous sunshine, are so rare in Ireland that it is not surprising that folk still recall with accuracy the hot summer of 1921. It is said that never before or since were there so many bright and cloudless days, with dry heat that reduced rivers to trickling streams, and dried to concrete hardness the beds of dykes and watercourses which had not been emptied within memory of man. Week after week, the scorching days followed in unbroken succession. In towns and villages, flagged sidewalks were hot under foot before the stroke of noon, and roller shades to protect shop fronts from injury by the sun appeared a permanent feature of every street.

In the middle of May that year the Auxiliaries came to Millstreet. The white dust lay inches deep on the winding roads of Muskerry and Duhallow. Across the dry fields and brown heather of the hills the republican units moved in the purple dusk of the warm nights.

What was the military situation in north Cork as the spring evenings lengthened towards summer? How stood the morale, the record, and the dispositions of the opposing forces? The answers show that most things went well with the national fight. Several heavy strokes against the enemy had been dealt by the men of the columns, and places such as Drishanebeg, Clonbanin, Ballydrohane and Tureengarriffe had given their names to actions that were talked of with pride by the people, not alone in north Cork but wherever else throughout the length and breadth of the land that news of them had penetrated the rigid censorship maintained by the British. All were serious enemy reverses. Add to these and others the various smaller operations carried out in battalion and company areas, such as ambushing patrols, sniping barracks, trenching roads and destroying bridges and railways, and a general idea of the military problem that confronted the British in north Cork, can be formed.

It will be asked what the British did by way of retaliation and counter-action. How were they disposed? The larger posts held full garrisons. Fermoy, Moorepark, Buttevant and Ballyvonaire, were big permanent training and mobilisation centres. Early in 1921 Kanturk workhouse was occupied by the Gloucester Regiment and a company outpost was established at Newmarket. Mallow had long been a permanent post. Black and Tans were in the RIC barracks at Kanturk, Banteer, Millstreet, Newmarket, Milford, Charleville and Dromcollogher. Every IRA engagement of note brought vindictive and brutal reprisal. Houses were raided and burned, men shot out of hand, children fired on as they played and women subjected to indignities. Such unsoldierly conduct merely steeled the men of the columns to sterner effort.

Such was the general picture when, following the Clonbanin fight, the leaders of the IRA in north Cork considered their plans for the future. At Clonbanin the IRA columns were unable to press home their advantage to complete victory by capturing the arms and ammunition of a badly mauled convoy, because the Vickers machine gun in a 'ditched' armoured car still dominated the road on which the dead and wounded British lay. That situation was bound to repeat itself in increasing measure, for it proved to the British the advisability of using armoured vehicles more extensively. A method of dealing with armour had to be found by the IRA and an obvious solution to this anticipated problem lay in the more extensive use of mines. But the difficulties were twofold. In the first place, men with the technical knowledge necessary for the manufacture and laying of effective road mines were almost as scarce in north Cork as the proverbial Red Indian on Manhattan. Secondly, chlorate of potash, which was the raw material, was difficult to secure in the required quantity. It was forbidden to sell more than about two ounces of it at a time, so that a tedious and widespread collection of the explosive had to be made over a period, before the quantity necessary for the manufacture of a few mines could be accumulated. In every town and village in north Cork, republican agents were ordered to purchase, on one pretext or another, the few ounces of chlorate of potash allowed by law. The purchases were canalised into a central pool and by these methods the second difficulty was eventually surmounted.

About that time, a reorganisation of IRA commands took place. General Liam Lynch, who had been brigade O/C, was appointed officer commanding the 1st Southern Division. The brigade area was divided up and two brigades were formed in the area in which one had previously operated. Seán Moylan, who had been commandant of the Newmarket Battalion, became O/C of the brigade which comprised the Mallow, Kanturk, Newmarket, Charleville and Millstreet Battalions, while George Power, who had been brigade adjutant, was given command of the brigade area covered by Fermoy, Castletownroche and Mitchelstown Battalions.

The days were lengthening, a factor favourable to the British, as it gave them more hours of daylight for the widespread and large-scale raids which they had been carrying out since the end of March. These big raids continued all through the spring and early summer months. Large sectors of the countryside were marked out, and thousands of troops converging from posts and barracks in many parts of the county, would move across them in skirmish line, raiding houses, combing woods and valleys, and scouring villages. Parties of troops dropped by lorry at various points on the roads of north Cork would move across country until picked up by their transport in the evening, at pre-arranged places. Frequently they went into bivouac for the night and continued the work next day. It was a technique designed to comb the countryside, field by field and house by house, until the elusive IRA columns were found and wiped out; an all-out effort to corner the republican army. Neither men nor materials were spared. On the ground the troops used lorries, armoured cars, mules and bicycles. Overhead planes flew low on reconnaissance, trying to spot IRA movements or concentrations. Colossal in conception and intense in execution, these operations proved as ineffective as they were costly and spectacular. They did result in the capture and shooting out-of-hand of individual officers and Volunteers. Skirmishes took place too, but the organised units so persistently sought always succeeded in slipping through the cordons.

In the early stages of this campaign in north Cork, General Lynch and his staff had a narrow escape. It happened in the dawn of a March morning at their headquarters in a valley of the Boggeraghs, above Nadd, that columns of troops from Fermoy, Buttevant and Ballincollig moved in on them under the guidance of an ex-British soldier who had been 'planted' in the Kanturk column by the enemy for espionage purposes and who had vanished from the area some days before the encirclement took place. He was present in Tan uniform on the memorable morning at Nadd. That was the last heard of him, though IRA intelligence tried hard to track him down, both in this country and in England. With the protecting Kanturk and Mallow columns, Lynch and his officers escaped through the one rapidly closing gap in the line of khaki thrown around the mountain glen that morning. Not far from the headquarters building, five members of the Mallow column were surprised asleep in bed in the house of a Volunteer named Herlihy. All five were taken with Herlihy to the rear of the house to be shot, when two of them, Joe Morgan and John Moloney, leapt over a nearby fence and made a daring escape. Both were wounded. Lieutenant Waters of Mallow and Volunteers Kiely, Herlihy and Twomey of Nadd were shot out-of-hand, in cold blood. Waters, Kiely and Herlihy died where they stood in their stockinged feet. Twomey, who attempted to escape, was shot crossing a field near the road below the house. Murder had been perpetrated. But the principal quarry, General Lynch and his staff, were not caught in the net. Higher up the glen, Mick Courtney, Martin McGrath, Jack Winters and Jimmy Hayes of the Kanturk Battalion column and a Volunteer named Ring, of Ballyclough, were billeted that morning in Jerh Riordan's house at Nadbeg, which overlooked the brigade headquarters. On hearing the shooting they dashed out of Riordan's and fought a successful rearguard action across the mountain. They came up with the wounded John Moloney of Mallow and brought him to safety. During the action they were joined by Captain Joe Hinchon of the local company and by Tadhg McCarthy, who was the first to spot the British and who had raised the alarm.

It was also in March that Charlie Reilly, of the Newmarket Battalion column, was shot when he, Seán Moylan and John D. Sullivan, of the same unit, had a brush with a party of troops at Coolagh Bridge, outside the town. Reilly fell riddled with machine-gun bullets while crossing the bog adjacent to the bridge.

The threat to its existence caused by the widespread raids and rounding-up tactics brought a ready and effective response from the IRA. With the object of preventing the enemy from using his lorries and armoured cars, bridges were demolished and roads trenched from one end of north Cork to the other. In every company area, from Araglin, on the border of Waterford, to Millstreet, on the bounds of Kerry, across fifty odd miles of County Cork, the men of the Volunteer army were ceaselessly at work on demolitions and trench cutting. Wherever a trench was filled it was destroyed in a matter of hours. Every movement of the British was watched and reported. Their swift convoys sallying forth from different centres in the area were observed, their directions noted, and the information flashed across the hill by scouts who used horn blasts by day and beacon signals at night. Many miles ahead of the advancing British columns the news of their movements was flashed or sounded. With the passing of each week the activities of the local companies of the IRA increased as their methods of dealing with the British raids became more effective. Scouts watched from selected hills all over the area, whilst at night working parties opened trenches and made other road blocks to deny the use of the highways to enemy transport and fighting vehicles.

So the task went on through the month of April and the early weeks of May in that momentous year of 1921.

The 16 May was a date made memorable by the arrival at Millstreet of a detachment of 120 Auxiliaries, the much talked of *corps d'elite* of the forces of occupation in Ireland. A month previously Mr Denis Henry, the Attorney General, had said that the strength of the Auxiliary Division of the RIC was 1,481, composed entirely of ex-officers. He said that the list of decorations held by members of the force was: one VC, two CMGs, twenty-two DSOs (one with three bars), 130 MCs (sixteen with bars), twenty-three DCMs (two with bars), sixty-three MMs, forty Foreign Orders and one Tank Corps OM. In addition, 350 members had been mentioned in dispatches during the war. In a special train 120 of these dreadnought mercenaries arrived at Millstreet station, which is situated about a mile north of the town. In the old Union Workhouse buildings, about a mile to the west of Millstreet and lying against the rugged northern slope of the mountain, they made their beds on their first night under Clara. Their stores they had left in wagons at the railway station. The unloading was a task that could wait for the morrow; or so they thought. As they slept that night in the old workhouse wards, appropriately enough Victorian relics of the Famine era, their precious stores and the wagons that held them were set ablaze by the Dooneen Company of the IRA on the gleaming tracks that stretched westward towards Rathmore. When the Auxiliaries' transport arrived to collect the stores next morning, they found but the charred remains of the railway wagons. The men of Millstreet were no respecters of reputations.

But while the burning supply wagons lit up the dark woodland patches around Dooneen, scarcely a dozen miles away, an event of the first importance to the brigade was taking place. Over at Boherbue that night, Brigadier Seán Moylan and one of his officers, Jim Riordan of Kiskeam, were resting in a friendly house. A raiding party of the Gloucester Regiment from Kanturk was practically upon them when the alarm was given. The brigade O/C and Riordan got out of the house, partly dressed. To a shout of 'Hands Up' from the Gloucesters, they replied with rifle fire, and succeeded in getting through the enemy lines into the night, following a further exchange of shots. The British sought them all through the darkness, and when the early summer dawn came up over the horizon, Jim Riordan had succeeded in escaping, but Moylan had been captured. He was recognised, bound in chains and brought under heavy escort, first to Kanturk and then to Buttevant and Cork. He was subsequently court-martialled and sentenced to death.

The capture of the brigade O/C was a severe blow to the IRA. Into the breach thus created stepped Commandant Paddy O'Brien of Liscarroll, on whom then devolved the duty of military leadership in the western portion of the north-east Cork area. His command embraced the battalion districts of Mallow, Charleville, Kanturk, Newmarket and Millstreet, and it was in this stretch of country that IRA agents collected the little quantities of chlorate of potash required for the mines to deal with the enemy armoured vehicles. About eight pounds of explosive went into each mine, so the number of two-ounce lots that had to be collected and pooled can be calculated. What of technicians? One was found, but it was the irony of things that on the very evening when he and the brigade O/C had completed the making of a mine, they ran into a party of the enemy. The brigade O/C made off in one direction and the mine-expert followed another. The enemy elected to pursue the technician and succeeded in capturing him. So it was that a mine-maker was found only to be lost again.

The brigade staff then set about the training of mine-makers. A man was found for the task, and about the middle of May he had trained a number of men in the technique of manufacturing and laying mines. The armament of the brigade at the time consisted of about twelve to twenty rifles in each of the five battalions which composed it, apart from shotguns and a number of other weapons. The brigade also possessed one Hotchkiss light machine gun. When a number of mines were made, the brigade was ready to strike again and the staff set about making plans. It did not have a long wait for action.

From Commandant C.J. Meaney of the Millstreet Battalion, came news that the Auxiliaries stationed there were loud and blatant with talk of their anxiety to come to grips with the IRA. Airing their reputation as a fighting force, and with their freedom from normal military discipline, they swashbuckled and swaggered around the Millstreet area in a manner which was bound to have a detrimental effect on the morale of the civilian population, if permitted to continue unchecked. From the workhouse the 'Auxies', as they were known, had moved to Mount Leader House, about three-quarters of a mile to the south of the town. Shortly afterwards it was reported that the workhouse was to be occupied by military. So the Clara section of the Millstreet Company of the IRA struck swiftly to prevent this, and one night the steep sides of the mountain were lit up by the blazing roofs of the building. In Millstreet itself curfew had been proclaimed and a reign of terror instituted. Undoubtedly, the 120 Auxiliaries in Mount Leader House believed they spoke the truth when they frequently told the people that they had the fear of either God or the devil driven into the IRA. Such was the situation when June came in with the sun of an extraordinary summer beating down on the white roads and brown fields as day followed day.

West of Banteer the railway line into Kerry had been put completely out of action by the IRA so that the Auxiliaries were obliged to collect their supplies at the Banteer railhead and take them by road in their armoured tenders along the eight or nine miles to Mount Leader House, outside Millstreet. The bridges on this road had been demolished like those on other north Cork roads; but the exceptionally warm weather had dried up the river beds so that the Auxiliaries were able to take their vehicles through. The IRA made no further effort to deny the enemy the use of the road between Banteer and Millstreet, with a purpose that will be seen.

Acting on orders of Commandant O'Brien and the brigade staff, the Millstreet IRA Battalion kept careful note of the movements of the Mount Leader garrison. It was observed that a convoy of armour-plated lorries travelled to the Banteer railhead for supplies on a couple of days each week. The observers noted that the lorries, which contained about eight or ten men each in addition to the driver, were covered with steel wire mesh to ward off bombs or grenades, and had machine guns mounted. It was also noted that the strength of the convoy varied between two and four lorries, which travelled an estimated distance of 300 yards apart. The watch on the convoy continued until the IRA leaders were satisfied that the journey between Mount Leader and Banteer was made invariably on Tuesdays and Fridays.

Furthermore, the important fact was established that if the convoy made one trip to Banteer in the forenoon, it always repeated the journey in the afternoon. Following consultation with the Millstreet Battalion, the brigade staff decided to attack the convoy, and to strike when it would be making a return journey in the afternoon. There were three main reasons for this decision:

(1) Having travelled the road three times in one day, the Auxiliaries would be less likely to expect attack on the fourth journey, thus enabling the IRA leaders to exploit the element of surprise to the full.

(2) By allowing the enemy to pass and repass along his route, the watching Volunteers would be afforded the opportunity to view what they would have to fight, in the actual place of battle. They would be able to note the distance covered by the entire convoy, its armament and strength. The distances between vehicles would be observed, as would the approximate position of each vehicle in relation to each ambushing section.

(3) To attack the enemy on his last return journey would mean a fight when the day was dying and would provide ideal conditions for the withdrawal of the IRA columns at the end of the engagement. Approaching darkness would make British aircraft ineffective for 'spotting' purposes.

Out to the men of the battalions in the Mallow, Millstreet, Charleville, Kanturk and Newmarket districts went the order to mobilise at Rathcoole Wood on the night of 15 June. In this mobilisation at Rathcoole is an example of the discipline and readiness of the IRA units in north-west Cork at the time. Many of the men were engaged in civilian occupations. Others were on the run. But all belonged to the brigade and every unit reported as ordered, even though the mobilisation order allowed very little time in which to do so.

Rathcoole Wood covered several acres. It lay some 500 yards south of the road between Banteer and Millstreet, and as near as makes no matter, was half-way between the two points. Occupying a slightly elevated position, it protected the assembling Volunteers from aircraft and ground observation while enabling them to keep the Banteer-Millstreet road under view. North of the road, and more or less parallel to it, ran the railway line that had been rendered impassable by the IRA since April. To the north and also roughly parallel, flowed the River Blackwater. South of the road the land sloped upwards to the wood and the foothills of the Boggeraghs.

On the night of Thursday 15 June, the riflemen of the battalion marched towards Rathcoole. From Charleville, on the border of County Limerick, they marched long, weary miles by Dromina, Freemount, and Meelin, leaving Newmarket town to the south and on their left. On they tramped to Kiskeam, where they contacted the Newmarket Battalion, and thence by Derrinagree to Keale Bridge, at which point the combined Newmarket and Charleville columns crossed the Blackwater and arrived at Rathcoole. From the Lombardstown district came the men of the Mallow Battalion with their rifles and a Hotchkiss gun sent to them from Dublin. At Nadd, the Mallow men met the Kanturk Battalion and together they moved down towards Rathcoole. Millstreet had already mobilised, for the fight was to be on their doorstep.

Some 130 armed men assembled under the pine trees of Rathcoole Wood that night. About sixty-five rifles were there in addition to fifty shotgun men of the Millstreet Battalion. Under the friendly trees they sheltered as the first rays of the sun of 16 June began another day of scorching heat. It was the day and the place of battle to which they had come. Out of the wood and over the glistening mountain dew the brigade officers led their section leaders down the 400 or 500 yards to the road.

The sixty-five riflemen were divided into eight sections and

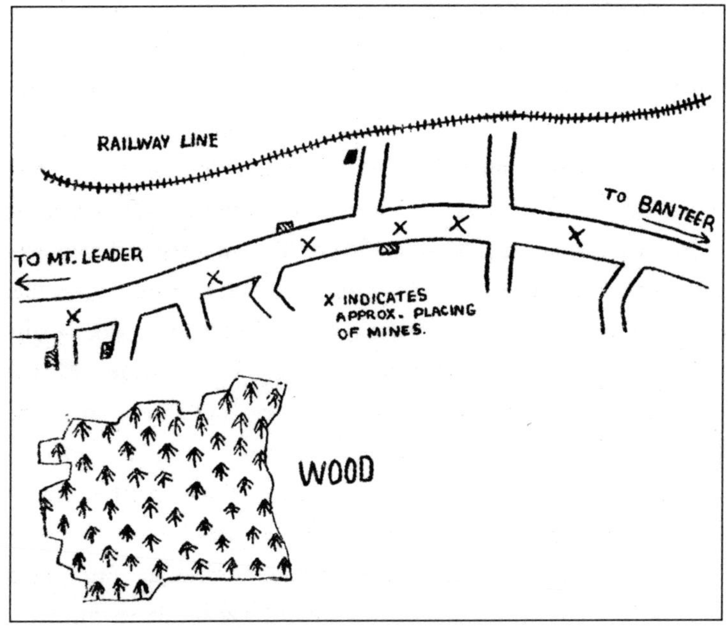

reinforced with shotguns. The plan of attack was that all the sections, with the exception of one, would occupy positions south of the road, on the same side as the wood. The other section would occupy a position north of the road at the extreme western end of the stretch of three-quarters of a mile marked out for the ambush, and with its back to the railway line and the Blackwater river. It was so placed because no suitable spot could be found for it on the same side as the others. Like all roads in mountain foothills, the Banteer-Mount Leader road winds more or less according to the contours of the terrain, and presumably conforms to the whims of the original road builders. At the ambush position, however, it was relatively straight except for an occasional slight curve and one appreciable curve towards its western end. Along this stretch of road it had been decided to place six eight-pound mines at intervals of approximately 150 yards. Those were the distances which the IRA leaders considered best for blowing up or disabling the enemy's vehicles, an operation which had in it a considerable element of chance, as, in addition to many other unpredictable factors, it was impossible to anticipate the speed of the vehicles or the distances between them.

Leading from the wood to the road were three ravines or dried water courses which were to be used as withdrawal routes for the different sections should it be found necessary to pull them out of the engagement. Men moving along the ravines could not be seen from the road, and so had splendid cover from view and to a great extent, cover from fire. Section commanders were shown where they were to place their men, and these positions varied between eighty yards and fifty yards from the road, according to the size of the fields. The sections were to endeavour to isolate each of the enemy lorries with a view to preventing the Auxiliaries from acting as a cohesive, co-ordinated force. Should an IRA withdrawal become necessary it was to be achieved by way of the ravines. In such event, each section was specifically instructed to maintain communication with that on its right and left, so that one section could cover the other during the retreat. While a section would be withdrawing, the other would keep the enemy's head down with well-directed fire. The lone section north of the road would withdraw towards the river and cross it at Keale Bridge.

By seven o'clock, the column commanders, having made sure that the section leaders were familiar with their positions and instructions and understood the tasks allotted their sections, retired with them to the shelter of the friendly wood in which the men were resting. The Millstreet Battalion had been mobilised to a man, and it provided scouts who were posted all round the area. It was also the task of the Millstreet men to supply flank protection and signallers, as well as to organise food supplies. Breakfast was procured from adjacent farmhouses, and the men were ordered to get what sleep they could in the wood in which it was anticipated they would spend most of the day. All of them had been more than twenty-four hours on their feet, and the majority had made long night marches to Rathcoole from their local area. So, while the scouts watched, the men rested under the protective foliage as the hot sun rose in the sky.

Silence reigned in the wood as the morning wore on and the men rested. About half past ten the scouts signalled the approach of enemy vehicles travelling towards the east. On the road below, they passed on towards Banteer, on the outward course of the first journey. The sight of them greatly pleased the watchers in the wood, for the morning journey definitely indicated that another would be made in the afternoon. The enemy passed out of sight and all was quiet again. Towards midday he returned to Mount Leader, and when he had passed, the waiting men of the IRA had a meal, supplied from neighbouring farmhouses. Afterwards, they settled down to wait again, and the hours of the afternoon passed. About four o'clock the convoy was once more signalled, and four armour-plated lorries, each with a complement of ten men and each vehicle carrying a mounted machine gun, passed by on their second journey to Banteer.

The thick white dust raised by the lorries settled down gently on the fields bordering the road. Out of the shelter of the wood emerged the waiting column to move down to their positions covering the road. Six mines had been laid on the highway, and with the dust inches thick on the untarred road, it was easy to cover the marks of mine-laying. The mines were placed at distances calculated to make them effective against each of the enemy lorries at a given time. Each mine was covered by a number of riflemen and by Volunteers armed with shotguns. East and west of the minefield were flanking parties of riflemen. By surrounding roads Volunteers waited to throw up barricades to impede all traffic, once the firing had commenced. Quietly the riflemen and the shotgun men moved into position. The Mallow and Kanturk Battalion columns were at the Banteer or eastern end, while the Newmarket, Millstreet and Charleville columns occupied the western end. A number of men from the Newmarket and Charleville columns formed the section north of the road, and it was these who would have to fall back towards the river in the event of withdrawal. All the other sections were south of the road, with the wood more or less to their backs. Signals had been arranged between adjoining sections. The mines were numbered off from west to east, and the sections of riflemen and shotgun men were also numbered. The IRA leaders had brought all the experience at their disposal to bear on this operation, and had assembled for it all the arms, equipment and trained men they had available. Months of effort were required to surmount the formidable difficulties encountered in the preparation and collection of materials and equipment. Weeks of careful planning had preceded it. At last the final stage had been reached. Everything was in readiness.

Through the ambush position the rough, dusty road wound like a narrow white ribbon on a brown-green patchwork. High up south the Boggeraghs were blue in the bright sunlight; to the north the Blackwater rippled gently from west to east. Behind a thin veil of haze in the drowsy afternoon, the Kerry mountains cut the horizon in the far west. Patiently, the men of the North Cork IRA waited as the hands of their watches approached six o'clock.

Some time between six and half past the hour, the four enemy vehicles approached from the east. They passed into the ambush position one by one until the fourth lorry was over the most easterly mine. The operator pulled his switch and the mine exploded. It was the signal for the commencement of the attack.

The IRA were confident that the last lorry would be blown up immediately and its occupants destroyed with it. When constructing their mines, however, they did not make due allowance for the soft, boggy foundation of the road in which they were to be laid. As a result, most of the mine blast was absorbed by the boggy sub-soil, and the effect on the lorry was of little account beyond stopping its engine. Fire was immediately opened on it from the sections covering that part of the road. The IRA Hotchkiss gun was employed against it also, but jammed after a short period. Auxiliaries attempting to leave their stalled vehicle were prevented by the IRA, but were able to return fire through the loopholes in its armoured sides.

By that time the second and third lorries had halted, and had come under a withering fire from the IRA sections nearest them. Neither was sufficiently near any of the mines to allow these be blown with effect.

There was a mine between the second and third lorry, and another between the third and fourth.

The leading lorry continued westwards and the watching sections of IRA waited for it to reach the last mine, at the extreme western end. It never did. Having heard the firing, its occupants decided to reverse to the assistance of their comrades. The IRA sections concerned held their fire. Back went the lorry. When it was plumb on top of the second most westerly mine over which it had passed minutes previously, the operator threw his switch. The explosion lifted the vehicle to its side with one of its wheels blown away. Out tumbled some of the occupants, who were met by a heavy and well-directed fire from the sections covering them. These sections closed in to capture the vehicle, but were held off by the machine gun it mounted.

Up at the fourth lorry the attacking sections also closed in for a capture, but the machine-gun fire from the third lorry kept them off the road. Out of this third truck jumped a daring group of four or five Auxiliaries who ran along the road with the object of out-flanking the nearest IRA sections. As they passed over one of the mines, they were blown into eternity. None of the group is believed to have survived the blast.

The fight was now raging. Some of the enemy who had succeeded in taking up positions on the road were giving back a heavy return of lead, supported by the machine guns mounted on the trucks. From all round, the IRA rifles and shotguns were pouring in deadly fire. There was no doubt about the fighting qualities of the Auxiliaries. Time and again they attempted to assume the offensive and made several efforts to outflank the attackers. Each time they were driven back by the IRA. Along the road smoke spiralled upwards as the rifles cracked and bursts of machine-gun fire beat a tattoo. It was a fierce and unrelenting engagement and it lasted most of an hour while determined men on both sides endeavoured to outfight and capture the other. As happened at Clonbanin, the machine guns in the armoured vehicles exercised a decisive influence by preventing the capture or complete destruction of the enemy. So the IRA leaders decided to break off the engagement with not a single casualty on their side. Nearly half of the Auxiliary force lay dead on the roadway and many more were wounded.

By the pre-arranged routes the columns withdrew in perfect order, each section alternately covering the other, according to plan. North of the road the section from the Charleville and Newmarket Battalions fell back on the river which it crossed at Keale Bridge. South of the ambush position the column retreated westwards to Caherbarnagh and Rathmore, and in the process passed a point about a mile-and-a-half from the Auxiliary headquarters at Mount Leader House. Through the night the enemy laboured to remove his dead and wounded and his disabled vehicles to Mount Leader. Whilst he was thus engaged a section of the Millstreet column sniped the building. By the next day the IRA columns were back in their own areas.

Apparently, it was the opinion of the British that the operation had been carried out by local men for, on 23 June, they carried out at Rathcoole the most extensive and concentrated comb-out of an area ever undertaken in the south. Troops converged on Rathcoole from Buttevant, Kanturk, Ballyvonaire, Ballincollig, Macroom, Killarney and Tralee. They cordoned off an area about five miles square. It need scarcely be stated that they failed to capture the IRA column which had inflicted such demoralising losses. By that time the leaders of the brigade were laying their plans for a campaign along the Limerick border.

British reprisals were of a useless and savage nature. On the morning of the big round-up Michael Dineen, a Volunteer of the Kilcorney Company (Millstreet Battalion) was taken from his brother's house at Ivale, Kilcorney, by a party of Auxiliaries. They took him some distance away and rifle and machine-gun fire was heard later. When the British moved on, the relatives of Mick Dineen found his mangled remains 300 yards from the house. His arms and legs had been broken by the blows of British rifle-butts before they murdered him. On the evening of 1 July, a party of Auxiliaries fired on two youths who were cutting hay on Murphy's farm at Rathcoole, and killed Bernard Moynihan of the Kilcorney Company. The wood at Rathcoole was burned too. But the IRA was not deterred by such vindictive deeds, and were it not for the coming of the Truce the Mount Leader gang would again have found themselves called upon to fight for their lives.

The urgency with which the Auxiliaries removed their dead and hauled their disabled lorries from the scene of the fight at Rathcoole can be gauged by the fact that, on the following day, IRA scouts collected thousands of rounds of rifle and machine-gun ammunition which the enemy had abandoned on the roadway. In fact, the IRA thus recovered more ammunition than they had expended during the engagement.

INDEX

C

D

E

F

M

N

O

P

Q

R

S

T

U

V

W